Family Matters in Indian Buddhist Monasticisms

Family Matters in Indian Buddhist Monasticisms

Shayne Clarke

University of Hawai'i Press
Honolulu

Printed in the United States of America

19 18 17 16 15 14 6 5 4 3 2 1

Library of Congress Cataloging-in-Publication Data
Clarke, Shayne Neil, author.
Family matters in Indian Buddhist monasticisms / Shayne Clarke.
pages cm
Includes bibliographical references and index.
ISBN 978-0-8248-3647-4 (cloth : alk. paper)
1. Monastic and religious life (Buddhism)—India. 2. Buddhist monks—Family relationships—India. 3. Buddhist nuns—Family relationships—India. I. Title.
BQ6160.I4C53 2014
294.3'6570954—dc23
2013031366

University of Hawai'i Press books are printed on acid-free paper and meet the guidelines for permanence and durability of the Council on Library Resources.

Designed by Wanda China
Printed by Sheridan Books, Inc.

Contents

Acknowledgments vii
Abbreviations xi
Conventions xiii

Chapter One. The Rhinoceros in the Room: Monks and Nuns and Their Families 1
1. Indian Buddhist Monasticisms 2
2. Conflicting Visions of the Ideal Monk 10
3. Indian Buddhist Monastic Law Codes 18
4. The Family 21
5. A Preview of the Inquiry 27
6. Reading Indian Buddhist Monastic Law Codes 29
7. A Note on the Scope of the Present Study 36

Chapter Two. Family Matters 37
1. Family Ties Set in Stone 39
2. From Home to Homelessness 45
3. Close Shaves with Monkish Assumptions 56
4. The Family That Eats Together 58
5. The Family That Stays Together 62
6. Like Father, Like Son 63
7. Incidental Incidents and Pugnacious Parents 68
8. Families on Different Paths 72
9. Conclusions 74

Chapter Three. Former Wives from Former Lives 78
1. Monastic Education Concerning Sex with One's Wife 80

2. Monks Arranging a Marriage for Their Children 87
3. Procedures for Formal Marital Dissolution 92
4. Relations between Married Monastics 96
5. A Monastic Family: Udāyin, Guptā, and Their Son, Kumāra-Kāśyapa 99
6. Mahākāśyapa and His Wife: Ascetic Values in Indian Buddhist Monasticisms 106
7. Married Monastics beyond India 115
8. Conclusions 118

Chapter Four. Nuns Who Become Pregnant 120
1. Mothers Becoming Nuns 121
2. Nursing Nuns 124
3. Monastic Motherhood 129
4. Nuns Becoming Mothers 134
5. Child Care and Nannying Nuns 144
6. Conclusions 146

Chapter Five. Reconsidering Renunciation: Family-Friendly Monasticisms 150
1. A View of the Evidence 150
2. Family-Friendly Monasticisms 152
3. Family-Friendly Monasticisms in a Competitive Religious Marketplace 155
4. A Scholarly Misperception 162
5. Comparative Monasticisms 163
6. On the Utility of *Vinaya* Texts for the Study of Indian Buddhist Monasticisms 165

Notes 171
Works Consulted 229
Index of Texts 263
Index of Authors/Subjects 267

Acknowledgments

This book has taken shape over many years and through the kindness and generosity of many, not all of whom are mentioned here. One person in particular, however, deserves special mention. To Professor Gregory Schopen I owe a profound debt of gratitude, both scholarly and personal (for among numerous other things, his gallant, albeit ultimately unsuccessful, attempts to teach me the rudiments of basketball). In 1998, I was studying under Professor Paul Harrison, the first of many great teachers, at the University of Canterbury in Christchurch. Paul invited Professor Schopen to deliver a series of lectures on "Monks and their Money." These lectures shattered all notions I had about Buddhist monasticism, and irrevocably changed the trajectory of my research. The seed of what was later to become the present book was undoubtedly planted at this time, although it would take several more years for it to begin to take any definite shape. First, I had to study under some of the world's finest *vinaya* scholars: Professors Sasaki Shizuka and Yamagiwa Nobuyuki in Kyoto, and finally Professor Schopen at the University of California, Los Angeles.

Professor Schopen has always given greatly of his time and encyclopedic knowledge of Indian Buddhism in general and the *Mūlasarvāstivāda-vinaya* in particular. His unpublished anthology of stories from the *Mūlasarvāstivāda-vinaya* was invaluable in the early stages of this work. His scholarship continues to provide inspiration and an ideal to work toward, no matter how unattainable it still seems. And that is perhaps as it should be: ideals, like that of the Rhinoceros Horn, probably function best when they are unattainable. I continue to learn much from our now too infrequent conversations. Indeed, every time I think I have a good idea, it is accompanied by a lingering suspicion that the seed of that idea, if not the idea itself, was planted by Professor Schopen.

Throughout the course of this project, I have benefited greatly from numerous comments, criticisms, and suggestions proffered by many, beginning with, at an early stage, William Bodiford, Robert Buswell, and Jonathan Silk. I would also like to thank the two anonymous reviewers for the Press: John Strong and Daniel Boucher. Both reviewers graciously revealed their identities, and offered important advice and critical suggestions for the manuscript's improvement. Although I struggled in particular with many of Daniel's criticisms, the struggle has improved the book immeasurably.

A number of former and current colleagues in the Department of Religious Studies at McMaster University read through the manuscript, some of them twice, offering encouragement and sound advice from fields far removed from *vinaya* studies: James A. Benn, Annette Y. Reed, Mark Rowe, and Peter Widdicombe; I thank them for their keen insights, friendship, and good counsel over many years. Readers may join me in thanking them for improving the readability of the book immensely. I have likewise benefited from comments and suggestions made by a number of careful readers: Ven. Anālayo, Oskar von Hinüber, Ute Hüsken, Petra Kieffer-Pülz, Gregory Schopen, Peter Skilling, Stephen Sharp, and Tim Ward. Petra in particular went through the manuscript at several different stages, offering further references, valuable advice, and good humor. Two of my students, Chris Emms and Chris Handy, helped collect and check references, and caught a number of errors. Stephanie Balkwill read a draft and offered useful comments. Despite the sound advice received from many, I alone remain responsible for all errors and infelicities in the present work.

Although the initial research for this book was conducted prior to joining McMaster University, the present work has benefited from research supported by McMaster's Arts Research Board and Canada's Social Sciences and Humanities Research Council. I also wish to acknowledge financial support from the Arts Research Board and Dean Charlotte Yates, Faculty of Social Sciences, for the indexing of this volume.

At the University of Hawai'i Press, Patricia Crosby was enthusiastic about the project right from the beginning. I thank her for her encouragement, and especially her patience. Ann Ludeman oversaw production of the book. Stuart Kiang, copyeditor extraordinaire, went above and beyond the call of duty, making the electronic copyediting adventure almost enjoyable, certainly educational, and only minimally nerve-racking; to him I remain greatly indebted for many a smoother turn of phrase and for finding my endnotes once thought lost in the black hole that exists between Mac and PC worlds.

In a book about the importance of family, it seems only fitting that I acknowledge my own family. I thank my mother, Lyn, for her love, support, and encouragement over many years, and especially for letting me go my own way, to exotic far-off lands such as America and now Canada. I thank my sister, Lisa, and brother, Graham, who have always found time for me on my infrequent visits back home. Finally, I would like to thank my wife, Masami, and daughter, Kira, for filling my days with smiles and joy. Masami and Kira have been extremely patient, and have sacrificed much while my attention has been focused on this and other projects. Without their love and support, this book would have taken even longer; their warmth has gone a long way to making the frigid temperatures of the north bearable for this flightless kiwi. I thank my family for teaching me in ways that the *vinaya*s could not that family matters.

Abbreviations

BD	*The Book of the Discipline* (Horner [1938–1966] 1996–1997)
BHSD	*Buddhist Hybrid Sanskrit Dictionary* (Edgerton [1953] 1998)
Chi.	Chinese
GMs	*Gilgit Manuscripts* (Nalinaksha Dutt [1942–1950] 1984)
Mahāvyutpatti	*Bon-zō-kan-wa shiyaku taikō hon'yaku myōgi taishū* 梵藏漢和四譯對校飜譯名義大集 (Sakaki [1916] 1998)
Skt.	Sanskrit
Sp	*Samantapāsādikā* (Takakusu and Nagai [1924] 1975–1976)
T.	*Taishō shinshū daizōkyō* 大正新脩大藏經 (Takakusu and Watanabe 1924–1935)
Tib.	Tibetan
sTog	*The Tog Palace Manuscript of the Tibetan Kanjur.* 109 vols. Leh, Ladakh: C. Namgyal Tarusergar, 1975–1980.
Vin	*The Vinaya Piṭakaṃ* (Oldenberg [1879–1883] 1969–1982)
VSPVSG	Vinayasūtra's Pravrajyāvastu Study Group
VSS$_{\text{MsB}}$	*Vinayasūtravṛttyabhidhānasvavyākhyāna.* Guṇaprabha's autocommentary to his *Vinayasūtra.* Sanskrit manuscript preserved in dBu med script, published by VSPVSG at Taishō University.

Conventions

An asterisk denotes reconstructed Sanskrit forms, unless otherwise noted.

Square brackets have been used to indicate additions to quotations or translations. Unless otherwise indicated, all translations are mine.

Romanization and other such conventions will be clear to those interested in such matters and irrelevant to others.

In citing line numbers from the Taishō, where a certain register (a, b, or c) contains irregular spacing (i.e., less than 29 lines) before the lines I cite, I have counted line numbers backwards from the last line, which I have taken to be line 29.

Family names containing particles are alphabetized in the indexes and list of works consulted under the first capitalized letter in the family name—for example, van Buitenen is under B.

Family Matters in Indian Buddhist Monasticisms

Chapter One

The Rhinoceros in the Room

Monks and Nuns and Their Families

> A nun gave birth to a baby boy. Not knowing what to do, she informed the Buddha of this matter.
>
> The Buddha said, "I authorize a twofold ecclesiastical act for appointing a nun to attend her." ...
>
> The two nuns held the child, and produced doubt [as to whether they had committed an offense].
>
> The Buddha said, "There is no transgression."
>
> The two nuns slept together with the child, and produced doubt.
>
> The Buddha said, "Again, there is no transgression."
>
> Having adorned the child, together [the nuns] fawned [upon him].
>
> The Buddha said, "That should not be done. I authorize you to bathe and to nurse him. If he [is old enough to] leave the breast, you should give him to a monk, and let him go forth [into the religious life]. If you do not wish to have him go forth [into the religious life], you should give him to relatives, and have him brought up."[1]

This series of four rules introduces monastic legislation to accommodate any pregnant nuns who give birth to baby boys within Indian Buddhist nunneries. Translated here from the *Mahīśāsaka-vinaya,* an Indian Buddhist monastic law code (*vinaya*) preserved in a fifth-century C.E. Chinese translation, the narrative recounts how a particular Buddhist "nun," a *bhikṣuṇī,*[2] gave birth to a baby boy. Without any explicit or even implicit criticism of the birth of a son to an ordained Buddhist nun, the authors or redactors of this monastic law code, canonical Indian Buddhist jurists, put into the mouth of the

Buddha a series of rules to appoint a fellow nun to attend the newly delivered mother-nun.[3]

This narrative and other similar stories preserved in the extant corpus of Buddhist monastic law codes complicate generally accepted scholarly and popular views of Indian Buddhist monastic life. Scholarly consensus has painted a picture in which Indian Buddhist monks and nuns severed all ties with their families when they left home for the religious life; monks and nuns remained celibate, and those who faltered in their "vows" of monastic celibacy were immediately and irrevocably expelled from the Buddhist order.

But the vision of the monastic life that emerges from a close reading of "in-house" monastic law codes challenges this conventional picture and some of our most basic scholarly notions of what it meant to be a Buddhist monk or nun in India. The narratives in these monastic law codes often depict monks and nuns as continuing to interact and associate with their families. Far from renouncing familial ties, some monastics are described as leaving home for the religious life together with their children. Although we are not accustomed to thinking about the marital status of monks and nuns, Indian Buddhist monastic law did not require monastics to dissolve their marriages upon entrance into the religious life.[4] Indeed, men and women are depicted within *vinaya* literature as sometimes even leaving home for the religious life together, as married monastic couples. Moreover, the authors/redactors of the extant monastic legal codes—the monks who quite literally made the rules, the authors of canonical Indian Buddhisms—legislated to accommodate not only pregnant nuns and monastic motherhood, but in certain circumstances even those who breached clerical celibacy.

1. Indian Buddhist Monasticisms

Modern Western understandings of Indian Buddhist monasticisms seem to have been based largely on two sets of images: (1) European notions of medieval Christian monasticism and (2) visions of the ideal monk from within modern, particularly Theravāda, Buddhist traditions and their canonical texts. Each of these images has served to shape the course and selectivity of scholarship on Indian Buddhist monasticisms.

Some of the earliest modern European references to Buddhist monks come from explorers and missionaries who traveled in Asia.[5] Early travelers and subsequent scholars have referred to the Buddhist *bhikṣu,* the full-time vocational religious specialist, by a variety of names, including almsmen, bonzes, clerics, friars, monks, priests, and talapoins.[6] Today, the most widely used term for Sanskrit *bhikṣu* (Pāli *bhikkhu*) (lit. "beggar") seems to be "monk," and this can be traced back at least as early as 1828, to Brian Houghton Hodgson.[7] One of the founding fathers of Buddhist studies, Hodgson equated the Buddhist *bhikṣu* with his Christian counterpart; he tells us that "Buddhist monachism agrees surprisingly with Christian. . . ."[8]

In the nineteenth century, scholarly understandings of terms such as "monk" and "monasticism" appear to have been shaped by medieval Benedictine notions of the monastic ideal. Susanna Elm suggests that, until very recently, "the historiography of monasticism as a whole, regarding its history both before and after Benedict, remains dominated and deeply influenced by the notions exemplified by Benedictine monasticism and its related concerns."[9]

Recent studies in Christian monasticism, particularly in the field of late antiquity, are beginning to move beyond the idea of a monolithic monastic ideal or norm as represented by the (later) Benedictine Rule.[10] By comparison, the field of Buddhist studies has been slow to reevaluate its own assumptions concerning the religious life. The name of Benedict may not necessarily spring to the minds of scholars of Buddhist history. Yet, I would argue that it is this image of the monastic ideal that is ingrained in many scholars' presuppositions concerning the religious life of the Buddhist *bhikṣu.*[11]

A scholar of late antiquity might now find it reasonable to ask whether fourth-century Egyptian or Byzantine monks continued to interact with their families.[12] For many scholars of Buddhist studies, however, such questions may seem misplaced. Indeed, Buddhism is about renunciation of one's family—or so runs the received wisdom.[13] Why would a nun or monk continue to associate with a family member whom s/he had just renounced or abandoned? It is precisely assumptions such as this that have guided the questions scholars of Buddhist history have asked and, more important, not asked. I contend that the assumption of a complete lack of contact between monastics and their family members has contributed to the construction of a scholarly and popular vision of Indian Buddhist monasticisms that is not supported by the preponderance of our premodern evidence.

When early scholars looked at canonical Buddhist literature with certain preconceptions about the monastic life, the images of "monks" and "nuns" that they saw largely confirmed their assumptions. Yet what they accepted as representative of Buddhist monasticisms was, I suggest, highly romanticized and rhetorically charged. Here we might consider an important example from some of the earliest known strata of Buddhist literature:[14] the *Rhinoceros Horn Sūtra,* a Gāndhārī version of which is preserved on a birch-bark scroll from, according to Richard Salomon,[15] perhaps the first century B.C.E. The following verses typify the renunciant ideal lauded by this text:[16]

> Having given up son and wife and money, possessions and kinsmen and relatives... (*one should wander alone like the rhinoceros).[17]
>
> Casting off the marks of a householder like a mountain ebony tree shorn of its leaves, (*leaving home, wearing) the saffron robe, (*one should wander alone like the rhinoceros).
>
> Having broken the ties of a householder, like a bird who has torn a strong net, not returning (*as a fire [does not return] to what it has burnt, one should wander alone like the rhinoceros).[18]

The *Rhinoceros Horn Sūtra* contains explicit exhortations to abandon kith and kin, forsake wealth and material gain, and go forth and wander alone like the rhinoceros (or its horn).[19] Something akin to this ideal arguably forms the cornerstone of modern scholarly understandings of Buddhist monasticisms.[20] A few examples should suffice to establish not the validity but the centrality of this image as a vision of the Buddhist monastic ideal in scholarly literature.[21]

In his 1881 introduction to the translation of the *Sutta-nipāta,* the collection within which the Theravāda or Pāli version of the same *sūtra* is found, V. Fausböll comments that "in the contents of the Suttanipâta we have, I think, an important contribution to the right understanding of Primitive Buddhism, for we see here a picture not of life in monasteries, but of the life of hermits in its first stage."[22] Indeed, readers are not left to make up their own minds as to what constitutes "the right understanding of Primitive Buddhism." Fausböll introduces his translation of the *Rhinoceros Horn Sutta* as follows:

> Family life and intercourse with others should be avoided, for society has all vices in its train; therefore one should leave the corrupted state of society and lead a solitary life.[23]

It is here, I suggest, in "the life of hermits," the abandonment of family and society in general, that we see Fausböll's—and subsequent generations'—"right understanding of Primitive Buddhism," a Buddhism that is clearly to be differentiated from that of "life in monasteries." In other words, Fausböll seems to posit two Buddhisms: a pure or original form of Buddhism as exemplified by the Rhinoceros Horn ideal, and a later, presumably degenerate, monastic form.

Fausböll seems to have taken the *Rhinoceros Horn Sutta* as a window on what, in 1889, Monier Monier-Williams would call "true Buddhism...the Buddhism of the Piṭakas or Pāli texts,"[24] a Buddhism which Monier-Williams clearly contrasted with "the changes Buddhism underwent before it died out in India," including "its corruptions in some of the countries bordering on India and in North-eastern Asia."[25] More than half a century later, B. G. Gokhale repeats Fausböll's earlier and still prominent view, suggesting that "the spirit of early Buddhism" is to be found in the *Rhinoceros Horn Sutta.*

> If there is any one text in the whole expanse of Pāli Literature reflecting the spirit of early Buddhism it is the Khaggavisāṇa Sutta....The ideal described in the sutta...is that of the lonely *arhat,* who has completely turned his back on the world and wanders alone like "the horn of the rhinoceros."[26]

A few years later, in 1970, Melford Spiro, a cultural anthropologist known in the field of Buddhist studies for his work on Theravāda Buddhism among the Burmese, reiterates the received wisdom on the Rhinoceros Horn ideal, although this time in the abstract. For Spiro, this now seems to be a pan-Buddhist ideal, not simply a "primitive" or "early" one.

> To renounce the world, according to Buddhism, means to renounce all ties—parents, family, spouse, friends, and property—and to "wander alone like the rhinoceros."[27]

In a 1975 article on Buddhist understandings of the Indian notion of karma, Richard Gombrich invokes the *Rhinoceros Horn Sutta* to make the point that "the first Buddhists were asocial, even anti-social,"[28] a point often made about Indian renunciation:[29]

> Once one had taken the Buddha's message seriously enough to act on it, one abandoned all social ties, and had as little human company as possible—'Go lonely as the rhinoceros'.[30]

It may be countered that views from the late 1880s or even the 1970s are not only old but also outdated, that they no longer hold any currency. Old they may be, but similar sentiments continue to feature in recent scholarship. Examples attesting to the ubiquity and centrality of the image of the Rhinoceros Horn may be found in a range of scholarly opinions, from anthropologists of Southeast Asia to specialists in East Asian Buddhism to scholars of Indian religions.[31] Take, for instance, Gananath Obeyesekere's 2002 statement that "Buddhism insisted that the monk should live 'lonely as the single horn of the rhinoceros,'"[32] or Bernard Faure's 2003 statement, in his book on gender in Buddhism, that "the early ascetic or monastic attitude... posits that 'a bodhisattva should wander alone like a rhinoceros.'"[33] Although admitting the existence of other Buddhisms in their 2003 work on the sociology of early Buddhism, Greg Bailey and Ian Mabbett tell us that "the monks who received the earliest Buddhist message were expected to live it as homeless mendicants, severing all ties with society."[34] Not surprisingly, Bailey and Mabbett cite the *Sutta-nipāta* in general and the *Rhinoceros Horn Sutta* in particular as "a probable *locus* for an early stage of Buddhist thought about a monk's life."[35] In 2004, Gavin Flood contends that "the ideal monk has renounced the world and family ties, renounced a settled life in a home and wanders in order to seek his own liberation.... The *Sutta-nipāta,* for example, compares the solitary ascetic wanderer to a rhinoceros horn."[36] Finally, and most recently, in a section entitled "Monks and Their Families" in her 2012 book on maternal imagery in Indian Buddhism, while clearly recognizing that life "on the ground" was much more complicated, Reiko Ohnuma maintains that "early Buddhist discourses such as the famous *Rhinoceros Horn Discourse*... likewise make it clear that the life of the ideal Buddhist renunciant necessarily involves a rejection of familial ties."[37]

For the most part, the scholars quoted above are careful not to conflate a prescriptive exhortation with a descriptive account of what Buddhists did.[38] Others, however, have understood the exhortation as evidence of actual Buddhist practice in India.[39] Although there is scholarly debate as to whether this ideal is in its origins pre-Buddhist, original, primitive, early, or otherwise,[40] the quotations above offer an indication of the privileged position that the *Rhinoceros Horn Sutta* holds not only in the early construction but also in recent scholarly understandings of the ideals of the religious life of the Indian Buddhist *bhikṣu*.[41]

But the Rhinoceros Horn may well turn out to be a red herring altogether: the renunciant ideal espoused by the *Rhinoceros Horn Sutta* is certainly not the ideal of mainstream monasticisms as known to us from the extant monastic law codes. In fact, Buddhaghosa, the fifth-century C.E. purported author of the *Paramatthajotikā,* a text in which we find a commentary to the *Rhinoceros Horn Sutta,* seems to have had trouble with the concept of monks who wandered alone, having abandoned kith and kin. This conservative commentator appears to have made sense of this form of the religious life only by explaining it away as something that not monks but solitary buddhas (*paccekabuddha*s; Skt. *pratyekabuddha*s) do.[42] Indeed, as Rupert Gethin has noted, the image of the Rhinoceros Horn seems to have appealed more to scholars of Indian Buddhism than Indian Buddhists themselves.[43]

What is missing from scholarly discussions of the Rhinoceros Horn ideal is a recognition of its function as rhetoric. In discussing the "domestication of asceticism," Patrick Olivelle has argued that "Indian ascetic traditions . . . were never totally asocial or antisocial. . . . Nevertheless, . . . in their rhetoric, images, and rituals [they] tended to accentuate their separation from familial and social life."[44] This accentuation is exactly what we see in Buddhist *sūtra* literature, and exactly what seems to be missing from "in-house" monastic law codes, a genre of Buddhist literature written solely for monastic and not lay consumption.[45] As we will see, the Rhinoceros Horn ideal is perhaps best understood as ascetic rhetoric. I do not mean to suggest that this rhetoric has not played an important part in Buddhist renunciatory traditions. The image of the forest-renunciant has been a key figure in the history of Indian Buddhism, providing "a specific ideal of complete renunciation of which later Buddhists were well aware and to which they could return at moments of personal and collective crisis."[46] Yet one must clearly differentiate between the ideals of an ascetic tradition and those of settled monasticism, the subject of our inquiry. Indeed, it makes little sense to talk about "the ideal renunciant" as if there were only ever one ideal.

To be sure, in recent decades, the utility of the image of the Rhinoceros Horn for the study of Indian Buddhist monasticisms has been questioned, particularly in terms of monks' continued involvement in financial and business matters.[47] Moreover, there has been some degree of recognition that Buddhist monks in India did not always sever their ties with kin.[48] Uma Chakravarti, for instance, wrote that the

Buddha made "exceptions to a large number of *vinaya* rules" on the basis of kinship bonds, and that "*Bhikkhus* were allowed to maintain contacts with members of their families."[49] However, old assumptions are nothing if not persistent. Serinity Young, for instance, writes that "the *vinaya*s...required [monastics] to abandon all family life."[50] Axel Michaels states that "Buddha...did—like Jesus—demand a radical break with family...."[51] Of course, abandoning family life is not to be confused with abandoning one's family, but the above scholars do not make this distinction. More often than not, such distinctions are in fact blurred. This is clear, for instance, in Môhan Wijayaratna's work on Theravādin Buddhist monastic life:

> The first step in becoming a monk or a nun is to abandon lay life, which means to leave one's family. Buddhist monasticism led many married persons to renounce their wives or husbands; single men and women renounced the possibility of marriage.[52]

Wijayaratna's statement concerning the abandonment of family echoes similar sentiments expressed by Fausböll, Monier-Williams,[53] Étienne Lamotte,[54] and other leading luminaries.[55] Wijayaratna bases his study solely on Theravāda sources and primarily the Pāli Vinaya. His sources alone, however, cannot account for his conclusions. Indeed, should one choose to look for them, there are any number of passages in the Pāli Vinaya that suggest quite the opposite to the picture of Buddhist monasticism presented by Wijayaratna.[56] Here I can conclude only that Wijayaratna is guided by his own preconceived notions and assumptions about the nature of Buddhist monasticism. This in turn dictates which passages he selects to tell his story. To my mind, Wijayaratna's comments attest only to the pervasiveness of our modern assumptions about the nature of Indian Buddhist monasticisms.[57]

I will introduce here but one further example of the assumptions vis-à-vis family underpinning scholarship on Buddhist monasticisms. In her 1996 study *Horrific Figurations of the Feminine in Indian Buddhist Hagiographic Literature,* Liz Wilson writes:[58]

> The homeless life was quintessentially a wifeless life, for the early monks of the primitive monastic community. And so it is today, among most of the Buddhist communities of South and Southeast Asia....Higher ordination (*upasampadā*) in the Buddhist *sangha* dissolves familial and

> matrimonial ties. If one is married at the time of ordination, that bond is dissolved; spouses are thereafter referred to as "former" spouses. If one is not married at the time of full ordination, one renounces the possibility of marriage.[59]

Wilson's depiction of the monastic life may be an adequate summation of Buddhism as practiced in some contemporary Theravādin monastic communities. Yet it is a leap to suggest that this was the case in India some two millennia ago. These views—from Fausböll to Monier-Williams, Wijayaratna, and Wilson—are neither argued nor debated; they are simply presented and accepted as the basic "facts" from which scholars proceed with their particular inquiries.

An uncritical adoption of the image of the Rhinoceros Horn as the ideal of Buddhist renunciation is not the only[60]—or perhaps even the best—way to account for modern scholarly notions of Buddhist monastic life. The scholarly opinions presented above go further and reflect ingrained assumptions about the nature of Buddhist monasticisms. Assumptions, by their very nature, are not usually expressed in explicit terms and hence are difficult to identify. Yet their presence may be discernible in the comments scholars make about the "nature" or "spirit" of Buddhist monasticisms. These assumptions, in my estimation, run something like this: Buddhist monasticism is antifamilial; one who becomes a monk or nun severs—or ideally should sever—all ties with family members: parents, spouses, and children; monastics have—or should have—no further contact with their former families; the act of renunciation somehow dissolves marriages; monks and nuns cannot remain married; pregnant women and nursing mothers cannot become nuns; nuns cannot have babies, and certainly cannot raise children in convents; monks and nuns must be—and supposedly therefore were—celibate; those who transgress the rule of celibacy are expelled without hope of redemption.[61]

If assumptions like these are accepted as the basic "facts" of Indian Buddhist monasticisms, we close the door to important questions about the lives of monks and nuns in India: Other than that of the Buddha himself, whose own son, wife, aunt and stepmother, and cousins are said to have joined the early monastic community, were there biological families in Indian monasteries? Did husbands and wives leave home for the religious life together? If so, could they take their children with them? What happens if a nun becomes pregnant? Can she have a baby and still remain a nun? If it is possible for nuns to have babies, are nuns' babies brought up in a monastic environment? If so, who looks after the infants? What happens when the children grow up? What happens if a Buddhist monk or nun falls from the celibate ideal?[62]

These are questions not usually asked in the field of Buddhist studies.[63] I contend that they are not only worth asking but to a certain extent also answerable. To begin to answer them, however, we must turn away from the image of the Rhinoceros Horn and look to the evidence of the extant *vinaya*s or Buddhist monastic law codes. We must turn away from what Buddhism may have been in its original conception. Given the dearth of early materials,[64] what it may have meant to be a monk in the first few decades or even centuries after the Buddha's passing is all but out of our reach. Indeed, if we know anything about monks who followed the exhortations of the *Rhinoceros Horn Sūtra*, it is perhaps only of their failures. Any monk who successfully cut off all ties to the world and wandered around like a rhinoceros would leave only the same traces in the sands of history as the rhinoceros himself. If in fact we know—and can know—anything at all about Buddhist monks in India, then it should be self-evident that the monks about whom we can legitimately talk were not the wandering rhinoceroses; the latter's tracks, if they left any, remain well covered. Rather, we must turn to what Indian Buddhist monasticisms had become by the time they can be tracked in the writings of the authors/redactors of our extant monastic law codes.[65] Moreover, since later Central Asian, Chinese, Japanese, Mongolian, Newar, Sri Lankan, Tibetan, and other forms of Buddhist monastic practice are often judged against a perceived ideal of Indian Buddhism, a view of Indian Buddhist monasticisms that takes into account the voices of Indian monastic lawyers as heard through their own stories holds the potential to transform our scholarly narratives about the development of Buddhist monasticisms more broadly.[66]

2. Conflicting Visions of the Ideal Monk

All known Indian Buddhist traditions accept at least two genres of texts as canonical, namely, *sūtra* or discourses, and *vinaya* or monastic law codes.[67] Whereas *sūtra* materials were accessible in some form to Buddhists both lay and monastic alike, the *vinaya*s are presented as strictly for monastic eyes and ears only.[68] Unlike the *sūtra*s, the *vinaya*s are internal documents. Their importance for the study of

Buddhist monasticisms lies, I suggest, in the fact that they transmit an "in-house" vision of what monks and nuns should and were thought to do, and how they ought to behave. Of course, this is not to be confused with what in fact monks and nuns did, and how they behaved. The vision of the monastic life that emerges from a study of the extant monastic codes is not what Buddhist monks told others, particularly the laity. Rather, it seems to reflect what they told themselves, what monks told other monks about their own institutions and traditions, and how they understood Buddhist monastic religiosity. Plainly stated, the *sūtra*s deal primarily with abstract spiritual and philosophical matters; the monastic law codes deal with concrete, corporate, and institutional religious concerns: the nitty gritty of how best to run a successful monastic institution. The authors/redactors of the extant *vinaya*s are primarily concerned not with ethics or morality[69] but with the preservation of the religious institution and its public image.[70] Indeed, as Gregory Schopen has observed, "the *vinayas* are, in fact, preoccupied—if not obsessed—with avoiding any hint of social criticism and with maintaining the status quo at almost any cost."[71]

The monastic lawyers' concern with the preservation of their institution's public image is discernible on almost every page of the monastic law codes. Most, if not all, monastic rules are presented as promulgations in reaction to criticism ensuing from specific actions of particular monks or nuns. Social censure comes from a number of quarters: from fellow monks and nuns, from other heterodox religious wayfarers, from kings, and, most prominently and trenchantly, from the laity.[72] More often than not we are simply told that the laity, that is, brahmins and householders, to use Schopen's translation, "were contemptuous, critical, and complained."[73] In a number of places, however, the content of this abridged criticism is fleshed out. In perhaps the most colorful expression, in the *Mūlasarvāstivāda-vinaya* brahmins and householders charge, for instance, that "the mendicancy of the Buddhist mendicants has gone up in flames; the holy life has gone up in flames."[74] The Buddha is made to react to such criticisms equally colorfully, indicating the seriousness with which the monastic jurists react to lay disparagement: "the criticism of brahmins and householders falls like a thunderbolt," he declares, before "therefore" (*de lta bas na*) promulgating a *vinaya* rule.[75] Moreover, when rules are established, the Buddha is usually said to see ten benefits in the promulgation of such rules. Two of these benefits are telling with regard to the connection between social criticism and its potential deleterious impact on the monastic institution, particularly in terms of patronage.[76] The establishment of a *vinaya* rule curtailing certain actions is said to "make unbelievers believe" and "increase the faith of those who are already believers."

Occasionally, one does get the impression that the monastic authors/redactors became so carried away in protecting their institution's corporate image from any hint of scandal or rumor that they lost sight of the very issue they were trying to negotiate. Take, for instance, the rule concerning the teaching of the Dharma to laywomen brought about by the monk Kālodāyin, also known as Udāyin, whom we will encounter in Chapter 3. According to the version preserved in the *Dharmaguptaka-vinaya,*[77] Kālodāyin went to the house of a prominent householder for alms. In front of the mother-in-law, he whispered the Dharma into the ear of her son's bride. Wondering what was going on, the mother-in-law asks her daughter-in-law what the monk had said. When the daughter-in-law replies that he was instructing her in the Dharma, the mother-in-law states that the Dharma should be preached in a loud voice so that all can hear, not whispered in one's ear surreptitiously. When another monk happens to overhear this, he reports it back to other monks who, in turn, inform the Buddha.[78] In response to this situation we might expect that the Buddha would state, for instance, that a monk must teach the Dharma in a loud voice, as suggested by the mother-in-law, or that at the very least it not be whispered like sweet nothings into a laywoman's ear. In fact, the monastic jurists here make the Buddha declare it to be an offense for monks to teach the Dharma to laywomen period.[79] However, the ruling as formulated proves untenable when laywomen want to hear the Dharma.[80] Eventually, after several amendments, the Buddha is made to state that a monk incurs an offense in teaching a laywoman more than five or six stanzas of Dharma unless in the presence of an intelligent man, viz., one who knows right from wrong.[81]

In the eyes of the ever-vigilant monastic lawyers (some would argue, the Buddha), only certain interactions seem to have required legislation lest they invite lay contempt. Continued familial and, to a certain extent, even marital relations seem to have posed little threat to the success of the monastic movement. That one could renounce the world together with one's family or visit lay family members after renunciation, for instance, seems not to have elicited lay criticism and thus required little, if any, monastic legislation. Issues surrounding pregnant nuns and questions concerning clerical celibacy, however, clearly presented the monastic legislators with delicate and difficult situations to diffuse. Here, as we will see in detail in Chapter 4, the jurists juggle the need to accommodate pregnant nuns and their desire to protect the image of the monastic corporation from aspersions. As one might expect, Buddhist monasticisms as viewed in "in-house" monastic law codes, in which we see the legal minds of our monastic lawyers at work to avoid any hint of social censure, offer a markedly different view of the religious life from that espoused in *sūtra* texts.

In order to highlight the value of *vinaya* texts for the study of Indian Buddhist monasticisms, I will survey three short passages that counterbalance the evidence from the *Rhinoceros Horn Sūtra*. While a more detailed discussion of these passages will emerge in Chapters 2 through 4, my aim here is simply to illustrate how different genres of canonical Buddhist literature can afford different views of monastic life. By way of experiment, let us consider a view of Indian Buddhist monasticisms based solely on passages from "in-house" *vinaya*s. In what directions might the field have developed with these passages as the touchstones of received knowledge of Buddhist monasticisms? Let us go back to a time well before Hodgson. Imagine an early scholar who, knowing nothing about Buddhism, tries to describe or reconstruct a vision of religious praxis primarily on the basis of the extant monastic law codes.[82]

A story from the *Dharmaguptaka-vinaya,* preserved only in Chinese, recounts how a young monastic is sent to find his father, a *bhikṣu,* who had wandered off on his own for breakfast.[83] In doing so, the father had awkwardly kept the rest of the monastic community waiting. A confrontation ensues. The father grabs his son, who in turn pushes his father, accidentally killing him. The boy is not found guilty of any offense, but only told that he ought not to have pushed his father. This story is not explicitly about fathers and sons; it is about murder, monastic definitions thereof, and whether the son is guilty of homicide. What is of interest to us, however, is the manner in which the story is introduced:

> At that time there was a *bhikṣu* who left home [for the religious life] late in life. Taking his son he left home [for the religious life] (將兒出家). At breakfast time he went to another layman's house. The *bhikṣu*s asked his son, saying, "Where did your father go?"[84]

The full story will be dealt with in Section 7 of Chapter 2. For now it will suffice to mention that nowhere in the story is any implicit or explicit criticism made about this *bhikṣu*'s "renunciation of the world" *with* his son. This is presented as a commonplace occurrence. It is simply taken for granted that a monk could, and in this case did, leave home for the religious life with his son.

If this were the first passage our imaginary intellectual predecessor had encountered, what conclusions might he have drawn from it about the nature of Buddhist monasticism? A cautious reader would of course be wary of conclusions made on the basis of a single reference to a *bhikṣu*. Nevertheless, our reader must start somewhere, and he might infer that Buddhist *bhikṣu*s could leave home for the religious life with their sons. Whether Buddhist monastic law somehow required that the *bhikṣu* take his son is not mentioned, but certainly it would be impossible for a reader to conclude that Buddhist *bhikṣu*s abandoned their children on the basis of this one passage.

If this one passage had piqued our reader's curiosity, he might begin to look for further references to *bhikṣu*s, perhaps in other monastic codes. Consider, for instance, a passage from the *Mahīśāsaka-vinaya,* again preserved only in Chinese.[85] A jealous *bhikṣuṇī* sees her husband, a *bhikṣu,* smiling at another *bhikṣuṇī* with whom, we are told, he had an illicit affair as a layman. Taking a water jug, she smashes him over the head with it. The Buddha then establishes a rule about *bhikṣuṇī*s waiting upon *bhikṣu*s with water jugs and fans. The husband and wife, *bhikṣu* and *bhikṣuṇī,* are introduced as follows:

> At one time there was a husband and wife (夫婦) who, the two of them, left home [for the religious life] at the same time (二人俱時出家). That husband-*bhikṣu* (夫比丘) went begging for alms, brought them back to where the wife-*bhikṣuṇī* (婦比丘尼) dwelt, and ate.[86]

Were our early observer to base his vision of Indian Buddhist monastic life solely on this passage, he might conclude conservatively that some *bhikṣu*s were married and left home for the religious life with their wives. Whether this would mean that *bhikṣu*s had to be married to leave home would remain unclear.[87] Were he to recall the story of the *bhikṣu* who left home for the religious life with his son, then, on the basis of these two passages, he might infer that when *bhikṣu*s "renounced the world" they sometimes took their wives and children along, if they had any.

Finally, our imaginary scholar might consider a narrative from the *Mūlasarvāstivāda-vinaya* which suggests that *bhikṣuṇī*s could have babies.[88] In the *Mūlasarvāstivāda-vinaya,* as in other monastic law codes, we find a number of passages dealing with *bhikṣuṇī*s who give birth. According to Buddhist monastic law, *bhikṣuṇī*s were not supposed to sleep in the same room as males. When a certain *bhikṣuṇī* gave birth to a son, she is said to have left him outside at night for fear of transgressing this rule. But when the boy's crying causes a commotion, a series of rules is established with regard to living arrangements for newly delivered *bhikṣuṇī*s. Here, in this passage preserved in Tibetan and Chinese, we see the *bhikṣuṇī* formally request permission to spend the night in the same room as her son.

> The Blessed One said, "Henceforth, with authorization, the *bhikṣuṇī* Guptā must request a resolution from the order of *bhikṣuṇī*s to sleep in the same room together with her son (與子同室宿羯磨; *bu dang lhan cig tu khang pa gcig tu nyal bar dge slong ma'i dge 'dun las sdom pa*). The request should be made as follows:...
>
> 'May the noble order listen! I, the *bhikṣuṇī* Guptā, have given birth to a baby boy (我笈多苾芻尼生男; *bdag gub ta las bu khye'u zhig btsas te*)....'"[89]

Were our observer to generalize from this one narrative, he might construct a picture of Buddhist monasticisms in which not only did *bhikṣuṇī*s have babies, but they were also authorized by the Buddha to look after—or at least share sleeping quarters with—their children. The need to request permission might imply that this situation was not without problems, but that a formula was set forth detailing how to request permission in such cases suggests that it was not at all extraordinary. Indeed, it seems to have been common enough to require regulation. Our early scholar might well conclude that, under certain circumstances, *bhikṣuṇī*s were authorized to raise their babies.

Our hypothetical scholar might arrange the data from these three passages in a number of ways. He might conclude, for instance, that Dharmaguptaka *bhikṣu*s had or could have children, Mahīśāsaka *bhikṣu*s could have wives, and Mūlasarvāstivāda *bhikṣuṇī*s could have babies. To infer from this that Mahīśāsaka *bhikṣu*s could also have children and not just wives would be tenuous. Were he to find similar references in all three monastic codes, however, then he would be able to make conclusions about pan-Buddhist, or at least Dharmaguptaka, Mahīśāsaka, and Mūlasarvāstivāda, monasticisms.

Our early scholar, of course, is entirely fictional, and these *vinaya* passages were not taken into consideration in the formulation of our most basic notions of Buddhist monasticisms.[90] Rather, the founding fathers of our discipline seem to have started with visions of the ideal *bhikṣu* such as those espoused in the *Rhinoceros Horn* and other *sutta* materials.[91] These texts have been the field's main points of reference and departure.

Lest my position be misunderstood, let me make clear that I do not advocate basing our knowledge of Indian Buddhist monasticisms solely on one or even all of the above *vinaya* passages. Rather, I suggest only that a balanced study of Indian Buddhist monasticisms cannot continue to ignore these and other similar voices from the textual record. We must consider all of the available evidence, and bring this evidence to bear on our scholarly assumptions. Incidental sightings such as those surveyed above of monks and their children or spouses in the extant *vinaya*s can perhaps be best understood with reference to what Jan Nattier, borrowing from New Testament studies, refers to as the principle of irrelevance: "We may draw with some confidence on data found within a normative text . . . when incidental mention is made of items unrelated to the author's primary agenda."[92] Our monastic jurists are not making a case for continued contact between monastics and their spouses, or between monks and nuns and their children. For them, no case needed to be made. That men and women might leave home for the religious life with, as opposed to abandoning, their spouses or children was simply part of Buddhist renunciation as known to our monastic lawyers. The canonical jurists, however, do make a case for the accommodation of pregnant nuns. This was something that had to be carefully negotiated and legislated given the probability that the presence of pregnant nuns would give rise to criticism concerning the celibacy of the community.

The canonical texts of Indian Buddhist monasticisms do not present a single, uniform vision of the monastic life. Buddhist *sūtra*s extol a religious ideal in which monks abandon family, wealth, and all possessions in favor of the religious life. Yet Schopen has shown convincingly that Buddhist monastic law codes go into great detail about contracts, debts, interest, loans, money, property, rights of inheritance, and wealth.[93] The *vinaya*s speak, in other words, to the this-worldly concerns of monks following the religious life. Likewise, whereas *sūtra*s go into lengthy discourses on the value of meditation, for instance, Schopen has shown that Buddhist monastic law codes warn against rigorous engagement in contemplative exercises since it "makes you stupid"; in the law codes "ascetic, meditating monks... almost always appear as the butt of jokes, objects of ridicule, and—not uncommonly—sexual deviants. They are presented as irresponsible and of the type that give the order a bad name."[94]

As we will see in the following chapters, the image espoused by the *Rhinoceros Horn Sūtra* seems to be antithetical to the religious life as envisioned by the authors/redactors of monastic law codes. In the monastic codes, most passages dealing with Buddhist renunciation do not mention, much less require, the severance of familial ties, even though that is exactly how they have been interpreted.[95] How, then, are we to understand these two visions of the monastic life? Are they to be categorized, for instance, as old and new, ideal and realistic (or perhaps pragmatic), external and internal, or simply as different, incompatible, or inconsistent?[96] While a comprehensive answer must await further research, a number of things are already clear. To date, the study of Buddhism—and the study of religion more broadly—has focused generally not on realia or social history but primarily on doctrine, philosophy, and ethics.[97] This focus is another factor in shaping the picture of Buddhist monasticisms prevalent in modern scholarship, and may also help to explain the privileging of *sutta* texts. Moreover, as we will discuss at the beginning of the next section, when the monastic codes or *vinaya*s have entered the discussion, at least until recently, the rule of choice has been that of the Pāli or Theravāda tradition, almost to the entire exclusion of the other five extant textual traditions.[98]

The modern Western understanding of Buddhist monasticism and the prevalence of the view that Buddhist renunciation somehow entails the complete severance of all familial ties cannot be attributed, solely, to the privileging of one type of canonical text over another (i.e., *sūtra* over *vinaya*), nor to the reliance on one tradition's sources (i.e., Theravāda) at the expense of those of other traditions. Rather, I suggest that it stems from selective reading within the corpus of privileged traditions and genres, a selectivity guided by preconceived notions about what Buddhist monasticisms should look like and perhaps also by how they have been put into practice by schools of Buddhism in the modern world.

3. Indian Buddhist Monastic Law Codes

The number of Indian Buddhist *nikāya*s or monastic lineages is traditionally counted at either eighteen or twenty.[99] It is thought that each of these *nikāya*s transmitted its own monastic law code.[100] Only six such codes have survived in a form that may be considered complete: the Dharmaguptaka, Mahāsāṅghika, Mahīśāsaka, Sarvāstivāda, Mūlasarvāstivāda, and Theravāda *vinaya*s.[101]

Of these six monastic codes, the Theravāda or Pāli Vinaya is the only complete *vinaya* extant in an Indian language (Pāli), although even this has long been recognized to be a translation.[102] The Pāli Vinaya is the only Buddhist monastic law code to be translated into any modern language.[103] Mostly untranslated, and largely unedited to critical standards, the other *vinaya*s remain available only to specialists.[104] Perhaps as a result, and especially in the West and among Anglophones, until recently[105] scholarly discussions of Indian Buddhism in general and Buddhist monasticisms in particular have been almost wholly drawn from Pāli or Theravāda sources.[106]

To base our understanding of Indian Buddhist monasticisms on only one of six extant codes risks reducing what may have been a variety of religious traditions to one. To my mind, it is premature to accept one of six traditions as representative of Indian Buddhist monasticisms without first studying—reading, editing, translating, and rereading—the textual traditions of the other five. In the present study, I have attempted to make use of all extant Indian Buddhist monastic law codes preserved in Chinese, Pāli, Sanskrit, and Tibetan in order to ensure that what we see is not just an isolated viewpoint of a single tradition, but is broadly representative of the canonical jurists' handling of family matters in all extant *vinaya*s. The use of all available *vinaya*s allows us to begin to build an argument for the trans-*nikāya* and pan-Indian ubiquity of our findings.

Moreover, as I will discuss immediately below, although the dating of the monastic law codes is not without problems, the use of all extant *vinaya*s may allow us to suggest that the picture which emerges from this study is not a late "corruption" of the monastic ideal but rather a very old vision of the religious life. Although the extant sources disagree about the dating, in the first few centuries after the demise of the Buddha, a great schism in Indian Buddhism is said to have resulted in the development of what we in Buddhist studies refer to, somewhat problematically, as sectarianism:[107] the Sthavira–Mahāsāṅghika split.[108] If we can show that the same or similar regulations as those found in the extant *vinaya*s of the Sthaviras (i.e., Dharmaguptaka, Mahīśāsaka, Sarvāstivāda, Mūlasarvāstivāda, and Theravāda *vinaya*s) are also found in the Mahāsāṅghika tradition(s), this, then, according to conventional wisdom and the principle of higher criticism, would suggest that these rules are in fact very old, dating from a presectarian tradition.[109]

As already mentioned, the task of dating our texts presents particular problems. We must be careful to differentiate between dates, where known, of composition or authorship of the extant monastic law codes and those of redaction and translation. Moreover, we must also distinguish dates associated with the content of the texts (composition/redaction/translation) from those of the manuscript evidence that has survived down to the present.

Catalogues and colophons of Chinese translations record the dates and names of translators, and, if accurate, these take us back centuries beyond the dates of our generally late extant Chinese printed editions and even manuscripts. For the Dharmaguptaka, Mahāsāṅghika, Mahīśāsaka, and Sarvāstivāda *vinaya*s, extant primarily only in Chinese translation,[110] this means the first quarter of the fifth century C.E.[111] Yijing's 義浄 (635–713 C.E.) incomplete Chinese translation of the *Mūlasarvāstivāda-vinaya* dates to the early eighth century (700–712).[112] Of course, these are only the dates of translation, not the dates of extant manuscript evidence. The earliest Chinese *vinaya* manuscripts date perhaps from the fifth to eighth centuries for the Dunhuang manuscripts,[113] or the eighth century for the Shōgozō 聖語藏 manuscripts.[114] It is not until much later that we find more complete manuscript copies or printed editions of a canon:[115] the Nanatsudera 七寺 canon, for instance, was copied between 1175 and 1180,[116] while the second carving of the Korean edition was completed in 1251 C.E.[117] The standard edition used by scholars today is the Taishō edition, compiled in Japan between 1924 and 1935, on the basis of the second carving of the Korean edition and collated with several other printed editions and manuscript collections.[118]

Approximately one-quarter[119] of the *Mūlasarvāstivāda-vinaya* has survived in Sanskrit in an incomplete manuscript from Gilgit dated to between the sixth and seventh centuries.[120] What appears to be a complete, or very nearly complete, Tibetan translation of the *Mūlasarvāstivāda-vinaya* dates to the ninth century.[121] We have a few early fragments of a handwritten copy of this Tibetan translation from Tabo dating perhaps from the tenth century onward,[122] and Dunhuang fragments that may be roughly contemporaneous.[123] The earliest complete extant printed edition of the Tibetan translation of the *Mūlasarvāstivāda-vinaya* dates from the fifteenth century, although this edition is not accessible.[124] The earliest editions currently available to scholars date from the seventeenth century.[125]

There are at least two dates that are often associated with the Pāli Vinaya, neither of which are the dates of composition. The earliest is that of the Aluvihāra redaction in Sri Lanka under Vaṭṭagāmaṇī Abhaya (29–17 B.C.E.).[126] Yet we have no way of confirming what the canon looked like at this early time; extant Pāli manuscripts do not go back this far. Excepting four folios found in Nepal and dated on paleographic grounds to the ninth century,[127] the earliest manuscripts we have for the Pāli Vinaya are from the late fifteenth century, the time at which Oskar von Hinüber tells us that "the continuous manuscript tradition with complete texts begins."[128]

The other date associated with the Pāli Vinaya is the fifth century C.E., when the tradition was locked into a close word commentary in the *Samantapāsādikā*.[129] The commentary itself, however, is also extant only in those same late manuscripts. If we accept that the fifth century is the earliest knowledge we have of the contents of the Pāli Vinaya, then this puts us roughly in line with the fifth-century translations of the *vinaya*s of the Dharmaguptaka, Mahāsāṅghika, Mahīśāsaka, and Sarvāstivāda.

The dates discussed above are primarily those of translation and transmission, not of composition. The painstaking work of tracking and tracing developments outside the texts by Schopen and others before him has placed the *Mūlasarvāstivāda-vinaya* in northwest India around "the first or second century of our era."[130] As Schopen has noted, all extant *vinaya*s presuppose a fully developed monasticism replete with durable goods and dwellings, and a highly organized infrastructure.[131] Our *vinaya* texts mention doors, guards, keys, land acquisitions, locks, permanent endowments, safes, saunas, sharecropping agreements, slaves or serfs, and much more.[132] However, evidence for this kind of monastic institution does not appear in the archaeological record until around the beginning of the Common Era.[133] The monasticisms assumed already in the canonical legal texts, then, cannot plausibly be so early as to be contemporary with the Buddha or his first few generations of followers. If all of our *vinaya* texts presuppose what are only late developments in the archaeological record, then it seems to follow that all of the texts are, as Schopen has suggested, uniformly late.[134]

Very little work has been done on the dating of the composition of the *vinayas* of the Dharmaguptaka, Mahīśāsaka, Mahāsāṅghika, and Sarvāstivāda. Although it may be that they came into existence only shortly before they were translated into Chinese in the early fifth century, at present I see no reason to place their composition any later (or earlier) than the *Mūlasarvāstivāda-vinaya,* and certainly not by centuries. As a working hypothesis, then, I accept that all of our monastic law codes date to around the first few centuries of the Common Era, with the provision that a couple of centuries either side of this is a manageable margin of error.[135] For the most part, the dating of the *vinayas* is of little consequence for the present study. An earlier or later dating of the composition of the *vinayas* would result only in a shift of the time frame, and would have little, if any, impact on my general observations about the importance of family matters in Indian Buddhist monasticisms as viewed through *vinaya* literature.

4. The Family

At the heart of this study lies the question of monks and nuns and their continued familial relationships. Before we get into the body of the study, it might be helpful here to say something about the family as it relates to the study of Indian Buddhist monasticisms. We will start by looking at what we know about the Buddha's own family.

Soon after attaining enlightenment, Siddhārtha Gautama, scion of the Śākya clan, is said to have been surrounded by friends and family members, whether as renunciant wayfarers or lay well-wishers. A small band of ascetics first followed in his footsteps in the hope of attaining awakening. Eventually, an organized community of monks (and later nuns) developed, at first comprised mostly of the Buddha's friends and family. This is what canonical texts, biographies, hagiographies, and legends tell us.

Details differ among the sources. One tradition, that of the Mūlasarvāstivādins, records in varying detail tales such as that of the Buddha's half-brother, Nanda. After struggling to leave his lovely wife to follow his brother, the Buddha, in the religious life, Nanda landed in trouble by doting over and drawing her image on rocks when he was supposed to be engaged in meditation or recitation.[136] We also find stories about the Buddha's cousins, Ānanda, Aniruddha, Bhadrika, and Devadatta, who are all said to have joined the monastic order.[137] There are stories about the Buddha's mother,[138] Mahāmāyā,[139] and his aunt and stepmother, Mahāprajāpatī Gautamī, who pleaded with the Buddha, and solicited the help of her nephew, Ānanda, to allow women to participate in the holy life as nuns.[140] One might recall the stories of the Kāśyapa brothers of Urubilvā, who brought with them their one thousand disciples;[141] the royal decree of King Śuddhodana, the Buddha's father, according to which a son from every family of the Śākya clan was to enter the monastic order;[142] the five hundred clan members who were tonsured by Upāli and subsequently ordained;[143] the conversion of Udāyin, son of King Śuddhodana's royal chaplain (*purohita*) and playmate of the Buddha;[144] the Buddha's uncles, Amṛtodana and Droṇodana, who, each together with some seventy thousand kinsmen, attained the first fruits of the Buddhist awakening, the stage of stream-enterer.[145] One might mention two of the Buddha's three wives—Gopikā and Mṛgajā—who, likewise, became stream-enterers, or his main wife, Yaśodharā, who entered the order of nuns and attained religious perfection;[146] or even the Buddha's son, Rāhula, who himself became a monk and, following closely in his father's footsteps, attained arhatship, a religious goal achieved by both his mother and father—in fact, one achieved by many, if not most, of Gautama's own family.[147] Similar stories suggesting the importance of the Buddha's own family abound in the narratives told by Indian Buddhist authors.

Despite the undeniable emphasis on the founder's family in many of the texts detailing the biography of the Buddha,[148] more often than not scholars have emphasized Gautama's initial act of renunciation with very little recognition that his own family followed him into the monastic life. With regard to the fate of married women in Buddhism, Young, for instance, suggests that "the Buddha did not fulfill his obligations to his father, his son, or his wife. He deserted them all as part of his rejection of worldly life in favor of the ascetic life, and most of the sixty men who joined the order of monks in the first few months of its existence also deserted wives and families."[149] Likewise, Ohnuma states that "in his biography, the Buddha himself, on 'going forth,' dramatically leaves behind his wife, son, and parents, and forever renounces the worldly roles of husband, father, and son."[150] Ohnuma then observes that although the Buddha "continues to be referred to as the 'father' of Rāhula, he is equally depicted as the 'father' of all monks and nuns within the Saṃgha.[151] Though he continues to recognize his former relationship with his family . . . it is clear that he is relating to them *as a buddha* rather than as a member of the family."[152]

Lest I be misunderstood, there is no doubt that the Buddha's initial "renunciation" of his family is dramatic, even if his family did subsequently follow him into the monastic life. Moreover, to be sure, one would not want to claim that the Buddha related to family members solely as a family member, and not "as a buddha." However, I do see as problematic the fact that there is little, if any, indication in the above statement by Ohnuma, for instance, that Rāhula, the Buddha's own son, and many other members of the Buddha's own family, also became monks and nuns. Unless I am mistaken, scholars have tended to highlight only one-half of the story.

Statements such as those quoted above give the impression that having gone forth from the home into homelessness, the Buddha and—if his renunciation is to be taken as a model for emulation—monks and nuns after him were no longer in contact with their families. One might even go further and suggest that Buddhist monks and nuns were, for all intents and purposes, socially dead. This is what has been suggested by Wilson, among others, who discusses the idea of Buddhist renunciation as "a death to the social world that leaves grieving relatives in its wake."[153]

Given the assumptions that seem to undergird the study of Buddhist monasticisms, it is perhaps not surprising that many scholars simply have accepted the received knowledge without questioning it.[154] In Spiro's introductory essay to a volume entitled *Religion and the Family in East Asia,* for instance, Buddhist monasticism is described as follows: "Beginning with the Buddha himself, 'leaving home' has meant abandoning not only parents, but also . . . wives and children as well."[155] Spiro goes on to suggest that "it is not living in a family-like structure as such that the 'goer-forth' rejects in 'leaving home,' but rather living in his own biological family. And make no mistake about it. 'Leaving home' *is* a rejection of the latter family, despite the monks' attempts to rationalize it."[156] Most recently, albeit in a much more nuanced fashion than Spiro, Ohnuma has stated that "it is clear that this act [i.e., renunciation]—ideally speaking, at least—*does* involve the rejection of one's family and the severance of ordinary family ties."[157]

By contrast, I suggest that the authors/redactors of Indian Buddhist monasticisms take for granted that biological kin might leave home for the religious life together. It is not simply allowed or permitted. Rather, I argue that renunciation *with* or *as* a family is tightly woven into the very fabric of Indian Buddhist renunciation and monasticisms as envisioned by the authors/redactors of our monastic codes. Moreover, even "ideally speaking," at least when speaking of the ideals of the authors/redactors of the extant *vinaya*s, there seems to have been little, if any, expectation that when one left home for the religious life one would either reject one's family or sever all family ties.[158] As we will see in Section 6 of Chapter 3, in the story of Mahākāśyapa, the Buddhist ascetic *par excellence,* even the strictest Buddhist asceticism, at least as presented in the *Mūlasarvāstivāda-vinaya,* far from requiring complete severance of all contact with one's "former" wife, actually requires a monk to share his alms with her in times of adversity.

A further indication of the prevalence of these received views can be seen in Alan Cole's entry on Buddhism and the family in the *Encyclopedia of Buddhism.* The entry begins as follows:

> Given that Buddhism is regularly understood as a monastic movement dedicated to "leaving the family" (*pravrajyā*), the technical term for becoming a monk or nun, it might seem odd to ask about Buddhism's relationship to the family. Why, after all, would Buddhism as a religion of renunciation have anything to do with family life? However, a closer look at the structure of Buddhist rhetoric, as well as Buddhism's various societal roles, reveals that Buddhism's relationship to the family and family values has several unexpected layers.[159]

Unhappily, Cole's entry replicates a number of problematic assumptions common to the study of the history of religions in general and Buddhist studies in particular.[160] Cole's assertions aside, it is his discussion of the role of family in Buddhism that warrants our immediate attention:

> Arguably there are at least four basic categories of Buddhist discourse that focus on familial issues: (1) a discourse on the negative aspects of family life, the language of renunciation; (2) a symbolic language in which identity within the monastic setting is understood as a kind of replication of the patriarchal family, a kind of corporate familialism; (3) guidelines for correct conduct at home, pastoral advice from the Buddhist establishment; and (4) specific lineage claims that sought to

establish an elite family within the monastic family, a more specialized form of corporate familialism.[161]

The third and fourth categories proposed by Cole are outside the purview of the present study in the sense that they do not deal with Indian Buddhist monastics and their families per se. Pastoral advice given by monks and nuns to laymen is found, to be sure, in certain genres of Buddhist texts. Likewise, lineage claims are also a part of Buddhist monasticisms (particularly Chinese and Japanese, but also Tibetan). Neither of these categories, however, has much to do with mainstream Indian Buddhist monastics and their families, either biological or matrimonial.

With regard to his first category, Cole suggests that the language of renunciation focuses on "negative aspects," "the unsatisfactory and even dangerous aspects of family life."[162] To be sure, some aspects of "Buddhist discourse" focus on "negative aspects" of family life; this we have already seen in the *Rhinoceros Horn Sūtra,* a text quoted at length by Cole in his contribution to *Sex, Marriage, and Family in World Religions.*[163] Here one might also cite part of the stock phrase found, for instance, in the *Mūlasarvāstivāda-vinaya* that often introduces a householder's motives for entering the religious order, viz., "I am now old and cannot pursue wealth. Furthermore, my relatives are all dead. I ought to forsake the lay life and leave home [for the religious life]."[164] We might also consider the claim leveled at the Buddha in the Pāli Vinaya, for instance, in reaction to the ordination of "very distinguished young men belonging to respectable families of Magadha," viz., that renunciation breaks up families, "making (us) childless . . . making (us) widows. . . ."[165] According to Bailey and Mabbett, however, this complaint occurs only once in the entire canon.[166]

Cole's second category, that of symbolic language used to create a monastic "family," draws on a common trope in studies of monasticism.[167] At least in the case of Indian Buddhist monastic law codes, however, there is little in the way of familial language used to address other members of the monastic community.[168] This was established long ago by I. B. Horner in reference to Theravāda monasticism: "neither Order looked to anyone or to any kind of being as their 'father' or their 'mother.'"[169] In attempting to arrive at an acceptable translation for Pāli *bhikkhu* (Skt. *bhikṣu*), Horner notes that "*bhātar,* the accepted word for 'brother,' and one in current terminology, was never apparently regarded as synonymous with *bhikkhu,* and indeed never seems to have been connected with members of the Order."[170] Moreover, with regard to the term for 'sister,' Horner states that "with this absence of *bhātar* as a term used in the religious life, it is curious that monks used its opposite, *bhaginī* [sister]. But it should be noted that they addressed laywomen as well as nuns as *bhaginī*. Hence the word *bhaginī* is clearly precluded from containing any unique reference to *bhikkhunīs*."[171]

To my mind, Cole provides another excellent example of the degree to which modern assumptions about the nature of Buddhist monasticisms and renunciation have constructed and constricted scholarly inquiry. We do not ask questions about monastic families, monks' wives, or nuns' children simply because, like Cole, we do not expect them to have any.[172] Were the present study to be limited to Cole's "four basic categories of Buddhist discourse that focus on familial issues," I would have little to say about Buddhist monks and nuns and their families. In contrast to Cole, this study addresses the continued biological and matrimonial relationships between monks and nuns and those whom they have "abandoned" in favor of the religious life, whether among family members who have likewise entered the religious life or among those who have not.

To be sure, not all scholars have overlooked the importance of family and the continuity of kinship ties in Indian monastic Buddhism; certain themes vis-à-vis family have been studied. Valuable contributions have been made by those who have seriously delved into the depths of the monastic law codes, texts in which one cannot help but notice the frequent mention of monks and nuns and their children, parents, siblings, and spouses. André Bareau, for instance, has dealt with the reactions of families to monks' ordinations.[173] Likewise, Schopen has written on the rights of monks to inherit family property,[174] their obligations to support their parents,[175] and Indian notions of filial piety.[176] John Strong has discussed the Buddha and his family, in particular his wife Yaśodharā and son Rāhula, and their "family quest" for enlightenment.[177]

In Japan, where studies in Buddhist monastic law are more commonplace than in the West, Nobuyuki Yamagiwa has discussed a number of monastic rules that allow monks to interact in various ways with laymen and laywomen to whom they are related, interactions that would otherwise incur offenses.[178] Yamagiwa has also dealt with monastics' obligations to prescribe medicines for sick parents.[179] In a short section on "renunciants and their families" in his work on

Indian Buddhist monastic life,[180] Shizuka Sasaki mentions continued contact between "renunciants" and their families, and states in this regard that "Buddhism does not deny this kind of familial affection" and that "it was never the case that severing connections with former relatives was encouraged."[181]

With the possible exception of Schopen's, however, these particular studies have had a limited impact on the wider field of Buddhist studies or religious studies. Though Schopen's work is widely read and cited, his focus is predominantly on Indian Buddhism in terms of the legal and financial aspects of monasticism. Moreover, Schopen's work has often highlighted the differences between Mūlasarvāstivādin monasticism and the monasticism presented in the (Theravāda) Pāli Vinaya, and hence in our modern handbooks.[182] Indeed, given his emphasis on the *Mūlasarvāstivāda-vinaya,* there has been, I suggest, a tendency to see the weird and wacky world of Mūlasarvāstivāda monasticism as portrayed in this monastic code as somehow unrepresentative of Indian Buddhism. In contrast to the work of Schopen, the present study highlights the similarities between the Mūlasarvāstivāda and Theravāda traditions, and all of the others in between. The study of family matters suggests that the Pāli Vinaya is not so different from the other *vinaya*s, especially when reread in light of the other, often narratively richer, monastic codes. Moreover, far from being aberrant, I contend that the *Mūlasarvāstivāda-vinaya* may be very much representative of what Indian Buddhist monasticisms had become in the first few centuries of the Common Era.[183] All extant Indian Buddhist monastic law codes suggest that monks and nuns could continue to interact with family members both lay and monastic. While this has been known to most specialists of Buddhist monastic law, the full religious and social implications of this for the study of Buddhism in India and beyond have yet to be laid out. The present study attempts to do just that.

5. A Preview of the Inquiry

Chapter 2, entitled "Family Matters," introduces a number of early Indian inscriptions in which monks, nuns, and laymen are identified in terms of familial relationships: So-and-so, mother of monk Y or nun Z. We also find inscriptions referring to nun X, mother of So-and-so, or nun Y, along with her daughter(s), or to laymen who are identified as sons or daughters of monastics. These inscriptions could be explained away as records of children who were abandoned and forsaken by their parents when the latter "left home for the religious life." Extant Buddhist monastic law codes, however, preserve stories about men "leaving home" to become monks with their young children, and children who, after joining the monastery, still call their monk-fathers "Daddy." We also encounter narratives of mothers and daughters who leave home for the religious life together. Here the monastic law codes may allow new interpretations of the inscriptional evidence.

Narratives from the monastic law codes raise questions of interpretation with regard to the phrase "to go forth from home into homelessness." This phrase has generally been understood literally. I argue that evidence from Buddhist monastic law codes suggests that it is best understood figuratively. For the monastic legislators, the authors of Indian Buddhist legal codes, there seems to have been no question that monks and nuns could take their families with them into homelessness. Moreover, in texts which are commonly accepted as belonging to among the earliest strata of Buddhist literature available to us, we find presupposed within monastic communities the existence of monks and nuns who were biologically related to each other. In my view, this throws doubt on the scholarly assumption that monks and nuns were required to forsake their families.

Chapter 3, "Former Wives from Former Lives," investigates the status of monks' "former" lay wives. These women have often been overlooked in the study of Indian Buddhism, and it is generally assumed that we know nothing about them.[184] In the case of Buddhist monks' wives, however, there is ample evidence in Buddhist narratives. In some stories, these "abandoned" women are presented as hostile to their husbands; in others they are depicted as still very much attached to them. We not only see stories about monks' visiting (and sometimes being seduced by) their wives, but we also catch a glimpse of the financial situation of some of these "deserted women." Furthermore, in some stories, monks and nuns act as go-betweens in arranging marriages for their own children. Accordingly, in this chapter I discuss the marital status of married men and women upon entering Buddhist monastic orders. Although various forms of marital dissolution were known to the authors/redactors of some monastic law codes, monks and nuns were not required to dissolve their own marriages; "former" wives, that is, lay wives, are not to be confused with divorced wives. Far from always and necessarily abandoning their wives, the monastic authors/redactors seem to have envisaged that monks might go forth into the religious life together with their wives.

Chapter 4, "Nuns Who Become Pregnant," looks specifically at issues surrounding monastic motherhood. Indian Buddhist epigraphical records tell us that some nuns had children; they do not, however, specify whether mothers became nuns or nuns became mothers. In the corpus of monastic law codes, however, we see that monastic jurists not only envisaged the possibility that pregnant women might enter nunneries, but—even if only to keep it under wraps in order to control their community's public image—they also legislated a place for motherhood in Indian Buddhist nunneries. All known Indian Buddhist monastic law codes allow pregnant nuns to give birth to children and to breast-feed and raise their newborns within the convent while practicing the Dharma.

In Chapter 5, "Reconsidering Renunciation," I suggest that a close examination of the issues surrounding family matters both presupposed and legislated by the authors/redactors of the extant monastic law codes may shed more light on the religious life of Indian Buddhist monks and nuns in the first few centuries of the Common Era than the romanticized portrayals based primarily on Pāli *sutta* literature that are prevalent in modern scholarly and popular literature. I also suggest that family-friendly forms of monasticism may have been more common in India than previously thought.

6. Reading Indian Buddhist Monastic Law Codes

Sources for the study of monastics and their families in Indian Buddhism are, in general, few and far between. In part, this is to be expected. John Boswell, for instance, has noted that "conjugal relations, reproduction, and the interior life of the family are, in fact, among the most reclusive and private respects of human existence, jealously guarded from public view in most cultures, and less likely than almost any other interpersonal activity to leave written records."[185] Although Boswell is writing on Christendom, there is no reason to think his observation concerning written records for family life is any less applicable to Indian Buddhism. Moreover, in the case of India the situation is particularly difficult since we lack many of the historical and social records that historians of the same time period in China, for instance, might reasonably expect to have at their disposal.

For the study of Indian Buddhist monasticisms, by far the richest sources are monastic law codes.[186] However, these *vinayas* are not a direct window on what monks and nuns actually did. Rather, the law codes provide us with records of what some monks (some would argue, the Buddha) seem to have thought other monks and nuns should and should not do. Yet few of the questions which I ask of our sources are ones that Indian Buddhist traditions ever seem to have formulated explicitly or dealt with in any great detail.

The extant monastic codes all follow a twofold division into (1) rules of comportment and deportment for individual monks and nuns (*prātimokṣa* rules) and (2) institutional law governing the activities of the monastic corporation or *saṅgha,* collected in what are known in Pāli as *khandhakas* and attested in the *Mūlasarvāstivāda-vinaya* as *vastus*.[187] In the first division, approximately[188] two hundred and fifty rules for monks and three hundred and fifty rules for nuns are arranged hierarchically in terms of the gravity of the infraction, ranging from the most serious, *pārājika* offenses, covering among other things breaches of celibacy and the taking of a human life, to the least serious, *śaikṣā* rules concerning matters of minor etiquette, such as not slurping one's meal. The second division, the *khandhakas* or *vastus*, are arranged thematically. They contain sections dealing with various topics such as, alphabetically, the allocation of corporate (monastic) chattels, confessional ceremonies, disciplinary proceedings, medicines, ordination, schisms, and so forth. However, there is no section in any known *vinaya* that deals specifically with monastic families. If the *absence* of specific texts devoted either wholly or even partly to our topic in the monastic corpus is significant, then family may have been of little concern to our monastic authors/redactors. In other words, matters surrounding monks and nuns and their families seem not to have been perceived as necessitating any serious monastic legislation.

But if there are no Indian Buddhist monastic legal texts dealing specifically with the question of family matters, how then are we to answer the questions that we might ask of our texts? I have attempted to bridge this gap by exploring a wide range of *vinaya* narratives dealing with issues that are seemingly unrelated to each other and most of which, at first sight, appear to have nothing whatsoever to do with the question of family. Evidence often comes from the most improbable of contexts. Passages dealing with topics as diverse as monks' visiting barbers, monastics' seeking meals, and nuns' personal safety often reveal important insights into the religious life as the elaborate narratives unfold.

All of the extant *vinaya*s contain an enormous amount of narrative material, some more than others. Sylvain Lévi describes one of these monastic codes—the most elaborate, that of the Mūlasarvāstivādins—as "written with art, overflow[ing] with miscellaneous matter of all kinds. The rules often have the appearance of being mere pretexts for relating long histories, heroic, comic, fabulous and romantic... a complete canon in itself."[189] In addition to lengthy narratives of previous lives and various *sūtra*s embedded within the monastic codes, many of which also circulated as independent texts or in anthologies such as the *Divyāvadāna,* most of the hundreds upon hundreds of *vinaya* rules are introduced with a frame-story outlining how each rule came about.

The frame-stories introducing *vinaya* rules relate incidents set, at least narratively, in the lifetime of the Buddha. As discussed above, the actions of a certain monk or nun, and often a group of monks or nuns, give rise to lay criticism of Buddhist monastics. The incident is then reported back to the Buddha, who thereupon promulgates a rule making the action performed by the monk or nun in question to be a monastic offense, the exact type of which is determined by the gravity of the incident. The monk or nun protagonist whose actions bring about the establishment of the rule is generally neither found guilty of any offense nor punished, since, according to the common legal principle *nulla poena sine lege,* there was as yet no law to transgress. The protagonist is generally referred to in *vinaya* literature as an *ādikarmika,* a term which is often translated, perhaps confusingly, since technically there is no offense, as the "first offender."[190] Although the rules and regulations of Buddhist monastic law are presented as the Buddha's reactions to accounts of what monks and nuns did, we might step back and interpret this legislation as early monastic lawyers' reactions to what monks were said to have done, were thought to do, or might foreseeably do, reactions mostly intended to protect the public image of the monastic institution.

Generally, these frame-stories explicitly address only one issue at a time. Inadvertently, however, they provide us with a rich array of incidental or secondary details. In addition to what the authors/redactors of these texts may have wanted to tell their readers, or even themselves, they reveal to us information about their assumptions concerning the religious life of monks and nuns in India. It is precisely the very casual and unselfconscious nature of such details that offer us candid glimpses of monastic life as envisioned by the authors/redactors of the extant law codes. To give but one example, in a stock phrase found throughout the *Mūlasarvāstivāda-vinaya,* monks and nuns who are seen constantly going to the houses of barbers and other craftsmen are assumed to be going to the houses of their relatives or families.[191] Although the narratives in which this stock phrase is found tell us nothing about monks' visiting their relatives or families, the point remains that in Indian Buddhist monastic literature, when a monk is seen frequenting a lay house, the natural conclusion to which the authors/redactors have other monks jump is that the monk is visiting his relatives. While the modern reader might assume that the monk is being criticized when he is mistakenly thought to be visiting his family, in fact there is not a hint of criticism, either expressed or implied. Rather, this stock phrase suggests the degree to which visits home by monks may have been not only unproblematic in the eyes of the monastic jurists, but also entirely commonplace in Indian Buddhist monasticisms. It is precisely assumptions such as those implicit in this and other stock phrases and narratives employed and crafted by the monastic authors/redactors that I seek to highlight and contrast with our own.

Broadly speaking, then, the *vinaya*s preserve two types of monastic law: rules governing the activities of individual monks and nuns, and those regulating the activities of the monastic community as a corporate entity. In this study, I will discuss examples of both types of monastic legislation. The rules for individual monks and nuns are found in *vinaya* literature in two different contexts. They are collected in lists known as *prātimokṣa*s, short texts that probably were used primarily for ritual recitation at confessional ceremonies. The exact same rules also appear in much longer sections known as *vibhaṅga*s, in which the rules are presented along with rich frame-stories and various other canonical legal interpretation, including word commentaries and detailed exceptions to the rule, presumably intended to guide monastic jurists in the application of said rule. Rules such as those found in the *prātimokṣa*s stating, for instance, that nuns should not ordain pregnant women appear at first sight relatively clear cut. Yet these so-called prohibitions in fact tell us very little. They do not tell us, for example, whether nuns ordained pregnant women; only that they were not *supposed* to ordain them. Neither can we tell how successful the rule was: did nuns thereafter stop ordaining pregnant women? The very existence of the rule and the provision of some type of punitive procedure for a lack of adherence admits the possibility that it would not always be followed. We cannot tell from the rule itself exactly why it was enacted. Were pregnant women presenting themselves for ordination in such numbers that a rule needed to be established? If so, why? And what precisely does the rule seek to prevent? Is it the ordination of pregnant women per se, or are there other factors such as social censure and lay criticism at play here? While the rules as embedded in the *prātimokṣa*s do not throw light on such questions, as we will see, the detailed legal traditions explicated in the *vibhaṅga*s do.

In fact, when the family members of monks and nuns are mentioned in the *prātimokṣa*s, it is generally, if not invariably, only to introduce exemptions to rules, none of which deal with family matters themselves. A monk, for instance, commits a minor offense in sewing a robe for a nun to whom he is unrelated, such as a stranger, a friend, a former lover, or even his own wife; there is no offense, however, if he sews a robe for a nun to whom he is biologically related, such as his mother, sister, or daughter. Similar rules not only presuppose the existence of kith and kin within the monastic confines, but they also allow the otherwise unallowable in cases of interaction with a monastic's own family members.

Although the *prātimokṣa*s, which are thought to belong among the earliest strata of Buddhist monastic law, presuppose continued contact between monks and nuns and their families almost from the beginning of Indian Buddhist literature,[192] they turn out to have less value for the purposes of the present study.[193] It is not that their content is unimportant or insignificant. Rather, the *prātimokṣa*s lack both narrative context (i.e., frame-stories) and canonical legal interpretation, as discussed above. Indeed, while it has been commonly held that *vinaya*s are dry, boring, legalistic texts,[194] those characterizations would squarely hit the mark if confined to the *prātimokṣa*s. Yet the *prātimokṣa*s represent only a tiny fraction of the extant corpus of Buddhist monastic law codes; as for the rest, nothing could be further from the truth.

The second type of monastic legislation is made up of rules governing the monastic community as a corporate body, not the activities of individual monastic practitioners. Like the *prātimokṣa* rules, this type of legislation is usually embedded in thick narrative. Unlike the *prātimoḳṣa* rules, either within or without a narrative context, these regulations often come in the form of blanket prohibitions lacking any sanction or directive to be applied in case of noncompliance. For the purposes of this study, the main difference between the two types of monastic legislation is perhaps best illustrated by contrasting the legal effectiveness of a *prātimokṣa* rule, which makes it an offense to ordain a certain type of person, with a blanket prohibition, such as those found in the *vastu*s or *khandhaka*s, which bans the ordination of another class of persons. Take, for instance, the *prātimokṣa* rule discussed above which makes it an offense to ordain a pregnant woman. This rule does not prevent the ordination. Rather, it stipulates the punishment to be meted out to a nun who ordains a pregnant woman. In other words, the ordination itself is and remains valid; the pregnant woman's new status as a nun is in no way affected by the minor offense incurred by the ordaining nun. This is one of the limits of this type of monastic legislation.

Although the existence of a *prātimokṣa* rule may act as a deterrent, the rule itself neither proscribes nor necessarily prevents the action it is designed to curtail. In Buddhist monastic law, the only way to prevent certain activities is to ban them outright with a blanket prohibition or direct command directed not to individual monks or nuns but to the monastic community as a corporate entity. We find this type of legislation predominantly in the thematically arranged chapters (*vastu*s or *khandhaka*s) of the *vinaya*s. In the *Chapter on Ordination,* for instance, certain people—the deformed, the sick, and the ugly, for example—are specifically barred from ordination.[195] Unlike the *prātimokṣa* rule, this type of monastic legislation does not allow any wiggle room: noncompliance is not an option—unless, of course, one ignores the legal system entirely, but that is a very different matter. A monk or nun does not incur an offense in ordaining such people; quite simply, they cannot be ordained.

In the following chapters it will be important to recognize these two different types of monastic legislation and their limitations. This will allow us to understand better not only the rules and regulations that were promulgated, but the choices made by and options available to Indian Buddhist monastic jurists. As we will see, it would have been a simple matter to prohibit the ordination of pregnant women entirely by adding them, along with the bald, blind, deaf, and mute, to the list of those who may not be ordained.[196] This, however, was not done; indeed, what the monastic lawyers chose not to do is often more telling than the choices they made.

In discussing family matters in Indian Buddhist monasticisms, I have found it useful in the following chapters to marshal two types of evidence from the extant monastic law codes. The first comes from reading the *vinaya*s not for the information they purport to report, but for the incidental details that betray the authors/redactors' assumptions vis-à-vis the monastic life. I have used this type of evidence predominantly in Chapter 2 in discussing monks and nuns and their continued familial relationships, and in Chapter 3 with regard to monks and their "former" wives. The second type of evidence is more straightforward. At least as they are presented in Buddhist monastic law, issues surrounding nuns' pregnancies and monastic motherhood are dealt with head on by our monastic legislators. The jurists legislate these issues not through rules for individual monastic practitioners, but in terms of corporate policies dictating how the monastic community is to deal with such situations. Accordingly, in Chapter 4, in connection with the phenomenon of monastic motherhood, there is little need to read the texts against the grain for incidental details that might throw light on the authors/redactors' presuppositions.

Although it is impossible to know for sure what Indian Buddhist monks and nuns did or thought some two thousand years ago, we can know what the Indian authors/redactors of extant Buddhist monastic law codes told other monks and nuns about their traditions. Buddhist monastic law codes or *vinaya*s provide us with much more than merely normative monastic visions of the religious life as envisioned by their authors/redactors. The present study is a survey of what Indian Buddhist "in-house" narratives reveal about the monastic life in general and the concerns and values of their authors/redactors in particular. Where possible, I have tried to verify or support the data from these internal monastic law codes with sources external to Indian Buddhist traditions, such as epigraphical, literary (Sanskrit drama), textual (civil legal documents from Central Asia), and modern ethnographic sources. When the external evidence is found to corroborate the internal, the probative value of the monastic codes seems to be confirmed, if not increased. This is especially so in the case of Sanskrit drama, which is often ambivalent, if not antagonistic, toward Buddhist monasticisms. When, for example, we read in both Sanskrit dramas and Buddhist monastic law codes that monks and nuns were acting as matchmakers for marital and sexual liaisons, we would seem to be on relatively firm ground in asserting that this was a problem not just in our monastic texts or in our authors/redactors' minds, but also in the cultural milieu of the India of the monastic jurists. The veracity of these claims is further increased when corroborating evidence is found in other genres of Indian literature, such as learned brahmanical treatises, texts that share an ambivalence and antagonism toward heterodox religions such as Buddhism.

7. A Note on the Scope of the Present Study

Rather than engaging in an in-depth study of one particular monastic tradition in this book, I have chosen to sketch out in broad brushstrokes various stances vis-à-vis monks and nuns and their continued familial relationships as portrayed in the six extant monastic law codes. It is impossible to deal with every passage in which mention is made of monastics' kith and kin. Many of the narratives presented exist in multiple versions. In general, I present only one version of a specific passage since anything else would burden the reader with an excess of detail. I have introduced only as much as I thought necessary to make a case for the continued importance of familial relationships between monks and nuns and their families, both lay and monastic.

The present study is an attempt to show how and why a close reading of Indian Buddhist monastic law codes is essential for a nuanced understanding of Buddhist monasticisms in India. In highlighting the richness of the *vinaya*s, I hope to make apparent what should have been self-evident. However unfashionable, I intend to call attention to what we still lack but so sorely need even after more than a century of scholarship: detailed studies, critical editions, and annotated translations of the entire corpus of extant Indian Buddhist monastic law codes. These basic resources will enable us to fill in the gaps in our knowledge with studies of individual monasticisms, studies that in turn will allow us to reconfigure the contours of the Indian Buddhist monastic landscape. The present study is experimental and exploratory. My findings are intended as a reconnaissance report to lay the groundwork for future studies of individual monasticisms.

Chapter Two

Family Matters

The present chapter establishes a foundation for our inquiry into the place of family in the narrative landscape of Indian Buddhist monastic law codes. In Section 1, I survey the corpus of Indian Buddhist inscriptions. The epigraphical record is our earliest datable evidence for how a range of Indian Buddhists viewed themselves and the world around them. Here we find references to monastics making religious donations together with brothers and sisters, sons and daughters, mothers and fathers. These inscriptions provide us with the first hints of continued interaction between Buddhist monastics and their biological kin in India outside canonical Buddhist texts.

In Section 2, I move from inscriptions to an examination of narratives in Buddhist monastic law codes. Here I focus on the phrase "to go forth from home into homelessness" (*agārād anagārikāṃ pra√vraj*), which often has been taken as implying the monk's abandonment of family.[1] I shall look at two important instances in which this phrase appears, both drawn from narratives attached to various monastic regulations, the first suggesting and the second confirming that the phrase is to be understood figuratively. I begin with the case of the monk Sudinna, who seems to continue to reside with his family although he has "left home" for the religious life. Only later is this monk said to leave home physically. Even then, however, he returns home for alms. I next turn to the story of the nun Dharmadinnā, a woman who is initiated and ordained into the religious life through a messenger while living at home. Additionally, I discuss the case of

Saṅgāmaji, a monk whose wife demands that he support her and her young son, a demand that seems to imply that a monk's wife and child could join him in homelessness. The narratives discussed in this section all suggest a figurative rather than a literal understanding of the phrase "to go forth from home into homelessness."

In Section 3, we deal with a short narrative about a monk who frequents the house of a barber only to be told to come back another day. As he is seen coming and going from this house, a fellow monk asks whether he is visiting friends or family. Here we catch a glimpse of the type of assumption a monk might make upon seeing a fellow monk visiting the same house day after day: that he was visiting family.

In Section 4, we examine rules authorizing proper protocol for monks who return home to eat with their families. We also see an instance in which a monastic regulation intended to ensure the physical safety of nuns is relaxed in order to accommodate their need to return home for meals when food is scarce. These narratives further suggest that "leaving home" did not necessarily imply severing ties with one's family.

In Section 5, I introduce a regulation in which it is declared that a nun commits no offense in staying in the house of a relative. Together with a narrative in which we catch sight of a nun living not in a nunnery but in a lay house, this regulation suggests the possibility that, in certain circumstances, nuns may have resided in the houses of their own kith and kin.

If leaving home for the religious life did not require the severance of familial ties, then it may follow that some monks and nuns might have gone forth not *from* family but *as* a family, and this is exactly what we see in Section 6. The various *vinaya*s preserve stories about fathers who take their sons with them when they leave home for the religious life, and this too points to continued familial ties within the monastic life.

To establish the degree to which the authors/redactors of Indian Buddhist monastic law codes assumed that monks would embark on the religious life *with* their children, I then consider, in Section 7, further stories in which the renunciation of father and son together is mentioned incidentally. These passing comments in the monastic codes reveal a great deal about what our authors/redactors thought it meant to be a Buddhist renunciant in India.

In Section 8, I discuss a few passages that throw light on the utility of Buddhist monastic codes for our understanding of notions of world renunciation in India in general. I conclude with one last piece of evidence suggesting that right from the very beginnings of Buddhist literature the canonical authors presupposed in their religious communities the existence of monks and nuns who were biologically related to each other.

1. Family Ties Set in Stone

The sizable corpus of Indian Buddhist donative inscriptions may aid us in better understanding the degree to which Indian Buddhist monastics actively associated with those very family members they are often said to have deserted: mothers, fathers, brothers, sisters, husbands, wives, and children.[2] The following survey of epigraphical evidence is not intended to be exhaustive. It will suffice to show that outside the monastic law codes, that is, in inscriptions recording their acts of giving, monks and nuns continued to associate with family members.

One particularly rich site of donative inscriptions is Sāñcī in central India. Here our knowledge of a number of specific individual Buddhists and their activities can be contextualized to around the first century B.C.E.[3] In these inscriptions we find mention of many monks (*bhikṣu*s) and nuns (*bhikṣuṇī*s). How they are identified is worth considering. There are a number of discernible patterns. The donation of one monk, for instance, is recorded in stone simply as follows:[4]

> Gift of the *bhikṣu* Kāda.
>
> (Lüders 1912 §167; Majumdar §34; Tsukamoto [Sāñcī] §20)

The gift of a group of nuns is recorded only with reference to their place of origin or residence:

> Gift of the *bhikṣuṇī*s from Vāḍivahana.
>
> (Lüders 1912 §163; Majumdar §22; Tsukamoto [Sāñcī] §8)

Some donations are recorded with the donor's name and place of residence, in addition to religious titles:

> Gift of the *bhikṣu* Arahadina, inhabitant of Pokhara.
>
> (Lüders 1912 §337; Majumdar §101; Tsukamoto [Sāñcī] §87)

This monk and the group of nuns from Vāḍivahana are identified only by the locale where they lived or were born. If they lived in a specific monastery or nunnery, for whatever reasons, this is not recorded. Other monks are referred to with the addition of honorific titles:

> Gift of the *bhikṣu* Noble Pasanaka.
> (Lüders 1912 §174; Majumdar §144; Tsukamoto [Sāñcī] §130)[5]

More interesting for our immediate concerns are a number of inscriptions, again from Sāñcī, in which monks and nuns are identified in terms of their familial relations.

> [Gift] of the *bhikṣu* Upasijha, brother of Phaguna.
> (Lüders 1912 §294; Majumdar §233; Tsukamoto [Sāñcī] §219)

This monk is identified as the brother of Phaguna, presumably a layman. Other inscriptions record gifts made by mothers of monks or nuns:

> Gift of Koḍā, mother of the *bhikṣu*. . . .
> (Lüders 1912 §647; Majumdar §653; Tsukamoto [Sāñcī] §711)

> Gift of the mother of the *bhikṣuṇī* Dhamayasā from Ujenī.
> (Lüders 1912 §410; Majumdar §60; Tsukamoto [Sāñcī] §46)

> Gift of the mother of Noble Rahila, the Sāphineyaka.
> (Lüders 1912 §198; Majumdar §352; Tsukamoto [Sāñcī] §338)[6]

Here it seems that laywomen are identified in an act of religious giving with reference to children who had chosen monastic vocations, and this may tell us something about not only these mothers' cultural values, but also the local reception of Buddhism.

From other inscriptions, it seems that some nuns were also mothers. That this should be so is hardly startling. Elderly women, for instance, often may have become nuns, especially when widowed. Of course, this is not the only possible interpretation, even if it is the most common. What might be surprising is that being nuns seems in no way to have barred these mothers from identifying themselves in relation to their children. We find, for instance, the following:

> Gift of the *bhikṣuṇī* Isidāsī from..., mother of Sagharakhitā.
> (Lüders 1912 §590; Majumdar §674; Tsukamoto [Sāñcī] §732)

Slightly later at Kārli, but still around the turn of the Common Era, we find a railing inscribed with the following donative inscription:

> The railing, gift of the *bhikṣuṇī* Koṭī, mother of Ghuṇika, was made by Naṃdika.
> (Lüders 1912 §1104; Senart §18; Tsukamoto [Kārli] §31)

From these inscriptions, it is clear that these two women—the nuns Isidāsī and Koṭī—had children. It is not specified whether they became nuns after having and raising children or whether these children were born to monastic parents and raised in monasteries, a phenomenon that we will explore in Chapter 4. For our present purposes, what is important is that these nuns are identified as mothers.

Similarly, at Bhārhut we find an early inscription recording the gift of a nun who is identified in terms of her matrilineage:

> Gift of the *bhikṣuṇī* Badhikā, daughter of Mahamukhi, inhabitant of Dabhina.
> (Lüders 1912 §718; Lüders 1963 §A42; Tsukamoto [Bhārhut] §33)

A number of centuries thereafter, in the second century C.E., we find the gift of a hall at Śailārwāḍi. The inscription records that the gift was donated by two women, Saghā and Budhā, and at least one of them is said to be a daughter of the female mendicant (*pravrajitikā*) Ghaparā, a disciple of the elder, Reverend Siha:[7]

> The religious gift of a Cetiya-Hall is made by Budhā and Saghā, the daughter of the female mendicant Ghaparā, a female disciple of the Elder, Reverend Siha....
> (Das Gupta; Tsukamoto [Śailārwāḍi] §2)

Similarly, at Amarāvatī we find the gift of a leather worker by the name of Vidhika, tentatively dated to around 100 C.E.:

> The religious gift of...by the leather worker Vidhika, son of the Upādhyāya Nāga, with his mother, with his wife, with his brothers,

> and his son Nāga, with his daughters, with his relatives, friends, and relations.
>
> (Lüders 1912 §1273; Sivaramamurti §41; Tsukamoto [Amarāvatī] §70)

Vidhika is identified first by his profession, and second as the son of the *upādhyāya* Nāga. If we take this to be a Buddhist *upādhyāya* or preceptor, then by most definitions he is a monk of at least ten years' standing, a monk in charge of (or qualified to be in charge of) the religious education of junior monastics.[8] This particular preceptor seems to have had not only a son but also a namesake grandson.

At the same site, we find a reference to a monk-donor also named Vidhika in an inscription dating from around 200 to 250 C.E.:

> Gift of... by the young *bhikṣu* Vidhika, disciple of Reverend Nāga, resident of Kudūra, and by his female disciple Budharakhitā, and by her granddaughter Cūla-Budharakhitā.
>
> (Lüders 1912 §1295; Sivaramamurti §99; Tsukamoto [Amarāvatī] §88)

Here, in the inscription of a young monk's gift, we find reference to a female disciple by the name of Budharakhitā (Protected by the Buddha) and her granddaughter Cūla-Budharakhitā (Little Budharakhitā).

A somewhat different relationship is attested in the gift of a lion-throne, again at Amarāvatī. Here we read of a gift made by an elder, the Venerable Budhi, also called the *cetiya* (*caitya*) worshipper (or pilgrim), and his sister, the nun Budhā:

> Gift of the Elder, the Cetiya-Worshipper, Reverend Budhi, and his sister the *bhikṣuṇī* Budhā—a religious gift of a Lion-Throne.
>
> (Lüders 1912 §1223; Tsukamoto [Amarāvatī] §29)

It is possible that this inscription preserves a reference not to a biological sister, but merely to Budhi's sister in the Dharma, although that is not made explicit.[9] Moreover, there is no good reason to doubt that siblings entered the religious life together. This elder made a gift with his sister, and perhaps even traveled with her.[10] The same could also be said about the inscription recording the gift made by the nun Budhā, sister of the Reverend Budhi and Cula-Budhi:

> [Gift] of the young *bhikṣuṇī* Budhā, sister of Reverend Budhi of...and Cula-Budhi, residing in the Piduvana....
> (Shizutani §159; Sivaramamurti §96; Tsukamoto [Amarāvatī] §153)

Also notable in this regard is the following inscription, in which we see a nun associating with her daughters in an act of giving:[11]

> Gift of the *bhikṣuṇī* Budharakhitā of..., the female disciple of the Elder, Reverend Budharakhita, resident of Rājagiri, superintendent of construction of the railing,[12] with her daughters, and of Dhamadinā and Sagharakhita.
> (Lüders 1912 §1250; Sivaramamurti §69; Tsukamoto [Amarāvatī] §49)

Again at Amarāvatī we find what seems to be a Buddhist family. The inscription mentions three generations of women and their religious gift:

> Success! Gift of the female mendicant Sagharakhitā residing in the Jetaparavana, and her daughter the female mendicant Haghā, and her daughter Jiyavā—a religious gift of an upright slab.
> (Lüders 1912 §1262; Shizutani §64; Sivaramamurti §31; Tsukamoto [Amarāvatī] §61)

All three women are identified by name: Sagharakhitā, Haghā, and Jiyavā. Jiyavā seems to be the daughter of Haghā (Skt. Saṅghā), who is in turn the daughter of Sagharakhitā. Both Haghā and Sagharakhitā are identified as mendicants (*pavajitikā*s). Whether this means that they were Buddhist nuns is not certain; they are not identified as *bhikṣuṇī*s, a term that was known at Amarāvatī.[13] Both mendicants, however, have easily identifiable Buddhist names (Saṅgharakṣitā and Saṅghā), unlike the granddaughter Jiyavā.[14] Whether or not these were their birth names is also not clear.[15] Apart from the fact that we have three women, two identified as mendicants, and two identified as daughters, very little is known of them. However, I see no reason to assume, as has Vidya Dehejia on the basis of this and other similar inscriptions, that "the implication seems to be that women often joined the Buddhist monastic order later in life, giving up their married lives."[16]

Finally, it is worth considering one last series of inscriptions, those connected with the famous *bhikṣu* Bala. On an enormous standing image of the Bodhisattva (i.e., the Buddha) dated to the third year of the reign of Kaniṣka and established by *bhikṣu* Bala "at Bārāṇasī, where the Blessed One used to walk," we find the following donative inscription:

> ...[gift] of *bhikṣu* Bala, master of the Tripiṭaka and companion of *bhikṣu* Puṣyavuddhi, together with his parents, with his preceptor and teachers, his companion pupils, and with Buddhamitrā versed in the Tripiṭaka...for the welfare and happiness of all creatures.
>
> (Lüders 1912 §925; Shizutani §1689; Tsukamoto [Sārnāth] §4; J. Vogel §iii.a)

On the pedestal of an equally impressive Bodhisattva image at Mathurā, dated to the year thirty-three of Huviṣka, we read:

> ...a Bodhisattva [image] was set up at Mādhuravaṇaka by the *bhikṣuṇī* Dhanavatī, the niece of the *bhikṣuṇī* Buddhamitrā, who knows the Tripiṭaka, a female pupil of the *bhikṣu* Bala, who knows the Tripiṭaka, together with her mother and father....
>
> (Bloch §B; Lüders 1912 §38; Shizutani §572; Tsukamoto [Mathurā] §11)

In the latter inscription, the donor, *bhikṣuṇī* Dhanavatī, is identified as the niece of *bhikṣuṇī* Buddhamitrā, who has mastered the *tripiṭaka,* the canon of Buddhist scriptures. Although both Bala and Dhanavatī mention their parents in these inscriptions, there is no reason to think that either of these monastics collaborated with their parents in the act of giving itself. Their parents are mentioned here, most probably, only so that they may share the merit of the religious gift. What is of interest to us is the fact that *bhikṣuṇī* Dhanavatī appears with her aunt, the famous *bhikṣuṇī* Buddhamitrā. Here the familial relationship between these two "world renouncers," one of them an expert in Buddhist doctrine and law, is recorded quite happily in stone, with, it seems, none of the unease exhibited in the scholarly literature.

In discussing the formulaic inclusion of all sentient beings in dedicatory inscriptions in general and those of *bhikṣu* Bala in particular, A. L. Basham, for instance, tells us that "the monk Bala concluded his dedications with a formula like this, forgetting (like many other Buddhist monks before and since) that theoretically he had abandoned all his family ties, and that therefore his seeking to benefit his parents before others was an admission of his failure to 'give up the world' completely."[17] It seems to me entirely unwarranted to view *bhikṣu* Bala's concern for his parents as an admission of any type of failure at the monastic experiment. The failure is wholeheartedly ours; we have clearly failed to understand what Buddhist renunciation entailed (and what it did not) in the canonical traditions of the learned monk and nun Tripiṭaka Masters Bala and Buddhamitrā.

The epigraphical material surveyed so far offers snapshots of religious activity, frozen in time, unchanged and unaltered by subsequent redactors and unhindered by the processes of transmission. It provides us with the closest thing we have to direct evidence for Buddhist monks and nuns in India around the turn of the Common Era. Buddhist monks and nuns such as *bhikṣu* Upasijha (brother of Phaguna), *bhikṣuṇī* Isidāsī (mother of Sagharakhitā), and *bhikṣuṇī* Badhikā (daughter of Mahamukhi) are identified in relation to their family members, both lay and monastic. This evidence attests to the fact that, at least in acts of religious giving, Indian Buddhist monks and nuns continued to associate—or be associated—with biological kin, whether parents, children, or siblings.

The monks' and nuns' association with family members in religious acts such as those recorded in donative inscriptions, however, cannot be taken, in and of itself, as evidence for continued contact between monastics and their lay or fellow renunciant relatives. The inscriptional evidence may be constrained by social, literary, and cultural conventions surrounding self-identification and religious giving that are still not fully understood.[18] Moreover, parties mentioned in donative inscriptions are often associated with these religious acts merely to ensure their dividends in the karmic rewards. But if the above survey of epigraphical evidence provides the first hint of sustained interaction between monastics and their families, this is fully confirmed by our next body of evidence: Indian Buddhist monastic law codes.

2. From Home to Homelessness

In Buddhist literature, when men and women "renounce the world" in favor of the religious life, they are said to "go forth from home into homelessness," or often simply just to "go forth."[19] Whether in Sanskrit, Pāli, Tibetan, Chinese (or Japanese), this phrase lies at the very heart of our understanding of the nature of Buddhist renunciation. However, in the monasticisms envisioned and sanctioned by the authors/redactors of Buddhist monastic law codes, the act of going-forth into homelessness does not seem to require the severance of familial ties.

In perhaps the most detailed and sophisticated treatment of this phrase to date, Steven Collins "reconstructed the social and psychological resonances of house-imagery."[20] Collins identifies three progressive stages in the act of going-forth: physical, psychological, and ontological. Yet even Collins's first stage is predicated on the assumption that "one must leave home physically by abandoning household life for the monkhood."[21] Although figurative and nonliteral meanings have been noticed,[22] more often than not scholars have simply accepted this phrase at face value.[23] Few, if any, have noted that the Buddhist *bhikṣu* may leave home for the religious life with his wife (or wives) and children. Indeed, scholars have tended to equate if not conflate the going-forth with the abandonment of family.

Spiro, for instance, tells us that "when the young man 'goes forth,' he does more than leave home—that is much too passive a term to characterize this process.... Rather, he *abandons* home, that is, he actively severs his ties with his parents and siblings, and he refrains from forming expectable ties with a wife and children."[24] In other words, Spiro takes this phrase literally as implying, to quote J. Moussaieff Masson, the Buddhist monk's "denial of the basic human needs of companionship (in his living in isolation), affection, and family ties."[25] Spiro and Masson, however, are not alone in their assumption that Buddhist monks and nuns leave or abandon their families when they go forth for the religious life.[26] In her work on Daoist monasticism, Livia Kohn, for instance, tells us that "in Buddhism, many stories tell of the complete separation of monks from their families.... In Daoism, however, monks did not give up relations with their native families.... *Chujia,* or 'leaving the family,' in medieval Daoism therefore did not mean the complete severance of all worldly ties."[27]

Here I do not mean to question the commonly accepted translations of this phrase; grammatically, lexically, and syntactically it is straightforward. My question is what the phrase meant to Buddhists in India, specifically the authors/redactors of our extant monastic law codes, some two millennia ago. The only way to determine the range of meanings of any word or phrase in Buddhist texts is by context. Dictionaries, glossaries, and other lexicological works provide a range of possible meanings, a semantic field (or ball park) at best. In order to establish the meaning of one of the most central and fundamental phrases surrounding Buddhist renunciation, I will examine two important instances of its usage within canonical Buddhist monastic law codes. Taking the good advice of Patrick Olivelle, I will attempt to "examine how the Indian renouncers themselves understood their condition as renouncers,"[28] at least as that self-understanding is presented in the texts.

We start with the story of Sudinna, the son of Kalandaka.[29] With some degree of variation, the story of Sudinna is found in all of the extant *vinaya*s.[30] According to the version preserved in the *Mūlasarvāstivāda-vinaya,* in the thirteenth year after the Bodhisattva's—that is, the Buddha's—awakening, Sudinna took a wife from a family of equal standing, sported, enjoyed himself, and made love with her—as the stock phrase habitually expresses it.[31] Then, at another time, he rejoiced and took refuge in the Buddha, the Dharma, and the Saṅgha. He cut off his hair and beard, and, having put on saffron-colored robes, through faith went forth from home to homelessness (*dad pas khyim nas khyim med par rab tu byung ngo;* 便以正信捨家趣非家).[32]

An almost identical story line is found in the *Majjhima-nikāya,* in the story of Raṭṭhapāla (Skt. Rāṣṭrapāla), a monk who is deemed to be foremost among those who have gone forth through faith.[33] The question that few seem to have asked, however, is exactly where Sudinna—or, for that matter, Raṭṭhapāla—went when he entered into homelessness. According to the version preserved in the *Mūlasarvāstivāda-vinaya,* in which there may be some ambiguity concerning the exact nature of his living arrangements, our monk,[34] Sudinna, having *left* home, *appears* to have continued to live *at* home. At least that is what the following passage seems to suggest: "Having left home [for the religious life] he continued to interact with his relations just as he had formerly as a layman."[35] According to the story as it is developed by the authors/redactors of this monastic code, our monk has "left home." He has renounced the world for the religious life, but this does not seem to have required that he sever ties with his family, or perhaps even physically leave them at all. Our monk continues to interact with his relations just as he had done as a layman, just as he had before his renunciation. Although the ambiguity as to whether Sudinna was still living at home or simply just associating with his family may cast some doubt on the suggestion that the phrase "to go forth from home into homelessness" is best understood figuratively, as we will see, there is no room for any such doubt in the story of the nun Dharmadinnā.

The story of Dharmadinnā sets a legal precedent for ordination by messenger in absentia.[36] The establishment of this form of ordination is found in all extant *vinaya*s, although outside the *Mūlasarvāstivāda-vinaya* the nun-protagonist is more commonly Ardhakāśī.[37] According to the version preserved in the *Mūlasarvāstivāda-vinaya,* two affluent householders in the city of Śrāvastī agreed to arrange a wedding between their unborn children when they reached the age of marriageability. Dharmadinnā, the daughter of one householder, was betrothed to Viśākha, the son of the other householder.[38] As an infant, Dharmadinnā constantly cried. However, when a monk visited in order to preach a sermon for her father, she listened attentively to the Dharma without crying at all. On account of her love for the Dharma at such an early age, she was named Dharmadinnā.[39]

As a young girl, Dharmadinnā wanted to become a nun. However, since her father had already betrothed her, he would not allow it.[40] Once, when the nun Utpalavarṇā happened to be visiting, Dharmadinnā confided to her her desire to leave home for the religious life. Dharmadinnā asked Utpalavarṇā to initiate her secretly on the spot since her father would not allow it.[41] Utpalavarṇā praised her desire to leave home for the religious life and explained to her the five demerits of sexual desire and the five merits of renunciation.[42] Agreeing to initiate Dharmadinnā, Utpalavarṇā asked her to wait while she sought the Buddha's advice on how to proceed.[43] The Buddha thereupon ordered Ānanda to assemble the community of nuns and have them confer upon Dharmadinnā the Three Refuges and Five Precepts making her an *upāsikā* or devoted laywoman. The Buddha also commands that Dharmadinnā is to be tonsured and made to leave home for the religious life while still *at* home (於家中剃髮出家; *gnas de nyid du rab tu 'byung bar*).[44] Utpalavarṇā is then sent as a messenger to inform Dharmadinnā of her new status and confer upon her the ten rules-of-training making her a novice nun.[45]

Hearing a sermon by Utpalavarṇā, Dharmadinnā attains the first of the four stages of religious attainment, that of a stream-enterer.[46] When Utpalavarṇā reports this back to the Buddha, he then tells Ānanda to have Utpalavarṇā confer on her the two-year *śikṣamāṇā* training, again while she is at home.[47] During this two-year probationary period, Dharmadinnā not only attains the second stage, that of a once-returner, but she also matures into a beautiful young woman.

Both families then decide to set a date for her wedding and proceed with the wedding plans.[48]

Knowing of the scheduled wedding, the Buddha declares that it is no good for Dharmadinnā to remain at home. He orders Ānanda to have the *bhikṣuṇī saṅgha* confer the *brahmacaryopasthāna-saṃvṛti,* what we might consider a type of certification of her successful completion of the two-year probationary status.[49] This is related to her again by Utpalavarṇā with a message that she should be ordained soon.[50] Hearing another sermon, Dharmadinnā attains the state of a nonreturner.[51] The Buddha then has Ānanda assemble both monastic communities and perform Dharmadinnā's ordination in absentia, sending Utpalavarṇā again to inform Dharmadinnā of her successful ordination as a nun.[52] After another sermon, Dharmadinnā attains arhatship.[53]

Having attained arhatship, Dharmadinnā informs her parents, stating that she wishes to go to the nunnery.[54] Her parents decide instead to invite the Buddha and the *saṅgha* for a meal. At the same time, they send word to the parents of her betrothed, Viśākha, suggesting that they quickly perform the wedding under duress.[55] The following day, Viśākha and father show up with a large retinue at Dharmadinnā's house.[56] When the Buddha and his monks are about to leave, Dharmadinnā goes to follow the Buddha out.[57] But just as she is about to leave, Viśākha grabs her. Manifesting her newly attained magical abilities, Dharmadinnā soars into the sky.[58] Viśākha and his retinue fall to the ground, seeking forgiveness. Coming back down to earth, Dharmadinnā preaches the Dharma to the crowd, causing innumerable hundreds and thousands to attain the various fruits of religious attainment, including arhatship.[59] On account of this miraculous display, the Buddha declares Dharmadinnā to be the foremost in preaching among the nuns' assembly.[60]

Although the rest of the narrative of Dharmadinnā, including a story of a previous life, need not detain us, it is worth noting that Dharmadinnā is not the only nun to have been initiated and ordained by a messenger at home against the will of her parents. Indeed, in a previous lifetime, under the Buddha Kāśyapa, Dharmadinnā is said to have acted as a messenger herself in the initiation and ordination of another young woman.[61]

The narrative of Dharmadinnā establishes beyond any doubt that the canonical phrase "to leave home for the religious life" must be understood figuratively. Indeed, this is the only way to make sense of the story of a woman who has "left home" while still residing *at* home. Moreover, regardless of how we understand Sudinna's continued "interaction with his relations," there can be little doubt that, at least in the *Mūlasarvāstivāda-vinaya,* staying at home while or even after renouncing the world is presented as a valid understanding of the religious life. That, however, is not to say that it is the ideal. Indeed, returning to the Sudinna story, this is the very next point raised by the authors/redactors of this monastic code:

> Then the Venerable Sudinna thought as follows, "How can I go forth in the well-spoken Dharma and Vinaya, in order to realize that which I have not yet realized, to attain that which I have not yet attained, and yet continue to interact with my relations?[62] I now ought to part with my relations. I will take my bowl and robe and go journeying about the countryside."[63]

Here, then, we seem to have our first explicit statement about the nature of Buddhist renunciation. In the narrative world of our monastic authors/redactors, one who has gone forth in the well-spoken Dharma and Vinaya (i.e., the teachings of the Buddha) appears to be able to remain living at home with his family. Sudinna, however, seems to have realized that there would be no gain in staying home, that is, it would not be conducive to his religious advancement.

It could be argued that we have here a monastic endorsement of a form of renunciation involving physical separation from one's kin, but it is certainly not a *vinaya* rule in any sense. To my knowledge, physical separation from one's family was never made a formal requirement for renunciation. Moreover, this kind of explicit comment regarding modalities of religious practice is uncommon in the extant monastic codes. The present passage may well provide the closest thing available to evidence for a justification for physically leaving one's home in the *vinaya*s.

The text goes on to confirm that our monk, Sudinna, did in fact do what he said he would:

> Thereupon the Venerable Sudinna, son of Kalandaka, in order to part with his relations, took his bowl and robe and went journeying about the countryside.[64]

Here, then, we seem to have a clear cut case of a monk who has severed ties with his family. Our monk seems to have rejected one form of religious practice for another; he, perhaps unlike others, has left home for the religious life both figuratively and physically. As we shall see, however, there is more to world renunciation than meets the eye: religious supermen they may have been, but men they still were, and hungry they grew.

At that time, a famine was feared, and forest-dwelling almsmen had difficulty acquiring food; parents had difficulty providing for their own children, let alone for almsmen. Sudinna then decides that "since I have relations possessed of great wealth, I will go to the village of Kalandaka and approach my relatives and have them prepare food for the monastic community." Sudinna returns to the village of Kalandaka and stays in a small hut. Then, while wandering about in the village in search of alms, he arrives at his "own house" (*rang gi khyim*), and here the text is quite specific: it is not said to be his former house. An old servant woman, seeing that Sudinna was departing without having received an offering, goes and informs his mother accordingly. Sudinna's mother, desiring an heir to the family line, tries to persuade him to come back home. Sudinna declines. Eventually, however, negotiations reach a middle ground: Sudinna will not return to the lay life,[65] but he agrees to have sex with his wife so as to ensure the birth of a son[66] and thereby save the family wealth from the clutches of the king.[67]

To be sure, the story of Sudinna is much richer than has been previously recognized. At least in this version, the going-forth of our monk, the first monk encountered in all of the *vinaya*s, initially seems to be entirely figurative: he appears to have "left home" while still residing there.[68] It is only later that he leaves home physically in order to further his religious goals. Even this, however, does not bar him from subsequently returning home to receive alms and to request food for the monastic community.

This version of the Sudinna story is a particularly striking example of the degree to which familial ties seem not to have been severed subsequent to entering the monastic order. Here also we have an explicit, albeit in the monastic codes rather rare, statement about the value of living apart from one's family. If the monastic authors/redactors wished to proscribe further contact, interaction, or association between lay and monastic family members, one would expect them to do so here. Although the authors/redactors could have made it a requirement of the religious life for monks and nuns physically to leave home when they "go forth into homelessness," we find no such requirement in the extant Indian Buddhist monastic law codes.

Not all versions of the Sudinna story afford us this degree of insight into what I call "family matters." In the shorter versions presented in the Pāli and Mahīśāsaka *vinaya*s, for example, there is no suggestion that Sudinna was dwelling at home as a monk. Even there, however, we still see a number of important assumptions concerning the religious life. In the Mahīśāsaka monastic code, Sudinna asks his parents for permission to leave home for the religious life. He is refused, and as a consequence he cannot become a monk.[69] Sudinna then goes on a hunger strike.[70] His friends step in, assuring his parents: "If you allow him to leave home [for the religious life], you may still see him from time to time."[71] His parents finally accede, but they ask Sudinna to promise to come back and see them. Sudinna's parents are presented as somewhat apprehensive about their son's joining a religious order: "We consent, son, to your leaving home to cultivate *brahmacarya* (the pure practices of the religious life), but you must make a promise to return from time to time to see us."[72] When he finally departs, their concern is repeated: "But do not forget your promise to return and see us from time to time."[73]

No matter how we understand this story, one thing is clear: for this lay Indian family, having a son leave home for the religious life, that is, having him become a Buddhist monk, did not mean that they would never see him again or that the bonds of kinship would be severed. That was not a potential consequence of Sudinna's renunciation as understood by his parents and friends, again as filtered through our monastic authors/redactors.[74]

According to the Indian Buddhist monastic law codes surveyed so far, Buddhist renunciation, the going-forth from home into homelessness, seems not to require physical separation from the home, much less the forsaking of kinship or social bonds. The same holds for the renunciation of Raṭṭhapāla.[75] He too promises to return home, and return home he does. But in doing so he makes what may well be a statement characteristic of, and even peculiar to, *sutta* literature: the assertion that those who have gone forth do not have homes. It may be telling that this statement is not found in the otherwise almost identical *vinaya* tale.[76] Indeed, the absence of this comment in the story of Sudinna is interesting considering the fact that it appears in the Pāli *sutta* materials as a response to an identical question found in both sources delivered by the monks' respective fathers.[77]

There are, of course, more *sutta* passages that seem to reinforce the popular image of monks as having abandoned their families, wives, and children. For our purposes, one more example will suffice.

The Pāli *Udāna* contains the tale of the monk Saṅgāmaji.[78] According to the text preserved in the Pāli canon, Saṅgāmaji had arrived in Sāvatthi (Skt. Śrāvastī). His "former" wife (*purāṇa-dutiyikā*)[79] heard that he was in town and decides to pay a visit. Taking her young son, his wife approaches and demands that Saṅgāmaji support her: "Nourish me, recluse, for I am one with a small son!," in Masefield's translation.[80] Saṅgāmaji remains silent even though he is thus entreated thrice.[81] Eventually his wife seems to change tack. Putting down her son, she departs, saying, "This is your son, recluse; nourish him!" But Saṅgāmaji will have no part in it. His wife comes back, picks up her son, and leaves. The Buddha, we are told, had seen these events unfold with his divine eye, and what he saw is "impropriety of such a form on the part of the venerable Saṅgāmaji's former female partner."[82] Here we seem to have a relatively clear-cut assertion of Buddhist values regarding the support and maintenance of abandoned family members. Monks care not, and that is how things should be: they after all had forsaken worldly ties. Or so it would seem if we read the text without reference to its commentary.

When we turn to the *Udāna* commentary, in which the story is fleshed out, what might have been taken as a straightforward statement concerning the unimportance of family appears in a very different light.[83] Having accompanied lay followers to the Jetavana to hear the Buddha, Saṅgāmaji, who at the time was childless,[84] decided to join the monastic order. He was refused initiation, however, since he had not secured parental permission. The commentary suggests that the details of his negotiations with his parents do not differ from those of Raṭṭhapāla or Sudinna, as discussed above. Indeed, the reader is directed to fill in the gaps from the *Raṭṭhapāla-sutta*.[85]

Like Raṭṭhapāla and Sudinna, Saṅgāmaji leaves having promised his parents that "he would let them see him after he had gone forth."[86] Saṅgāmaji then returns to Śrāvastī not only to see the Buddha but also "with the aim of discharging his promise to his mother and father."[87] When his parents hear that he has returned, his mother, father, relatives, and friends all go to his *vihāra* to visit. They try to convince him to give up the religious life and return home. The reason—as in the cases of Sudinna and Raṭṭhapāla—is to prevent the king from seizing the family wealth.[88] When their efforts fail, they enlist the help of his wife. She sets off with her young son to see him. She asks thrice to be nourished and supported since she has a young child. Masefield translates the relevant section of the commentary as follows:

> ...you went forth abandoning me whilst I was still with child; that same I am now one with a small son, with a son who is still a child. This performance on your part of the Dhamma of a recluse after abandoning one such as me is improper. Therefore, recluse, you must support me, who am one with a son as partner, with fodder and coverings and so on.[89]

Saṅgāmaji, however, remains uninterested. He is presumably aware that his family was taking care of his wife and son, as clearly they had the means to do so—the destitute seldom need to avoid taxes.

Eventually, the wife puts her son down and departs with the following words: "This is your son, recluse; nourish him!"[90] Again, Saṅgāmaji does not budge. Finally she comes back to pick up her son. The Blessed One, we are told, sees "that impropriety of... Saṅgāmaji's former female partner."[91] What is improper is not her demand for support and nourishment, but—according to the commentary—"placing a son in the lap, which is not good form where those gone forth are concerned."[92]

The most revealing aspect of this tale, however, may be Saṅgāmaji's wife's suggestion that she and her son be supported "with fodder and coverings," which, Masefield notes, "refers to food and clothing of very poor quality."[93] At first glance, this does not seem to make sense. Saṅgāmaji's family and friends had just tried to convince him to give up the religious life: "this going forth is not good enough—come, my dear, forsake it."[94] Saṅgāmaji is introduced in the commentary as "the son of a certain wealthy merchant of great means."[95] Masefield understands the story to suggest that "Saṅgāmaji's wife is trying to tempt him back home, where he would no doubt have resumed his lifestyle of some opulence." Thus, Masefield is puzzled by the reference to "fodder and coverings."[96] In light of what we have already seen in the story of Sudinna, I suspect that Masefield squarely hit the mark when he asks, "Does this imply that she expected to join him as a recluse and share his meagre sustenance?"[97] Indeed, the wife concludes not that Saṅgāmaji should return home, but rather that he ought to support his family. That a monk might have his wife and child join him in the religious life may strike us as somewhat odd. As we will see, however, when reread in light of *vinaya* materials, passages suggesting the presence of monastic families do not seem out of place.

So far we have concentrated primarily on the monk Sudinna,

but we have failed to mention his family.[98] According to the Dharmaguptaka, Mahīśāsaka, Mūlasarvāstivādin, and Sarvāstivādin traditions, Sudinna's son, Bījaka, went on to leave home for the religious life.[99] The Theravādin tradition records that Sudinna's wife, Bījaka's mother, also went forth into the religious life with Bījaka when he was seven or eight years old.[100] Sudinna's family, then, seems to have "gone forth from home into homelessness," and this suggests that the homeless state was not necessarily a family-less state. A monk's biological and matrimonial kin were free to join him in homelessness, even if husband and wife would no longer dwell together as they previously had as a lay couple.

How Sudinna's family's renunciation might have been viewed by his co-religionists is difficult to know. To be sure, the story of Sudinna is, in many respects, and indeed is intended to be, one of monastic failure: a monk who has sex while still a monk could not be otherwise. That, of course, is Sudinna's role in this literature: a foil intended to teach other monks how to behave correctly through his own misdeed. It is worth noting, however, that the authors/redactors of these law codes include within this very narrative an account of Sudinna's son's attainment of the fruit of arhatship, the goal of the religious life as formulated and espoused by the authors/redactors of our Buddhist monastic codes.[101] Moreover, in what scholars generally view as the most conservative of these monastic law codes, the Pāli Vinaya, we find reference to the attainment of arhatship by Sudinna's wife, known as Bījakamātā, Mother of Bījaka. Sudinna himself becomes known as Bījakapitā, Father of Bījaka.[102] Arguably, by renaming Sudinna and his wife after their son, an arhat who succeeded where his own father failed, the monastic authors/redactors all but state that Sudinna's story, the story of a monk who was rebuked but not expelled for fulfilling his familial duty of begetting a son, was one of both religious and familial success.

Although chronologically Sudinna is not portrayed as one of the first to join the Buddhist order, this tale is the first narrative of renunciation encountered in all extant Buddhist legal codes. Sudinna and his monastic family set the scene for monks and nuns who knew their *vinaya*s, their own monastic traditions. The story of Suddina's family suggests that, for the authors/redactors of the *vinaya*s, the presence of a monk's wife and child as co-religionists within Indian Buddhist monastic life was quite unremarkable. Indeed, our monastic lawyers begin the compilation of their lawbooks with a tale about a father and son, and in the Pāli tradition also a mother, who live the monastic life together. Not only is co-renunciation presented as an entirely unproblematic interpretation of the monastic life, but its implementation recorded in the first few folios of Indian Buddhist legal literature is presented as an eminently successful one. Arguably, the story of Sudinna and his family should not be seen as a tale of monastic failure but rather as a religious success story.

3. Close Shaves with Monkish Assumptions

What the monastic authors say, what they explicitly sanction, is clearly of importance; they, after all, wrote the rules that defined Indian Buddhist monasticisms. By paying too much attention to their purported message, however, it may be easy to overlook what is implicit in their own understandings of renunciation. In this section, I shall return to a stock phrase concerning monks' visits to craftsmen that was mentioned briefly in Section 6 of Chapter 1. This stenciled narrative highlights the authors/redactors' assumption that a monk might return home or visit relatives even on a daily basis.

In pursuit of the religious life, monks and nuns might well have left the world, but some things cannot be left behind. No matter how supermundane their quest for religious goals, some things kept monks' feet firmly planted on terra firma: hair grows, sandals snap, and bowls break. Our monastic authors/redactors were prepared for it all. Here, in the negotiation of these and other issues, in a stock phrase found throughout the *Mūlasarvāstivāda-vinaya,*[103] we catch a somewhat unexpected glance of the inner workings of the monastic mind, including assumptions vis-à-vis family.

The narrative begins as follows:

> The Buddha, the Blessed One, was dwelling in Śrāvastī, in the Jetavana, in the Park of Anāthapiṇḍada.
>
> A certain monk's hair had grown very long, and having gone to the barber's, he said, "Sir, you must cut my hair!"
>
> The barber thought to himself, "Since these mendicant Sons of the Śākyan [i.e., followers of the Buddha] are very importune and commission work without payment, if I were to cut this one's hair, one after another will come when they hear of it, so I will continue to put him off, and he will go away of his own accord." So thinking he set a time.

> "Noble one, you must go away and come here tomorrow, or the day after, in the morning, or afternoon, or at noon."
>
> Since the monk was deceived by him, he went again and again.
>
> The monk had a friend who was also a monk, and having seen him going [to this house] again and again, he said, "Venerable one, why do you come here again and again? Is this the house of a relative, or the house of your family?"
>
> The monk replied, "Venerable one, that is neither the house of a relative nor the house of my family. Rather, it is the barber to whom I said, since my hair has grown very long, 'You must cut my very long hair; the merit will come to you!' He fixed a time, but has not cut it."[104]

The tale continues, and our monk's friend reveals to him that he too is skilled in cutting hair, but that his hands are tied since the Buddha has not authorized monks to cut another's hair. This is reported back to the other monks, and finally to the Buddha himself. The authors/redactors of our monastic code then have the Buddha establish a rule by which a monk who is knowledgeable in such matters may cut hair as long as it is done out of the public eye (Tib. *phyogs dben par;* Chi. 於屏處; Skt. **pratigupte pradeśe*).[105]

This little story is of interest for a number of reasons. It might, for instance, tell us something about the demographics of those who joined, or were thought to join, the monastic order: some of them might have had backgrounds in the crafts, which in the case of India tells us a good deal about their castes given the perceived pollution attendant on those occupations. Our story also tells us a thing or two about how such monks might have thought they were perceived outside the monastic order (with perhaps even a dash of self-reflection). Craftsmen may well be portrayed as somewhat cunning and dishonest, but this is also exactly how craftsmen are made to view monks: they come around commissioning work for free, promising only to pay in the currency of merit.[106]

What is of most interest to us, however, is a point that is incidental to the development of the story. Our monk is seen by another monk coming again and again to the same house. The monk's friend comes to what would seem to be the only possible conclusion, namely, that this monk was visiting either family or relatives. This is not criticized at all; one who has left home for the religious life is not castigated when he is thought to be returning home or dropping in on relatives even on a daily basis. This evidently is what some monks seem to have done in the course of the day. Contrary to the expectations of his co-religionist, his brother in the Dharma, our monk was not visiting family or relatives. Yet it remains that when he is seen frequenting a lay house, this possibility is presented as the natural conclusion to which a fellow religious might jump.

4. The Family That Eats Together

Unlike the previous section, where the monk was only assumed to be returning home, in this section I shall discuss three narratives in which monks and nuns most certainly did visit family and relatives.[107] Buddhist mendicancy requires that some monastics venture out for alms in the morning. Daily interaction with the laity, particularly with housewives, must have presented its fair share of tricky situations, especially for celibate monks. Yet even here in the most mundane of monastic routines we find further evidence of continued and sustained contact between ordained monastics and their lay family members. Take, for instance, the following story from the monastic law code of the Mahīśāsakas dealing with what are clearly brahmanical concerns of purity and pollution vis-à-vis food.

> A monk went to the house of his relatives.
>
> The relatives said, "We are not strangers, and we are not impure. Why do you not eat with us?"
>
> [Other] monks told this matter to the Buddha.
>
> The Buddha said, "I authorize you to eat together [as long as you ensure] the presence of mindfulness—but you must not let your hands touch."[108]

Here we see confirmation that, at least in the narrative world of our Buddhist lawyers, a monk did indeed visit and eat with his own relatives. In a passage directly preceding this one, the monastic authors/redactors had responded to brahmanical questions of pollution by putting into the mouth of the Buddha an injunction concerning the sharing of dishes with laymen.[109] At least narratively, our monk took heed of this and seems to have taken one more step, one that turned out to be a misstep—he decided not to eat with his relatives at all. The relatives were presumably somewhat offended, as is suggested by the castigation of their monkish kin: "We are not strangers, and we are not impure. Why do you not eat with us?" The Buddha is then made to clarify the monastic position: monks may share meals with their relatives, but they are to be mindful not to let their hands touch. Here too it is taken for granted that monks visit family. Monks also sit down to meals with their families, and this too is taken as a given. Here no censure or criticism is made with regard to monks' visitation of lay houses, whether of kin or not.

A similar situation is seen in a rule in the *Mahīśāsaka-vinaya* introducing monastic protocol with regard to the acceptance of meal-invitations.

> If in [lay] houses there are these kinds of delicious foods: milk, curds, ghee, oil, fish, meat; and if a monk, without being ill, seeks and obtains these for himself, and eats them, he incurs a *pācattika* offense.[110] If he seeks them for a sick monk; if they are from the house of a relative; if he seeks them at the house of an acquaintance, in all of these cases there is no transgression.[111]

At least as they are commonly depicted in modern scholarship, monks and nuns have not embarked upon the religious life for fine food.[112] This rule, however, suggests that epicurean ecclesiastics may have presented problems for monastic authors/redactors.[113] Some monks were dining in the homes of laymen, and, it seems, also in houses of their own kin. Delicious or gourmet foods were, according to our text, only to be procured and consumed by monks if they were sick. Otherwise a monk would incur a *pācattika* offense, a minor transgression that requires a monk to confess his offense to another monk. In other words, clerical consumption of fine foods incurs a minor offense only if a monk is in good health.

Perhaps most telling are the exceptions. There is no offense if the monk is ill; such a monk, it seems, may eat as he pleases. Furthermore, all monks, whether sick or not, may dine on fine cuisine if it is procured from their friends or families. The point here is perhaps not immediately clear. Monastic gastronomes going from house to house seeking sumptuous specialties might invite lay contempt or criticism. As we will see, the monastic authors/redactors were worried above all else about how they were viewed by the laity, and not necessarily about what monks actually did. When monks ate with their own kin, there was little need to worry about the public eye.

Times, however, were not always easy, and our texts suggest that food was sometimes scarce. We see this, for instance, in a story in the

Mūlasarvāstivāda-vinaya about a nun who is having trouble obtaining alms and who therefore goes back home to her father.

> At one time there was a prominent householder who took a wife in marriage. Before long a daughter was born. When she had grown up, she abandoned secular ties and left home [for the religious life] in the Buddha's Dharma.
>
> At one time, food being scarce, it was difficult to obtain [alms] by begging. Going around families begging for alms, she eventually reached her father's house.
>
> Her father, seeing his daughter coming, straightaway approached her and asked, "Noble lady, how do you now subsist?"
>
> Thereupon she informed her father, "Begging for alms by going around families it is truly difficult to obtain [alms]. Although one goes to much trouble, still one's hunger is not satisfied. It is extremely difficult to endure being burned by the fire of hunger."
>
> Hearing these words, her father was dispirited and unhappy. Thereupon he informed his daughter, "If you were lay and not a monastic, even without sympathy for you, you would necessarily always be served. From now on, every day that goes by you may come home and accept meals."[114]

This text suggests that a nun, a woman who has left home for the religious life, might return home in times of need. Here the authors/redactors seem not to have seen anything incongruous in the suggestion that a nun might come home for meals, even every day.

> Having accepted the invitation, thereupon, on another day, she again came to her father's house [this time] with a companion, and received the invited meal.
>
> The father informed the daughter, saying, "At present I do not have the capacity to sustain two [extra] people. You should come on your own and take meals."
>
> The daughter informed her father, saying, "The World-Honored One does not permit a woman to travel alone."
>
> "If the Buddha were to permit it, you would not be faced with these troubles."[115]
>
> Then the nun told the above matter in detail to the monks.
>
> The monks told this matter to the Buddha.
>
> The Buddha said, "If in times of food scarcity it is difficult to obtain

> [alms] by begging, and one cannot maintain one's sustenance, I authorize nuns to petition the assembly for permission to go and return to their parents' house (聽苾芻尼從衆乞法於父母舍而作往還)."[116]

As it stands, the text is relatively straightforward. The nun's father suggests she might come home for meals, but when she does so, she brings home a companion. This presents the nun's father with a slight problem: times are tough, and although he is able to feed his daughter, another nun is really out of the question. The daughter, however, cites security concerns: nuns are not allowed to travel alone. When the Buddha is approached, he relaxes the injunction on solitary sojourns in order to address such cases: "I authorize nuns to petition the assembly for permission to go and return to their parents' house." We seem to have before us, then, a case of safety regulations being relaxed to allow nuns to travel home for meals.

As the text continues, we find details of the formal ecclesiastical act by which nuns are to petition the monastic community for leave to return home:

> [She] should petition thus, "Reverends, may the community of nuns listen! I, nun So-and-so, have now met with a frugal year and I am having trouble acquiring food and drink. If I have no food or drink, I will not be able to sustain myself. I, So-and-so, now from the community of nuns petition for the formal ecclesiastical act [of permission] to return and stay with my relatives (我某甲今從尼僧伽乞於親族邊作往還住止羯磨)."[117]

This formula then concludes with a ruling put into the mouth of the Buddha:

> If the great assembly of nuns has finished granting the formal ecclesiastical act [of permission] to return to one's lay relatives (諸俗親往還羯磨), this nun may travel alone without any offense. Going to her family home, she may eat as she likes. But in plentiful times, then she should not go [alone]—were she to go alone she would incur an offense of transgression against the rule of law (越法罪).[118]

It is important to be clear about exactly what is and is not being allowed here. It is not that a nun is granted permission to travel to her family home for meals when food is scarce. Rather, with this ecclesiastical act she is granted a one-time leave to travel alone. In other words, nuns did not need special permission to return home for meals. Permission was needed to travel alone. Likewise, a nun may still continue to return home in times of abundance. If she travels alone in those cases, she would incur a transgression against the rule of law, a very minor type of offense. For our purposes, however, it will suffice to note that the monastic authors/redactors seem to have seen no problem in nuns returning home for visits or meals; their concern was primarily for the nuns' personal safety.[119] We cannot know how common it was for Indian Buddhist monks or nuns to return home to their families for meals.[120] But it was presumably common enough that the monastic authors/redactors felt the need to legislate a set of rules prescribing proper protocol for such situations.

5. The Family That Stays Together

We have seen a good deal of evidence suggesting continued and sustained contact between ordained monastics and their lay families. We have not, however, seen strong evidence that this contact consisted of anything more than short visits.[121] So far we have little reason to think that monks and nuns actually stayed or lived with their families. Indeed, given the strictures of monastic life as it is usually depicted in modern scholarly literature, it seems hard to imagine how monks and nuns could possibly have stayed or dwelt amid the laity. In this section, I shall introduce two *vinaya* narratives that provide just such evidence, suggesting that nuns, for instance, were allowed to stay overnight in lay homes, and even in the homes of their own kin.

We first turn to a passage from the *Mahīśāsaka-vinaya:*

> At one time nuns spread out bedding and stayed with lay families with whom they were acquainted. [Other] laymen criticized them, saying, "How can you leave your houses for the religious life, and yet stay at the houses of others? We do not delight in seeing this inauspicious sight."
>
> The senior nuns heard this and criticized them in various ways.... *down to*[122]
>
> [The Buddha said:] "Now I will set forth a rule for the nuns.—*Again as expounded above.*—If a nun, without asking a layman, at his house unceremoniously spreads out bedding and stays, it is a *pācattika.* Pro-

> bationary nuns and novice nuns [incur an offense of] wrongdoing.[123] If one stays at the house of a relative, one commits no offense."[124]

We see here that nuns incur a minor offense requiring only a confession for staying the night at a layman's house without permission. But, as before, exceptions are made for families. It is not an offense to stay in the house of a relative; there, nuns may stay without incurring any offense at all.[125] In other words, the monastic authors/redactors seem not to see any problem with the prospect of nuns staying overnight in the houses of their own kin; this appears not to have been a practice that needed to be legislated against, or in any way controlled, restricted, or prevented.

If the above passage from the *Mahīśāsaka-vinaya* suggests the possibility that some monastics may have stayed or even lived in lay homes, then this seems to be confirmed by another passage, this time from the *Dharmaguptaka-vinaya*.

> At one time there was a nun who dwelt in a layman's house. She saw the husband kissing with his wife, touching her body, and grabbing her breasts. The young nun, having seen this, thereupon produced thoughts of discontent toward the Buddha's Dharma.
>
> The nuns told the monks, and the monks told the Buddha.
>
> The Buddha said, "I authorize the separate construction of a dwelling place for nuns."[126]

This passage is unambiguous. A nun was staying at a layman's house, and she happened to see the husband making love to his wife. The nun—and she is described as a young nun—thereupon became somewhat disenchanted with the religious life. The Buddha was then made to allow the construction of separate dwellings for nuns. This ruling may suggest that at least initially nuns did live in lay homes, whether their own or those of others.[127] If nuns could dwell in lay homes, then we might infer that they could certainly dwell in their own homes, especially given the dispensations already seen with regard to family members.

6. Like Father, Like Son

As we have seen in the preceding sections, leaving home for the religious life did not necessarily entail severing all ties with kith and kin, according to the authors/redactors of Indian Buddhist monastic law codes. Monks and nuns seem to have been free to visit and/or stay with their families and relatives at will. Yet contact between a monk and his family was in no way limited to visitations or short stays. In this section, I shall introduce a narrative in which co-renunciation with one's children is taken for granted. As we will see, for the Buddhist renunciants depicted in monastic law codes, leaving home for the religious life sometimes seems to have meant moving one's family to a monastery.

The following tale from the *Sarvāstivāda-vinaya* serves as the origin story for the rule introducing a minimum age requirement for novices.[128] In the city of Śrāvastī, a certain householder's wife and relatives had all died, and his wealth was all gone; the householder, the father, was left with his two children.

> The householder thought to himself, "Among the followers of various [religious] paths it is only the mendicant Sons of the Śākyan who benefit from offerings, and are without grief and suffering. Having gone forth (*chujia* 出家) in this [religion], there will be no problems."[129]

The householder then took his two children and went to the Jetavana seeking initiation into the religious life (將二兒到祇園中求出家). The term which I have translated as "initiation into the religious life" is not problematic at all; *chujia* 出家 literally means "to leave home,"[130] and is a standard translation of Sanskrit *pra√vraj* "to go forth" or "to leave home and wander forth as an ascetic mendicant."[131] At least from this passage, then, it would seem that going-forth does not necessarily imply the abandonment of family, much less the severing of all family ties. Indeed, here the householder takes his children, and all are either initiated or ordained. In our text, no condemnation of this action is made explicit, and the only thing that might be construed as a light criticism, or perhaps even a disclaimer, is a statement to the effect that "the monks, *not knowing his intentions*, thereupon granted him (and presumably also his children) the going-forth."[132] The monks, however, receive no condemnation or censure for ordaining a layman along with his children.

A few days afterwards, in narrative time, our newly ordained monk sets out for alms. He dons his robe, takes his bowl, and leading his two children he enters the city of Śrāvastī to beg for alms. Visiting restaurants, bakeries, sweet stores and other food shops, his two hungry children see the breads and say, "Daddy, give us some food, give us some bread" (阿父、與我食與我餅). The father replies, "Although you may ask, without any money who is going to give it to you?" The two children follow behind their father crying. Witnessing this incident, householders rebuke the monk, saying, "The mendicant Sons of the Śākyan do not sever desire! Within the monastic cells, together with the nuns, they give birth to children" (沙門釋子不斷欲。僧坊内共比丘尼生兒).[133] One person told two, two told three, and aspersions spread throughout the city of Śrāvastī. Eventually word gets back to the Buddha, who is then made to promulgate a rule to this effect: "Henceforth those not a full fifteen years old are not to become novices."[134] As we will see, this rule was later amended to allow the initiation of boys in some cases as young as seven years old.

We might fruitfully consider the above narrative on a number of levels. This passage is found in the *Chapter on Ordination* and deals, ostensibly, with the age requirement for novices. On another level, the story reflects the assumptions of the authors/redactors of this monastic code vis-à-vis co-renunciation. Moreover, we also seem to glimpse a layman's assumptions about renunciation with one's children. The authors/redactors portray this householder as assuming that he can leave home for the religious life *with* his two children. The authors/redactors neither critique nor condemn his actions. Rather, they take it for granted that such a situation might arise. Laymen renouncing the world with their children was not the problem that this rule sought to prevent.

The authors/redactors were worried, however, about the corporate image of the monastic order. The problem for the monastic lawyers seems to have been that monks with children calling them "Daddy" in public were bound to raise more than a few eyebrows.[135] Laymen were likely to misconstrue the situation and accuse monks (and nuns) of sexual impropriety. It is this, the charge of unchastity, that the monastic authors/redactors seem to have sought to avoid. Yet this concern never moves the authors/redactors to proscribe the initiation of father and son into the monastic order. Rather, they simply introduce a minimum age for the initiation of novices, one that is subsequently lowered. According to this monastic code, then, a layman may renounce the world and become a monk while taking his children along with him as novices so long as they were over a certain age. For the monastic authors/redactors, going forth from home into homelessness did not require that family—our monk's children—be abandoned or deserted.

This story is not unique to the *Sarvāstivāda-vinaya*. Variant versions of the same basic tale are also recorded, for instance, in the *Dharmaguptaka-vinaya*.[136] There, an elder (長老)[137] is said to have "gone forth taking his son" (將兒出家已). At the marketplace, when the son stretches out his arm asking for food, householders are likewise critical, saying, "Mendicant Sons of the Śākyan know no shame. They transgress celibacy!" The World-Honored One is then made to establish a rule that one may not initiate those under twelve years old.

The *Mūlasarvāstivāda-vinaya*'s account of this rule is somewhat longer, but there too no criticism is made concerning the ordination of one's own children—in this version there is only one son.[138] When the baker refuses to give the bread, the father grabs his son by the fingers, lifting him up and making him fall on his back. When the boy starts crying, onlookers address the monk, saying, "Who is this novice to the venerable one?" When the monk replies, "My son" (*bu yin no*), the onlookers castigate him. Even the criticism, however, is revealing. The monk is not criticized for having a son, but rather for what nowadays some might call child abuse: "Is this what a mendicant does to his own flesh and blood?"[139] It would seem, then, that in no extant version of this story is the monk at all criticized for leaving home with his son(s). Renunciation with one's children appears to have caused other problems, but the monastic lawyers legislate around them, rather than proscribe the practice.

What I take to be the corresponding story in the *Mahīśāsaka-vinaya* does not mention a baker.[140] A certain family had been plagued by nonhumans, leaving just father and child alive. The father, fearing that the calamities were not yet over and that there would be a famine, considers where he might escape. He thinks to himself, "The mendicant Sons of the Śākyan have many resources and medicines for the sick. Right now, I ought to take my son and go forth and receive ordination" (我今便可將兒出家受具足戒). The father does so, but later on he enters the city for alms carrying his son in one arm and his bowl in the other. When seen by the laity he is accused of not cultivating celibacy. Others step up to his defense, "[No,] he had this child before he went forth. However, why do the monks not wait until he [i.e., the boy] has grown up and then initiate him? Instead they make this man carry his son when he goes for alms. Who would not think he had broken his celibacy?"[141] The Buddha is then made to state:

"One should not initiate little children" (不應度小兒).[142] Here too the authors/redactors take for granted the fact that monks may leave home for the religious life with their children, but the monastic lawyers identify a potential problem in the eyes of the almsgiving public. The solution put into the mouths of the laymen is not the severance of familial bonds. Rather, they suggest that the monks should wait until the boy has grown up before initiating him into the religious life. The perceived problem, then, is neither the initiation of family members nor the entering into homelessness as a family, but rather the presence of toddlers on an alms round, something that was bound to attract unwanted rumor.

The rule that children under a certain age should not be admitted as novices is also found in the Pāli Vinaya, although, as far as I know, its implications have never been fully articulated.[143] Here the Pāli is quite explicit in its narrative: "They (i.e., father and son), having gone forth among the monks, still went for alms together" (*te bhikkhūsu pabbajitvā ekato 'va piṇḍāya caranti*). Unlike Chinese translations, which can be ambiguous if plurals are unmarked, the nature of a heavily inflected language such as Pāli allows us to confirm that the father and son (they: *te*—plural) both went for alms (*piṇḍāya caranti*—again plural) having gone forth (*pabbajitvā*). It is interesting to note, however, that even in this rule, tucked away in the depths of the Pāli Vinaya, no criticism or condemnation is put into the mouth of the Buddha. Laymen misunderstand the situation thinking that the monk had broken the rule of celibacy, but here too the Buddha is portrayed as moving only, it seems, to curtail lay criticism: "Monks, a boy less than fifteen years old should not be initiated."[144]

The rule expressly forbidding the initiation of boys under the age of fifteen in the Sarvāstivāda, Mūlasarvāstivāda, and Pāli *vinaya*s, under the age of twelve in the *Dharmaguptaka-vinaya,* and young boys of an unspecified age in the *Mahīśāsaka-vinaya* is then amended to allow, under certain circumstances, the initiation of much younger boys, usually as young as seven, and usually conditional upon their ability to chase away crows.[145] Confining her comments to the Pāli account, Horner describes this as "a most singular exception to the general rule forbidding the going forth of a youth under fifteen years of age."[146] Exceptions to the rules are in fact rather widespread.

The amendment admitting male novices as young as seven years old into the religious life is interesting for a number of reasons. In the account preserved in the *Sarvāstivāda-vinaya,* for instance, the two boys in question are specifically said to be relatives of the Buddha's cousin Ānanda.[147] The idiot—so the authors/redactors of this *vinaya* characterize him—Viḍūḍabha had just killed the Sons of the Śākyan in the city of Kapilavastu, home of the Buddha. The Buddha and Ānanda happen to be in the city, and the two boys, who presumably had been orphaned in the massacre, run up to their relative, Ānanda. Ānanda gives them some food, and the Buddha, although he knows the answer—the authors/redactors hasten to add—asks, "Whose children are these?" Ānanda replies they are his relatives, to which the Buddha asks, "Why do you not let them go forth?" Ānanda explains that the Buddha has already promulgated a rule prohibiting the initiation of boys under fifteen years old. The Buddha asks whether the boys are able to chase away crows from the monastic community's food. When answered in the affirmative, the Buddha amends his previous position. Here, then, we see another case in which a general amendment to Buddhist monastic law is made to accommodate the initiation of relatives, this time specifically tied to a story about the plight of the now orphaned relatives of the Buddha's own cousin, Ānanda.[148]

Even our limited foray into the narrative depths of Buddhist monastic codes in this section suggests that, according to the authors/redactors of canonical *vinaya* texts, the "going-forth" was not necessarily an act of severing ties with children, parents, and siblings. According to our Indian Buddhist monastic jurists, when men went forth from home to homelessness in India, it seems that they could take their children with them.[149]

7. Incidental Incidents and Pugnacious Parents

The rules in the preceding section dealing with the age at which a boy may be initiated into the religious life were all found where we would expect them: in the *Chapter on Ordination* in our monastic codes. These frame-stories allowed us to confirm that at least the authors/redactors of the so-called Sthavira *vinaya*s (Dharmaguptaka, Mahīśāsaka, Mūlasarvāstivāda, Sarvāstivāda, and Theravāda) seem to take it for granted that a monk may leave home for homelessness with his children. As briefly discussed above, in Section 3 of Chapter 1, any claims concerning pan-*nikāya* or transsectarian understandings of Indian Buddhist monastic religiosity must also take into account the *vinaya* of the Mahāsāṅghikas. As is well known, the structure of the *Mahāsāṅghika-vinaya* differs from that of the Sthavira *vinaya*s,[150] and this slightly complicates our task.

Although the *Mahāsāṅghika-vinaya* does recognize the "scare-crow provision,"[151] the frame-story attached to this piece of monastic legislation does not allow us to confirm this *vinaya*'s position vis-à-vis co-renunciation. Accordingly, we need to look elsewhere in the *Mahāsāṅghika-vinaya* for evidence that a monk could take his children with him when he went forth into homelessness. In this section, I shall introduce a frame-story from the *Mahāsāṅghika-vinaya* in which co-renunciation with one's children is presented as commonplace. Moreover, in order to make sure that co-renunciation in the Sthavira *vinaya*s is not limited to the narrative discussed in the previous section, I will introduce one further example from a Sthavira *vinaya* suggesting again the unproblematic nature of co-renunciation with one's children.

The narrative world of these monastic codes presents us with a wealth of information even in the most improbable of places. Snapshots of a purported conversation or incident, details often entirely incidental to the rule being delivered, provide us with valuable evidence, all of which bespeaks the degree to which familial relations were ingrained in the very fabric of the Indian Buddhist monastic culture known to our canonical jurists. The following story from the *Mahāsāṅghika-vinaya* concerning monastic protocol vis-à-vis food storage and preparation provides us with just such an unguarded glimpse of our monastic lawyers' assumptions about the religious life.[152]

> The Buddha was traveling through the kingdom of Kosala and arrived at the brahmin hamlet of Old *Śaila.
>
> At one time there were barbers: an old man, the father, and his son. Having left home [for the religious life] they dwelt in this hamlet. Then the old man heard that the World-Honored One was coming, and thereupon spoke to his son, saying, "You must take the barbering tools and enter the hamlet. Seek rice, beans, ghee, oil, and crystallized sugar. The World-Honored One is arriving; we must make various gruels."
>
> Thereupon the son entered the hamlet. Crowds of people asked him, saying, "What do you hope to obtain by barbering?"
>
> He replied, "I require rice, beans, ghee, oil, and crystallized sugar."
>
> "What will you use those for?"
>
> He replied, "Tomorrow the World-Honored One is arriving; I must make various gruels."

> Then the householders, having heard this, delighted, and with thoughts of faith they doubled what they gave him.
>
> Thereupon he brought this back to his dwelling place.
>
> The World-Honored One had arrived, and the old man himself had made various gruels. The following morning the Buddha and the community of monks sat down, and the old man washed his hands and personally served the gruel.
>
> The Buddha—although already knowing—intentionally asked, saying, "Monk, what is this gruel?"
>
> He replied, "World-Honored One, formerly when I was a layman, I used to make offerings to the monks, and I always had this thought, 'When will I be able to make offerings to the World-Honored One with my own hands?' Therefore, now I have made this gruel."
>
> The Buddha said, "Where did you obtain the rice?"
>
> He replied, "My son took clients as a barber and obtained it."[153]

The text then goes on to clarify this monastic code's position on the acceptance and storage of food, a complicated topic that has not received adequate treatment to date. The Buddha is made to list various types of food that are not allowed: food stored or cooked inappropriately, and food, among other things, obtained by taking clients in occupations such as barbering, which is considered polluting in brahmanical society.

The exact details of monastic food preparation aside, this short story affords us a number of insights into the world of Buddhist monasticism as envisioned by our monastic authors/redactors. We see here another case of a father and son leaving home for the religious life together. Moreover, although their cooking of food obtained through barbering is deemed to be inappropriate, the fact that this father and son joined the monastic order together is here nothing more than a narrative flourish. The inadvertent or incidental nature of this narrative detail, in my view, makes it of even greater import than something which the monastic authors consciously reveal to us.[154] The authors/redactors of our monastic code are not making an argument for world renunciation with family members. For them, no case need be made. Rather, they seem to assume that one can leave home for the religious life with one's family. It is precisely the irrelevance of many of these details that assures us of their relevance.

We next turn to a more explicit case, this time from a section on murder in the *Dharmaguptaka-vinaya,* a frame-story briefly discussed above, in Section 2 of Chapter 1, in relation to our imaginary intellectual predecessor. Here the familial relationship between the monastics plays a slightly larger part in the narrative, but again it is never called into question; it is simply accepted as part and parcel of established Buddhist monasticism. Here too we see the very real possibility that when laymen renounced the world and went forth into the Buddha's Dharma they could take along their children.

In Śrāvastī a patron had invited the Buddha and the monastic community for a meal. The World-Honored One had arrived with 1,250 monks. As is the usual practice of Buddhas—add the authors/redactors—food or drink was not accepted until the monastic community was fully assembled.[155] The rest of the story is short enough to give in full:

> At that time there was a monk who left home [for the religious life] late in life. Taking his son he left home [for the religious life] (將兒出家). At breakfast time he went to another layman's house. The monks asked his son, saying, "Where did your father go? On his account the World-Honored One is made to wait without eating."
>
> The boy replied, "I don't know."
>
> A monk said, "You must go and search for him."
>
> He searched and found him.
>
> The boy said to his father, "Where did you go? On account of waiting for you, father, the Buddha and community are unable to take their meal."
>
> The boy's father became angry and grabbed his son. The son pushed himself free. The father fell to the ground and thereupon passed away. The boy suspected [he might have committed an offense].
>
> The Buddha asked, saying, "Sir, what were your intentions?"
>
> He replied, "It was not done with the intention of killing."
>
> The Buddha said, "There is no offense, but you should not have pushed your father."[156]

As noted previously, this story is not about father and son monastics. Rather, it is a discussion of culpability in the case of death resulting from the pushing of one's father.[157] Like the examples examined above, this short passage is predicated on the notion that monks and nuns do not sever family ties when they enter the state of homelessness. Our monk has not deserted his son. Rather, they have embarked on a religious sojourn together. This relationship is recognized by the other monks in the story, as evinced by their question, "Where did your father go?" Likewise, even the Buddha is made to acknowledge this relationship in his suggestion to the boy, "You should not push your father." This father and son entered the religious life together, associated within the monastic community together, and continued to acknowledge each other as father and son. The authors/redactors of our legal codes make not only the other monks but even the Buddha tacitly acknowledge this enduring familial relationship. Here, then, we find another example in which the bonds of kinship continued to be very much a part of the monasticism depicted by the authors/redactors of this canonical *vinaya* text.

8. Families on Different Paths

Although the tales we have seen in the Buddhist monastic codes so far deal primarily with Buddhist renunciation, a number of others also address the interface between Buddhism and other heterodox religions in India. As such, the Buddhist monastic codes may have implications for the study of Indian religions in general. When family members renounce the world together, they do not necessarily have to agree on their religious paths; sometimes they go their separate ways when entering monastic orders.

In a story in the *Mahāsāṅghika-vinaya,* we encounter a mother and daughter who leave home for the religious life together (母子出家). The mother joins a non-Buddhist community, and the daughter becomes a Buddhist nun.[158] The non-Buddhist nun, the mother, makes an interesting comment, one that reveals a number of presuppositions about Buddhist religious life which the authors/redactors portray a newly ordained, non-Buddhist nun as holding.

This nun, a follower of an unspecified non-Buddhist path, invites her daughter, a Buddhist nun, to come and live with her: "We are still mother and daughter; why should we be apart in life? You may come here and we will dwell together."[159] The daughter, however, replies that she needs a reason to leave the Buddhist order. Accordingly, she goes, it seems, to pick a fight with her co-religionists. She starts by renouncing the Buddha, the Dharma, and the Saṅgha, and then claims that other religious sects are superior and that she would be better off cultivating *brahmacarya* there. Her fellow nuns try to get her to stop saying such things, but, it seems, ultimately fail. The Buddha is then made to enact a rule by which a nun incurs an offense if she does not abandon such talk after three admonitions.

Our text explicitly addresses neither interactions between Buddhists and non-Buddhists, nor continued contact between a mother and daughter. Rather, this tale introduces the rule about not giving up talk of abandoning the religious life. In the frame-story, however, we see that the non-Buddhist nun fully envisages—or is made to envisage—a form of world renunciation in which mother and daughter can still live together. The Buddhist nun is portrayed as being open to this form of religiosity, one that presumably would not differ significantly, as we have seen, from Buddhist understandings of world renunciation in terms of continued contact between ordained family members. Arguably, the only reason that our nun does not invite her mother to join her in a Buddhist convent is that this would not fulfill the requirements of a frame-story for a rule about a nun intent on giving up the Buddhist religious life. Here, then, there is at least a hint that Buddhism may not have been the only family-friendly monasticism in India.[160]

Another rule in this monastic code is introduced with a frame-story involving parents on a different religious path than their son's. Gartodara leaves home for the religious life with his parents; they become Buddhist renunciants (父母在佛法中出家), but he follows another, unspecified tradition.[161] Without a robe during a spell of cold weather, Gartodara carries around an animal to keep warm. He goes and sees his mother, a narrative detail again suggesting that family ties were not severed in either Buddhism or this non-Buddhist renunciatory tradition. The Buddhist nun, taking pity on her son, gives him a new robe. Wearing this he goes into a tavern (*pānāgāra;* 酒店), where he is criticized for wearing the emblem of a sage (*ṛṣidhvaja;* 聖人幖幟). This is reported to the head of the nuns' order, Mahāprajāpatī Gautamī, the Buddha's aunt and stepmother, who in turn reports it to the Buddha. The canonical authors/redactors thereupon have the Buddha make it an offense for nuns to give robes to followers of other paths with their own hands.[162]

In addition to the numerous examples surveyed in the preceding sections, these two short examples should be enough to suggest that a number of assumptions about the nature of Indian renunciatory traditions may not be as clear-cut as they have previously been made out to be. Louis Dumont, for instance, in an article that has been described as "justly influential"[163] and "seminal,"[164] states "there are two kinds of men in Hindu India, those that live in the world and those that have renounced it."[165] Dumont points out that "it is well known that classically whoever seeks liberation must leave the world and adopt an entirely different mode of life. This is an institution, *saṃnyāsa,* renunciation, in fact a social state apart from society proper."[166]

While I do not necessarily wish to call into question assumptions about non-Buddhist Indian renunciation, Indian Buddhist notions of the going-forth—at least as viewed through the eyes of our monastic authors/redactors—seem to present problems for this classical formulation of Indian world renunciation. It probably is true, as Olivelle suggests, that "Dumont's structural dichotomy between the renouncer and the man in the world is tenable only at the level of ideal types: the lived reality of both the ascetics and people living in society was much more complex and much less tidy."[167] If we accept, however, that our Buddhist monastic codes present monastic ideals as envisioned by their authors and subsequent redactors, then we would seem to be forced to accept that even the religious life in an idealized formulation as understood by the authors/redactors of Buddhist monastic law codes did not demand the renunciation or abandonment of family. The "social state apart from society proper," at least as envisioned by the authors/redactors of the *vinaya*s, seems not to have been predicated on the dissolution of familial ties, and this seems to hold not only for Buddhists in India, but also for non-Buddhist renunciation as viewed through the lens of our monastic authors/redactors.

9. Conclusions

As we saw in the epigraphical record, family members are mentioned in the donative inscriptions of Buddhist monks and nuns in India around the turn of the Common Era. In our monastic law codes, leaving home for the religious life might not have perforce required the ordinand physically to leave the home at all, although this decision is sometimes presented as important in terms of religious advancement. The stories we have examined assume that monks and nuns continued to interact, associate, and at times even stay with lay family members. In fact, actions that would otherwise incur minor monastic offenses are oftentimes declared to be nonoffenses if done with or for a monk's or nun's family member. Moreover, our texts assume that in Indian Buddhist monasticisms—and perhaps even non-Buddhist forms—one could renounce the world *with* one's children.

Should the monastic authors/redactors have wanted or needed to do so, it would have been a simple matter either to prohibit the initiation and ordination of biological kin, or to require that family members enter the religious life elsewhere than with each other. During the ordination ceremony, the candidate was asked a series of questions in order to ascertain whether he is free of debt and disease, human, not a thief, not in the king's service, not a slave, and so forth.[168] Here the candidate could easily be asked about his family, and whether or not any were ordained Buddhists, but this was not a question asked at the ordination ceremony. Here the ordination of prostitutes is likewise instructive. The *Dharmaguptaka-vinaya,* for instance, discusses how, when a prostitute is ordained, she is to be taken five to six *yojana*s away from where she plied her old trade lest she be confronted by former johns.[169] Biologically related kin and spouses could easily be required to be ordained down the road, so to speak, but this again was not made a rule. Neither of these rules was established, it would seem, simply because the presence of kin within the monastery was not a problem that required monastic legislation.

One's understanding of what it meant to be a Buddhist monk in India changes dramatically depending on which source materials one consults. Previous scholarship has tended to privilege one side of the story, reconstructing Indian Buddhist monasticisms primarily on the basis of *sutta* materials. As we have seen, however, our *vinaya* texts present Indian monastic Buddhism as a religion in which the family was not shut out or cut off; this holds true for whatever *nikāya* we examine, whether it be Dharmaguptaka, Mahāsāṅghika, Mahīśāsaka, Mūlasarvāstivāda, Sarvāstivāda, or Theravāda.

It might be argued that the view of Indian Buddhist monasticisms in which continued contact with one's family is not merely tolerated but accepted as a normal part of the religious life is late and thus does not represent pristine monastic Buddhism, should we admit the existence of such a thing at all and should we still be interested in reconstructing and studying it. To make such an argument, however, requires that we accept that all sources for monastic Buddhism in India are uniformly late; of course, precisely this has been argued before.[170] But even if we accept that this view of the family in monastic Buddhism is a relatively late one, this would still require that we accept the importance of family in Indian monastic Buddhisms by at the very latest the early fifth century C.E., the date of the translation into Chinese of the Dharmaguptaka, Mahāsāṅghika, Mahīśāsaka, and Sarvāstivāda *vinaya*s.

To turn this around, then, again using only the dates of the Chinese translations, we might likewise argue that this view is representative of Buddhism as late as the eighth century, when Yijing translated the *Mūlasarvāstivāda-vinaya* (or even later for the Tibetan translation). In the opposite direction, we might go back to the Aluvihāra redaction of the Pāli Vinaya in the first century B.C.E. (29–17 B.C.E.),[171] or even a century beforehand with the use of inscriptional material. In doing so, however, in writing off the importance of family in Indian Buddhism by regarding such a monasticism as "late," we will be forced to accept the currency of these views for almost a millennium, from the first century B.C.E. through the eighth or ninth century C.E.—in other words, for the greater part of the history of Buddhism in India.

Although Indian Buddhism may have become a family-friendly institution by the first few centuries of the Common Era, was this always the case? How far back can we push these views? For the moment, let us concede, along with Thomas William Rhys Davids and Hermann Oldenberg, that the *prātimokṣa*s, the lists of rules to be observed by individual members of the monastic order, represent "one of the oldest, if not the oldest, of all Buddhist text-books."[172] If we accept the early age of these *prātimokṣa*s, then we must also somehow explain the existence almost at the very beginning of Buddhist literature of rules found in these so-called textbooks that not only take it for granted that monks and nuns might continue to interact with their relatives, but also that monastic communities may have as members monks and nuns who are biologically related to each other.

The sixth *nissaggiya-pācittiya* of the Pāli *Bhikkhu-pātimokkha,* for instance, makes it an offense for a monk to "ask for robe material from a householder or householder's wife, not related [to him]."[173] Implicit in such rulings is the fact that there is no offense if the householder involved is a relation of the monk. Moreover, what is here only implicit is made explicit in the *vibhaṅga,* wherein we are told that "there is no offence if... [the robe material] belong[s] to relations."[174] Here and in other similar rules, exceptions are made in the case of a monk's or nun's kinfolk.[175] Likewise, rules such as the fourth and fifth *nissaggiya-pācittiya*s state that a monk incurs an offense by having "an old robe washed or dyed or washed by beating by a bhikkhunī not related [to him]" or by accepting "a robe from the hand of a bhikkhunī not related [to him]."[176] In these rules, the fact that a monk might be related to a nun—defined in the *vibhaṅga* as "related on the mother's side or on the father's side back through seven generations"[177]—is taken as a given by some of the earliest authors of Buddhist literature. Certain rules already have built into the canonical text expressions that presume the presence of nuns to whom a monk might be biologically related within the same monastic community. In other words, family is woven tightly into the very fabric of Indian monastic Buddhism from the very beginnings of Buddhist literature.

Chapter Three

Former Wives from Former Lives

> Pig went over to Squire Gao, tugged at his coat, and said, "Sir, may my wife come out and pay her respects to these two gentlemen?"
>
> "Brother," said Monkey with a laugh. "You've entered the church now and become a monk. Don't ever talk about a wife again. Only Taoist priests can have families—we Buddhist monks never marry."
>
> —*Journey to the West*[1]

In the preceding chapter, I suggested that for the authors/redactors of Indian Buddhist monastic law codes, embarking on the religious life did not require the severance of all familial ties. Indeed, numerous monastic narratives are predicated on the assumption that monks and nuns would have continued interaction with their families. Moreover, I argued that leaving home is not to be confused with abandoning or even necessarily leaving one's family. In the narrative world of the monastic codes, men and women sometimes left home for the religious life *as a family*.

In this chapter, my aim is to explore the contours of the narrative landscape of Indian Buddhist monastic law codes further by building on these observations concerning monastics and their families. Our focus here is on continued marital, as opposed to familial, relations. The authors/redactors of Buddhist monastic law codes seem to have envisioned the formal maintenance of marital ties not only between monastics and their lay spouses, but also between married monks and nuns. Although aware of legal provisions for the dissolution of marriage, Buddhist jurists seem not to have required monks or nuns to dissolve their marriages. Rather, the canonical lawyers negotiated the boundaries between acceptable and unacceptable behavior not only for monks and their "former" lay wives, but also for married monastic couples.

We start, in Section 1, with a story of monastic education and the need to inform new ordinands not to have sex. Although our story is primarily about monastic education and celibacy, the authors/redactors of this tale seem to take for granted that monks might return home to see their wives. This story confirms our observations from Chapter 2 and extends them to monastic spouses, thereby allowing us to start to question whether men and women who were already married remained so upon entering the religious life.

In Section 2, we turn to a story about two monks who arrange marriages for their children. By acting as marital go-betweens, the monks get into trouble and reveal to us the concern felt, or believed to have been felt, by some monks with regard to traditional obligations toward their wives, children, and families. Although we cannot prove (nor, for that matter, disprove) that this represents an historical reality, non-Buddhist materials—including sources generally ambivalent if not antagonistic to Buddhism such as Sanskrit dramas—reveal to us a similar picture. I argue that this external testimony may confirm the verisimilitude of the internal evidence found in the monastic codes.

In Section 3, I discuss marital dissolution and divorce in the Indian context. Despite the oft-made claim that "divorce" was not recognized in Indian society, there are a number of passages in Buddhist monastic law codes that, although not well known, make it clear that some form of marital dissolution was available to Indian couples. If monastic authors/redactors were aware of provisions for the dissolution of marriage, why do they not require ordinands to dissolve their marriages? As we will see, it appears that monks and nuns in India may have continued to remain legally married to their lay partners after their initiation and ordination into the religious life. In the monasticisms envisioned by Buddhist monastic authors/redactors we see the very real possibility of married monks in India.

Monks and nuns may have been able to remain legally married to lay partners, but could a monk be married to a nun? In Section 4, I deal with a number of *vinaya* narratives that address nuns' engagement in seemingly mundane matters such as serving water to, and fanning, monks. Here the monastic authors/redactors introduce stories involving husbands and wives who have left home for the religious life together: husband and wife, monk and nun. Such monastic couples receive no comment or criticism, and are presented almost as a commonplace.

In Section 5, I introduce a narrative of one monastic couple, Udāyin and Guptā, and the birth of their son, Kumāra-Kāśyapa. This is a story of a monk and nun, husband and wife, who conceive and raise a child in a monastery, a child who grows up to be a religious success, an arhat, and the foremost in eloquence among the Buddha's disciples. This story gives a good sense of the full range of complex marital and familial relationships assumed possible, and perhaps also somewhat problematic, within Indian Buddhist monasticisms. Here we catch our first glimpse of a monastic family: not only husband and wife, but a son, too, born within the monastic confines.

In Section 6, I discuss two presentations of the life story of Mahākāśyapa, the foremost ascetic in Buddhist literature. The first version emphasizes his ascetic qualities to a lay audience of brahmin housewives. The second story is one told to monks and nuns about the ascetic *par excellence*'s married life and his co-renunciation through several lifetimes with his wife, the beautiful Kapilabhadrā. As we will see, at least as envisaged by the authors/redactors of the extant monastic law codes, even strict Buddhist asceticism in no way ruled out continued interaction with one's wife.

The picture that emerges from this chapter is one that stands in contrast to much that we have been told about Buddhist monasticisms and the marital ties of ordained monastics. What we see, however, is in fact not as strange as one might have first thought. As I shall discuss in Section 7, parallels confirming the existence of married monks and monastic families are found in varying degrees in premodern and modern forms of Central Asian, Kaśmīri, Newar, Sri Lankan, and Tibetan Buddhisms, all of which point not to a corruption of a pure Indian ideal but perhaps to a continuation of forms of Buddhist monasticisms somewhat closer to those envisioned by our monastic authors/redactors.

1. Monastic Education concerning Sex with One's Wife

We begin with a *vinaya* story concerning monastic education and the need to inform newly ordained monks of the four *pārājika*s immediately upon ordination, lest, unbeknownst, they commit one of these major offenses.[2] The story comes from the *Mūlasarvāstivāda-vinaya* and deals with a householder who goes forth in the religious life.[3]

At one time, when he had lost his relatives and wealth, he thought to himself, "I am now old and cannot pursue wealth. Furthermore, my relatives are all dead. I ought to forsake the lay life and leave home [for the religious life]."

Having thought this he said to his wife (*chung ma;* 妻), "Dear (*bzang mo;* 賢首), I am now old and cannot pursue wealth. Furthermore, the relatives are all dead. I want to leave home [for the religious life]."

The wife replied, "Fine, but do come and see me from time to time" (*dus dus su ltar byon cig;* 善、然可時時看問於我).

The husband replied, "Certainly."

This passage presents a householder who, in his old age, while contemplating becoming a monk, consults his wife. The first part of the passage—the reference to old age, the inability to pursue wealth, and the death of one's relatives as a reason to enter the monastic order—is a stock phrase found throughout this monastic code.[4] Here, however, the wife asks her husband to visit from time to time. Her expectation, a lay Indian housewife's expectation, albeit seen through the eyes of the monastic authors/redactors, is that a monk could from time to time visit his wife. This is then reinforced by the husband's reply that, as a monk, he will do so. Our Indian householder and his wife are portrayed as entertaining the same preconceptions of Buddhist monastic life: being a monk would not prevent one from returning home to visit one's spouse.

The husband, we said, is leaving home to enter the Buddhist order. He is not parting with his family, just his wife; his relatives, we are told, are already dead. The husband travels to the Jetavana Grove and receives initiation and ordination in the well-spoken Dharma and Vinaya. After two or three days, when the newly ordained monk had been taught the rules of customary behavior (Tib. *kun tu spyad pa'i chos;* Chi. 法式; Skt. **āsamudācārika-dharma*), the content of which is not stated, he is told to go to Śrāvastī and beg for alms there.

While out on his alms round, our monk sees a woman who looks just like his wife (*rang gi chung ma 'dra ba'i bud med cig;* 一女人形似其妻). The monk then recalls that he had promised his wife that he would stop by from time to time. Lest she be disgruntled, he decides to pay her a visit. It is perhaps useful to note here that the text alternates between "wife" and "former wife." The term translated here as "former wife" (Tib. *sngon gyi chung ma;* Chi. 故二; Skt. **purāṇa-dvitīyā*) seems to mean, quite simply, a wife from one's "former" lay life.[5] The alternation between "wife" and "former wife" in the text is probably indicative of little more than the interchangeability of the two terms. Since the question of divorce will become important later in this chapter, let us be clear that a "former wife," one's lay wife, is not to be confused with a wife whom one has divorced.

Turning back to our narrative, the monk returns to the Jetavana and addresses his preceptor as follows: "Upādhyāya, I have a former wife and since I promised her that after going forth into the religious life I would come to see her, on account of that might it be permitted and I shall go." The monk is then granted permission to go and see his "former" wife: "Go, son, although you must guard your thoughts."[6] The canonical authors/redactors are here setting the stage for what is to come; the preceptor recognizes a possible danger in a monk's meeting up with his "former" wife, and he warns his pupil accordingly. It is noteworthy, however, that the newly ordained monk's informal request for permission to visit his wife receives no criticism from his preceptor. The text suggests that the authors/redactors of this monastic code accepted the idea that monks might visit their quondam partners as a commonplace of monastic life. This was not a matter that needed to be prohibited or even made an offense, although it did warrant a warning to be on one's guard.

When the monk arrives back home, his "former" wife, seeing him from afar, joyfully hurries to meet him. "Noble son, welcome, welcome," she says, greeting him. "It has been a long time since I have seen you." Then she begins to touch him.

> "What are you doing?" he asked.[7]
>
> "I am taking your robes so that you can rest."
>
> "Don't touch me," he said.
>
> "Why not?"
>
> "My preceptor told me that I must guard my thoughts."
>
> "Noble son," she said, "although you may well guard your thoughts, am I forbidden?"

As the text continues, the wife attempts to seduce the monk. Having taken his robes, she washes and anoints his feet. Here Yijing's Chinese translation offers a few details not found in the Tibetan:

> Thereupon she took his robes and bowl, spread out a seat, made him sit down, and brought water to wash his feet.

"What are you going to do?" he asked.
"I was about to wash your feet," his wife said.
"Do not touch my feet," he replied.
"Why not?" she asked.[8]

The monk again explains to his wife that he had been told to guard his thoughts; she again explains to him that while that is all very well, it in no way prohibits her from washing his feet—the Buddha's regulations, after all, apply to him and not her. The monk allows her to wash his feet, and the two go back and forth in the same manner when his wife attempts to anoint his feet with oil. She then offers him some food, and sits down to eat with him. The monk asks, "What are you doing?" She replies, "Noble son, it has been a long time since I ate with you." After eating together, she arranges the bed, saying, "Noble son, on this bed you must rest your weary back." The monk reclines, and she attempts to lie down beside him. Again, predictably, the monk says, "What are you doing?" "Noble son, as it has been a long time since I lay down together with you, you must not scold me." The monk replies, "My preceptor told me that I must guard my thoughts." "Noble son," she replies, "although you may well guard your thoughts, am I forbidden? As it has been a long time since I lay down together with you, surely we can lie down together." The monk is unwilling, however. Then, thinking to herself, "After embracing him, he will be mine," she embraces him. The text goes on to give what is a frequent editorial insertion in this monastic code when dealing with the seduction of monks. It states, in no uncertain terms, that women are poison to the touch (*bud med ni reg pa'i dug yin pas;* 女是觸毒).[9] The text then states that the two, husband and wife, had sex.[10]

After staying there for a long time—the Chinese states many days—the monk finally says to his wife, "Dear, I am going" (*bzang mo 'gro'o //*).[11] The term of address here is one that we have seen before: it is exactly the same term that our monk used to address his wife when he first told her of his intention to join the monastic order. In other words, as a monk he continues to address his wife just as he did as a layman.[12] Likewise, the wife consistently refers to the monk with a term of address appropriate for one's husband: **āryaputra* (noble son).[13] Here, then, we have before us one of the first indications that the marriage of this couple may be anything but formally dissolved.

Before considering the rest of this story, it will be useful to review what others have said about the marital status of those who enter the Buddhist monastic order. In his classic study of Indian Buddhist monasticism according to the Theravādin textual tradition, Oldenberg concluded that "both the marriage tie and the rights of property of him who renounces the world, are regarded as *ipso facto* cancelled by the 'going forth from home into homelessness.'"[14] Oldenberg goes on to state that "the monk, who is resolved to remain true to the spiritual life, looks upon his marriage as dissolved, his property as given away. The wife whom he has forsaken, is strictly termed in the texts 'his quondam partner.' ... He addresses her, like every other woman, as 'sister.'"[15]

Oldenberg's observations about the terms of address used for a monk's quondam partner certainly do not hold for our monastic code. Oldenberg, however, may be right about the *ipso facto* cancellation of marital ties, but this is by no means legally binding. We see here the same ambiguity pointed out by Schopen with regard to the renunciation of personal property: it is not "effected by the fact of ordination itself but would depend on the individual's spiritual resolve."[16] In other words, although Oldenberg himself seems to admit that a monk might, or perhaps even should, regard his marriage as dissolved, this is simply a question of the individual monk's resolve: a moral imperative not a legal one.[17] For our present purposes, it will suffice to note that there is absolutely no talk of divorce or the dissolution of marriage in the narrative. This was clearly not an issue for the monastic authors/redactors.

In our story, when the husband tells his wife that it is time for him to return to the monastery, the wife offers him money for the road: "Just so, noble son, go! But you must take some cash (*kārṣāpaṇa*s)[18] for provisions on the journey."[19] The monk, apparently already aware of the rule that monks may not touch money, declines: "Dear, when monks do not touch valuables, how am I to accept it?"[20] The wife then puts the valuables in a covering, ties it up, and binds it to the lower end of his staff (*'khar gsil;* 錫杖), allowing the monk to take it without touching either the cash or the letter of the law.[21]

When the monk finally reaches Śrāvastī, the Venerable Upananda happens to be hanging around the gate of the Jetavana, as was the custom of those in the Group-of-Six, a merry band of mischief-making monks whose actions account for many if not most of the rules established in monastic law codes.[22] Upananda, the monk in this and other *vinaya*s most usually associated with greed, sees this monk coming with "hair like the flower of the crane tree, brows drooping," and—confusing age with seniority—thinks he is an elder (*gnas brtan;* 尊者).[23] Upananda greets him, saying, "Elder, welcome, welcome." The monk, however, addresses Upananda as Ācārya (*slob dpon;* 阿遮利耶), a term of address restricted to one's own personal teacher.[24] Upananda thinks to himself, "Alas, this is just some old fellow.[25] He knows neither his *ācārya* nor his *upādhyāya*!"

Upananda asks the monk, "Old fellow, where have you come from?" The monk replies, "Ācārya, I have a former wife; I went to see her and I am coming back from there." "Old fellow, excellent...," replies Upananda, who then goes on to quote the Blessed One on the subject of gratitude. Upananda continues:

> "Did you see your former wife?" (*sngon gyi chung ma mthong ngam /*; 得見妻不)
>
> "Yes, I saw her."
>
> "Was she in good health?"
>
> "Yes, in good health."
>
> "Old fellow, that I understand, but what is that hanging on the lower end of your staff?"
>
> "Ācārya, she gave me some *kārṣāpaṇa*s for travel provisions."
>
> "Old fellow, look at you! While you have made some merit and also seen your former wife, you have also succeeded in [making] a profit."
>
> "Ācārya, your words are very kind."

Upananda continues to question the monk, who eventually tells him what had transpired. Upananda then—mischievously but all too characteristically—says to the old monk, "Old fellow, you must tell all that to your preceptor. Your preceptor will be most pleased."

Upananda is setting the monk up for a fall. The monk has just visited his wife, but the visit was fully sanctioned by his preceptor. The old monk has also brought back some cash, but this too was unlikely to land him in trouble: there was technically no offense, or even any suggestion of one, as he had not "touched" the *kārṣāpaṇa*s. Moreover, as we saw in Chapter 2, the fact that he went home and stayed with his "former" wife for several days was not a problem from a legal standpoint. What is at issue, then, is the narrative event of this monk's breaking of the rule of celibacy, as is made clear when he tells his preceptor.

The preceptor in turn tells the other monks, and they inform the Buddha. The Buddha states—according to the Chinese—that "that old fellow does not know right from wrong; he did not intentionally transgress [the rule]."[26] Here, then, the monk is not found guilty of a *pārājika* offense. The monk had had sex, and he had broken the rule of celibacy. But as a newly ordained monk, he had not yet been informed that monks were not supposed to have sex.[27] At least narratively, it had not yet been made a part of the basic monastic curriculum. This is exactly the legal loophole that the authors/redactors of this monastic code sought to close, and this they did with characteristic legal precision.[28] The Buddha is made to say in Yijing's Chinese translation: "If the four *pārājika*s have not yet been expounded to him, he thereby has not transgressed [any rule]. You, monks, on account of this incident, should immediately expound the four *pārājika* rules [to a monk] once he has been ordained. If one does not expound them, one incurs an offense of transgression against the rule of law."[29]

The Tibetan text is slightly more problematic since it involves a textual variant, but it may be rendered as something like the following: "He does [not] incur a *pārājika*. Henceforth, with authorization, as soon as one has gone forth the four *pārājika* rules must be explained in detail, and in this there is no offense."[30] In the sTog Palace recension, a negative particle (*ma;* "[not]") has been added above the line indicating an emendation, a sign that at some time in the recensional history of this edition someone felt the need to correct the text, to make it say that our monk does *not* incur a *pārājika*.[31] Context—not to mention the Chinese translation—also makes it clear that this should not be a *pārājika* offense: our monk has not yet been told what constitutes a *pārājika,* and this, arguably, was the point of the elaborate narrative.[32] Indeed, the monk seems to be presented as a "first offender," one whose actions brought about the establishment of a new monastic rule. As we noted in Section 6 of Chapter 1, these figures are not usually culpable.

The narrative, then, is about monastic education and the need to tell newly ordained monks the ground rules before they break them. This ruling could have been delivered with a frame-story that involved any of the other *pārājika* offenses: stealing (taking something of value that is not given), killing (a human being, not an animal), or lying (not in general but about religious attainments). It could also have been presented with a narrative concerning a breach of celibacy without any mention of a monk's "former" wife. Yet the choice was made to frame the story in terms of a monk's visit home and seduction by his "former" wife, events that may have presented the greatest air of plausibility to a celibate male monastic audience.

As we have seen, the authors/redactors of this Buddhist monastic law code addressed the need for monastic education concerning the *pārājika* offenses by presenting the rule perhaps most probable to be broken by newly ordained men of the world, monks who had been—and perhaps continued to be—married. That the authors/redactors chose to illustrate their point about monastic education by having a monk visit his "former" wife suggests not the severance but the continuation of some form of marital ties between monks and their "former" wives, at least in the monasticisms envisioned by these *vinaya* authorities. Indeed, not only is the plot of this tale dependent upon this narrative event, but, and perhaps more important, the monk's visit home receives no direct censure—neither from the Blessed One, nor from the monastic authors/redactors. In this story, the visit is in fact sanctioned by his preceptor and thus also, by extension, by the authors/redactors of the monastic code. In my view, this narrative casts doubt on the commonly held assumption that marital ties were perforce severed when married men and women went forth from home to homelessness. Monks were free to go home and visit their "former" wives; they just needed to avoid their wives' womanly wiles.

2. Monks Arranging a Marriage for Their Children

To be sure, not all stories of monks who visit their "former" wives paint a rosy picture of the plight of these women. Indeed, with regard to the impact of Buddhist renunciation on the "grieving relatives [left] in its wake,"[33] scholars have asserted that renunciation "breaks up the family, leaves the woman abandoned and grieving, and otherwise conflicts with . . . traditional obligations to wife and children."[34] Here it may be worth evaluating the evidence for such claims in the extant monastic codes.

An indication of the extent to which Buddhist monks may have continued to take seriously their familial obligations can be seen from a short passage in the monastic code of the Mahāsāṅghikas. The narrative below deals with two monks who go home to see their respective wives and children. The monks' wives' reactions offer us a rare insight into the dynamics of a family broken up by Buddhist renunciation.

The Buddha was residing in the city of Śrāvastī.

There were two old men. One old man had abandoned his wife and son, and left home [for the religious life]. The other old man had abandoned his wife and daughter, and left home [for the religious life]. Both of them had been traveling through the country. Coming back to the city of Śrāvastī they stayed in the same cell together.

The one who had abandoned his wife and daughter thereupon thought to himself, "I ought to return home and see my former wife and daughter." Donning his village-entering robe, he went to his former home.

His wife saw the old man coming from afar, and thereupon became angry, saying, "You old man, of little merit and inauspicious,[35] you are unable to support your wife and daughter. Moreover, avoiding the state service you abandon your home and run far away. Your daughter is now grown up and unable to get married. What do you want coming back now? Quick, be off with you! If you don't go, I'll break both of your legs! Who do you think would be happy to see you?"

Then that old man returned to his previous dwelling place. Like a merchant who has lost his wealth, he dwelt in melancholy and pain.

Then, when the one who had abandoned his wife and son and left home [for the religious life] returned home [his experience] was also like this.

[The two monks] stayed together in the same cell. The one who had left home [for the religious life] abandoning his son had a touch of wisdom. Speaking to the second old man, he said, "Elder, why are you dwelling in melancholy and pain?"

"Elder, why must you ask about this matter?" he replied.

Again, [the monk] said, "Certainly I wish to know. How can the two of us share the same cell and yet not share[36] the good and the bad with each other? If you do not tell me, whom else would you tell?"

That old man thereupon told him of the foregoing incident in detail.

The old man who had abandoned his son said, "Why are you so depressed? My family was also like that. Do you not realize [what we can do]? It has just occurred to me that you should make your daughter my son's wife."

"Excellent!" the old man replied.

Thereupon the two old men both incurred an offense of transgression against the rule of law.[37]

This narrative is of interest for a number of reasons, partly for what it tells us about the kind of behavior for which a monk would incur a minor infraction and partly for what it seems to take for granted: what a monk might do without censure or criticism. We see, for instance, that the two old monks incurred an offense of transgression against the rule of law, but we are not told exactly what they did wrong.[38] Here, legally speaking, no formal rule has yet been established, although the monastic authors/redactors are slowly building up to one.

This ruling is found under the fifth *saṅghāvaśeṣa* offense for monks, a rule that makes it an offense for a monk to act as a go-between in sexual or marital liaisons.[39] What the two monks have done so far does not constitute a breach of this rule; they have not yet acted as go-betweens for any marital or sexual engagement, although this is the direction in which they are heading. As we will see, it is the meddling of monks in marital matters that the authors/redactors sought to curb with this ruling.

It is difficult to know how much we may read into this narrative. Whether we may take the first monk's reluctance to share his problems with his cell mate as representing a monastic ambivalence about preoccupation with paternal brooding is unclear. Arguably, the passage's importance has less to do with the issue it explicitly addresses, that of monks acting as go-betweens, than with what it passes over, without censure or comment, as a commonplace of monastic life: monks engaged in visiting and interacting with their "former" families and, in some sense, taking seriously their obligations to wives and children—in this case, arranging a marriage for their children, even if this lands them in trouble.

In other words, this passage requires that we accept that the Mahāsāṅghika authors/redactors—not unlike the Mūlasarvāstivādin jurists encountered in Section 1—were of the opinion that monks could continue to visit their wives and families.[40] These monastic lawyers clearly thought, or wanted their monkish audiences to think, that such interactions were possible and perhaps even probable. It is hard to see the lack of censure, condemnation, or criticism as anything other than a tacit acceptance that such visits were commonplace. At least in the eyes of these monastic authors/redactors, it seems that a monk physically could leave his wife and family in his religious quest, but this did not prevent him from continuing to associate and interact with them.

The monks in this narrative shared not only a cell but also their problems. They had visited their wives and children, only to be told, quite understandably and in no uncertain terms, to get lost. But this was not to be the final word. The story continues with the monks getting deeper and deeper into trouble as they try to make good on at least some of their familial responsibilities.

> These old men, the following day, when the [appropriate] time had arrived, donned their village-entering robes, and when they returned to their respective former homes, the one who had abandoned his daughter said to his wife, "I have found you a son-in-law!"
>
> The wife thereupon asked, "Whose family is this son from?"
>
> "He is the son of such-and-such a family," he replied.
>
> The one who had abandoned his son and left home [for the religious life] said to his wife, "I have found you a wife for our son!"
>
> "Whose family's daughter?" [the wife] asked.
>
> "She is the daughter of such-and-such a family," he replied.
>
> When they spoke thus, both incurred a *sthūlātyaya* offense.[41]
>
> When that boy and girl were playing in the village streets, one of the old men said to his daughter, "He will be your groom."
>
> The second old man said to his son, "She will be your wife."
>
> When they spoke thus, both incurred a *saṅghāvaśeṣa* offense.[42]

This is exactly what the monastic authors/redactors found objectionable: monks engaged in acting as go-betweens and arranging marriages. What is neither criticized nor condemned is the ability of monks to visit their wives or children, or to have continued contact with their "abandoned" families; that seems to have been an accepted part of Buddhist monasticisms in the India of our monastic lawyers. In fact, the whole story turns on such visits.

We must be careful about extrapolating from Buddhist narratives to historical fact. We have, as yet, very little evidence that what we have seen so far amounts to anything more than stories that some monks, albeit monks with voices of canonical authority, told other monks. Although all of the extant Indian Buddhist monastic law codes specifically address the issue of monks and nuns acting as go-betweens, only the Mahāsāṅghika version seems to describe monks actually arranging a marriage between their own children.[43]

The rule making it an offense to act as a go-between is common to the orders of both monks and nuns. In the *Mūlasarvāstivāda-vinaya,* we find two frame-stories: one involving the Group-of-Six monks, and another with the Group-of-Twelve nuns, the female counterparts to the Group-of-Six. These troublemaking nuns were busy matchmaking, conveying messages from men to women, and from women to men, in order to facilitate both marriages and illicit sexual liaisons.[44] The *bhikṣuṇīs* are then rebuked by the Buddha, who is moved to establish a rule about acting as a go-between after his nuns come under fire from nuns of an unspecified heterodox tradition.[45]

That Buddhist and non-Buddhist nuns engaged in the practice of acting as go-betweens in India seems to be independently confirmed by sources external to the tradition, sources that are ambivalent if not antagonistic to Buddhist monasticisms. In his study of "False Ascetics and Nuns in Hindu Fiction," Maurice Bloomfield noted some ninety years ago that in brahmanical literature "female ascetics, nuns, or other religious women figure for the most part in love-affairs as go-betweens and abettors of amorous couples."[46] This has been noted by others since,[47] and specific examples are easily found. In Kṣemendra's (eleventh-century) *Narmamālā* or "Garland of Satires," for instance, we find "a certain Buddhist nun called Vajrayoginī...a master go-between to adulterers, women's dating-deity in the initiation ceremonies of intercourse with men."[48] Likewise, in Daṇḍin's *Daśakumāracarita,* "The Ten Princes" (sixth to seventh century), we find the nuns Arhantikā and Dharmarakṣitā in similar roles.[49] The nuns Kāmandakī, Avalokitā, and Buddharakṣitā all play a part in the matchmaking between Mālatī and Mādhava in Bhavabhūti's eighth-century *Mālatīmādhava.*[50]

With regard to these "go-betweens," Bloomfield further states that "Brahmanical texts love to cast a slur upon these people by making them out to be Buddhist or Jaina nuns."[51] But if brahmanical authors cast a slur on go-betweens by accusing them of being Buddhist nuns, then what, if anything, might this tell us about Buddhist monasticisms in India during this time? From the internal evidence, it seems that Buddhist monastic jurists tried to prevent such behavior. But by legislating against it, much like Sanskrit dramatists, the monastic authors/redactors in fact attest the practice. That the authors/redactors of Buddhist monastic law codes explicitly sought to prevent monks from acting as go-betweens may suggest that this was, in every sense, a real problem in the Indian cultural milieu of these canonical jurists. Indeed, similar reports not only in Sanskrit dramas, wherein we might well expect to find occasional pokes at heterodox religious, but also in learned brahmanical treatises such as the *Kāmasūtra* and *Arthaśāstra* seem to confirm this.[52]

If we accept that monks acting as marital or sexual liaisons presented a somewhat uncomfortable situation for monastic authors/redactors, one that had to be delicately negotiated, then we likewise must acknowledge that monastics' interaction, association, and visitation with their "former" spouses presented no such unwelcome situation or occasion for legislative reform. Unlike the meddling of monks in lay marital affairs, visits to their "former" wives seem to have been of little interest or consequence to our monkish authors and audiences. Indeed, the monastic lawyers deliver these stories with only a light warning to be on one's guard against the seductive powers of "former" wives.

3. Procedures for Formal Marital Dissolution

Before we discuss the lack of any requirement in Buddhist monastic law for men and women formally to dissolve their marriages before entering into the religious life as monks and nuns, it may be useful to give a brief sketch of the issue of marital dissolution in Indian society more generally. In the broader Indian context, scholars speak of marriage as "a sacrament":[53] it is "sacred," and as such "irrevocable" and "indissoluble."[54] This, however, does not mean that a wife cannot be superseded or abandoned.[55] Indeed, P. V. Kane tells us that, according to Indian *Dharmaśāstra* or brahmanical law, "a man was allowed to supersede a wife and marry another or others or to abandon his wife altogether in certain circumstances. But that does not amount to divorce (i.e. dissolution of the marriage tie); the marriage is still there intact."[56] As Kane tells us, "divorce in the ordinary sense of the word... has been unknown to the dharmaśāstras and to Hindu society for about two thousand years (except on the ground of custom among the lower castes)."[57] Such statements require clarification, and fortunately a good start in this direction has already been made by P. K. Virdi. Having narrowly defined divorce as "dissolution of marriage whereby the status of husband and wife ceases to exist as such, marital rights and duties are severed by law and the spouses are free to remarry," Virdi tells us that divorce in this sense "was not recognised at Hindu law by the *sastra*."[58]

Although "divorce" in this sense may not have been recognized by brahmanical legal authorities,[59] this does not mean that some kind of marital dissolution was either unknown or unavailable in the India of our canonical Buddhist lawyers.[60] In fact, the monastic law codes provide good evidence that more than one form of marital dissolution was available to unhappy Indian couples.[61] In the *Mahāsāṅghika-vinaya,* for instance, two forms of marital "release" (*fang* 放) are enumerated.[62] The first is by "sale" *mai* 賣, the second by *lihun* 離婚, a term we can hardly translate as anything other than "divorce," both etymologically and in terms of social practice.[63] According to this monastic code, the first of these two forms of marital "release" is in accordance with the customs of the (as far as I know unidentified) kingdom of *poli* 頗梨: "if one has a wife whom one despises even a little, thereupon one sells her."[64] While this may sound somewhat strange to modern sensibilities, we must bear in mind the fact that, as elsewhere in the premodern world, to brahmins contemporaneous with the monastic authors/redactors, a wife was little more than "a piece of property that may be alienated at will."[65]

In brahmanical law, the sale of a wife is explicitly proscribed. The lawbook of Manu, for instance, states that "a husband could not release his wife by sale or repudiation."[66] What we see being negotiated in the monastic law codes, however, is probably an early confirmation of the fact that, as noted by Lingat, "law and custom have in India entirely different natures."[67] The India of the canonical authors/redactors was governed not only by law, but also by custom. As noted by Lingat, "From a very early period, the rules and customs observed in the various social groups, castes, corporations or guilds, families, etc., or in different regions of India formed a sort of special law within the bosom of the common law."[68] Or, in the words attributed to Nārada (ca. third to fifth century C.E.),[69] "When there is a contradiction between a dharma text and custom, it is right to apply common sense, for custom prevails over dharma."[70]

As we have already seen, the authors/redactors of the *Mahāsāṅghika-vinaya* were aware of the possibility of marital dissolution by sale. The second form of annulment mentioned by the monastic jurists, however, is of interest for our present purposes since it provides us with a rare insight into the options available to Indian couples caught in miserable marriages. *Lihun* 離婚 is defined as follows:

> There is a custom (*fa* 法) of the land by which [if] a husband and wife who are not enjoying being together thereupon visit the king, pay three and a half coins[71] and two lengths of *kārpāsa* (cotton),[72] and seek termination [of their marriage], it will be permitted for them to get divorced.[73]

Apart from providing us with specifics of the legal procedures and fees or taxes involved in the annulment of a matrimonial bond, this Buddhist law code seems to confirm the assertion already found in the *Arthaśāstra* that "by mutual disaffection (alone) a divorce (shall be granted)."[74] The *vinaya* passage, however, is important not only for what it tells us about brahmanical society in general, or Indian marriage customs in particular, but also for what it tells us about a topic that it addresses neither explicitly nor implicitly.

The passage above is not an isolated reference to the dissolution of marital bonds. Both the Mūlasarvāstivāda and the Sarvāstivāda *vinaya*s contain a list of seven different types of wives, or forms of marriage,[75] and although a number of parallels can be discerned, these do not correspond well to the eight forms of brahmanical marriage known from Indian dharma literature.[76] At this stage of our knowledge it is perhaps safe to say only that the authors/redactors of the Buddhist monastic codes, here the *Mūlasarvāstivāda-vinaya*, seem to recognize the following forms of marriage (technically, types of wives):[77]

1. *udakadattā* (*chu tshigs kyis byin pa;* 水授婦): "(a wife) given with water"; a woman given, not sold, by her parents to the groom with a ritual pouring of water over the groom's hands[78] (cf. Brāhma marriage)
2. *dhanakrītā* (*rin chas nyos pa;* 財娉婦): "(a wife) bought for a price"[79] (cf. Āsura marriage)
3. *dhvajāhṛtā* (*btsan phrogs su thob pa;* 王旗婦): "(a wife) seized under a [military] standard," i.e., abducted by force (including abduction by brigands, and so forth)[80] (cf. Rākṣasa marriage)
4. *chandavāsinī* (*dang sam du 'dus pa;* 自樂婦): "(a wife) dwelling [there] out of her own desire"[81] (cf. Gāndharva marriage)
5. *paṭavāsinī* (*gos zas kyis 'tshos pa;* 衣食婦): "(a wife) dwelling [there] for cloth [and food]"[82]
6. *samajīvikā* (*kha dum pa;* 共活婦): "(a wife) in a partnership [wherein both parties combine their property]"[83]
7. *tatkṣaṇikā* (*thang 'ga' phrad pa;* 須臾婦): "(a wife) for a few moments"[84]

To my knowledge, this list has never been studied in any great detail.[85] Until more references to these types of marriages are found and examined, our discussion must remain tentative. What is of importance here, however, is not the exact nature of these marriages, but the fact that provisions for what seems to be their annulment were known to the canonical authors/redactors. In this connection, the *Mūlasarvāstivāda-vinaya* lists seven steps to, or ways of, annulling a marriage. It provides detailed guidelines clarifying the offense committed by a monk who reconciles married couples at each of these seven stages. Unfortunately, however, these stages are not entirely clear.[86]

Just as monks were not supposed to act as go-betweens, so too were they not to provide marriage counseling or reconcile broken marriages, lest they be accused of meddling in matters in which a monk should not become embroiled.[87] The *saṅghāvaśeṣa* offense for matchmaking is only technically incurred in certain circumstances when reconciling marriages. A monk would be guilty of the very minor and lesser offense of wrongdoing if, for instance, he were to reconcile and make harmonious a relationship in which husband and wife[88] are still quarreling,[89] but have not yet finished their quarrel,[90] have not split asunder,[91] have not strewn stones in three directions,[92] have not abandoned daily obligations such as the washing of one's husband's feet,[93] the husband has not declared the wife to be no longer a wife,[94] and have not sounded the bell.[95]

A monk has to go a lot further in reconciling a marriage in order to infringe the *saṅghāvaśeṣa* rule, and the *vinaya* passage makes this clear in painstaking detail.[96] If the married couple has proceeded to the second stage, namely, if they have finished quarreling, then a monk commits two offenses of wrongdoing in reconciliation, and so forth. When the couple has hit the fourth stage, when they have strewn stones,[97] then a monk commits three offenses of wrongdoing and a *sthūlātyaya* offense.[98] The sixth stage in annulling or dissolving a marriage is relatively clear: this stage involves a declaration that the woman in question, one's wife, is in fact no longer one's wife (*chung ma ma yin par bsgrags pa;* 言非我婦離). The Sanskrit terminology underlying both the Tibetan and Chinese is preserved in Guṇaprabha's *Vinayasūtra,* a fifth- to seventh-century digest of this enormous monastic code, and the form given there is *abhāryānuśrāvitatva,* which we might translate as "the state of being declared not to be a wife." This is coupled with the seventh stage, which appears to refer to one who is publicly declared or proclaimed [no longer to be a wife].[99] The Chinese adds to all seven steps the word *li* 離 "separation,"[100] indicating that this is some form of parting, if not dissolution or even divorce.[101]

The exact nature of these last two stages or procedures for what seem to be forms of marital dissolution, and the legal status of a woman who has been thus declared, one who is said to be "no longer a wife," remain out of reach. For our purposes, it will suffice to note that the authors/redactors of this legal code, like their Mahāsāṅghika counterparts, seem to have recognized some kind of marital dissolution or annulment.[102] It is important to note, however, that the monastic authorities neither require nor even recommend that men or women legally dissolve their marriages when they "leave home for the religious life." Whereas some might expect that married ordinands must first declare their wives "no longer a wife," this seems never to have been made a part of monastic legislation. Moreover, until we have a better sense of the significance and implications of "divorce" in our monastic law codes, it would be unwise to expect this to be a prerequisite for entrance into the monastic life. Indeed, the men who become monks in our law codes are not presented as being unhappy in their marriages. Accordingly, renunciation seems to have been in no way connected to marital dissolution, even though the latter was known and presumably available to the monastic authors/redactors. The monastic law codes do not require a married woman who seeks ordination to obtain a divorce. Rather, she must obtain permission from her husband and parents.[103] A male candidate requires only parental permission, regardless of his marital status. Here, then, the monastic authors/redactors seem to reveal not that "Buddhist monks never marry,"[104] but that they in fact never divorce.

4. Relations between Married Monastics

In the preceding sections we saw several stories predicated on continued contact between monks and their "former" wives. We have also reviewed evidence that the authors/redactors of Buddhist monastic legal codes were aware of customary provisions for the dissolution of marriage and yet never seem to have required that ordinands dissolve their marriages before embarking upon the religious life. In this section, I will argue that contrary to Elizabeth Wilson's assertion that "the homeless life was quintessentially a wifeless life,"[105] it is not uncommon in the narrative world of the monastic authors/redactors for husband and wife to leave home for the religious life together.

We see this, for instance, in a story from the monastic code of the Mahīśāsakas, discussed briefly in Section 2 of Chapter 1, in which a nun waits upon a monk, her husband, while he dines.[106] The text begins as follows:

> At one time there was a husband and wife (夫婦) who, the two of them, left home [for the religious life] at the same time (二人俱時出家). That husband-monk (夫比丘) went begging for alms, brought them back to where the nun-wife (婦比丘尼) dwelt, and ate. His nun-wife held a jug of water and stood in front of him, fanned him with a fan, gave him water, and in a coquettish manner[107] enquired as to whether he was cool enough.
>
> That husband-monk lowered his head and ate without looking at or talking with her.
>
> That husband-monk, formerly, when he was a white-robed householder, had an illicit relationship with a woman. Having left home [for the religious life], she too was dwelling there. When he saw her coming the monk thereupon smiled.
>
> His nun-wife became jealous, and thereupon hit the monk over the head with the water jug, smashing it to pieces.[108]

The story ends with the Buddha's being made to legislate against the actions of nuns who wait on monks with water and fans.[109] Delivered with a characteristic touch of humor, the point of the story is that nuns should not wait on monks as they might have done their "former" husbands. But perhaps inadvertently, the authors/redactors reveal much more. They seem to assume that monks were able to enter nuns' residences freely, and to eat in the presence of their wives. These activities receive no comment or censure; they are simply taken for granted.[110] Moreover, the informal interactions between monks and nuns attested by this short passage do not seem to be affected by the fact that the monastics happened to be husband and wife, a situation full of potential dangers that we might well expect the monastic authors/redactors would have sought to defuse.

In the Chinese translation of this text, the only language in which this *vinaya* survives, the wife in the passage is not referred to as a "former" wife, but merely as a wife. The same can be said for the husband. The designations *fu-biqiuni* 婦比丘尼 (nun-wife) and *fu-biqiu* 夫比丘 (husband-monk) may be narrative devices, ones to which we should not attribute too much significance.[111] What is not in doubt, however, is the fact that the authors/redactors depict this couple, husband and wife, as leaving home for the religious life *together* to become monk and nun.

The same frame-story is also found in the *Mahāsāṅghika-vinaya.* There we see a story about a husband and wife who leave home for the religious life together among the Śākyas (有夫婦二人釋種中出家).[112] When the husband starts talking about the past, the wife becomes angry and throws water in his face, hits him on the head with a fan, and accuses him of being ungrateful. A rule is thus formulated to address the danger posed by nuns' waiting on monks with water and fans. As is often the case, the exceptions listed after the word commentary provide us with a number of important insights. The exceptions state, for instance, that it is not an offense if a nun serves water to, or fans, many monks.[113] This would appear to confirm that the rule is designed to curb marital-like behavior, if anything, and not service to monks per se.

The text goes on to state that "if among the assembly [a nun] has a father or brother (若衆中有父兄者), there is no offense in fanning him with a fan. Thus it was taught by the Blessed One."[114] What we see here is an exception to monastic rules allowed to fathers and brothers but not to "former" spouses. This passage highlights the entirely unproblematic nature of continued paternal and fraternal relationships in Indian Buddhist monasticisms. The monastic authors/redactors pass over these narrative details without so much as a word of censure or criticism.[115] At the same time, this *vinaya* narrative seems to confirm that for the authors/redactors of the monastic codes, continued contact between spouses—now monk and nun—may have been not only commonplace but also, because it was so common, fraught with potential problems. Nevertheless, such situations did not necessitate outright prohibitions on continued contact between husband and wife, monk and nun.

There are many more stories about husbands and wives renouncing the household life together throughout Buddhist monastic law codes, much more than can be discussed or even noted here.[116] Any definitive statement on married monastics in Indian Buddhism must await further research. Yet the monastic attitude toward co-renunciation with one's spouse may be summed up well in the words placed by the authors/redactors of the *Mūlasarvāstivāda-vinaya* into the mouth of the Buddha's aunt and stepmother, Mahāprajāpatī. When a husband tells his wife that he is old and will leave home for the religious life, his wife replies that she will join him. The husband takes his wife to Mahāprajāpatī, the founder and leader of the order of nuns. Mahāprajāpatī praises them in a motherly fashion, stating that it is splendid that a husband and wife should set out to enter the religious life together.[117] Conjugal co-renunciation, then, is not critiqued but rather commended in our canonical corpus.

5. A Monastic Family: Udāyin, Guptā, and Their Son, Kumāra-Kāśyapa

In this section I introduce a narrative account of a monastic family: husband and wife, monk and nun, and their son. This narrative brings together in one elaborate story many of the aspects of family-friendly monasticisms encountered already, including the continued marital ties discussed in this chapter and the familial ties surveyed in Chapter 2. In addition, it previews our discussion of monastic motherhood in Chapter 4. As we will see, a number of provisions for the monastic life were put in place to deal with problems that could arise when monks encountered their "former" lay wives as nuns.

At least narratively, the problems seem to have started when a certain monk, the Venerable Udāyin, a key member of the Group-of-Six and the monk in monastic law codes associated more than any other with sex and sexuality,[118] encounters his "former" wife. The story itself is remarkably long and convoluted, and perhaps as suitable to a Bollywood movie as to a Buddhist monastic law code.[119] Our treatment of this story will be necessarily cursory.[120]

The monastic authors/redactors pull out all the stops for this story, starting with the birth of the Buddha, the prediction that he would become either a *cakravartin* ("wheel-turning" king) or a great sage, and his sojourns outside the palace.[121] Eventually we are told about diplomatic missions between various rulers and are introduced to the key characters of the drama that is about to unfold. Whenever King Prasenajit of Kosala sent an emissary to King Śuddhodana, the Buddha's father, he would send his prime minister, Gupta (*sbed pa;* 密護).[122] After conducting the king's affairs and dealings, Gupta would stay at the house of Udāyin, son of the royal chaplain to King Śuddhodana.[123] Whenever Śuddhodana sent an emissary to Prasenajit, he would send Udāyin, who would stay at the house of Gupta. Now, Gupta had a wife (*chung ma;* 婦), Guptā (*sbed ma;* 笈多), fair in body, pleasing to behold, beautiful, and charming. Udāyin—noted for his fondness of women—seems to have entered into some kind of relationship with her, although its exact nature remains unclear.[124] When Gupta found out, he thought of murdering Udāyin[125] but realized that if he were to kill a brahmin, then both kingdoms would go to war.[126] Fearing he had been found out, Udāyin flees. Gupta later dies. Since he has died sonless, his estate goes straight to King Prasenajit's royal vaults in accordance with brahmanical law.[127] Hearing of this, Udāyin, who although narratively still a layman would have been familiar to his audience as a monk, hatches a plan and uses his political connections and influence to get King Prasenajit to offer him Guptā, the house, and the estate.

That Udāyin is successful in getting Guptā as his wife is confirmed later in the narrative when Udāyin, who has now joined the Buddhist order, encounters an elderly monk—a *mahallaka,* or old uncle—a stereotypical fool in Buddhist monastic law codes.[128] Thinking the old monk to be an elder, Udāyin greets him, "Welcome, Elder, welcome. Homage!" The old monk replies, "Homage, Ācārya!" This response tips Udāyin to the fact that this is no elder, just some old monk; he knows neither his *ācārya* nor his *upādhyāya.* Just as the two are about to enter the monastery, Udāyin asks, "Old fellow, where have you come from?" When the old fellow replies, "Śrāvastī," Udāyin takes interest anew: "Since if I first and foremost enquire about news of Guptā I will be scoffed at, I should ask first having enquired in this manner."[129] Feigning interest, Udāyin then proceeds to enquire about the Blessed One, the communities of monks and nuns, the assemblies of *upāsaka*s and *upāsikā*s, the elders Ājñātakauṇḍinya, Mahākāśyapa, Śāriputra, Mahāmaudgalyāyana, and the other elders, and then on to King Prasenajit of Kosala, and various others. Finally, Udāyin gets around to asking what he had wanted all the time: "Venerable one, now, do you happen to know Guptā, the householder's wife?"[130]

The old monk replies, showing that he is not as dumb as he looks. He has outsmarted Udāyin, and it is here that we get our first confirmation that Guptā, now a Buddhist nun, had been married to the Reverend Udāyin:

> "Reverend Udāyin, I know her. She is the former wife (*sngon gyi chung ma;* 昔日之妻) of the Reverend Udāyin!"
>
> "Elder, I know the story."
>
> "Do you still think she is the householder's wife? She has left home [for the religious life]."

"Who initiated her [into the religious life]?"
"Mahāprajāpatī Gautamī."[131]

Here the monastic authors/redactors paint the monk Udāyin as anxious to have tidings of his "former" wife, an emotion that might invite some ridicule from his co-religionists. Nevertheless, despite a hint of possible ridicule, the monk's anxiety for his wife invites no formal censure. Udāyin then welcomes the old monk and tells him to stay. The old monk replies stating that since he is a *caitya* pilgrim, he does not wish to stay there.[132] Udāyin, however, hands him the lock and keys. Manipulatively and all too characteristically, Udāyin then quotes the Blessed One on the subject of leaving *vihāra*s empty.[133]

Now himself free to leave, Udāyin heads away to Śrāvastī and sets himself up in a cell. Guptā hears that Udāyin is back in town. Prompted by other nuns, but against her better judgment, she heads off to his cell.

Guptā knocks on Udāyin's cell door.
"Who is it?" says Udāyin.
"It is I, Guptā," says Guptā.
"Guptā, the householder's wife, welcome."
"Am I still a householder's wife to you? But why? I have left home [for the religious life]!"
"Who initiated you [into the religious life]?"
"The noble sister Mahāprajāpatī Gautamī."[134]

After a brief exchange, Guptā pays homage to Udāyin's feet and then sits down in front of him to listen to the Dharma.[135] Udāyin begins to expound the Dharma, yet in doing so starts to remember the good old times: the laughs, the fun they had, the frolicking, and the lovemaking.[136] Here Udāyin provides some insight into notions of dating and courtship in the India known to our monastic authors/redactors: "Guptā, do you remember when the two of us at such-and-such a pleasure park, and meeting place, and temple (**devakula*),[137] ate this and that sort of food, prepared this and that sort of drink, drank this and that sort of drink?"[138]

Meanwhile, in the course of expounding the Dharma, Udāyin has become sexually excited. Guptā notices and makes an excuse, "I am going outside; I will come back later." Udāyin thinks to himself, "Surely she must want to go to the latrine."[139] Having gone outside and trussed up her waist-cloth, Guptā starts to run for it. Hearing the noise, Udāyin runs after her yelling, "Shaven-headed nun, whither are you fleeing?"[140] He evidently catches up to her, as the text then states that with the touch of her thigh he ejaculated.[141] Seeing that he had calmed down, Guptā approaches him and offers to abandon the religious life. Clearly, it would not do to have monks and nuns, married or not, running around having sex, especially with each other.

Udāyin then takes the moral high ground. Having quoted the Blessed One to the effect that "when one guards oneself, others are guarded, and when one guards others, oneself is guarded," Udāyin delivers his own statement on religious practice, a sermon, the spiritual significance of which does not seem to move Guptā. She simply replies: "Noble one, give me this undergarment; I will wash it."[142] Our story does not end here. In fact, it is only here that the point of this incredibly convoluted and elaborate narrative becomes apparent: monks, as we will see, are not to have unrelated nuns do their laundry.[143]

Guptā thereupon becomes somewhat nostalgic, and takes the semen and impregnates herself with it.[144] When the other nuns are critical of her, a now pregnant nun, Guptā defends not herself but the good name of the Venerable Udāyin: "Sisters, that monk is endowed with virtue; never before since I left [home for the religious life] has he so much as laid even a hand on me."[145] But the nuns are not easily convinced: "If without touching you he still gets you into a state such as this [i.e., pregnant], what kind of state would he get you into if he touched you!"[146]

The nuns in this narrative were not the only ones who had trouble believing that Guptā could have fallen pregnant without having sex. Indeed, even the canonical authors/redactors felt the need to explain how this had happened, and their explanation suggests that they were somewhat uncomfortable: "Since the maturation of the actions of beings is difficult to fathom, she came to be with child."[147] The authors/redactors of this monastic code—presumably very learned monks—are here forced to admit that some things are beyond them, the authors of the Word of the Buddha: they resort to an explanation of these events as the mysterious workings of the doctrine of karma, one of the central doctrines of not only their Buddhist faith, but of Indian religions in general.

It seems to me that here the authors/redactors are being uncharacteristically coy. Unless I am mistaken, what is at issue in this story is not simply the question of nuns who become pregnant as nuns, but rather nuns who have been impregnated by a monk. I suggest that the tale of artificial insemination is in fact a red herring. Even if we do accept the circumstances of Guptā's conception at face value, the fact remains that what is being discussed is the issue of a nun who is impregnated by a monk, however circuitously. To be sure, the authors/redactors of the extant *vinaya*s were generally anything but shy in discussing sexual matters. Indeed, it was not enough for our jurists simply to state that all manner of sexual activity incurred monastic offenses. These canonical lawyers went on to provide graphic frame-stories for nearly every conceivable sexual activity, including bestiality and necrophilia.

Contrary to what has been commonly assumed and asserted solely on the basis of the Pāli Vinaya, a monk who has had sex—and Udāyin is said not to have—was not necessarily expelled or even excommunicated.[148] All known Indian monastic law codes, bar the Pāli Vinaya, allow a monk who has had sex to remain a member of the monastic community, if truly remorseful.[149] The monk is granted a special penitential status known as the *śikṣādattaka,* a status in which he is neither barred from the fruits of further religious attainments nor from complete participation in the activities of the monastic community. Likewise, nuns who had sex could also be granted a reprieve from the loss of communion associated with the commission of a *pārājika* offense. Canonical Buddhist law allowed such *bhikṣuṇī*s to remain within the monastic community as penitent nuns or *śikṣādattā*s, a status found in all extant *vinaya*s except for the Pāli Vinaya, the monastic code on which so much of our "knowledge" of Indian Buddhist monasticism is based.[150] This status allowed penitent nuns who had broken their celibacy to continue to practice the Dharma within their monastic communities.

As I have discussed in detail elsewhere, Nandika, the famed meditator-monk whose sexual indiscretion and subsequent repentance brought about the establishment of the rules for *pārājika* penance, went on to attain the state of an arhat, or religious perfection as known to the traditions of mainstream Indian Buddhist monasticism.[151] Indeed, his story is not one of failure but of remarkable religious success. It is perhaps not a coincidence, then, that in the narrative of Nandika, this meditator-monk has sex neither with a nun, nor even with a human woman. The legal precedent allowing monks who have had sex, monks who commit *abrahmacarya,* to repent and remain within the monastic fold is set by a monk who has sex with one of the daughters of Māra, the Buddhist personification of evil.[152] Although the monastic authors/redactors legislate to allow monks who have had sex to remain within the ecclesiastical fold, they do appear to be reticent to provide a canonical ruling that would in effect legitimize breaches of celibacy on the basis of a story about a monk who has sex with a human woman. And it is this very same reticence, I suggest, that has forced the hands of our monastic authors/redactors into penning the narrative of Guptā's not-so-immaculate conception. Whether the canonical authors/redactors believed that any or all of this happened, whether they thought it possible that Guptā in fact could have fallen pregnant in this manner is not directly relevant to our present purposes.[153] The story could have been changed or rewritten so as not to require this editorial insertion attributing Guptā's pregnancy to the mysterious workings of karma.[154] What is noteworthy is that this is how our Indian monastic jurists decided to frame their discussion of monks' laundry when it was done by nuns to whom they were unrelated[155]—and thus legitimate sexual partners.[156]

The story continues with the Blessed One being brought in to defend the nun Guptā: "Monks, that nun has not committed a *pārājika*...."[157] In other words, the Buddha is made to support her claim that she has not broken her celibacy. Guptā then delivers the baby, the boy Kāśyapa or Kumāra-Kāśyapa.[158] He grows up to be a fine and, like his father, religiously successful monk: he becomes an arhat, and the foremost in eloquence among the Buddha's disciples.[159] After all of this, the rule is finally delivered:[160] "Whatsoever monk would have a nun who is not a relative of his wash or dye or beat old robes incurs an offense requiring confiscation."[161] The point here seems to be that monks are not to have nuns who may be sexually attracted to them, or to whom they themselves may be sexually attracted—women, that is, to whom they are unrelated by blood—wash their underwear as a lay wife might for her husband. This is the message that our story purports to convey. Here, however, I suggest that the monastic authors/redactors betray a trace of nervousness about the possible pitfalls of allowing such close interaction between married monastics, those who were not related to each other biologically.

Unlike the Mūlasarvāstivādin authors/redactors who may have been somewhat distracted by the spinning of a great yarn, their Mahīśāsaka and Mahāsāṅghika counterparts suggest that the problem with having nuns wash and dye monks' robes was that the nuns became so busy doing laundry that it interfered with their recitation and meditation. The laity saw this and criticized them as being no different from themselves.[162] Here too, then, the monastic authors/redactors, as usual, are not seeking to prevent married or related monks and nuns from associating with each other, but rather only to protect the public image of the monastic corporation.

The richness of detail in the narrative of Udāyin and Guptā allows us to confirm a number of issues that, while perhaps important to us, seem to have been nonissues for the monks who wrote these monastic law codes. This story is predicated on the assumption of continued contact in a monastic setting between a monk and nun who were husband and wife, a relationship of which there seems not to have been—nor would we expect—any annulment or dissolution.[163] Udāyin and Guptā, "formerly" husband and wife, now monk and nun, interact and associate with each other in this monastic setting, and this is neither criticized nor censured by the monastic authors/redactors. That Guptā ended up pregnant was clearly of some concern, but only to the extent that the authors/redactors of this monastic code felt compelled to set down rules about monks' dirty laundry. Contact and interaction between monk and nun, husband and wife, is in no way proscribed, or, for that matter, even addressed. Fraternization resulting in a nun's pregnancy may not have been common in Indian Buddhist monasteries. Yet even this one story, one which our monastic authors/redactors seem to have delighted in telling and retelling, should be enough to cast doubt on a number of old and persistent assumptions concerning the religious life in Indian Buddhist monasticisms.[164]

Oldenberg, for instance, suggested that there was little interaction between members of the two monastic communities. He asserts that "strict separation prevailed between monks and nuns," and that "even the monk, who had to preach to the nuns, was not allowed to set foot in the nunnery, except when one of the sisters lay ill and required his consolation."[165] Akira Hirakawa asserts that "contact between the two groups was strictly regulated" so as "to ensure that monks and nuns remained chaste and above suspicion."[166] This narrative from the monastic law codes, however, presumes no obstacles to informal interactions between monk and nun, regardless of whether or not they formerly had been husband and wife. What we see in the story of Udāyin and Guptā, a tale which Indian Buddhist monks told other Buddhist monks for centuries, is only partly reflected in

I. B. Horner's summation of spousal interaction among those who had entered upon the holy life:

> Yet, as a rule, almsmen were not lured away from the higher life by retrospective qualms of conscience concerning their wives in their absence, or by remembering them with longing. It was on the occasions when they went to visit at their old homes, or when the wives came to visit them at the vihāra with this purpose in their minds, that they recognised anew their physical charms, and terrified of capitulating, they either stood their ground, and sometimes converted their wives, or rushed out into the safety of the open.[167]

The authors/redactors of Indian Buddhist monastic law codes could clearly—and as we have seen, very vividly—depict a husband and wife, now monk and nun, sitting down together to discuss the Dharma. As suggested by Horner, they appear to have envisioned that in such cases the husband might feel nostalgia for his former lay life and perhaps even become sexually excited at his own reminiscences. Moreover, the monk might make untoward advances toward the nun, his "former" wife. Yet these were not actions that the monastic jurists sought to proscribe or prevent. The authors/redactors seem to have been content not to address the issue of continued contact between connubial couples within the conventual confines. Rather, as was often the case with our monastic lawyers, they were concerned primarily with the corporate image of the monastic institution and how best to deal with their dirty laundry.

6. Mahākāśyapa and His Wife: Ascetic Values in Indian Buddhist Monasticisms

The canonical authors/redactors might well have taken great delight in recounting tales of spousal interaction in connection with monks such as the Venerable Udāyin, the archetypical lecherous monk whose actions bring about most of the ecclesiastical rules relating to sexual matters. But surely he is the exception to the rule. If he is representative of anything other than the monastic jurists' comedic genius, then Udāyin represents the extreme end of the celibate ideal, a monk struggling and fighting at every turn with the monastic imposition of celibacy. Unlike Benedict of Nursia (ca. 480–ca. 550), who is recorded as "overcoming his temptations by rolling naked in the thorn thickets,"[168] some Indian Buddhist monks are portrayed as never, at least not in this lifetime, struggling with their religiosity and sexuality.

Here we might consider the life story of Mahākāśyapa, a figure who is generally acknowledged as the foremost of Buddhist ascetics, the renunciant *par excellence*. Mahākāśyapa is no average ascetic. As the embodiment of Indian Buddhist ascetic values, Mahākāśyapa is unlikely to have been representative of most Buddhist monks in India from the time of the Buddha onward. Mahākāśyapa's ascetic practice probably represents the upper limit of what Indian Buddhist authors felt was acceptable Buddhist asceticism, but even here, where we might most expect it, there is no indication that continued interaction with one's "former" wife, now a nun, was to be eschewed.

In this section, I examine two episodes connected with the life story of Mahākāśyapa. The first provides us with a vivid example of how Mahākāśyapa is said to have been described to an audience of potential lay patrons. This characterization of our monk is broadly representative of the scholarly romanticization of Indian Buddhist monasticism and asceticism, and it is also how corporate monastic lawyers, I suggest, wanted to brand asceticism to the laity.

The second version, on the other hand, seems to represent an "in-house" discussion of the asceticism of Mahākāśyapa. This version goes into great detail about Mahākāśyapa's interaction with his wife, not only before but also after they both joined the Buddhist monastic order. Unfortunately, this presentation of the asceticism and religiosity of Mahākāśyapa and his wife seems not to have informed modern scholarly opinions on Buddhist monasticism, even despite the fact that much of it has been available in an English translation since 1882.[169]

Although we cannot know how the figure of Mahākāśyapa was perceived by brahmins or Buddhists of his day, preserved within the *Mūlasarvāstivāda-vinaya* we have an account of how one monk is said to have introduced Mahākāśyapa to pious brahmin ladies. A brief look at this text may afford us a view of how the authors/redactors of this monastic code thought—or at least wanted others to think—the pinnacle of Buddhist asceticism should be presented to a brahmanical audience.[170]

The first tale starts with the Venerable Udāyin, who, as usual, was hanging around the gate of the famous Jetavana monastery.[171] Having seen a group of brahmin ladies approach, Udāyin greets them:

"Welcome, ladies, welcome."[172] After a brief exchange, the ladies state that they wish to enter the monastery and pay reverence to the feet of the Blessed One, the elders, venerables, and monks.[173] Udāyin naturally offers to show them around.[174] The text itself is too long to present in anything more than a few highlights, but Udāyin's tour runs something like this.[175]

> This, ladies, is the Perfume Chamber of the Blessed One, where during the six watches of day and night the Buddha, the Blessed One, constantly surveys the world with the Eye of a Buddha....[176]
>
> This is the Elder Ājñātakauṇḍinya's cell, he who was first to have the Eye of Dharma cleansed by the Blessed One with the collyrium stick of wisdom when the world was in the darkness of ignorance, without a guide, and without a leader....[177]
>
> This is Venerable Mahākāśyapa's cell, a brahmin [with wealth that extends] like a great Sāla tree, who went forth [into the religious life] renouncing one thousand less one yoke of plough oxen; had sixty tens of millions in riches; possessed eighty stores of golden barley, eighteen slave villages, sixteen villages promoting trade and commerce; had as his wife Kapilabhadrā (迦畢梨; *ser skya bzang mo*), whose body surpassed the golden [statue]. [All this] he renounced like a ripe ball of phlegm....[178]
>
> This is Venerable Śāriputra's cell. He is a son of a noble brahmin family. He renounced lay life, leaving home [for the religious life]. At the age of sixteen he fully understood Indra's treatise on grammar[179] and defeated all opponents....[180]
>
> This is Venerable Mahāmaudgalyāyana's cell. He is the son of a royal chaplain, who renounced the crownless reign and left home [for the religious life]....[181]
>
> This is Venerable Aniruddha's cell....He is the Blessed One's father's brother's son....[182]
>
> This is Venerable Ānanda's cell. He is the Blessed One's father's brother's son....[183]
>
> This is Venerable Sundarananda's cell. He is the Blessed One's younger brother....[184]
>
> This is Venerable Rāhula's cell. He is the Blessed One's son....[185]
>
> This is—here introducing the other members of the Group-of-Six monks—Nanda's cell; this is Upananda's, Aśvaka's, Punarvasuka's, and Chanda's....[186]
>
> And this is my cell. Would you like to see this too?[187]

Inviting them into his cell, Udāyin offers them a few drinks,[188] and then ends up getting into trouble for fondling the brahmin ladies,[189] all part of his job as the authors/redactors' sounding board for monastic boundaries vis-à-vis the female sex. Udāyin's misconduct here brings about the establishment of the second *saṅghāvaśeṣa* rule, concerning touching the body of a woman.[190]

The authors/redactors' recounting of Udāyin's tour of the Jetavana is interesting from a number of angles, but of particular interest to us is the clear emphasis given to the familial relationships of the Buddha's chief disciples. As our monastic tour guide points out the local sights within the monastic compound, he introduces Aniruddha and Ānanda first and foremost as the Buddha's cousins, Sundarananda as his brother, and Rāhula as his son. There is no attempt to disguise the fact that many of the Buddha's most accomplished disciples were from his own family. The existence of kinfolk in the monastic life is not portrayed as something that would in any way invite lay contempt, a concern about which the monastic jurists were ever vigilant. Rather, together with the emphasis on the brahmanical backgrounds of some of the Buddha's leading disciples, the prominence of the Buddha's own kin is, arguably, even one of the selling points in Udāyin's attempt to impress the ladies. What is perhaps of most interest, however, is Udāyin's introduction of Mahākāśyapa and the emphasis on his ascetic qualities to these pious laywomen.

Not unlike Prince Siddhārtha himself, Mahākāśyapa's greatness—his position as foremost among the Buddha's disciples who extol the ascetic practices or *dhūtaguṇas*[191]—seems to derive from the spiritual power associated with the renunciation of such vast resources. At least, this is how Mahākāśyapa is presented by our monastic tour guide to the brahmin ladies. Note, however, that we are specifically told that Mahākāśyapa had a wife, one Kapilabhadrā, whose beauty surpassed even that of a golden statue, but that Mahākāśyapa had renounced her and his other possessions like a ripe ball of phlegm. Here there is no indication that his wife also became a nun, or that the two of them continued to interact with each other as monk and nun. Indeed, this is not part of the public presentation of the life story of Mahākāśyapa.

This image of Mahākāśyapa, moreover, seems to be the one on which most scholarly pronouncements concerning Buddhist asceticism are made. To offer but one example, I cite Reginald Ray's influential work on *Buddhist Saints in India*. Not surprisingly, Ray's first choice in his discussion of "orthodox saints" in Buddhism is Mahākāśyapa. Ray tells us that "in the texts of the established monastic traditions," the "orthodox" and "paradigmatic" figures such as Mahākāśyapa are "cast in a consistently positive light as embodiments of the schools' highest ideals."[192]

There is, however, another side to Mahākāśyapa, one that is seldom heard and almost entirely absent from scholarly discourse such as that offered by Ray. The other side to the life story of Mahākāśyapa is not one that monks seem to have told to pious brahmin laywomen, but rather one which they told to themselves and their nuns.

The tale appears as the frame-story of the first *pārājika* ruling for nuns. Much of this episode has been known in the West since as early as 1882.[193] Unfortunately, the full text remains available only in Tibetan and Chinese. The frame-story is important for a number of reasons. In other monastic law codes for nuns, shared rules are generally not delivered with full frame-stories. This is the case in all but the *vinaya*(s) of the Mūlasarvāstivādins,[194] *pace* Hirakawa.[195] In most *vinaya*s, the first four *pārājika*s, being common to both *saṅgha*s, are either omitted, abbreviated, or simply stated without a frame-story.[196] Our story, then, is perhaps the only place in any of the extant Buddhist monastic law codes where the rule of celibacy for *bhikṣuṇī*s is delivered with a story bearing some relevance to the lifestyle of nuns. In other words, here the rule for nuns is said to come about in reference to the actions of a nun and not a monk. In the other *vinaya*s, nuns all too often seem to get landed with what is primarily monks' baggage.

The story starts with a wealthy brahmin by the name of Nyagrodha.[197] After much entreating of the gods, he is eventually blessed with a son, whom he names Kāśyapa.[198] Kāśyapa grows up into a fine young man but does not wish to marry. This irks his father, who wants someone to carry on the family business. Though recognizing that it is the custom for brahmins to remain chaste for forty-eight years, Kāśyapa's father wishes him to marry. His father tells him, "Son, since this is the way of the world, for the sake of the family lineage, you must take a wife."[199]

Kāśyapa reluctantly agrees but sets an impossible standard for his bride-to-be: a maiden has to be found who resembles a golden image he had commissioned. Four golden images are taken throughout the country and touted as the "goddess of maidens" (*bu mo'i lha mo;* 金神).[200] As it happened, a rich brahmin from the city of

Kapila had a beautiful daughter, named Kapilabhadrā.[201] She, not unlike Kāśyapa, had no desire to marry, but likewise had parents who thought otherwise. In order to appease her mother, she went to visit the goddess of maidens, who was said to offer, among other things, marriage in a lofty family.[202] As Kapilabhadrā approached the golden image, her beauty outshone it, making the goddess look pale like iron.[203] Word gets out. Brahmins sent by Kāśyapa's father ask for Kapilabhadrā's hand in marriage. Kāśyapa hears of this and is worried that such a beautiful woman would be full of desire, which is the last thing on his mind. Kāśyapa then hatches a plan to go and check out his bride-to-be.[204]

In the city of Kapila he goes door to door for alms.[205] Arriving at her door, he asks:

"Whose daughter are you?"

"I am Kapila's."

"Have you been given [in marriage] to another?"[206]

She explains that her parents have promised her to Kāśyapa. Without revealing his true identity, Kāśyapa asks what use she has for a husband like that. It would be like having no husband; he cares not for sensual desires. Bhadrā replies that this is excellent for she too cares not for sensual pleasures. She asks the young brahmin's advice, saying that she is powerless to do anything since she has already been betrothed by her parents.[207] Kāśyapa then reveals his identity: "I am that brahmin youth, Kāśyapa."[208] The two of them then enter into a celibacy pact, vowing not to touch each other after their marriage.[209]

Returning to the city, the brahmin youth marries Bhadrā (*chung ma blangs so*).[210] His parents see to it that Kāśyapa and Bhadrā live together, supplying them with two beds. The two remind each other of their previous vow and live not as husband and wife but like mother and son.[211] This gets reported back to Kāśyapa's parents. The parents blame themselves: "Why did we provide two beds?" They then give instructions for only one bed and a seat to be provided.[212] Bhadrā again reminds her husband of their previous vow. For the first watch of the night, she sleeps on the bed while he takes the seat. In the middle watch, he takes the bed, and she the seat. In the last watch, she sleeps and he stays awake on the seat.[213] When the seat is also taken away, they again remind each other of their previous vow. She sleeps during the first and third watches of the night, while he paces up and down. During the second watch, she paces up and down while he sleeps.[214] They continue like this for some twelve years, with a single bed in a single dwelling, but without even the slightest lustful thought between them.[215]

Śakra, lord of the gods, decides to test this extraordinary display of self-control. Changing himself into a snake, he takes up residence under their bed. Kāśyapa sees this venomous black snake. Asleep, Bhadrā had let one arm hang down. Being careful not to touch her, Kāśyapa lifts up her hand using the handle of a yak's tail fly-whisk. Awoken by the touch, Bhadrā, who is now upset, asks why he has touched her: "Is it not that you have touched me with lustful thoughts?" Kāśyapa explains the situation, denying the allegation. But Bhadrā declares that it would be preferable to be bitten by a venomous snake than to have Kāśyapa touch her, even with the jeweled handle of a yak's tail fly-whisk.[216] She explains, citing the famous case of Ṛṣyaśṛṅga,[217] that it is on account of the touch of women that the world goes to ruin.[218]

Kāśyapa's parents eventually die, and it occurs to him that he now has to take over the affairs of the household. He tells his wife to look after the housework while he oversees the fields. But after a short visit to the fields and a meeting with the dust-covered workers with callouses on their hands and feet, he tells his wife to take over the affairs of the household since he is heading off to the penance grove.[219]

Eventually, Bhadrā declares that she will follow Kāśyapa. But he asks how he can take a wife with him to the penance grove. After some discussion, the two decide to leave home for the religious life together.[220] The asceticism of the penance grove was out of the question with a wife, but "world renunciation" seems to present no particular problems. Kāśyapa and Bhadrā eventually go their separate ways. Bhadrā enters the order of the naked ascetics under Nirgrantha Pūraṇa.[221] The naked ascetics, however, are infatuated with the beautiful Bhadrā, and, with the permission of their leader, five hundred of them are said to have, in W. R. S. Ralston's idiom, "enjoyed her company every day."[222]

In the meantime, Kāśyapa encounters the Buddha, recognizes him as his teacher, and exchanges robes with him. Kāśyapa attains arhatship and becomes Kāśyapa the Great, or Mahākāśyapa.[223] This marks Kāśyapa's formal conversion to Buddhism. Later on, Mahākāśyapa heads off to Rājagṛha for alms. There he sees his wife, Bhadrā, and, noting her appearance, enquires as to whether she is still abiding in her celibacy.[224] Distraught, Bhadrā explains the situation. Upon hearing this, Mahākāśyapa suggests she become a Buddhist nun. Bhadrā, a little apprehensive at first, especially after her encounter with the naked ascetics, is then entrusted to Mahāprajāpatī, the Buddha's aunt and stepmother and founder of the order of nuns, by whom she is initiated and ordained.[225]

On another occasion, Bhadrā, now a Buddhist nun, sets out on her alms round. Mahākāśyapa does the same and coincidentally runs into his wife, Bhadrā. Mahākāśyapa enquires as to whether she is rejoicing in the teachings of the Blessed One. She replies that she is, but that not unlike a plump sheep she still seems to be attracting a large amount of attention from people who wish her harm.[226] Mahākāśyapa then suggests that she not go out to collect alms at all. Rather, if the Buddha would allow it, everyday he would give her half of his. The Buddha then rules that he should give her half.[227]

Mahākāśyapa's sharing of his alms in turn attracts the criticism of the Group-of-Six monks, in the Tibetan, and of the nun Sthūlanandā, in the Chinese: "We hear that when he was a householder, Mahākāśyapa dwelt together in the same house with Bhadrā for twelve years, and that not even occasionally did he engender thoughts of desire. Nowadays, however, he's giving her half his alms!"[228] It is difficult to know what to make of this criticism, but it does not seem to be a scathing critique of monks' sharing their alms with nuns, a practice that is here established with the Buddha's sanction. Moreover, in another section of this monastic code, when a husband and wife leave home for the religious life together, the husband receives abundant alms. The wife, however, struggles. The Buddha is then made to state explicitly that a monk *must* share his alms with a nun in times of hardship, and in this regard there is to be absolutely no uncertainty.[229] It is not, then, specifically the sharing of alms that is here criticized. Moreover, it is unlikely that the monks of the Group-of-Six are criticizing Mahākāśyapa for fraternizing with his wife. Indeed, this is something for which one of these troublemakers was himself in fact well known. As we saw in the preceding section, Udāyin, our monastic tour guide from earlier on, was married to Guptā, a nun who became pregnant after a Dharma talk by her husband that went horribly wrong. It seems more probable that the criticism lodged at Mahākāśyapa is reflective only of the general monastic ambivalence toward those of an ascetic bent.

Bhadrā, under the spiritual guidance of her husband, then goes on to attain religious perfection, the state of an arhat.[230] Shortly thereafter, Mahākāśyapa hears the monks scoffing. He states that that which ought to be done by a good spiritual friend has been done by him and that, since a wild animal does not nurture another wild animal,[231] Bhadrā should now go out for alms within her own sphere or range of activity.[232]

Bhadrā goes out for alms, but her beauty again lands her in trouble when she is arrested by one of King Ajātaśatru's ministers. Thinking that she would provide a good distraction for Ajātaśatru, who, having just killed his father, is somewhat depressed, the minister orders that Bhadrā be bathed, perfumed, garlanded, adorned, robed in a manner befitting royalty, and then offered to the king. The king sees her, and immediately becoming infatuated, makes love to her.[233]

Eventually, Bhadrā escapes by employing her supernatural powers.[234] The unfortunate event gets reported back to the Buddha. When asked whether she enjoyed (Chinese) or consented to (Tibetan) the act, Bhadrā replies that she has left behind worldly desires and therefore could not have enjoyed or consented to it.[235] She is deemed not to have committed an offense,[236] but this brings about the promulgation of the first *pārājika* rule concerning breaches of celibacy by nuns.[237] The monks, however, are somewhat perplexed and ask the Blessed One how it is that both Mahākāśyapa and Bhadrā have overcome their desires.[238] We are then presented with numerous past-life stories explaining the maturation of their actions. In some of these previous lives, Mahākāśyapa and Bhadrā were again husband and wife who renounced the world in favor of the religious life together.[239] One story relates how as a householder Mahākāśyapa once disturbed a *pratyekabuddha* who was meditating in the forest. The *pratyekabuddha* is described as asocial, preferring solitude and dwelling like a solitary rhinoceros, apart from the herd.[240] On this day, Mahākāśyapa and Bhadrā had become so engulfed in their lovemaking in the woods, oblivious to the Great Being at the foot of the tree, that they startled him, waking him from his *samādhi*. The shame of this incident led them both to vow to be reborn without desire.[241] The paragon of Buddhist asceticism, then, seems to have shared not only his alms but also several lifetimes and a very strong karmic connection with his wife.

As we have seen, it is not just monks who fail to live up to the highest ideals of Buddhist renunciation that continue to interact with their spouses after formally "renouncing" the world. Indeed, such relationships seem to be acceptable for the entire range of monastic aptitudes, from the lecherous and troublesome Udāyin to the pinnacle of ascetic practice, Mahākāśyapa.

7. Married Monastics beyond India

That Indian Buddhist monastics, at least in their own narratives, might continue to associate and interact with their "former" spouses and families, and that some monks could even co-renounce with their wives, should hold resonance for those familiar with Buddhism in Central Asia. The third-century C.E. Kharoṣṭhī documents from Chinese Turkestan provide us with a rich array of legal and administrative records, and correspondence.[242] Here we find references to Central Asian monks and novices, elders and *śramaṇa*s, *saṅgha*s and *saṅgha-ārāma*s, what seems to be a *vihāra*,[243] and local monastic regulations. Furthermore, manuscript discoveries confirm that canonical *vinaya* texts were known throughout Central Asia.[244] More pertinent to our immediate purposes, however, are a number of documents that mention *śramaṇa*s (i.e., monastics)[245] taking wives: *śramaṇa* Budhavarma, for instance, takes the adopted daughter of *śramaṇa* Śariputra as his wife;[246] *śramaṇa* Saṃgapala is also said to have taken a wife;[247] another *śramaṇa*, Aṭhamo, is said to have had two sons, Budhila and Budhaya, and is perhaps the same Aṭhamo who married the daughter of Budhavarma and his wife;[248] *śramaṇa* Suṃdara had a daughter named Supriyae;[249] and *śramaṇa* Budhaśira had a son called Budhosa.[250]

Not unlike our monastic law codes, reference to married monastics and *śramaṇa*s with children in the Central Asian material seems to attract no social or legal criticism within the textual corpus itself. In the Kharoṣṭhī documents it is almost taken for granted that these monastics were married and had children. As Ratna Chandra Agrawala noted some sixty years ago, commenting on what modern interpreters might be tempted to call corrupt monastics:[251]

> These Central Asian Buddhist monks and priests who happened to style themselves as *śramaṇa*s in the Indian manner were quite different from the Indian monks both in their attitude and actions. They were occupied in all sorts of worldly affairs, indulged in luxuries, followed a number of secular professions, kept slaves and led lives quite unworthy of a *śramaṇa*. . . . At the same time the monks were not absolutely ignorant of the rules of discipline and monastic life. They had some noble ideals before them, though it was yet early for them to come up to the high standard of the Indian *bhikshus*. Moreover, it was not at all obligatory for the monks to live in monasteries alone. They could lead household lives and were still entitled to be called monks.[252]

Clearly, Agrawala's "high standard of the Indian *bhikshus*" is not the vision espoused by the authors/redactors of our extant monastic law codes. In fact, as I argued in discussing our imaginary intellectual predecessor in Section 2 of Chapter 1, if our sole source of knowledge of Buddhist monks and their ideals were the extant *vinaya*s as opposed to *sūtra* materials and selective readings of the Pāli Vinaya, the highly romanticized traditions of Indian Buddhism would come crashing down to earth and look conspicuously like the allegedly degenerate religious practices found in Central Asian, Chinese, Japanese,[253] Mongolian,[254] Newar, and Tibetan Buddhisms—traditions often characterized as not upholding the *vinaya*s, however inaccurately the monastic codes have been understood or at times imagined.

Recalling the findings of contemporary anthropologists of Buddhism, one might have trouble distinguishing these Central Asian married monks from the Newar Vajrācāryas and Śākyas whose "unequivocal Buddhist identity," Gellner tells us, "is that they are monks, albeit married, part-time ones."[255] Michael Allen has summed up the Newar *bare bhikṣu* (i.e., the Śākyas)—a group who call themselves "Brahmacarya Bhikṣu"[256]—as "an endogamous hereditary community whose members have for some seven hundred years regularly inter-married and borne children, yet live in buildings which are both called and look like monasteries and are members of associations known as *sanghas*."[257] The same also seems to hold in part for Tibetan Buddhism, in which celibacy is strictly required apparently only by the Gelugpa,[258] or in which "*ngag-pa* priests are married."[259]

Even the scanty historical records available to us for India and Sri Lanka suggest that actual Buddhist practice, at certain times and in particular places, may have been much closer to the Himalayan or Central Asian models than previously thought. We see, for instance, in the *Rājataraṅgiṇī*, or *Chronicle of the Kings of Kaśmīr,* a *vihāra* built by the Queen Yūkadevī, "in one half of [which] she placed those Bhikṣus whose conduct conformed to the precepts, and in the [other] half those who being in possession of wives, children, cattle and property, deserved blame for their life as householders."[260] Likewise, Richard Gombrich tells us that prior to 1753 "there were no true monks left in Ceylon but only men called *gaṇinnānsē*. These had taken the lower ordination...and were not necessarily celibate; they lived in monasteries and kept the property in the family.... Conditions before 1753 thus seem to have replicated those before 1164, when 'in the villages belonging to the Sangha the good morals of monks consisted only in their supporting their wives and children.' "[261]

Moreover, although rather scanty, there is Indian epigraphical evidence that suggests that not all of those who dwelt in *vihāra*s were monastics.[262] There are, for instance, a number of interesting, although admittedly late (tenth-century), inscriptions from Kurkihar. One records the gift of Mūlakā, the wife of Mahiaru, whose husband is described as "a resident of the Āpaṇaka monastery."[263] Similarly, we find the gifts of Vāṭukā and Gaukā, both wives of one Gopālahino, who is also identified as a resident of the Āpaṇaka monastery.[264] What to make of this is unclear. It would seem that at least two interpretations are possible. Either that we have laymen, and possibly their wives, living in monastic complexes, or that we have monks—although not specifically identified as such—who seem to have had wives. Either way, it seems undeniable that a number of residents of this *vihāra* were or had been married.[265]

We might also consider the evidence from Mahāyāna *sūtra*s. In discussing the "corrupt" religious life of mainstream monastics, the *Rāṣṭrapālaparipṛcchā-sūtra,* for instance, states that "a householder is not as covetous with passions as these [corrupt monks] are after going forth. They would have wives, sons, and daughters just like a householder."[266] Likewise, the author(s) of the *Kāraṇḍavyūha-sūtra* put into the mouth of the Buddha a prophecy that three hundred years after the *parinirvāṇa,* those who bear the title householder in the monastery and who are surrounded by their sons and daughters will become worthy of veneration.[267] The authors of the *Rāṣṭrapālaparipṛcchā* and the *Kāraṇḍavyūha-sūtra* clearly found the idea that monks might have wives and children somewhat abhorrent.[268] But their acerbic attacks appear to attest the existence of such monks in India as they knew it.

Although the author(s) of the *Rāṣṭrapālaparipṛcchā* characterize these family-friendly monks as "hav[ing] no regard for the rules of training or for the *prātimokṣa* or *vinaya,*"[269] monks in our *vinaya* texts are in fact depicted as sometimes having wives, visiting wives, and even leaving home for the religious life with those very wives. Nuns are sometimes said to have babies, and both monks and nuns often seem to be surrounded by their sons and daughters in the religious life. All of this, moreover, is not against the *vinaya*s but rather presented as accommodations already allowed or presupposed by the authors/redactors of these monastic law codes. Given what we have seen of the evidence from Indian Buddhist monastic law codes, I suggest that we might fruitfully begin to consider later forms of Buddhist monasticism such as those found in Central Asia, Kaśmīr, Nepal, and Tibet not in terms of corruption and decline but of continuity and development of a monastic or renunciant ideal that we have yet to understand fully.[270]

8. Conclusions

In this chapter, I have shown that, according to Indian Buddhist monastic law codes, monks could continue to visit and interact with their "former" wives, that is, their lay wives, in full compliance not only with the letter but also with the spirit of the *vinaya* texts. We saw this in the story about an elderly monk seduced by his wife upon his promised return home. Whereas monks were advised to guard against their wives' sexual advances, the authors/redactors of the monastic codes seem content not to proscribe such visits.

Some Indian Buddhist monks' wives, however, seem not to have been eager to have their husbands come home to visit. We saw this in the story about monks who arranged a marriage for their children. The detailed narratives of the monastic codes suggest that some monks may have continued to take seriously their familial obligations to wives and children. If these stories hint that the matrimonial bonds of monks and nuns may not have been severed, this fact was confirmed in our discussion of divorce. Although marital dissolution of some kind was recognized by the monastic authors/redactors, it was not a prerequisite to the monastic life. Indeed, the status of "former wife" as designated in the monastic law codes in no way implied any marital dissolution or annulment. Indian Buddhist monks and nuns could remain legally married. At least as envisioned by the monastic jurists, Indian Buddhist monks were probably not living at home with their wives and children, even if we may catch a glimpse of this form of religiosity in a number of early Mahāyāna *sūtra*s, to say nothing of Buddhist practice outside India.[271] Ordination, however, seems not to have necessitated the end of any and all contact with one's marital partner(s) or family; monks and nuns were free to associate and interact with their quondam spouses and families, who—according to the narratives told by the monastic jurists—sometimes accompanied the former on their religious paths. Moreover, as we saw in the story of Udāyin, Guptā, and Kumāra-Kāśyapa—and also the tale of Mahākāśyapa and Kapilabhadrā—men and women united previously in matrimony but now in the Dharma as monk and nun could continue to interact and associate with each other. The jurists were interested not in proscribing interaction between members of monastic families, but in preserving the corporate image of the monastic community by diffusing difficult situations in which the celibacy of the community could be compromised or challenged.

Some of the greatest threats to a monk who had just renounced—although as we have seen, perhaps not necessarily abandoned or relinquished—not only his livelihood, property and wealth, but also his wife and family to embark on a spiritual quest into "homelessness" were the very things and people he had just "renounced," particularly his wife. Indeed, as it appears that this danger was still being negotiated as late as the redactions of the extant monastic law codes, it is probable that it was, in fact, never fully resolved. Pragmatic redactors may have come to the realization that although monks might well be monks, men were still men, and women women. No amount of monastic negotiation or legislation could change this. Moreover, this reality was undoubtedly brought even closer to home with the simple fact that—to quote Jean Leclercq writing on medieval Christendom—"many of these monks and nuns came to monasteries with definite knowledge of secular love."[272] Indian Buddhist monks appear to have neutralized some of the dangers presented by their "former" wives by allowing these women to participate in the religious life together with their husbands, as husband and wife, monk and nun, all under the watchful eye of their monastic lawyers.

Chapter Four

Nuns Who Become Pregnant

Get thee to a nunnery, why wouldst thou be a breeder of sinners?
—*Hamlet*[1]

We begin our discussion of monastic motherhood, in Section 1, by looking at what the authors/redactors of the extant monastic law codes have to say about the ordination of pregnant women. Taking our cue from work on modern legal theory, we will examine the nature of these rules, and this will allow us to identify a distinction recognized both in legal theory and Buddhist monastic law: the distinction between prohibition and rule of law.

In Section 2, we look at the rules in their narrative context in the *Dharmaguptaka-vinaya,* the only *vinaya* still used to govern monastic communities in which nuns are fully recognized in the modern world. This investigation will allow us to point out the dangers of conclusions based solely upon the study of *prātimokṣa*s, lists of monastic rules for ritual recitation *sans* the narratives, the word commentaries, the casuistry, and exception clauses.[2] When we examine the rules in their narrative context, we see that they prohibit neither the ordination of pregnant women, nor nuns' giving birth, as has often been assumed. Rather, the authors/redactors of the monastic law codes discuss how the community is to deal with issues surrounding pregnant and nursing mothers, and the ordination thereof.

In Section 3, we explore the issue of monastic motherhood in all extant *vinaya*s in order to show that the monastic position concerning the ordination of pregnant and nursing mothers discussed in Section 2 on the basis of the *Dharmaguptaka-vinaya* is not an aberration, and by no means limited to one monastic tradition.

In Section 4, we move from a discussion of pregnant and nursing women who become nuns to one concerning nuns who become mothers. Here the monastic jurists also consider what to do with ordained nuns who, some perhaps unwittingly, find themselves pregnant. The evidence from the *vinaya*s suggests that Indian Buddhist monasticisms were much more open to monastic motherhood than we might imagine from an examination of only the *prātimokṣa*s.

In Section 5, I discuss a *prātimokṣa* rule which, as it has been translated into English, seems to offer evidence that nuns should not raise children. A closer look at the rule, however, reveals that it in fact concerns nuns who look after not their own children but lay children, an issue that seems to have presented particular problems for the monastic lawyers.

In Section 6, I offer a few general remarks on the utility and limitations of various types of *vinaya* texts for the study of Indian Buddhist monasticisms. I also suggest that motherhood and the sisterhood were not as incongruous in Indian Buddhist monasticisms as some readings of the *prātimokṣa*s might lead one to assume.

1. Mothers Becoming Nuns

Modern scholarly assumptions about Buddhist nuns and motherhood in India, I suggest, have been shaped largely by the evidence of the *Bhikṣuṇī-prātimokṣa*s. In part, this is due to the fact that these short liturgical texts have been made available in translation. We begin by looking at one of these, the Dharmaguptaka *Bhikṣuṇī-prātimokṣa.* This is a compendium of rules for nuns belonging to the Dharmaguptaka *nikāya,* the monastic tradition most commonly followed in East Asia down to the present day.[3] It contains two rules concerning the ordination of pregnant women and nursing mothers. The two rules run as follows:[4]

> If a *bhikṣuṇī,* knowing a woman is pregnant, initiates and ordains her, [she commits] a *pāyantika* [offense].[5]
>
> If a *bhikṣuṇī,* knowing a woman is breast-feeding a child, ordains[6] her, [she commits] a *pāyantika* [offense].[7]

These rules are not unique to the Dharmaguptaka tradition. They are also found in the *prātimokṣa*s of the Mahīśāsakas, Mūlasarvāstivādins, and Theravādins.[8] Although the following discussion applies equally to these monastic traditions, for the moment we will restrict our comments to the Dharmaguptakas.

On the surface, in these rules we seem to have clear and seemingly incontrovertible prohibitions against the ordination of pregnant or nursing mothers, women to whom the door to full and equal participation in the religious life of a nun appears to be closed. Indeed, this is exactly how these rules have been interpreted. Here, however, it may be useful to consider how this type of monastic legislation works, as discussed briefly in Section 6 of Chapter 1.[9]

The rules presented above are in many ways representative of any other *prātimokṣa* rule, and we must note that they are most certainly not blanket prohibitions. Strictly speaking, they are not prohibitions at all. These rules are formulaic and read: if a nun does X, she commits offense Y. They are conditional clauses stating not that "X must not be done," but conversely that "if X is done, punishment Y is incurred." These rules, in fact, do not prohibit pregnant or nursing women from being ordained. Rather, at most, they might deter other nuns from ordaining pregnant or nursing women. Although it is a minor offense for a nun to ordain a pregnant or nursing mother, there can be no offense for a lay mother who presents herself for, or receives, ordination. Indeed, Buddhist monastic law applies solely to Buddhist monastics; it is not a set of rules governing lay behavior but rather one regulating monastic activities.

Here we should distinguish at least two different varieties of Buddhist monastic legislation. The first is typically found in the *prātimokṣa*s. These rules are perhaps best understood as being analogous to modern criminal law, which, according to the legal scholar H. L. A. Hart, "is something which we either obey or disobey and what its rules require is spoken of as a 'duty'. If we disobey we are said to 'break' the law and what we have done is legally 'wrong', a 'breach of duty', or an 'offence'."[10] Hart's observations on criminal law apply to our case almost as if he were writing on Buddhist monastic law:

> There is no law prohibiting murder: there is only a law directing officials to apply certain sanctions in certain circumstances to those who do murder. On this view, what is ordinarily thought of as the content of law, designed to guide the conduct of ordinary citizens [we would

> say, monastics], is merely the antecedent or 'if-clause' in a rule which is directed not to them but to officials, and orders them to apply certain sanctions if certain conditions are satisfied.... They are all of the form, 'If anything of a kind X is done or omitted or happens, then apply sanction of a kind Y.'[11]

This is almost exactly what we see in the Dharmaguptaka *prātimokṣa* rules above. Again, notice that those rules direct the monastic community (Hart's "officials") to charge nuns who ordain pregnant or nursing laywomen with certain offenses (Hart's sanctions). The rules do not bar such women from ordination. As we will see, in other contexts prohibitions do exist in Buddhist monastic law. A prohibition against the ordination of pregnant or nursing women, however, seems not to have been a priority for the authors/redactors of Indian Buddhist monastic law codes.

To understand the limited range of this type of legislation, it will be useful to consider alongside it another type of monastic rule, what we might justifiably refer to as "blanket prohibitions" and "direct commands"—prohibitions that are different in nature to the rules-of-training we have seen so far.[12] Unlike the rules for individual monks and nuns found in the *prātimokṣa*s, these prohibitions seem to allow for very little wiggle room.[13]

The Dharmaguptakas, for instance, in the *Chapter on Ordination* in their monastic code prohibit—and here I think we can for the first time legitimately use this term—the ordination of those[14] with a host of diseases,[15] those whose hands or other body parts have been cut off, those who are bucktoothed, or who have crooked fingers, warts, blue, yellow, or red eyes, or are bald, blind, mute, deaf, or—in some *vinaya*s[16]—are just plain ugly.[17] The passage presents an extremely long and detailed list of infirmities and concludes by stating that "such individuals may not be initiated or ordained" (如此人不得度受具足戒).[18] This clause does not make it an offense to ordain them. Rather, it categorically bars them from ordination.[19] The difference here is significant, even if the distinction between these two modes of monastic legislation has not always been recognized.

Here we see again the monastic lawyers at work protecting both the corporate image of the monastic community and its financial well-being on two fronts. First, Indian Buddhist monastic health care did not extend to preconditions. This made the sick ineligible for ordination. Second, individuals exhibiting deformities were unlikely to attract lay support. Accordingly, they are barred from the religious life. Although the monastic legislators easily could have included pregnant women and nursing mothers in their list of people who are categorically barred from ordination, for whatever reasons they appear to have demurred. Instead, the monastic lawyers made it a minor offense for nuns to ordain such women,[20] an easily expiated offense also incurred for numerous other minor monastic misdemeanors such as eating garlic,[21] making dildos,[22] or going to watch live entertainment.[23]

The *Dharmaguptaka-vinaya*'s position on the ordination of pregnant and nursing women, then, should be clear: although enactment of a prohibition would have been relatively simple, there is no *prohibition* against their ordination. Lest I be misunderstood, let me make clear that I do not mean to suggest that their ordination is something that is to be encouraged. To be sure, a nun who ordains a pregnant or nursing woman incurs an offense, albeit a relatively minor one. But the ordination itself is and remains valid. This also seems to obtain for the Mahīśāsakas, Mūlasarvāstivādins, and Theravādins, all of whose *prātimokṣa* codes contain similar rules.[24] Before we address these other codes, however, we might treat the *Dharmaguptaka-vinaya* in slightly more detail. As we will see, this text has much more to say about pregnant and nursing mothers than might be first thought, and all of which is missed in studies based solely on the *prātimokṣa*s.

2. Nursing Nuns

Fortunately, the *prātimokṣa*s are not the only—or, I argue, even the best—source to consult if we are interested in the full spectrum of legal negotiation surrounding the ordination of pregnant or nursing mothers, or nearly any other topic, for that matter. We now turn to the *Dharmaguptaka-vinaya* proper in order to highlight the differences between a close reading of the narratives of extant Buddhist monastic law codes and their *prātimokṣa*s.

The *Dharmaguptaka-vinaya* records an account of a nun who ordained a certain breast-feeding woman (度他乳兒婦女).[25] The woman had left her child at home, and afterwards had the child sent from home, presumably to her in the convent.[26] When this nun entered the village for alms carrying her baby she was criticized by the laity in what is, in part, a stock phrase in this monastic code: "Where is the True Dharma in this? Look at this renunciant who has given birth to a baby, and carries it going on her alms round!"[27] It is precisely this sort of social censure, or fear of it, that seems to have provoked the authors/redactors to put into the mouth of the Blessed One a rule stipulating that a nun incurs an offense in ordaining a breast-feeding woman.[28] This was later amended when nuns encountered another woman but did not know whether she was lactating, only to find out that she was after ordaining her.[29] The rule was then changed to state that it is an offense if they "knowingly" ordain a breast-feeding woman.[30] Whereas the *prātimokṣa* tells us, usually in one or two lines, generally only what is not to be done, the *vinaya* proper, the full monastic code, tells us what is to be done, what is acceptable, what constitutes an offense, and where and how to draw the line. In the copious detail provided by the monastic lawyers, we get our first glimpse at how one Indian Buddhist monastic legal tradition handled what were undoubtedly, at least potentially, somewhat sticky situations.

In addition to a detailed gradation of offenses incurred at each successive stage of the ordination,[31] the text states that there is no offense if not knowing they believe what the ordinand says, believe what one who is believable says, or believe the words of the ordinand's parents and then, having ordained her, she sends for the child.[32] The point here seems to be that the monastic community is to make a good-faith effort to ascertain whether the woman is nursing. If she is known to be nursing, then nuns commit an offense in ordaining her. However, if a woman or her parents were to lie, and she then were to send for her child after being ordained, then those performing the ordination commit no offense. The legal position is clear. The monastic community is not to recruit nursing mothers. However, if it happens that one is ordained, there can be no question as to the continued validity of her ordination—it is never revoked.[33] Ordaining a nursing mother incurs a minor offense for the ordaining nun, but the ordination itself is in no way invalid. As the monastic authors/redactors make perfectly clear, nursing mothers who are ordained as nuns are to have no doubts concerning their role as mothers. The canonical text continues:[34]

> That mother became doubtful, and did not dare to take [her baby] into her arms and nurture it.
>
> The Buddha said, "If [the child is] still unable to live on its own, I authorize [the nun] to nurse and nurture [her baby],[35] in accordance with motherhood (如母法), until she has weaned [the child] and stopped [breast-feeding]."[36]

This passage is quite remarkable given what we have been told about Indian Buddhist nuns. Here we see the Buddha being made to state that a nun must not only nurse her child as other mothers do, but that she should do so until the child is weanable.

There is much more of note in this short passage. Take, for instance, the verb used when the Buddha is made to speak: the Chinese term *ting* 聽 is sometimes translated as "to allow" but is most probably a translation of Sanskrit *anu√jñā,* which, as pointed out by Heinz Bechert, is often a direct command.[37] Accordingly, *ting* 聽 in this context is probably best translated along the lines of "to command" or "to order." In other words, the authors/redactors of this canonical law code have put into the mouth of the Buddha much more than a simple exhortation that nuns *may* nurse and nurture their children, or that they are *allowed* to do so. They are in fact *commanded, ordered,* or *authorized* to do so.

Although this piece of monastic legislation was made to carry the Buddha's own sanction, raising children in a nunnery, as we will see, was bound to present the monastic institution with a whole set of further issues to be negotiated. The story about the nun who was reluctant to nurse her child continues, and this time the sleeping arrangements present a problem, albeit one that is easily resolved.

> Later the mother spent the night in the same place with this child, and had doubts.
>
> The Buddha said, "Henceforth, I authorize one who has not yet weaned [her son to spend the night together with her son]—there is no transgression."[38]

Although not expressly stated, the issue here seems to be the baby's gender: nuns were not supposed to share sleeping quarters with males, and this nun's child was undoubtedly a boy.[39] The passage, then, presents the *Dharmaguptaka-vinaya*'s authorization for nuns to share sleeping quarters with their sons at least until the boys are able to be weaned. Since this was, and could only have been, a problem for mothers and sons, there seems to have been no problem in the case of daughters, and thus no need for any further legislation.

The Dharmaguptaka jurists' decision to make it a minor offense to ordain a breast-feeding mother intentionally, then, is in no way tantamount to disallowing the ordination of breast-feeding mothers. The distinction may be a fine one, but it is an important one.

These two short rules authorizing nuns to nurse and sleep together with their children clearly confirm that these legal texts are to be read historically in much the same way as Hart reads modern criminal law. The passages in no way suggest that breast-feeding mothers, for instance, were barred from ordination, or that once ordained—and clearly they could be ordained—their ordinations were questioned, much less invalidated. Indeed, as these two rulings show, these mothers were fully accepted and recognized as nuns by the canonical legal authorities. The authors/redactors of the *Dharmaguptaka-vinaya* have amended existing legislation in order to secure a place within the monastic community for nursing mothers to be *bhikṣuṇī*s.

If what we have so far seen of the *Dharmaguptaka-vinaya*'s stance on nursing mothers suggests the possibility that monastic jurists of at least this *nikāya,* and possibly others, would allow pregnant women to become nuns, and thereby in some cases perhaps even allow—although not necessarily encourage—nuns to give birth to children, then that suggestion is in fact fully confirmed by a close reading of another passage in this monastic law code. In a rule parallel to and directly preceding the narrative discussed above concerning nursing nuns, the *bhikṣuṇī* *Balā (婆羅) ordained a pregnant woman who subsequently gave birth.[40] The newly delivered mother-nun then took her newborn into the city while she begged for alms. Seeing this, the laity criticized her, saying, "These nuns know no shame.[41] They transgress the pure practices [of the religious life]. Outwardly they themselves proclaim, 'We cultivate the True Dharma,' but where is the True Dharma in this? Look at this renunciant with her newborn!" (看此出家人新生兒).[42] In reaction to this lay condemnation, the Buddha is here made to proclaim it to be an offense for a nun to ordain a pregnant woman.[43] This ruling is further modified to allow for the provision of ignorance, with the end result being the rule that a nun incurs an offense in knowingly ordaining a pregnant woman.[44] Just as in the parallel case of the ordination of nursing mothers, making it an offense in no way prevents or prohibits the ordination of pregnant women in the first place. Here we find explicit authorization for nuns to breast-feed their newborns:

> When she had given birth [the nun] doubted [the propriety] and did not dare to pick up and hold [her baby].
>
> The Buddha said, "If [the child is] still unable to be separated from its mother and live on its own, I authorize [in] all [such cases the mother] to nurse and nurture in accordance with motherhood (如母法)."[45]

Here we see a number of things worth noting. First and foremost, the authors/redactors of this law code seem to neither blink at the prospect of a nun giving birth in a convent, nor make the Buddha do so. When the sight of a mother and her newborn gives rise to unfounded rumors about the celibacy of the order of nuns, the authors/redactors have the Buddha criticize the nun *Balā for ordaining a pregnant woman, albeit with a cliché or stock phrase. The narrative event of a nun giving birth to a baby within a nunnery, however, receives no direct comment or criticism from the canonical jurists. Here, again, the monastic lawyers are chiefly interested in preventing damage to their corporate image. Their concern is not that a nun might have a baby within the cloister, but rather that a nun seen outside the convent with a baby might give rise to rumor and scandal, and, more important, create confusion and mistrust among the laity.

What we have here is the case of a pregnant woman who joined the order of nuns and later gave birth as a nun. There is, as far as I know, no rule that prohibits or even makes it an offense for nuns to give birth, but this is not to suggest that childbirth and child raising were entirely free of problems. Yet, at least according to the extant monastic codes, the problems that ensued from nuns giving birth and nursing their children all seem to stem from one issue: the male gender of their children. Nuns and their daughters seem to have presented no significant problems for the monastic lawyers. In other words, nuns having daughters, nuns sharing sleeping quarters with their daughters, nuns touching their daughters, taking them into their arms, and nurturing them were all, legally speaking, a nonissue. It caused few, if any, problems for the monastic lawyers and necessitated no negotiation, and no legislation—it was simply not an issue that needed to be resolved, although presumably the nuns were not to take their daughters out for alms either.

As we saw above in the case of the nursing nun, here too the newly delivered nun is made to display her knowledge of the monastic disciplinary code in her reticence about sharing sleeping quarters with her newborn son:

> Later [the mother] had doubts, and she did not dare to spend the night in the same room with this baby boy (男兒).
>
> The Buddha said, "If [the baby boy is] still unable to spend the night separated from his mother, I authorize [the mother] to spend the night together [with the baby boy], in the same place—there is no transgression."[46]

The problem again seems to be confined to mothers and sons, and this is confirmed by the clear identification of the child's gender. Here the authors/redactors of the text tacitly acknowledge another rule that seems to have already been in place: if a nun spends the night together with a male [she commits] a **pācattika*.[47] The Buddha is made to state, in effect, that this rule does not apply in cases where the male is a nun's own infant son. Mothers and sons are allowed to share quarters, at least until the son is big enough to leave his mother's breast.

So far we have seen that according to the Buddhist monastic law code of the Dharmaguptakas, pregnant and nursing women could be ordained as nuns and not only give birth, but also nurse and raise their newborns within nunneries. This, of course, does not mean that nuns were allowed to breach the rule of celibacy; pregnant women could become nuns, but none of the passages considered so far suggest that a nun's pregnancy would be tolerated. The cases presented above deal specifically and solely with the ordination of pregnant and nursing women, and not with ordained nuns who become pregnant—that is a very different matter. What we have seen so far is a monastic attitude to motherhood, and not one to celibacy.[48] The monastic authors/redactors seem to have opened the door to the religious life for expectant and nursing mothers, especially those who came knocking. Once open, however, it may have proved not only difficult to close; it may also have been difficult to control exactly who was let through the front door.

3. Monastic Motherhood

To what extent is the Dharmaguptaka understanding of monastic motherhood, as seen in the preceding section, representative of other Indian Buddhist *nikāya*s? To attempt to answer this question, we must examine other *vinaya*s. To identify each and every rule concerning monastic motherhood would be beyond the scope of the present study. What follows is a short survey of the terrain.

We first turn to the *vinaya* of the Mahīśāsakas, a tradition that is often reported to be very close to the Theravāda *vinaya* preserved in Pāli. In this *vinaya* the frame-story for the rule that makes it a minor offense to ordain a pregnant woman involves an expectant woman (懷妊女) who is ordained by nuns. When she enters the village to beg for alms, she is made fun of by the laity:

> "This nun carries a heavy load; we ought to give her some food quickly!"
>
> Some said, "Take a look at this belly!"
>
> Others said, "They do not cultivate *brahmacarya.*"
>
> [Still] others said, "This one cultivates *brahmacarya;* this is [simply the result of] an action [that took place] before she left home [for the religious life]."
>
> Thereupon chastising her the [other] nuns said, "Why did you not wait until after giving birth, and then leave home [for the religious life]?"[49]

In our previous discussion, we noted that the *prātimokṣa*s do not state that a pregnant woman cannot be ordained, but simply that if a nun knowingly ordains a pregnant woman, the ordaining nun becomes guilty of an offense. In the frame-story in this *vinaya,* the mother-to-be is ordained, and there is absolutely no question as to the validity of her monastic status. Her sisters in religion, however, are made to suggest that she should have waited to "leave home" until after she had given birth. As we will see, at least narratively, one nun did follow this advice.

In the very next narrative in this monastic code, when a nun goes out on her alms round with a bowl in one hand and her baby in the other, the laity tease the mother and child, saying, "Quick, give these two some food!"[50] This gets reported back to the other nuns, and eventually the Buddha makes it an offense to ordain a newly delivered mother (新產婦). Although it may appear that the laity are here portrayed as having some expectation that nursing mothers should not become nuns, what seems to be at issue for the monastic jurists is the lay criticism that a nursing nun might invite. Indeed, as we saw in the previous narrative, the laity have no way of knowing when a pregnant or nursing nun became pregnant. As we saw in that narrative, in the face of allegations that a nun had breached her *brahmacarya,* some speak up to defend her and her cultivation of celibacy, claiming in effect that she is a pregnant woman who became a nun and not a nun who became pregnant. The celibacy of the community, then, remains intact.

As I have argued above, it would have been possible to prevent the ordination of pregnant or nursing mothers. Here and elsewhere, however, the authors/redactors of this monastic code seem to be concerned with ensuring only that reasonable and not drastic precautions are taken to prevent social censure from the laity and any resultant financial fallout. In a general sense, this concern is confirmed by the following passage from the *vibhaṅga* of the *Mahīśāsaka-vinaya:*

> If one is about to grant ordination, one should first look at [the ordinand's] breasts; if there are no signs of children, it is not a transgression [to ordain her]. If only after the ordination is completed [the ordaining nun] finds out [that the ordinand] is pregnant, there is also [in this case] no transgression.[51]

As we saw with the Dharmaguptakas, the Mahīśāsakas actually provide for the possibility of ordaining pregnant women in their monastic code proper, even though they explicitly declare it to be a minor offense to ordain a pregnant woman or a newly delivered mother in their *prātimokṣa.*[52]

When we turn to the *Chapter on Nuns* in this *vinaya,* however, we move from rules governing the individual members of the monastic community to institutional law, rules that govern the actions of the community as a corporate body, the second of the two types of monastic legislation described above.[53] It is here, as we saw briefly in Chapter 1, that we get our first glimpse of how Mahīśāsaka communities may have dealt with the issue of monastic motherhood:

> A nun gave birth to a baby boy. Not knowing what to do, she informed the Buddha of this matter.
>
> The Buddha said, "I authorize a twofold ecclesiastical act for appointing a nun to attend her. One nun should declare amid the community, 'Sisters, may the community listen! This one, nun So-and-so, has given birth to a baby boy (此某甲比丘尼生男兒). Now we are to appoint nun So-and-so to attend her. If for the community the [right] time has arrived, may the community consent and authorize it.' Thus is the motion. 'Sisters, may the community listen! This one, nun So-and-so, has given birth to a baby boy. Now we are to appoint nun So-and-so to attend her. Those sisters who consent remain silent; those who do not consent speak up![54] The community has finished appointing nun So-and-so to attend nun So-and-so on account of the community's silence. Thus I hold this matter to be (i.e., motion carried).' "[55]

Here a nun has given birth to a baby boy, but this is neither deplored nor condemned by the community; it simply happened. The community accepted this, and—apparently without any lay criticism or censure to curtail—the Buddha is made to enact legislation to appoint a fellow nun to attend the newly delivered nun.

A number of issues connected presumably with the gender of the nun's newborn and the potential problems associated with bringing up a boy in a convent again come to the fore:

> The two nuns held the child, and produced doubt [as to whether they had committed an offense].
>
> The Buddha said, "There is no transgression."
>
> The two nuns slept together with the child, and produced doubt.
>
> The Buddha said, "Again, there is no transgression."[56]

These two passages present potential parenting problems which we previously encountered in the *Dharmaguptaka-vinaya.* The interpretation of these monastic authors/redactors is slightly different, although this is perhaps to be expected given that they have allowed for another nun to assist the mother-nun.[57] Here we seem to have a position that is far more lenient than that of the *Dharmaguptaka-vinaya,* in which only the mother-nun was allowed to sleep with the baby boy.

The Mahīśāsaka monastic authors/redactors, however, go one step further, and, in the process, they offer us a rare insight into monastic motherhood:

> Having adorned the child, together [the nuns] fawned [upon him].[58]
>
> The Buddha said, "That should not be done. I authorize you to bathe and to nurse him. If he [is old enough to] leave the breast, you should give him to a monk, and let him go forth [into the religious life]. If you do not wish to have him go forth [into the religious life], you should give him to relatives, and have him brought up."[59]

Here the Mahīśāsaka tradition clearly delineates a certain length of time during which the mother-nun is allowed to take full charge of her son's upbringing. Although not clearly stipulated, the period seems to be infancy.[60]

The authors/redactors of this monastic law code further allow for the initiation of young boys so long as they are able to scare away crows. The rule is delivered in reference to two boys aged seven and eight, respectively, but no age limit is stipulated. This ambiguity in the rule suggests that even younger boys may have been initiated in this tradition if they were able to meet the "scarecrow" requirement, viz., be of some use to the community.[61] Tentatively, and conservatively, we can conclude that a mother-nun could look after her son in the nunnery until he was big enough to join the order of monks as a novice around the age of seven. In effect, this piece of monastic legislation established legal provision and precedent for Indian Buddhist nuns not only to give birth and breast-feed, but also to raise their children until they were old enough to join a monastery officially.

When the child was able to be weaned, it seems that the mother had a number of decisions to make. If the mother did not want her son to follow in her footsteps in the religious life, she was to give him to relatives to bring up. The passage above suggests that the decision was the mother's and not the child's, as is perhaps natural in the case of legal minors.[62] In the case of a daughter, moreover, it appears likely that she would either stay right where she was, in the convent, or go and live with relatives when she was old enough to be weaned. In short, it would seem that one could very well be born into Indian Buddhist monasticisms, at least in the Dharmaguptaka and Mahīśāsaka traditions.

The rules that we have seen so far allowing and accommodating motherhood in the monastic institution are from *nikāya*s that have *prātimokṣa* rules expressly making the ordination of pregnant women a minor offense. Unlike their Dharmaguptaka and Mahīśāsaka brethren, however, the Sarvāstivādins and Mahāsāṅghikas seem not to have gone so far as to make the ordination of pregnant women an offense in their *prātimokṣa*s.[63] Nevertheless, when we turn to the law code of the Sarvāstivādins, we see that monastic motherhood there was just as much an issue. When a newly widowed laywoman joined the order of nuns, and later started to show signs of pregnancy, the nuns threw her out of her cell, accusing her of sexual (mis-)conduct.[64] This, however, was a misunderstanding; the nun had been celibate since joining the order, but was with child when she was ordained. In reaction to this situation, the canonical authors/redactors make the Buddha establish a two-year *śikṣamāṇā* training or probationary nun status.[65] The Buddha addressed the nuns as follows:

> You are not to say this nun [did] such things. She has not broken her *brahmacarya;* formerly when she was a laywoman she became pregnant. Henceforth, I authorize *śrāmaṇerī*s (novice nuns) to train in the six matters for two years. [Thus] you will be able to tell whether one is pregnant or not.[66]

This ruling sought to prevent the ordination of pregnant women with the imposition of a two-year probationary period. Once the rule was in place, there should have been no possibility of ordaining, as opposed to initiating, a pregnant woman. Presumably, a pregnant woman would first become a novice, and then undergo two years of training as a *śikṣamāṇā*, during which time her pregnancy would not only become evident but she would also give birth. Assuming that she had strictly maintained her celibacy during those two years, there would be no way for a pregnant woman to be ordained. The Dharmaguptaka *prātimokṣa* rule making it an offense to "ordain" pregnant women, then, seems to presuppose the absence, or to predate the appearance, of the *śikṣamāṇā* rules.[67]

Neither the *śikṣamāṇā* rules nor the *prātimokṣas* tell us much about monastic reactions to nuns who became pregnant.[68] Resolving problems associated with mothers who became nuns was one thing; dealing with nuns who became mothers was quite another. As we will see in the next section, accommodating pregnant nuns and child rearing in convents demanded further negotiation and legislation.

4. Nuns Becoming Mothers

In the previous sections, we discussed several *vinaya* narratives dealing explicitly with nursing or pregnant mothers who became Buddhist nuns. In Section 5 of Chapter 3, we also discussed a narrative in which the nun Guptā was said to give birth to the future arhat Kumāra-Kāśyapa, son of the Venerable Udāyin. However, we have yet to see any evidence suggesting accommodations within monastic legislation directed specifically to Buddhist nuns who become pregnant. Indeed, given the importance placed on celibacy and the need to maintain, if not project, the perception of a celibate community in the eyes of the laity, one might not expect to find rules accommodating pregnant nuns in the monastic law codes. Yet, as I suggested above, once the cloister was open to some mothers, the door may have been difficult to close. In this section, we shall investigate regulations concerning monastic motherhood for nuns who find themselves pregnant.

The *Sarvāstivāda-vinaya* contains a series of narratives concerning the motherhood of the *bhikṣuṇī* Guptā, the wife of the Venerable Udāyin, whom we encountered in Chapter 3. Although no details of the nun Guptā's conception are given in these frame-stories, it is clear that at least narratively Guptā had already been ordained as a *bhikṣuṇī*. Guptā and Udāyin feature as protagonists in a number of narratives in this *vinaya*, some with Guptā as a laywoman[69] and some with her as a nun.[70] The story of her conception, narrated twice in this monastic code,[71] makes it clear, however, that she was already ordained. In other words, the narratives surrounding monastic motherhood delivered in connection with the nun Guptā's pregnancy preserve for us rules not about the motherhood of pregnant women who were ordained during their pregnancy, but of nuns who somehow became pregnant.

In the *Sarvāstivāda-vinaya*, when Guptā the nun gave birth—and here we are explicitly told, to a baby boy (崛多生男兒)—she faced a dilemma: "I have given birth to this baby boy. What will I do now?"[72] The monastic authors/redactors negotiate the problem in two separate episodes. The first is delivered as Guptā's recollection of the rule against touching males,[73] and the second is about spending the night together with them.[74] In allowing exceptions to established rules in the case of nuns and their sons, the canonical authors/redactors of the *Sarvāstivāda-vinaya* seem to have reacted in a similar fashion to their Dharmaguptaka and Mahīśāsaka brethren.

In the Sarvāstivādin legislation, a number of points only implicit in the Dharmaguptaka and Mahīśāsaka rulings discussed previously are made explicit. In the first place, in the Sarvāstivādin ruling, the exception clearly applies only to the mother: "Other nuns should not touch him. If they touch him, they commit an offense."[75] Furthermore, the exception in the case of the mother is valid only until the boy is weaned: "If [the child is] able to be separated from the mother, and the mother touches him, [she commits] an offense of wrongdoing."[76] Similar exceptions are granted and restrictions put in place for sleeping arrangements: "If [the mother] spends nights together [with the baby boy] once he is weanable, the mother incurs an offense of wrongdoing. [If] other nuns spend nights together [with the baby boy, they incur] a *pāyattika*."[77] I assume that there would be no question of an offense in the case of a baby girl. Sleeping together in the same room or cell with one's daughter seems not to have been an offense for nuns. The issue here is the male gender of this nun's son. The same exceptions could have been made in the case of a nun's daughter, but such situations seem not to have concerned our cautious canonical clerics.

Finally, within this tradition, there was one more obstacle to overcome. At some stage, the monastic legislators seem to have realized that at least initially the sisterhood was not set up to deal with nuns' giving birth. Yet the monastic jurists eventually seem to have carved out a place within nunneries for pregnant and nursing mothers. In fact, the monastic lawyers established a formal ecclesiastical act for the very purpose.

> The Buddha was in Śrāvastī.
>
> At that time [the nun][78] Guptā gave birth to a baby boy, and thought thus, "The Buddha has expounded, 'A nun may not spend the night in a solitary cell even for one night. She must spend the night sharing a cell with one nun.'[79] What will I do now?"
>
> She reported this matter to the Buddha.
>
> The Buddha, on account of this matter, assembled the community, and told the nuns, "You are to perform the formal act of [assigning] a solitary cell for the sake of the nun Guptā. If there are further nuns like this, again you should perform the formal act of [assigning] a solitary cell for their sake."[80]

Here a number of things have been negotiated by the canonical authors/redactors, and all have been put into the mouth of the Buddha. First of all, we see that accommodation had to be made for the mother and her newborn within the monastic community. As we saw above, the rule stating that nuns were not to spend the night in the company of males was amended to allow for a nun who had given birth to a baby boy. Other nuns, however, were subject to a slightly more serious offense for sharing sleeping quarters with the baby boy. This seems to be the rationale for granting the mother-nun separate living quarters, a concern that is amply accommodated by this ecclesiastical act. Furthermore, we see here that the applicability of the monastic legislation occasioned by Guptā's situation was not limited to this one case. Indeed, the Buddha is made to say that any nun in a similar situation is to be likewise accommodated.

The ecclesiastical formula to be used in such cases is given in full in the text, and it provides further confirmation of the monastic lawyers' negotiation of a potentially delicate topic. The text is somewhat repetitive, but we will pick up the thread after Guptā's formal announcement of her situation and her request for the formal act of assigning a solitary cell:

> From amid this [assembly], one nun should declare amid the community, "Reverend [sisters], may the community listen! This one, Guptā, has

given birth to a baby boy. From the community [she has] petitioned for the formal act of [assigning] a solitary cell. If the community [deems that the appropriate] time has arrived, may the community assent and authorize the community to perform the formal act of [assigning] a solitary cell for the nun Guptā. This is the motion, [it is] a *jñapti-dvitīya karman.*[81] The community has finished performing the formal act of [assigning] a solitary cell for the nun Guptā. The community assents on account of its silence. Thus I hold this matter to be (i.e., motion carried)."[82]

As is evident from the ecclesiastical formula itself, the nun Guptā was granted formal permission to occupy a monastic cell, not with another nun, but alone so as to be able to raise her son. If the fact that this nun had just given birth to a baby was previously not known to the entire monastic community, it most certainly was now. Here it is publicly declared before the religious community. Moreover, the provision of a solitary cell in which she may raise her son is fully sanctioned by the *saṅgha.*[83] The authors/redactors of the *Sarvāstivāda-vinaya,* then, seem to have negotiated and secured a place amid the community of nuns for a nun who gave birth as a nun, one who was about to embark on motherhood and all of its attendant duties with the full ecclesiastical sanction of official Sarvāstivādin monastic jurists, a nun whose example provides both a legal precedent and an ecclesiastical formula for future pregnant nuns.

Closely related to the Sarvāstivādins are the Mūlasarvāstivādins. Indeed, some have suggested that these two *nikāya*s may in fact be one and the same.[84] Whether or not this is true, we are still left with the fundamental question of why we have two monastic law codes, one Sarvāstivādin and the other Mūlasarvāstivādin.[85] Although no satisfactory answer can be given here,[86] it is worth noting that the *Mūlasarvāstivāda-vinaya* also preserves similar rules to those found in all other *vinaya*s surveyed so far. This *vinaya* is one of the few monastic law codes that can be located at a given time and place. What it tells us can be placed securely in northwest India in the first few centuries of the Common Era.[87]

Here, again, the rules governing monastic motherhood are established by means of a narrative about the nun Guptā. A highly abridged version of the narrative of her conception is found in the *Kṣudrakavastu* (雜事; *phran tshegs kyi gzhi*) or *Chapter on Miscellany.*[88] Since the narrative in the *Mūlasarvāstivāda-vinaya* is very close to the one found in the *Sarvāstivāda-vinaya,* we will deal with it here only briefly. Without repeating the entire story, the authors/redactors of the *Kṣudrakavastu* allude to it and give a short statement of how Guptā came to be with child without having sex,[89] tacitly acknowledging that some monks may have had trouble accepting their explanation. Indeed, they conclude that "the maturation of the actions of beings is difficult to fathom."[90]

The authors/redactors then present us with a story about the nun Guptā's child-raising skills:

> Consequently, she became pregnant and gave birth to Kumāra-Kāśyapa. Then Guptā the nun did not dare to touch him.
>
> The child thereupon cried.
>
> Her relatives enquired, "Why is the child crying?"
>
> Some nuns heard this and remained silent; other nuns replied, saying, "The World-Honored One has set down a rule-of-training that [a nun] is not allowed to touch a male. Therefore she does not dare to approach, and he cries because of this."
>
> They thereupon replied, saying, "The World-Honored One is very compassionate; how could he not allow one to touch one's own son? If the mother does not touch him, how could he survive?"[91]

The nuns are then said to have praised this advice.[92] They report the incident to the monks, who in turn report the matter to the Buddha. The Buddha is then made to say, "One's own child one should touch. There is no fault in nurturing him and taking him in one's arms."[93] The Chinese here is relatively clear, although it lacks the precision and specificity that either a Sanskrit original or its Tibetan translation provides. The Tibetan text may be translated as follows: "Henceforth, with authorization he should be touched. He should be fed. He should be nurtured. He should be brought up."[94] The Tibetan, then, confirms that this is not simply something that nuns may do if they feel so inclined; here the Buddha is made to authorize or command that nuns touch, feed, nurse, and raise their sons. Nuns who give birth to children are not to leave their sons unattended out of misplaced fear that they might break the rule against physical contact with males.

The genesis of this rule was not the result of anonymous lay criticism, as is usually the case. Here Guptā's own relatives are the ones who were critical of her negligent mothering. When the baby cried, her relatives asked why he was crying. We have here, then, a nun who has just given birth to a baby boy.[95] Her relatives, presumably laywomen, criticize her not for having a baby, but for neglecting him in his hour of need. Guptā's lay relatives proffer advice on motherhood. Their advice, moreover, is praised by the nuns, reported to the Buddha, and made to carry the Buddha's seal of approval.

Consistent with the patterns seen above in other monastic law codes, the *Mūlasarvāstivāda-vinaya* contains two further regulations governing nuns and their sons. When the other nuns, Guptā's coreligionists, heard that the baby should be fed, nursed, and brought up, the nuns all passed the baby boy from lap to lap. The boy, however, became emaciated and stopped growing. The relatives again step in, and the Buddha is made to say, "A nun must not touch another's child; if she does touch another's child she incurs an offense of transgression against the rule of law."[96]

Similarly, since the Buddha had said that nuns were not to share sleeping quarters with males, our nun made her son sleep outside. When the relatives heard him crying, they asked what was going on, and again criticized the mother. When the story is finally reported to the Buddha, he is made to say that Guptā is to request a formal resolution (*sdom pa*) from the community of nuns allowing her to sleep under the same roof with her son.[97] This is granted, and the whole procedure is given in full. When the nun Guptā is granted permission to share sleeping quarters with her baby boy, other nuns also sleep there. This is then made an offense, as was the mother's sharing of sleeping quarters with her son after he had grown up.[98]

There is at least one thing of interest in the Mūlasarvāstivādin account that is not present in the parallel stories. Here Guptā's mothering skills are constantly criticized by her relatives. When she puts her son, Kumāra-Kāśyapa, outside for the night,[99] the relatives are said to have heard the boy crying. Where exactly this took place is not clear. Narratively, the location seems to be within the convent, although this is not made explicit.[100] But if this is all happening in the convent, do we here have evidence of laywomen living in a nunnery, or was the nunnery located so close to the house of this one nun's relatives that they could hear the baby crying? These questions are not answerable at the present, but are perhaps worth considering as they may provide further insights into lay/monastic relations and the urban location of Indian Buddhist convents.[101]

So far we have dealt with only non-Mahāsāṅghika texts, that is, texts that all purport to stem from one side of the putative great split in Buddhism, mentioned in Section 3 of Chapter 1.[102] Below, we will discuss the story of Kumāra-Kāśyapa as found in the *vinaya* of the Mahāsāṅghikas. Whether or not we accept the antiquity of these rules concerning monastic motherhood on the basis that they may go back to a presectarian era, we will still be forced to conclude, at the very least, that the accommodation of motherhood into Buddhist monasticisms was not limited to one tradition but represents a pan-*nikāya* or transsectarian understanding of monastic religiosity.

The *vinaya* of the Mahāsāṅghikas records, albeit in a somewhat different context, the birth of Kumāra-Kāśyapa. The beginning of the account is short enough to translate in full:

> At that time, in the city of Śrāvastī, there were two sisters who were pregnant but had not yet given birth. At home [i.e., as laywomen] they had faith [in the teachings of the Buddha], and left home to follow the [religious] path. Other nuns saw the state of their bellies, and thereupon drove them out. They went and told this matter to the World-Honored One.
>
> The Buddha said, "They were pregnant when at home [as laywomen]; there is no offense."
>
> [One of] these nuns (比丘尼) later on gave birth to a baby boy, named Kumāra-Kāśyapa. When he reached eight years of age he left home for the [religious] path, and became an arhat.[103]

Although initially driven out by other nuns, the two sisters in our text seem to have been ordained. This is suggested by the canonical reference to them as *bhikṣuṇī* (*biqiuni* 比丘尼). The unquestioned validity of their monastic status is also further echoed in the words put into the mouth of the Buddha: "They were pregnant when at home [as laywomen]; there is no offense." As we have seen in other *vinaya*s, the implication seems to be that the mothers only began to show signs of their pregnancy after ordination and were then driven out by nuns who thought that they had acted inappropriately. When the Buddha is made to say that there is no offense, it therefore means that the pregnant nuns, now mother-nuns, have committed no offense, and not that there is no offense in ordaining them—that was not at issue here. In the *vinaya* of the Mahāsāṅghikas, then, the story of the birth of Kumāra-Kāśyapa to an unnamed nun makes it clear that pregnant women who had been ordained in this tradition were allowed to remain as nuns and give birth within the nunnery.

There is one final passage that we should briefly look at from the Mahāsāṅghika tradition. The passage is available in both Chinese translation and an Indian text known as the *Mahāsāṅghika-Lokottaravāda Bhikṣuṇī-vinaya.*[104] The nun Kālī had initiated Sudinnā, the wife of a royal minister, who, it turned out, was pregnant. The nuns suggest she should be driven out,[105] but when this was reported to the Buddha, the monastic authors/redactors vindicate her and her claim that the sexual encounter had taken place in her former lay life.[106] The following is put into the mouth of the Buddha:[107]

> If there is one like this, she should not immediately[108] be granted ordination; wait until she has delivered. If she gives birth to a girl, as soon as she has left the maternity chamber[109] she is to be granted ordination. If she gives birth to a boy, wait until the boy is able to be weaned, and afterwards she is to be granted ordination. If relatives or sisters say, "Give us this boy; we will raise him," in such a case she should be granted ordination [immediately].[110]

The position taken in both the Mahāsāṅghika and Mahāsāṅghika-Lokottaravādin traditions is not unlike that advocated by the authors/redactors of the other canonical *vinaya*s. As Hirakawa and others have noted, this *vinaya* does not seem to contain a *prātimokṣa* rule making it an offense to ordain pregnant women.[111] However, this narrative clearly suggests that pregnant women should not be ordained. Moreover, whereas the positions of jurists of other monastic traditions were often either ambiguous or only explicit with regard to nuns' giving birth to baby boys, here we have a straightforward ruling that covers both monastic sons and daughters. For these monastic jurists, a candidate for ordination into the order of nuns (i.e., one who had already "gone forth") was not to be ordained immediately if she had given birth to a boy; in that case she was to wait until her son was able to be weaned. This, of course, was only a question of her formal ordination, and may imply that she still would have been able to stay in the nunnery as a *śikṣamāṇā* or probationary nun and raise her son. Moreover, if family members offer to raise her son, then the newly delivered mother is to be ordained straightaway. If, on the other hand, she gives birth to a baby girl, then there seems to be absolutely no impediment to her ordination. In fact, she is to be ordained almost as soon as she has given birth.[112]

The Mahāsāṅghika position on the ordination of not only pregnant women but also newly delivered mothers, then, seems to be the strictest of all the traditions we have so far surveyed. This may tell us something about the Mahāsāṅghika tradition, one that has been accused—it would seem erroneously—of laxity in regard to monastic discipline.[113] Here it is most certainly the strictest: mothers of newborn sons are not to be ordained until the boy is weanable. This rule, however, seems to apply only to the ordination of pregnant women, and not to the pregnancy of ordained women.[114]

Not unlike the Dharmaguptaka, Mahīśāsaka, and Mūlasarvāstivāda monastic codes surveyed above, the Theravāda tradition also preserves rules that make it an offense to ordain pregnant and breastfeeding women. Yet, as we have seen already, the presence or absence of these rules is a poor indicator of a tradition's own attitudes toward monastic motherhood. Here too the *vibhaṅga* clarifies the position of the Pāli *pātimokkha* (Skt. *prātimokṣa*): the *vibhaṅga* explicitly states that it is not an offense to ordain such women if one thinks that they are either not "pregnant" or not "giving suck."[115] Unlike the *Dharmaguptaka-vinaya,* however, the rules in the Pāli Vinaya and the *Mahīśāsaka-vinaya* were not modified to incorporate this view. The Dharmaguptaka jurists amend the wording of their rules concerning the ordination of pregnant and nursing mothers to make it an offense to ordain such women only if one does so knowingly.[116] In the Theravādin and Mahīśāsaka traditions, however, this legal opinion appears to belong to the, presumably slightly later, stratum of legal decisions known as *anāpatti*s (lit. nonoffenses).[117] Unlike their Dharmaguptaka brethren, the monastic jurists of the Theravādin and Mahīśāsaka traditions have not subsequently modified the wording of their canonical rules in order to incorporate these legal decisions.[118]

Regardless of where or when it is established, the Theravādin position as it has come down to us, then, seems to be the same as most of the other *vinaya*s: if one happens to ordain a pregnant or breast-feeding mother, her ordination stands. The ordaining nun, not the ordinand, becomes guilty of a minor offense. This seems to be the extent of the implications of a rule making it an offense to ordain a pregnant or nursing mother as opposed to an explicit prohibition of such ordinations. When we delve deeper into the Pāli Vinaya, we see that this tradition also allows for, and indeed accommodates, pregnant women who slip through the cracks and end up as ordained nuns. The Pāli Vinaya records the following story, translated for us already by Horner:

> Now at that time a certain woman had gone forth among the nuns when she was already pregnant, and after she had gone forth she was delivered of a child. Then it occurred to that nun [*bhikkhunī*]: "Now what line of conduct should be followed by me in regard to this boy?" They told this matter to the Lord. He said: "I allow [*anujānāmi*] her, monks, to look after him until he attains to years of discretion."[119]

Here a nun—and she is clearly identified as a *bhikkhunī*—entered the monastic life when she was pregnant and subsequently gave birth as a renunciant. Here too, as above,[120] it seems that we must conclude either that this nun did not undergo the compulsory two years of training as a probationary nun or that narratively this probationary period was not yet established. At least in this, and some but not every other, *vinaya*, the *śikṣamāṇā* probation is required by one of the eight rules or *gurudharma*s that the Buddha's aunt and stepmother Mahāprajāpatī is said to have accepted as a condition of the formation of an order of nuns. Despite the fact that it is already provided for in some of the *gurudharma*s,[121] this two-year probationary period seems to have been introduced quite late.[122]

The authors/redactors of the Pāli Vinaya seem to have put into the mouth of the Buddha not a concession "allowing" nuns to look after their children, but a direct order requiring them to do so (*anujānāmi* "I authorize/command").[123] The authors/redactors present two further rulings. The first has the Buddha assign the mother-nun a companion (*dutiyaṃ*), as she had realized that "it is not possible for me to live alone, nor is it possible for another nun to live with a boy."[124] The narrative then turns to the companion nun (*dutiyikā bhikkhunī*), who has doubts as to what is permissible for her, and the Buddha is made to command companion nuns "to behave in regard to that boy exactly as they would behave to another man, except for sleeping under the same roof."[125] In other words, according to the Pāli Vinaya, the *dutiyikā bhikkhunī* is exempted from the rule against sleeping under the same roof as a male if she is acting in her, now official, capacity of companion to a nun who has just given birth to a baby boy.[126]

The Pāli Vinaya, then, far from contradicting the testimony of our other *vinaya*s, actually corroborates it, and this suggests that what we have seen in the legal texts is much more than simply *one* Buddhist position on monastic motherhood. Indeed, the monastic law codes of these six Indian *nikāya*s—Dharmaguptaka, Mahāsāṅghika, Mahīśāsaka, Mūlasarvāstivāda, Sarvāstivāda, and Theravāda—the only Indic Buddhist monasticisms for which we have anything more than scattered and fragmentary records, all concur. We appear to have established, to the extent possible at present,[127] what may be described as *the* Indian Buddhist attitude toward nursing nuns and monastic mothers.

5. Child Care and Nannying Nuns

There is one last *prātimokṣa* rule that we should examine. As translated into English from Tibetan, this rule seems to suggest that motherhood may have been incongruous with Indian Buddhist monastic life. This rule is reported only in the *vinaya* of the Mūlasarvāstivādins.[128] It is available to us in Tibetan and Chinese, and a French translation of the former was made by W. W. Rockhill as early as 1884. Taking the rule to be about looking after infants, Rockhill translated it as "Si une bhikshuni soigne un petit enfant, c'est, etc. [i.e., un péché qu'on doit confesser]."[129] In Karma Lekshe Tsomo's English translation, however, the rule is given as "If a *bhikṣuṇī* raises a child, she commits a *pāyantika*."[130] Here, at least in Tsomo's translation, we seem to have evidence that nuns would incur an offense for raising children. To be sure, the offense is only a minor one. Moreover, as we have already seen, legally speaking, the mere existence of this type of *prātimokṣa* rule would not in fact prohibit nuns from raising children, to say nothing of actual practice outside the legal texts. The rule, however, clearly deserves our attention.

There are a number of variants recorded in the various editions of the Tibetan *Bhikṣuṇī-prātimokṣa* for the verb translated by Tsomo as "raises":[131] *'tshong* [*ba*][132] "to sell"; *'tsho* [*ba*][133] "to nourish"; and *'tshol* [*ba*], perhaps meaning "to try to obtain."[134] However, it is not the verb that is particularly problematic here. Rather, the question is whose children should not be sold, nourished, obtained, or, probably, simply just looked after. Fortunately, here Yijing's Chinese translation offers us further clarification of the probable intent of this rule:[135] "Whatever nun looks after (給養) another's child (他孩兒), [she commits] a *pāyantika*." However we translate the verb,[136] clearly this rule specifically addresses how nuns should behave in regard to *another's* child and not their own children.[137] This, then, seems to be a rule about monastic interaction with the children of lay families, and not evidence of a rule against or even about nuns raising their own children.

When we turn to the *Bhikṣuṇī-vibhaṅga* of the *Mūlasarvāstivāda-*

vinaya, we see hints of exactly what kind of behavior the rule may have been intended to curb.[138] The nun Sthūlanandā had entered a house for alms, and saw that the wife had recently given birth.[139] Not knowing how to bathe her son, the wife says to the nun, "Noble lady, please bathe my son!"[140] Sthūlanandā replies, "Who will give me alms?" The newly delivered mother offers alms for the nun's attending menial novice, her preceptress, and the convent guard.[141] Sthūlanandā then lays aside her bowl and tucks up her robes, takes the boy into her arms, and rocks him for a moment. She rubs him with clay and warm water, pours eye drops into his eyes, marks his forehead with ash, and cleans his hair. After feeding him with honey and butter, she puts him into a crib and lays him down to bed. Thereupon, having collected a load of alms in return for her services, Sthūlanandā returns to the convent.[142] By helping this mother look after her newborn, however, the nun Sthūlanandā sets a narrative precedent, one that has surprising ramifications for other nuns who visit that same house.

The authors/redactors have here set the stage for a farcical encounter, the types of which are not uncommon in *vinaya* literature. On another occasion the nun Mahāprajāpatī Gautamī, the Buddha's aunt and stepmother and the head of the order of nuns, goes to that very house for alms. When she requests alms, she is asked to bathe the baby.[143] Mahāprajāpatī is taken aback and replies, "Sister, I bathed the Bodhisattva and since him I have not bathed another baby boy. Sister, you are talking to a nun endowed with morality! And yet you ask me to do the work of a maidservant? Notwithstanding that, Sister, where in such a manner have you seen or heard of a nun bathing a baby boy?"[144] The mother replies, saying that Sthūlanandā had bathed the boy, and it is in reaction to this that the Blessed One is made to say that nuns incur an offense if they look after another's (presumably a layman's) child. In other words, nuns are not maidservants and are not to do such work; if they do, then nuns are likely to be asked to help out whenever, and perhaps wherever, they go for alms. Clearly this would not do.

Unlike the "nuns" in the Tilokpur Nunnery founded by *bhikṣuṇī* Karma Kechog Palmo (Mrs. Freda Bedi), who, according to Yeshe Palmo, were required "to get up in the middle of the night and change diapers on the little ones,"[145] Buddhist nuns in India were not to look after laymen's children. They were not, in the words of the unknown author of the *Ārya-sarvāstivādi-mūla-bhikṣuṇī-prātimokṣa-sūtra-vṛtti,* to bathe, clean, dress, feed, or, it would seem, play with someone else's children.[146] Clearly, then, the narrative context of this piece of monastic legislation does not permit Tsomo's translation. In fact, this rule does not prevent and is not even about the raising of children by nuns. Rather, it is a rule against babysitting or nannying, a rule concerned with how nuns interact with lay families, presumably other than their own.

6. Conclusions

This survey of monastic motherhood narratives in the extant corpus of Indian Buddhist law codes reveals that those who wrote or redacted these *vinaya*s seem to have envisaged, and perhaps even encountered, not only mothers or pregnant women presenting themselves for ordination, but also nuns who somehow found themselves pregnant. For the Buddhist *bhikṣuṇī* in the India of our narratives, pregnancy, parturition, and motherhood seem not to have been major obstacles to the religious life. To be sure, the authors/redactors of the extant monastic law codes were concerned with the preservation of the corporate image of the monastic community. The contempt that might be invited by the sight of pregnant or nursing nuns on alms rounds undoubtedly would result in the loss of lay support. The monastic authors/redactors could have taken a hardline approach. But expelling pregnant and nursing nuns was likely to open them up to further and possibly more trenchant criticism. Rather than ignoring the problem, the monastic lawyers legislated a place within the monastic confines for the occasional pregnant or nursing nun. Arguably, addressing the issue in this manner would have allowed the canonical jurists better control of their community's corporate image.[147]

We are now in a position to offer a few general remarks. The first point concerns the utility of the *prātimokṣa*s for the study of Indian Buddhism. As we have already seen, the rules preserved in the *prātimokṣa*s generally tell us very little about Indian Buddhist legal opinions toward monastic motherhood, although, somewhat ironically, it is these very texts that have been the focus of much of the work in *vinaya* studies.[148] In the preface to her study of the Dharmaguptaka and Mūlasarvāstivāda *Bhikṣuṇī-prātimokṣa*s, Karma Lekshe Tsomo, for instance, justifies the translation of these two texts as follows:

> The Bhikṣuṇī Prātimokṣa texts constitute the foundations of spiritual practice and social organization for thousands of communities of

> women even today. The translation of these texts is no mere academic exercise, but has significance for the restoration and continuance of the order of Buddhist nuns in the modern world.[149]

Tsomo has chosen to stress the importance of the *prātimokṣa*s, but in doing so she has neglected the context in which these rules are said to have been delivered by the traditions themselves. In my view, this approach puts us in danger of missing their significance and even meaning. Indeed, reading Tsomo's translation of these lists of rules one might well assume that pregnant women or nursing mothers could not be ordained. Motherhood, at least in the sense of parturition and child raising, would appear to have little if any place in Indian Buddhist monasticisms. This seems to be the inevitable conclusion of any study of Buddhist monasticisms limited to the evidence afforded by the *prātimokṣa*s. As we have seen, however, all of the known *vinaya* traditions state just the opposite. The narrative contexts in which Tsomo's rules are framed by the authors/redactors of Indian Buddhist monasticisms categorically confirm that the Buddha commanded nuns who had given birth to breast-feed and raise their children within the convent. This should give us pause for thought, especially those of us interested in, as Tsomo puts it, the "spiritual practice and social organization for thousands of communities of women even today." Clearly, we must rethink the utility of the *prātimokṣa*s for the study of Indian Buddhist monasticisms.

The narratives of the various *vinaya*s preserve a transsectarian or trans-*nikāya* openness to the ordination of pregnant and nursing mothers. This evidence seems to reflect an acceptance that Indian Buddhist nuns might, finding themselves pregnant, give birth to children and raise them in nunneries. The authors/redactors of all of the extant monastic law codes endorsed, sanctioned, and legislated for this position. Of course, I do not mean to suggest that the monastic lawyers advocated that nuns fall pregnant or have babies. These monastic traditions—if the term "monasticism" is still useful—seem to have placed great emphasis on celibacy. But as we have repeatedly seen above, the monastic law codes cover both mothers who become nuns, and nuns who become mothers, and it is only in the case of the latter, pregnant nuns, that we find any suggestion of a breach of monastic celibacy.

It seems possible that the ordination of nursing mothers and women in the earliest stages of pregnancy may have paved the way for what was to follow. Once a place in Indian Buddhist convents was negotiated for nursing mothers and pregnant women, it would have been only a small step to accepting the inevitable: that some nuns would fall victim to sexual assault and rape, others would succumb to temptations of the flesh, and a number of nuns would end up pregnant. Pregnant nuns undoubtedly would have benefited from the legislation that had been enacted to cover the ordination of pregnant women. Indeed, pregnant nuns could not but attract the attention of our canonical lawmakers. To be sure, as we have seen above, there are cases in the extant monastic law codes in which pregnant nuns are said to have been driven out of the convent by other nuns. However, they are driven out not on account of their being pregnant, but rather because they were thought to have broken their celibacy. Indeed, in all but one case of which I am aware, the Buddha is made to step in and exonerate these "banished" pregnant nuns, claiming that either they were pregnant when they were ordained, or, like the nun Guptā, they were "miraculously" impregnated.

To my knowledge, in Indian Buddhist monastic law codes, the only pregnant nun who is said to have been expelled is the nun Mettiyā, but, until recently, the legal grounds for her expulsion have remained a mystery.[150] The Theravādin tradition, in which her pregnancy is not mentioned, holds that Mettiyā falsely charged an innocent monk with rape. The legal enigma, however, is that she seems to have been expelled even though making a baseless accusation against a monk is not grounds for expulsion in any Buddhist monastic legal tradition. As I have argued elsewhere, the reason for expulsion was not her false accusation, but her acknowledgment of guilt with regard to contravention of the rule of celibacy.[151]

As we have seen, it is clear that, according to our extant *vinaya*s, canonical sanction allowed nuns who became pregnant *before* they were ordained to give birth and raise their children within the cloister while remaining as *bhikṣuṇī*s. Moreover, contra Ohnuma's claim that "the accommodation of motherhood applied only to women who had become pregnant *before* being ordained as nuns,"[152] it is equally clear that nuns who became pregnant *after* ordination were allowed to do the same, as established in the extant monastic law codes on the basis of the legal precedent of the nun Guptā.

For Indian women in the first few centuries of the Common Era, then, being a Buddhist nun may not necessarily have entailed giving up one's children. Moreover, it was certainly not a religious choice limited to young virgins and elderly widows. For Buddhist women in

India there seems to have been no dilemma; they, unlike the contemporary Ladakhi women studied by Ria Reis, for instance, seem not to have seen the paths of "reproduction or retreat" as necessarily mutually exclusive.[153] Indian Buddhist jurists appear to have turned what might otherwise have been monastic failures into religious successes. Arguably, and even if only to control the public image of their religious institutions, by legislating pregnancy, parturition and even child raising within the conventual confines, the monastic lawyers found a way to defuse the otherwise difficult situations encountered when motherhood was integrated into the sisterhood.

Chapter Five

Reconsidering Renunciation

Family-Friendly Monasticisms

The picture that emerges from this study stands in stark contrast to much we have been told about the familial and marital relationships of Buddhist monks and nuns in India. Buddhist monks and nuns, we are told, went forth from home into homelessness. Scholars have generally understood this literally. World renunciation has been taken to imply, if not entail, that monastics severed all ties with kith and kin, that monastics were socially dead. The case, however, has never been set forth adequately, much less proven; the vital step between assertion and acceptance seems to have been overlooked. In the present study I have sought to open the case. Although I have probably raised more questions than I have been able to answer, this was in part to be expected: the present inquiry was intended to be both experimental and exploratory.

1. A View of the Evidence

As we saw in Chapter 2, early epigraphical evidence suggests that Indian Buddhist monks and nuns, those who had left home for the religious life, continued to be identified with their family members in acts of religious giving. Monastic law codes confirm this external evidence from within the Buddhist traditions in rich detail. Narratives from the monastic law codes depict monks and nuns returning home from homelessness for visits and meals and staying overnight and perhaps even longer in houses of their own kin. In fact, the phrase "to go forth from home into homelessness" seems to have meant nothing more than that one joins the monastic order, and in no way did it imply or require renunciation of familial ties. As we saw in the stories of Sudinna and Dharmadinnā, monastics may have chosen to separate themselves from their families physically, but Buddhist renunciation seems not to have required such strict physical or perhaps even psychological separation. Not only does it seem that under certain circumstances Buddhist monastics could continue to dwell at home, but when they went forth into homelessness they could even take their children with them. Homelessness was not necessarily a state devoid of family. Indeed, the inscriptional record suggests that monks and nuns continued to be concerned with making merit for their families.

In Chapter 3 we examined a *vinaya* story about a monk who succumbs to the seduction of his "former" wife, a somewhat ambiguous designation referring, it seems, to nothing other than his wife in his "former" lay life. Although the monk had been warned to beware of his wife's womanly charm, the monastic jurists did not move to prohibit monks from visiting their "former" wives or even staying overnight with them. We also noted a story about monks acting as go-betweens in arranging a marriage for their children. These narratives suggest both the degree to which ordained Buddhist renunciants continued to interact and associate with the very wives and families they had "left," and the degree to which some of them seem to have taken seriously their traditional familial obligations. That some Indian Buddhist monks and nuns meddled in marital matters, moreover, is partly corroborated outside our "in-house" monastic law codes by Sanskrit dramas and learned brahmanical treatises, sources external and ambivalent, if not antagonistic, to the Buddhist traditions in India.

While Indian Buddhist monks are generally understood to have been either unmarried or no longer married, evidence from the monastic law codes calls this assumption into question. Indian Buddhist monastic law codes make it clear that the authors/redactors of Buddhist monasticisms were aware of secular provisions for the dissolution of marriage. Moreover, not only were they aware of those provisions, but—and more important—they also never seem to have required their own ordinands to invoke them. In other words, the authors/redactors of the monastic law codes chose not to require men and women to dissolve their marriages prior to embarking on the religious life. Rather, they seem to have allowed them to remain legally married.

It has been widely assumed that in India when a married man left home to become a Buddhist monk, he also left his wife. As we have seen, however, *vinaya* narratives present married monastic couples as commonplace. Men and women, husband and wife, are often depicted in these narratives as co-renouncing. Even the foremost Buddhist ascetic, Mahākāśyapa, seems to have spent several lifetimes, including his last, co-renouncing with his wife. In addition to conjugal co-renunciation, Indian Buddhist monastic law codes provide elaborate evidence for the existence of monastic families. The degree to which the family was woven into the very fabric of Indian Buddhist monastic culture is suggested by the fact that one Buddhist school is said to have traced its roots back to the story of a monk born to monastic parents: our story of the monk Udāyin; his wife, the nun Guptā; and their son Kumāra-Kāśyapa, who, according to Lamotte, was the patriarch of the Kāśyapīya or Suvarṣaka *nikāya*.[1]

In Chapter 4 we saw that, according to the monastic traditions' own narrative contexts, *prātimokṣa* rules that have been previously understood as proscribing the ordination of pregnant women and nursing mothers in fact restrict nothing of the sort. Rather, the monastic lawyers seem to have accommodated, albeit perhaps hesitantly, not only pregnant women seeking ordination, but also ordained nuns who found themselves pregnant. In other words, the authors/redactors of the *vinaya*s seem to have negotiated a place within their religious institutions for monastic mothers. We see, for instance, rules authorizing nuns to breast-feed and share sleeping quarters with their children, and the appointment of nuns to help raise these children within the conventual confines. The evidence from the monastic law codes, moreover, may allow us to reread some of the epigraphical evidence dealt with in Chapter 2. It is possible that children mentioned in nuns' donative inscriptions may have been children born to nuns and raised in convents. While not conclusive, the testimony of the monastic codes at least opens up new avenues of inquiry; it allows us legitimately to think and rethink what was previously unthinkable.

2. Family-Friendly Monasticisms

In surveying all extant Indian Buddhist monastic law codes, we are presented with a pan-*nikāya* and pan-Indian picture of Buddhist monasticisms that is remarkably consistent in terms of its attitudes toward family. Whereas scholars have often assumed that monastic Buddhism must be antifamilial, that the family is somehow incongruous with the monastic life, these assumptions were clearly not shared by the authors/redactors of the *vinaya*s. If Buddhism is, as sources both internal and external to the religion would have it, a middle path, a happy medium between indulgence and asceticism, then surely one would not expect it to advocate antisocial and antifamilial practices. How could such a path be a middle way? Surely a religious life that embraced family and friends—the position that is, in my view, hinted at by a number of Indian Buddhist inscriptions and confirmed by monastic law codes—would be closer to a model of religious moderation than the wholesale abandonment of familial and social ties so often portrayed in scholarly discourse.

If we are confronted with a picture that differs somewhat from what scholars have said about the nature of Buddhist monasticisms, about the family vis-à-vis the monastic life, then this difference is undoubtedly due almost in its entirety to a difference in source materials. To date, scholars have been somewhat selective in what they have taken as representative models of Indian Buddhist monastic ideals; we have placed all of our eggs in one basket, the *Suttapiṭaka* of the Pāli canon.[2]

By contrast, a close reading of select passages from Indian Buddhist monastic law codes affords us insights into the narrative world of monastic lawyers. As we have seen, these authors/redactors were nothing if not highly pragmatic, and—perhaps like all good corporate lawyers—ever vigilant when it came to protecting the public image of their institutions. While they may have been aware of religious goals and ideals such as those expounded in the *Rhinoceros Horn Sūtra,* they also seem to have been acutely aware of the fact that, as Herbert B. Workman noted back in 1913, "renunciation, though it starts with the individualistic standpoint, cannot long content itself with this. By a law of being the renunciant cannot remain a law unto himself, or condition his salvation by himself."[3] The authors of Buddhist hagiography, legend, and narrative had recognized this long ago, too. The Buddha himself is said to have formed a community of religious, one initially comprised almost entirely of his own family, friends, and relatives. But such a development is only natural. Workman, for instance, points out:

> But so quickly did Monasticism pass through its merely individualistic stage, that we find, almost as soon as it emerges out of the mists of romance into the light of history, the solitary hermit...joining himself

> unto others, seeking to adapt his life to a common rule.... monachism gave place to cenobitism....[4]

The study of Buddhist monasticisms has suffered a similar fate to its Christian counterpart, which, as Workman colorfully observes, "has been obscured and hindered by the way in which for many centuries romance has been mistaken for fact. In popular writings the idea of a religious Robinson Crusoe has had a hold out of all proportion to its actual accomplishment."[5] Moreover, since the Indian model is taken as the yardstick for Buddhist monasticisms, Buddhisms in East, Central, South, and Southeast Asia have been measured against a view of the religious life that may never have been realized on Indian soil, a view that may have existed largely or only in the romanticized and rhetorically charged visions of Buddhist monasticisms entertained by our academic forefathers. In being held up to a romanticized ideal, Buddhist monasticisms outside India have often been shortchanged. Married monks in Central Asia, Mongolia, Nepal, or Tibet, for instance, have tended to be seen as "corruptions" of a purer form of the religious life. In viewing these traditions as corrupt, however, scholars are implicitly categorizing them as failures at the monastic experiment. But if they are failures, then the fault lies squarely at our door. When measured against the ascetic ideal of the Rhinoceros Horn, any form of monasticism comes up short. Indeed, how could it be otherwise? If, however, we accept that this romanticized ideal had little, if anything, to do with Buddhist monasticisms in India from almost the very beginning of the Buddha's ministry to the demise of Buddhism in India some fifteen centuries later, then so-called monastic corruptions or religious failures appear in a very different light. Suddenly, the monastic enterprise becomes a story of splendid success.

In the present study I have explored in some detail one aspect of mainstream Indian monastic Buddhisms. I have rarely mentioned those groups of monks usually now referred to, albeit in an oversimplification, as *the* Mahāyāna. Early Mahāyāna groups provide us with a number of acerbic attacks on mainstream monastics for having wives and children, and leading a religious life considered by many to be morally and legally (that is, in terms of Buddhist monastic law) corrupt.[6] As we have already seen, the vision of religious life under attack might not be too far removed from the realization of the monastic ideal as espoused by monastic jurists in their own law codes. To understand fully what it was that at least some of the early Mahāyāna groups were reacting to, it is important to place their critiques of this-worldly monasticism in their proper context.

Ironically, just as it is becoming increasingly clear that the early Mahāyāna was in fact much closer to what we used to think of as mainstream Buddhism,[7] mainstream Buddhism itself is starting to look surprisingly and increasingly like what we see in later Mahāyāna Buddhism in Nepal, for instance. Mainstream monastics, monks and nuns, the people against whom Mahāyāna monks and nuns were most probably reacting, seem to have had a very different idea of how best to live the religious life. These monastics were not ascetic forest dwellers wandering alone like rhinoceroses; they were most likely slightly portly, homely, easygoing family men and women who had chosen—some as families—to wander down the religious path and seek spiritual betterment (and, on occasion, perhaps perfection) as they knew it: they had come to the realization that family matters in Indian Buddhist monasticisms.

3. Family-Friendly Monasticisms in a Competitive Religious Marketplace

Some readers may wonder how Buddhist monasticisms remained competitive in the Indian religious marketplace while allowing not only co-renunciation and continued contact between monastics and their lay family members, but also the occasional pregnant or nursing nun and monastics who, again on occasion, failed to maintain their celibacy, however we understand this term.[8] Although there is good evidence for the existence of entrepreneurially savvy monks and nuns and their continued ownership of personal property and wealth,[9] as a rule, economically, Buddhist monasticisms relied on the generosity of the almsgiving public. The kind of financial support that made possible the construction of many of the finest monasteries ever erected on Indian soil was, most probably, predicated on a perception of the monastic community as offering a good rate of karmic return on investments. Monks and nuns were considered to be good "fields of merit," but the fertility of the field in which donors would reap their rewards varied according to the virtue—real or perceived—of the renunciants.[10] How, then, are we to understand the tension, if any, between the familial and marital relations maintained by monastics, to say nothing of the occasional breach of celibacy, and the monastic community's need to present a celibate, renunciant image to the laity?

Neither the monastic jurists nor the laity, I suggest, were particularly concerned about monks and nuns who maintained familial, and perhaps even marital, relationships. There is hardly a hint of nervousness on the part of the monastic authors/redactors with regard to continued contact with family members. Moreover, given what we know about the Buddha's own family's participation in and patronage of his religion, it is improbable that a monastic's contact with kinfolk was seen as much of a threat to the perceived purity of the monastic order. The practice of returning home to beg for alms, or even to dine, was not unknown in India. In his discussion of the fourfold classification of classical Indian renouncers, Olivelle, for instance, tells us that "a Kuṭīcaka, the lowest class, . . . begs, or, more accurately, eats at the house of his son or relative."[11] Even a monk's contact with his "former" wife was not likely to be a major concern for Buddhist lawmakers or the laity whose gaze so concerned them. Indeed, the "abandoned" former wife would usually still be residing at the family home, enjoying the support of the extended family. For the purpose of our analysis, then, we can consider contact with "former" wives in the form of visits back and forth simply as an extension of contact with the rest of the monk's kith and kin. The monastic authors/redactors warn monks to be on their guard with regard to their celibacy, but in this the jurists' primary concern was the celibacy of the monk and not what the laity might say if he were seen going home to his wife or family.

It is tempting to suggest that what may have raised more concern was co-renunciation with one's spouse. This would have seemed highly irregular to a brahmanical audience—irregular, that is, if we compare, perhaps unfairly, the Buddhist *bhikṣu* with the *saṃnyāsin,* the classical Indian renouncer. Here, however, it might be useful to compare Buddhist "renunciation" with the disengagement from the duties of the household, the so-called retiring to the forest, that is the third of the four stages of life in brahmanical society. As Olivelle notes, "a hermit has the option of taking his family with him."[12] Indeed, the lawbook of Manu, to cite but one authority, prescribes that the hermit "should go to the forest, entrusting his wife to his sons or *accompanied by her.*"[13]

Buddhist lawyers did not want their monks to appear lax. But co-renunciation was practiced by the competition in India. In his authoritative work on Jain monasticism, S. B. Deo tells us that "generally, when the husband became a monk, his wife or wives also became nuns."[14] Deo cites the cases of "Vāśiṣṭhī, the wife of a purohita, [who] renounced the world seeing that her husband and all her sons had become monks" and "Rājīmatī, [who] hearing the news of her would-be husband's renunciation, became a nun."[15] He also notes that "in certain cases even brother-monks had to protect their sister-nun."[16] In other words, Buddhism is not particularly unique in its family-friendly and even spouse-friendly form of monasticism. Co-renunciation and the presence of kin within the monastery can also be seen in Jain monastic traditions, even if, as Deo concludes, interaction between ordained Jain nuns and their "former relatives" may have been much more limited than in the case of the Buddhists.[17] In any case, since we have strong evidence that even the Jains allowed co-renunciation of husbands and wives, then it follows that the Buddhist practice of co-renunciation was neither a unique development in Indian monastic traditions, nor one that was likely to draw severe criticism from the laity. In fact, contra Har Dayal, we might consider not that Buddhists were abandoning "the old Indian ideal of the married sage (*ṛṣi*)," but rather that in some respects they were following it.[18] Indeed, as Olivelle notes in his discussion of Aśvaghoṣa's *Life of the Buddha,* "the wise brahmins declare that Siddhártha will become an 'Awakened Seer,' placing him squarely within the tradition of Brahmanical holy men."[19]

As I suggested above, the dangers that would most probably impact negatively on the monastic community's image in the eyes of the laity were misbehaving monks and pregnant or nursing nuns. The monastic lawyers knew exactly how the laity would react to rumors of impropriety and breaches of celibacy. In the eyes of these jurists, perhaps only one thing was more serious than the presence of unchaste monks or pregnant nuns, and that was the laity's finding out about them. Monks who *were known* to have had sex (not simply monks who had sex) would have presented serious headaches for these monastic jurists.

The monastic lawyers were faced with at least two options in negotiating this minefield: either deal with matters in-house, as I have argued they sometimes did, or expel pregnant nuns and errant monks. Yet the expulsion of a monk or nun would be tantamount to a public announcement of the monastic community's lack of purity, and, arguably, this would bring about the loss of lay support so feared by the monastic authors/redactors. As we saw in Section 5 of Chapter 3, monastic jurists seem to have come up with the status of the *śikṣādattaka* to allow penitent monks and nuns who breached their celibacy to remain within the religious community. By dealing with this problem in-house, the monastic jurists avoided bringing it to the attention of lay supporters, and this would have allowed them to preserve their corporate image. Of course, this is not to say that the most egregious offenders were not expelled, however we understand this term.[20] The same holds true for the eviction of pregnant nuns, although this was more complicated.

As discussed in Chapter 4, pregnant and nursing nuns would be criticized by the laity when going on alms rounds. To forestall this criticism, a rule was created making it an offense to ordain pregnant or nursing women. However, this rule neither categorically bans their ordination, nor addresses the issue of ordained nuns who later on become pregnant, either through willful breaches of their celibacy or as victims of rape. While a hardline position such as expelling a pregnant nun certainly would reinforce the community's image as one of hardcore celibates, arguably this kind of inflexibility would do more damage to the reputation of the monastic community than accommodating her within the religious life. Indeed, hardcore asceticism was not the market into which Indian Buddhist jurists sought to make inroads. Moreover, even the accommodation of pregnant nuns seems not to have been unique to Buddhist monasticisms.

Given the vulnerability of women in general and female "renunciants" in particular in India,[21] it is not surprising that the Jains also dealt with similar issues. Unlike the Buddhists, however, Deo tells us that the Jains included pregnant women in "the list of persons who were debarred from entry to the Order."[22] Moreover, as we might expect, even the Jains allowed exceptions. Deo cites the case of "Queen Padmāvatī of Campā who became a nun when she was pregnant but separated from her husband at that time."[23] Elsewhere, in discussing spells and magic, he mentions that "a certain parivrājaka named Pedhāla caused impregnation to a nun Sujyeṣṭhā, daughter of king Ceṭaka."[24] In addition to these magical pregnancies, Deo also discusses the fate of raped nuns. He states that a raped nun was to tell only her superior; the other nuns were not to be informed.[25] The nun, Deo tells us, "was not to be driven out of the order but was to be handed over for care to the guru or to the 'sejjāyara' (the person who lent them lodging)."[26] If, however, the incident were widely known, then "the raped nun was kept in the monastery (upāśraya) and was not allowed to go out for begging, etc. Other monks and nuns were to bring food for her. When she was advanced in pregnancy she was handed over to a devoted layman and her duties as a nun were suspended so long as her child sucked her. . . . She was not to be expelled on the grounds that she would harbour hatred against the monks."[27] To this we might also add a verse taken from the same source as that used by Deo, Saṅghadāsa's *Bṛhat-kalpa-bhāṣya*. The verse is conveniently translated for us by Mari Jyväsjärvi in her recent comparative study of Jain and Buddhist monastic attitudes toward female renunciation: "In the absence of such people, she should be placed with her relatives or [if that is not possible either] with an old monk who is her kin."[28]

Here, then, the Jain—or perhaps more correctly, this Jain—monastic attitude toward pregnant, raped nuns seems remarkably, or perhaps unremarkably, similar to the position held by the Buddhist lawmakers surveyed earlier. The major difference seems to be that the Jain jurist deals with the issue of rape head on; the Buddhists cover much the same ground not in terms of a discussion of rape, but rather in the case of a nun's pregnancy. So it appears that much of what we previously noted in regard to Buddhist monasticisms in India also holds for the Jains, a monastic order that was in direct competition with the Buddhists. Indian monastic jurists—both Buddhist and Jain—could better control their communities' public image by not expelling pregnant or nursing nuns, but rather by legislating to allow them to remain discreetly in the religious life. The difference between the Buddhist and Jain responses to these situations was that the Buddhists appear to have raised their nuns' children in convents whereas the Jains entrusted the babies to lay families, presumably until they could be weaned.

But what about the presence of children in a Buddhist monastery or nunnery? Surely this would be a clear indication that something was awry with the monastic life. Here we must be clear on what is not entirely clear: how exactly to define childhood. We know that Indian Buddhist monasticisms allowed boys as young as seven—and perhaps even younger, if silence is allowed to speak—to enter the religious life as novices. Girls—actually married women—could become novice nuns as young as ten years old, and *bhikṣuṇī*s at twelve.[29] Seven and ten, respectively, then, seem to be the earliest ages at which boys and girls could join a Buddhist monastery or nunnery as novices or professional Buddhists in training, to say nothing of the other categories of people and perhaps children present in monasteries.[30]

It is not only the Buddhists that attest the presence of young children in an Indian monastic setting. Phyllis Granoff tells us that in medieval Jain monasticism, "being ordained at a young age, sometimes as young as six, often at age eight, was not uncommon."[31] In fact, she mentions one exceptional case, that of the monk Vajra, who seems to have chosen his path at the age of three (or perhaps at birth).[32] The infant baby is "reclaimed" by his father, a monk, from his mother, who, Granoff tells us, "also becomes a nun, and...continues to visit him and nurse him while he is living with the lay family."[33] The presence of young children around the age of seven in a monastic setting, then, was unlikely to raise questions as to the purity of the monastic community and its worthiness of lay support.

The question, then, is what about children under seven? This seems to be the age bracket that might cause the most confusion among the laity, as well as culminate in claims concerning clerical celibacy. Schopen has recently drawn attention to a number of "monastic practices connected with the well-being of children."[34] One of these is the giving of children as "attending menials" (*paścācchramaṇa*) in the *Mūlasarvāstivāda-vinaya* and related *avadāna* literature.[35] The children seem to have been promised before birth, in part as a protective measure to ensure safe childbirth. Schopen states that in most but not all cases, the child oblates seem to have been either deformed or otherwise physically abnormal.[36]

Schopen also discusses the practice of giving children and wives to the monastery and then selling or auctioning them back to their parents or husbands, a practice also depicted in the famous *Vessantara Jātaka*.[37] How long these "children" and "infants" remained in the monastery is unclear, as are their exact ages, although they seem to have been referred to as either "cured," "recovered," or in some cases "grown up" when they left the monastery.[38] Given that the *Mūlasarvāstivāda-vinaya* and its commentarial tradition preserve discussions concerning compensation from the parents and grown-up children on account of their gratitude, it seems that the monks were offering a valuable social service. The mere presence of very young children in Indian Buddhist monasteries, then, was unlikely to have been a cause of considerable concern to lay donors. This is especially so given the attestation of a similar phenomenon in Jain monastic traditions, in which Granoff tells us "the donation or sale of children to the monastery" was likely to have been "a widespread practice."[39]

In sum, then, I suggest that the family-friendly forms of Indian

Buddhist monasticisms seen in the preceding chapters were not radically out of kilter with other "heterodox," that is, non-brahmanical, interpretations of the religious life in India. The difference between the Buddhists and the Jains, for instance, was probably one of degree and not of kind. It seems improbable that either the presence of family members, spouses, and young children—although not babies—inside the monastery or continued contact with lay relatives and spouses would have seriously harmed the perception of Indian Buddhist monastics as worthy recipients of lay support, support that often may have come from their very own families.

What probably would have hurt the image of the community, however, were claims—whether factual or baseless—about the celibacy of its members. Accordingly, the monastic authors/redactors took great care in dealing with misbehaving monks and pregnant nuns. Here, however, rather than automatically expelling or disbarring those who were undoubtedly, at least potentially, most harmful to the community's reputation, the monastic jurists seem to have legislated to accommodate some of them within the fold. Arguably, this allowed the corporate lawyers to maintain better control of their community's public image.

Of course, there probably always was dissent. Those of a more ascetic bent than the monastic jurists—the authors/redactors of the *Rāṣṭrapālaparipṛcchā-sūtra,* for instance—clearly were not happy with sedentary, institutionalized monasticism. They saw it as a corruption of the teachings.[40] Even if "accommodations" allowing family-friendly forms of monasticism were not publicized in traditional *sūtra*s but rather were kept in "in-house" monastic law codes, texts for monastic eyes and ears only, Indian Buddhist monastic authors were perhaps well aware that they would sometimes struggle in promoting their institution as a good "field of merit." They, or their brethren, however, had covered their bases from another angle, this time from a doctrinal one, in a message delivered in *sūtra* texts for the laity. In the *Dakkhiṇāvibhaṅga-sutta* of the *Majjhima-nikāya,* for instance, we read that even an individual offering to one who is immoral "may be expected to repay a thousandfold."[41] Gifts to the *saṅgha,* moreover, trump offerings to individuals, even to Buddhas: "in no way is a gift to a person individually ever more fruitful than an offering made to the Sangha."[42] In other words, to quote Daniel Boucher's analysis of the message of this sermon, "the merit deriving from a gift to monks is not affected by their moral worthiness."[43] This doctrinal innovation, then, may be one of the manifold ways in which Buddhist monasticisms were able to remain competitive in the Indian religious marketplace, even with the occasional errant renunciant.

4. A Scholarly Misperception

In the present study I have attempted to highlight a scholarly misperception in the study of Indian Buddhism. Scholars rarely discuss Buddhist monks' or nuns' families simply because they generally do not expect monastics to maintain meaningful relationships with those family members whom the language and rhetoric of renunciation tell us they have "abandoned." Moreover, neither introductory handbooks nor scholarly tomes discuss monastic motherhood.[44] We usually assume that there was no such thing. Indeed, we are told that monks and nuns who had sex were immediately and irrevocably expelled from the Buddhist order. Such statements leave little room to entertain the possibility that Indian Buddhist nuns could continue to stay within convents while giving birth, nursing, or raising their newborns, and, moreover, that they could do so with—not against—ecclesiastical sanction.

I have suggested that a major contributing factor to the construction of this scholarly misperception is a privileging of *sūtra*—and in particular Pāli *sutta*—over *vinaya* literature. Scholars have embraced the image of a monk's abandoning his family and wandering alone like the horn of a rhinoceros, an image that not only makes for a neat and tidy scholarly narrative but one that also conveniently confirmed early Western presuppositions concerning the ideal monk.

In Chapter 1, I asked how the field of Buddhist studies might have developed if it had taken into account some of the *vinaya* narratives discussed above in constructing our most basic notions about the life of the Indian Buddhist monk or nun. How might scholars have benefited from a consideration of canonical accounts of continued contact between monks and their families not as aberrations or irregularities of the monastic life, but as part of the very fabric of Indian Buddhist monasticisms? In part we might have avoided the scholarly narratives of decline that have hindered the field of Buddhist studies. As Philip Almond has demonstrated, from the middle of the nineteenth century Victorian scholars contrasted "an ideal textual Buddhism" with Buddhism on the ground in Asia. Needless to say, Buddhism as lived by Buddhists was found to be wanting, and eventually characterized "in the language of decay, degeneration, and decadence."[45] This divide between the ideal and the lived tradition is often put down to the, perhaps inevitable, gap between practice and precept. To be sure, Buddhist monastic life as reported in Central Asia, Mongolia, or Nepal, for instance, is a far cry from the high ideals of *sūtra* literature. But perhaps Buddhism in some sense always was "degenerate," right from its earliest beginnings. Degenerate, that is, in comparison with the "ideal textual Buddhism" created by our Victorian forefathers.

In the present study I have avoided highlighting gaps between Buddhist ideals and practice. Rather, I have questioned whether we have fully understood the ideals of the Indian authors/redactors whose texts have come down to us in the form of Buddhist monastic law codes. Have we simply projected our own ideals on them, ideals that we have been all too quick to derive from the philosophical *sūtra* literature? Have we confused the messages that our monkish authors/redactors told others in their *sūtra* literature with the messages both implicit and explicit in their own strictly "in-house" *vinaya*s? In other words, have we confused sermons meant for public consumption and propagation of the faith with texts restricted to monastic ears and eyes only? Have we uncritically accepted a story not unlike that delivered by the Venerable Udāyin, our monastic tour guide, to the pious brahmin women at the Jetavana? If we are to learn anything other than that which the authors/redactors of our extant texts wanted the laity to believe about the nature of Buddhist monasticisms and the Indian Buddhist religious experience, then it seems to me that we will need to part company with our tour party; we need to go off the sign-posted and well-trodden highways of Buddhist *sūtra* literature and continue to explore the still largely uncharted terrain of "in-house" monastic codes such as the *Mūlasarvāstivāda-vinaya*.[46]

5. Comparative Monasticisms

If the present study has implications for how we understand Buddhism in historical and contemporary situations in Asia, then it may also have ramifications for how we study Buddhist monastic life in comparative light. What, if anything, do Buddhist "monks" or "nuns" as envisioned by the authors/redactors of our monastic law codes have in common with their Christian counterparts? Might we legitimately begin to question the utility of the categories "monasticism" and "renunciation" to describe the full array of religious practices and lifestyles described in the extant *vinayas*?

By settling on "monk" as a translation for Sanskrit *bhikṣu,* we invariably end up pitting the Indian *bhikṣu* against his much younger and in many respects much more developed Benedictine brethren. While our wild rhinoceros may fare well in this arena, his somewhat domesticated fellow "renunciants" found in *vinaya* texts certainly do not. Our "monks" and "nuns" are probably better compared to their closer contemporaries in late antiquity, monks and nuns such as those in "the earlier period of Pachomian monasticism," wherein "monks were allowed to continue their relationships with their biological families after they had joined the monastery"[47] or those in Shenoute's White Monastery "where biological kin and those who renounced their families, parents, siblings, and children lived side by side."[48] But even the relatively family-friendly monasticism of Shenoute seems to have imposed strict separation of biological kin within monastic communities,[49] a separation made neither explicit nor implicit in the monastic law codes of Buddhist jurists.

Likewise, by referring to the Indian Buddhist *bhikṣuṇī* as a "nun," we may be burdening her with far more cultural baggage than she should shoulder. The story of the medieval Gilbertine nun of Watton as recorded by Aelred of Rievaulx, for instance, preserves the story of a young girl who had entered the nunnery at the age of four and "grew up into a frivolous and lascivious young woman"; "she went out a virgin of Christ, and she soon returned an adulteress."[50] Upon being found out, her sisters in religion "seized and beat the culprit, tearing the veil from her head, and were prevented only by the senior sisters from burning, flaying, or branding her. She was chained by fetters on each leg, put in a cell, and fed with bread and water. Even then she was saved from yet harsher punishments only by the fact that she was pregnant."[51] Delivered of her baby, the nun is miraculously and "completely restored... her belly had shrunk to normal,... her face had acquired a girlish if not virginal look."[52] The nun's baby was then taken away by the bishop and raised, presumably, outside the convent.[53]

Taken as an example of the wider genre of medieval European accounts of pregnant nuns or abbesses as discussed by Boswell,[54] the story of the nun of Watton suggests, at least to me, the incompatibility of pregnancy, childbirth, child raising, and motherhood with this medieval Christian vision of the monastic life. Indeed, Giles Constable describes the incident as "a shattering challenge to [the] most cherished norms [of a religious community]."[55] Although the stories of pregnant Buddhist nuns discussed in the preceding chapters did not involve any breaches of celibacy—at least not technically—to differing degrees both communities of nuns and their male monastic minders may have feared the same thing: public scandal and the concomitant loss of lay support. But whereas the medieval nun's baby is taken away by the bishop, our Indian monastic jurists introduce canonical law commanding nuns to give birth and raise their children, to nurse and nurture their babies, in accordance with motherhood. Our monastic lawyers allow and in fact require what their medieval Christian counterparts seek to avoid, even if both are working to protect the public profiles of their respective institutions.

But that an Indian Buddhist "nun" could give birth to a baby and remain with her child in the cloister, all with the sanction of canonical Buddhist monastic law, is not the story that scholars of Buddhism hitherto almost universally have told. Consequently, when information concerning Buddhist monastic life has been passed from specialists to generalists, the field of religious studies has ended up with comments such as those by Elizabeth Abbott noting on the one hand that Buddhist "monastic life was rigidly structured and governed by the Vinaya," and, on the other hand, that "compared to Christianity, Buddhism punished its sexual sinners harshly, for ejection from the religious community, especially for women, was tantamount to social death."[56] Abbott's view, and it is a common one even among scholars of Buddhism, is unlikely to find support in a close and critical reading of any extant *vinaya*. If we are interested in a nuanced understanding of comparative monasticisms, then surely the specialist must ensure that generalists have accessible to them a full range of texts representing the full range of Buddhist voices in the extant textual record.

6. On the Utility of *Vinaya* Texts for the Study of Indian Buddhist Monasticisms

Finally, a few words might be said about the utility of Indian Buddhist *vinaya* texts for the study of Indian Buddhism. Until recently, with few exceptions, Schopen being the most prominent, most scholars who have consulted *vinaya* materials have used the Pāli monastic law code. But this comparatively short and narratively sparse *vinaya* is only one of six extant codes. Although, as we have seen, the Pāli Vinaya is remarkably similar to the other *vinaya*s with regard to family matters, nuns' pregnancies, and child rearing, this is not the case with all topics. The Pāli Vinaya, for instance, is the only extant Indian Buddhist monastic law code that does not contain rules allowing monks and nuns who have committed *pārājika* offenses—those who have had sex, for example—to remain within the monastic community. Moreover, primarily on the basis of the *Mūlasarvāstivāda-vinaya,* Schopen has consistently demonstrated that we still have much to learn about the financial affairs of Indian Buddhist monks and nuns, much more than the Pāli Vinaya reveals to us. To be sure, the Pāli Vinaya is an important source of information for the study of South Asian Buddhism. However, it should not be treated unquestioningly as if it is the only or even the best source for the study of Indian Buddhist monasticisms. It should be taken for what it is: an—not *the*—Indian Buddhist monastic law code. Yet when even scholars of Tibetan privilege Pāli sources and their English translations over narratively richer untranslated texts such as the *Mūlasarvāstivāda-vinaya* preserved in Tibetan, things have gone too far.[57] The Pāli Vinaya—in fact, any *vinaya*—cannot be accepted as representative of Indian Buddhist monasticisms without first fully examining the other five monastic law codes; we must marshall all available evidence in rereading Indian Buddhist monasticisms.

Throughout this study I have stopped short of claiming that Buddhist monastic law codes offer us unfiltered access to Buddhism on the ground around the time of their compilation or redaction. I have cautiously framed the discussion in terms of the narrative world of our monastic authors/redactors. However, it is worth considering the extent to which we can reconstruct sociohistorical realities on the basis of the extant textual corpus.

For the most part, the visions of the monastic life both implicit and explicit in our monastic jurists' legislation and its framings do not represent mere figments of their imaginations. It may be true that some of the narratives introducing monastic legislation are products of overactive imaginations. Certainly, the extensive discussions concerning the myriad manners in which a monk is *not* to have sex give this impression. The modern reader might take with a grain of salt stories about monks who have sex with those of the nonhuman realm such as *nāga* maidens, female *yakṣa*s, goddesses, *gandharva* girls, and female *asura*s.[58] But one should not overlook the message behind such narratives, namely, that monks were not to have sex, no matter how creative they might be in skirting the law or redefining "sex."

With the possible exception of one detail, Guptā's miraculous conception, the narratives examined in the present study are of a different nature to those characterized immediately above. In the case of incidental sightings of monks and their families, the canonical authors/redactors are not making a case for or against continued contact with one's family. They simply take such interactions for granted. In the case of pregnant nuns, however, the monastic lawyers are making a case to accommodate nuns who found themselves pregnant. It is hardly probable that such legislation came about as anything other than a reaction to nuns in the real world who somehow found themselves with child. While such cases may have been rare and certainly not the norm, they were clearly enough of a concern to make their way into all extant Buddhist monastic law codes. While some may charge that this legislation represents exceptions to the rules, and as such the present study overemphasizes irregularities of the monastic life in Indian Buddhist monasticisms, at what point do the numerous exceptions to the rule in fact make the rule? Indeed, as we have noted above, the lived traditions of Buddhist monastic life in Asia, outside texts, throughout most of Buddhist history have also been found to be "irregular."

We must be careful not to discount everything that the monastic lawyers said by reason of the fact that we cannot establish what actually happened on the ground in Indian Buddhist monasteries and nunneries. Indeed, were we to reject the picture that emerges from the texts that have come down to us as merely historical fiction, then in applying the same standards—as surely we must—we would be forced to reject nearly everything that we know about Indian Buddhist monasticisms on the basis of other similar, and in some cases identical, sources. We cannot, or at least should not, accept the texts only when the message they deliver is what we want to hear.

The need to reevaluate and rethink what we know about Indian Buddhism has been noted numerous times by Schopen, particularly with regard to the continued financial activities of monks and nuns. What we have seen in the present examination of family matters in Indian Buddhism, however, suggests that even some of our most basic assumptions about Indian Buddhist monks and nuns and their continued familial and marital (and perhaps even sexual) lives also may need to be rethought. Indeed, with every new discovery we must reread the extant corpus, armed with our newly found knowledge, alert to new possibilities. Given that only one of six extant *vinaya*s has so far been translated into any modern language, what else might we be missing by relying solely on this one monastic code?

What do we know, for instance, about the range of Indian monastic jurists' positions on the performance of abortions by nuns, either their own or for laywomen? Although in the present study I have assiduously avoided the topic of abortion, which deserves a detailed, separate treatment, the simple answer is probably not much—not much because we have assumed that all Indian Buddhists maintained the same basic positions as those we know from the Pāli canon. What are we to make of the Mūlasarvāstivādin narrative in which the nun Sthūlanandā agrees to dispose of a married laywoman's illegitimate, aborted fetus lest her husband find out about her affair?[59] The rule delivered in reaction to this incident simply makes it a minor offense for a nun to carry a large alms bowl like the one which Sthūlanandā used to carry away the fetus. Is the mention of a nun's disposal of an aborted fetus simply a narrative flourish? Or do we need to take this account seriously? Should we consider the implications of a ruling making it an offense for nuns to make use of what seems to be an elevated or suspended latrine? This rule is said to have been brought about on the basis of lay criticism when a "rule-breaking" pregnant nun was seen aborting her own fetus.[60] Do we need to consider these narratives along with legal rulings on the hypothetical actions of monks and nuns who rub a woman's belly with the intention of killing the fetus but end up instead killing the mother?[61] And how are we to understand these rulings in light of the fact that these same monastic codes seem to suggest that monks and nuns may be fully rehabilitated into the *saṅgha* even after committing *pārājika* offenses such as the intentional taking of a human life, which in our *vinaya* texts may include abortions?[62]

Although it is still too early to tell how our vision of Indian Buddhist monasticisms might change if we take seriously the views both expressed and presumed by the authors and redactors of the extant canonical legal codes, it is beginning to appear that the Indian Buddhist *bhikṣuṇī,* for instance, may look very different from what we might assume and perhaps even from what some of us might want. There is good evidence, for example, that the economic activities of Indian Buddhist "nuns" may have included the running of not only taverns but also brothels, and this may give us further cause to rethink the stated position on abortion among other things.[63] Indeed, if we find that our own expectations and assumptions about Indian Buddhist monastic life collide with those of the authors/redactors of Indian Buddhist monasticisms, then eventually one side will have to give. To date, in constructing both scholarly and popular views of the history of Indian Buddhism, the voices of five out of six of our Indian Buddhist monastic jurists have been largely ignored. It is high time that the Indian Buddhist *bhikṣu* have a say in what was, after all, his story.

Notes

Chapter 1: The Rhinoceros in the Room

1. T. 1421 (xxii) 189c19–190a1 (*juan* 29).

2. Solely for convenience, I use the terms "monk" and "nun" for Sanskrit *bhikṣu* and *bhikṣuṇī,* respectively. The term "monk" in my usage excludes novices. I include novices, both male and female (*śrāmaṇeralśrāmaṇerī*), probationary nuns (*śikṣamāṇā*), and *bhikṣu* and *bhikṣuṇī* in the term "monastic." I have used "mendicant" for *śramaṇa,* a broad term encompassing both Buddhist and non-Buddhist religious wayfarers. Admittedly, the terms "monk" and "nun" are not without problems: they carry with them assumptions concerning stability of residence, poverty, and celibacy. See also Schopen 2007a. On problems with the use of the term "monasticism" to describe Indian Buddhist renunciation, see Schopen 2010d.

3. The extant monastic law codes have come down to us as *buddhavacana,* i.e., the word of the Buddha. Who wrote these texts and to what extent they were redacted, we cannot know. That the authors/redactors were monks (as opposed to nuns or laymen) is not controversial; beyond that, we know very little.

4. Note, however, Lingat 1937 on Southeast Asia.

5. Here I exclude discussion of references to Samaneans (i.e., *śramaṇas*) in early Greek literature such as Clement of Alexandria's *Stromata* (late second century C.E.).

6. See, for instance, Horner [1930] 1999 for almsmen/almswomen. For bonzes, see Costelloe's translation of *The Letters and Instructions of Francis Xavier* (1992, 299 and index, q.v.). For friars, see Hopkins 1906, 455, 457, 460; Barnett 1924, 281; 1930, 698, 699. See Kaempfer [1727] 1998, 69, and Bigandet [1879] 1979, 2:241, for talapoins/talapoi (also Phongyies and Rahans in the latter). See Coomaraswamy [1916] 1956, 147, for "Brother," "Religious Mendicant," and "Wanderer."

7. Hodgson [1828] 1972, 30: "The followers of Buddha are divided into regular and secular—a division exactly equivalent to the Grihastha Asrama and Vairágí or Sannyásí Asrama of the Hindoos—but *not* equivalent to Laics and Clerics. The regulars are all monastic. . . . They are all monks, and constitute the *congregation* of the *faithful,* or only *real* Buddhists; the seculars having always

been regarded as little better than heretics" (emphasis in original). Hodgson's "seculars" refer to the Vajrācāryas, on which see Gellner 1992. On the *Āśrama* system, see Olivelle 1993. On Hodgson, see, most recently, Lopez 2004. Of course, there are earlier references to "monks," such as those found in the writings of Francis Buchanan on the Burmese (1799, 274).

8. Hodgson [1828] 1972, 71 n. 4. The degree to which the Buddhist *bhikṣu* has been compared to Western monks can be seen in subsequent studies. See, for instance, the following chapter titles in R. Spence Hardy's ([1850] 1989) *Eastern Monachism:* Noviciate, Ordination, Celibacy, Poverty, Mendicancy, Diet, Sleep, Tonsure, Habit, Residence, Obedience. See also Oldenberg 1896, 104–105.

9. Elm 1994, 8.

10. Elm 1994.

11. Sukumar Dutt ([1924] 1996, 90) follows Benedict's classification of monks into four classes (Cenobites, Anchorites, Sarabites, and Gyrovagi) and suggests that the Buddhist *bhikṣu* originated in the wandering community of Gyrovagi. Note, however, that Benedict is very negative about both the Sarabites and the Gyrovagi, particularly the latter (see *Rule of St. Benedict* 1.6–.11 [Fry 1981, 169–171]). The origin, but not the etymology, of the term Gyrovagi is unknown (Caner 2002, 9 n. 27). On the Gyrovagi, see Dietz 2005, 78–81, 88–90. For a comparative study of Buddhist and Benedictine monasticisms, see Don Peter 1990. For a Weberian study of medieval Catholic and Theravāda monasticism, see Silber 1995.

12. Rousseau ([1985] 1999, 153), for instance, suggests that "families were not entirely severed by the walls around the communities." See also Talbot 1990; Krawiec 2002.

13. See the discussion immediately below. See also Chap. 2, p. 46.

14. On the age of the *Sutta-nipāta*, the Pāli collection containing the *Rhinoceros Horn Sutta,* see Fausböll 1881, xi–xii; Chalmers 1932, xiv–xvi; Norman [1992] 2001, xxxi–xxxiii; and Cousins 1985, 219. See also von Hinüber 1996, 48–50.

15. Salomon 2000, 23. Of course, this is only the date of the extant manuscript and not of its contents; on this distinction, see Sec. 3 below.

16. The message of the *Rhinoceros Horn Sūtra* is known to us primarily from Pāli sources; see, for instance, Norman [1984] 1996. The scholarly attention received by the *Sutta-nipāta* is impressive. On the various translations and editions, see Norman [1992] 2001, x.

17. The asterisks here and below are Salomon's and denote reconstructions, usually the "invariable refrain verse"; see Salomon 2000, 115. I have modified the punctuation slightly.

18. Ibid., 106–108; square brackets and parentheses in original. The first and second verses are not consecutive.

19. The meaning is debated; for a summary of the scholarship and his own views, see ibid., 10–14.

20. Some scholars might subscribe to only part of this image, accepting, for instance, the abandonment of family but rejecting the solitary ideal.

21. For a very early reference, see the report of Bardesanes (Bardaisan) (154–222 C.E.), "a Babylonian who... met the Indian embassy sent with Dandanis to the Emperor," as preserved in Porphyry of Tyre's *On Abstinence from Killing Animals* (late third century C.E.) (Gillian Clark 2000, 113 and n. 645; for the date, see p. 1). In discussing the Samaneans, Bardesanes states that one joining their order leaves home for the religious life "without another look or word for his wife and children, if he has any, and thinking they are none of his business. The king looks after the children, so that they have the necessities of life, and the relatives look after the wife." This passage has been discussed recently in Reed 2009, 67. It seems to me that we have here a similar case to the position ascribed to Derrett by Stoneman (1995, 108) with regard to the "identity of the sages met by Alexander," viz., "the commonsense view that what the Brahmans say to Alexander is what any Indian ascetic would say to any modern Western politician."

22. Fausböll 1881, xii.

23. Ibid., 6.

24. Monier-Williams 1889, vii. Unlike Burnouf, who advocated for the study of Sanskrit and Pāli Buddhist texts ([1844] 1876, 11–12; 2010, 64–65), Oldenberg, Rhys Davids, Müller, and even Monier-Williams seem to have decided that Buddhism was to be studied through Pāli texts. Monier-Williams (1889, ix), for instance, states that he has "brought to the study of Buddhism and its sacred language Pāli, a life-long preparatory study of Brāhmanism and its sacred language Sanskṛit." The shift of emphasis from Sanskrit to Pāli has yielded English translations of most texts of the Pāli canon, and in some cases multiple translations. Not surprisingly, the study of Sanskrit Buddhist texts has not fared well. Writing about "the middle period" of Buddhist studies (1877–1942), de Jong (1997, 27) notes that "after Burnouf's death in 1852, little work had been done in the field of Sanskrit Buddhist literature."

25. Monier-Williams 1889, 147.

26. B. G. Gokhale 1965, 354. See also Radhakrishnan [1929] 1971, 1:587: "In the Khaggavisāṇa Sutta family life and social intercourse are strictly prohibited."

27. Spiro [1970] 1982, 279; see also Spiro 1969, 346; [1984] 1986, 49–50.

28. Gombrich (1975, 216) is somewhat nuanced, suggesting that only "the first Buddhists were asocial, even anti-social." Bailey and Mabbett (2003, 162) quote Gombrich in support of their view of the asocial nature of early Buddhism. Gombrich cites Dumont 1960 as "in a sociological context the *locus classicus* for this argument." Dumont refers to renunciation as "a social state apart from society proper" (1960, 44) and clarifies with a remark attributed to J. F. Staal (Dumont 1960, 44 n. 18) that the renunciant renounces "the social world *(saṃsāra)* and not the material universe *(jagat)*." Others have been less generous in their appraisals; Hume ([1924] 1942, 69) says, "The main trend in Buddhist ethics is

negative, repressive, quietistic, individualistic, anti-social." Hume cites, among other texts, the *Rhinoceros Horn Sutta.* Sukumar Dutt ([1924] 1996, 93) cites verses from the *Sutta-nipāta* and *Dhammapada* to highlight the Buddhist emphasis on "unsocial life."

29. In discussing Indian renouncers, Sukumar Dutt ([1924] 1996, 31), for instance, noted that "they have one essential characteristic in common, viz. that they are all professed religieux, homeless wanderers without kinship or social bonds." Heesterman (1985, 199) maintained that "world renunciation... threatens to break up society"; and Silber (1981, 164) suggested something similar: "World-renunciation, a tenet having evident asocial or even antisocial implications, is venerated as a central idea in Theravāda Buddhist countries." Note, however, Olivelle's qualification of the antisocial rhetoric of Indian asceticism on p. 7.

30. Gombrich 1975, 216. Sukumar Dutt refers to the rhinoceros ideal as "the ancient charter of a Bhikkhu's life" (1957, 68) but notes that Buddhist practice as described in the *Vinayapiṭaka* had already departed from this early ideal (ibid., 67–69).

31. For earlier examples, see Basham 1966, 12: "The ideal Buddhist monk walks alone, 'like the rhinoceros' "; Ch'en 1968, 87: "The early ideal of the Buddhist monks was thus an eremitical one, wandering around with no settled place of abode.... It was also expressed in the refrain... 'Let him wander alone like a rhinoceros' "; and Wiltshire 1990, 19: "The injunction to emulate the rhinoceros and fare alone is a figurative way of urging a person to become a *pabbajita,* defined in the Pali canon as 'one who goes forth from a household to a homeless life' " (emphasis [bold] in original).

32. Gananath Obeyesekere 2002, 114.

33. Faure 2003, 9.

34. Bailey and Mabbett 2003, 1.

35. Ibid., 166–167.

36. Flood 2004, 127.

37. Ohnuma 2012, 182.

38. There are, however, hints that for some scholars the image of the Rhinoceros Horn might represent more than just an ideal. For B. G. Gokhale, for instance, this ideal "reflects the essentially asocial spirit of primitive Buddhism" (1965, 354). For Gombrich, the seriously committed Buddhist is one who has "abandoned all social ties" (1975, 216). Gananath Obeyesekere tells us that "Buddhism insisted" upon this vision of the religious life (2002, 114).

39. See, for instance, Bronkhorst 1986, 121: "the *Khaggavisāṇa Sutta* constitutes evidence that in early days of Buddhism monks did often live alone."

40. Some scholars suggest that this ideal is not monastic but an early or primitive one prevalent before settled monasticism became a part of Buddhism. Salomon (2000, 15) rejects this as "somewhat simplistic, even naive... there is no clear evidence that there ever was, in any meaningful sense, a 'pre-monastic period' of Buddhism." There is also debate as to whether the ideal is an as-

cetic or monastic one. Collins (1992, 273) maintained: "I think that in fact the solitariness in question here is to be understood sociologically as the 'single-ness' of being unmarried, leading the celibate monastic life, rather than the physical solitude of eremitic asceticism, and in that sense it is spiritually applicable to all monks and nuns." Salomon 2000, 15 and n. 14, responded: "...the Rhinoceros Sūtra and similar texts in the Sn [*Sutta-nipāta*] do clearly represent the ascetic tradition of forest-dwelling monks....I would not go so far as Collins, who thinks that the prescriptions...can be interpreted as referring to monastic life." Most scholarly opinions, however, are not as nuanced as those of Salomon and Collins. Ascetic and monastic traditions are commonly not distinguished, with the result being simplistic talk of *a* or *the* Buddhist ideal (see, for instance, the comment by Faure cited in n. 33 above).

41. For a discussion of the privileging of "original metaphysics over and against modern practices and institutions," see Masuzawa 2005, 125–131, esp. 127. Following Masuzawa's advice to consider the influence of Max Müller's *Sacred Books of the East* in the development of Buddhism as a "world religion" (ibid., 259–265), it is interesting to note that volume 10 of this series contains the *Rhinoceros Horn Sutta*. We might also consider why the incomplete *vinaya* volumes (17–19) in the same series, published between 1882 and 1885, did not attract similar attention. The degree to which the *Rhinoceros Horn Sutta* captured the Western imagination can be seen in the account of Nietzsche's borrowing of Coomára Swámy's 1874 translation of the *Sutta-nipāta* in 1875. Brobjer (2004, 10 and n. 34) reports that "in it [Nietzsche] found, among others, a motto he was most fond of: 'Thus I wander, lonely as the rhinoceros.'"

42. On the problematic ascription of this text to Buddhaghosa, see von Hinüber 1996, 129–130. For a study of the *pratyekabuddha* and a partial translation of the relevant section of the *Paramatthajotikā,* see Kloppenborg 1974, esp. 78–125; note also Norman 1983a. For a full translation, see Murakami and Oikawa 1985, 127–319. According to Murakami and Oikawa, a similar explanation is also found in the *Cullaniddesa,* a canonical commentary on the *Sutta-nipāta,* and this would seem to mean that the Rhinoceros Horn ideal struck even the authors/redactors of the Pāli canon as something that other religious did (ibid., 289 n. 1). Indeed, they too are forced to attribute it not to the Buddha but to *pratyekabuddhas*. Norman 1983b, 65, also notes that "the Niddesa...states that they [i.e., the verses] were uttered by *paccekabuddhas.*" See also Bronkhorst 1986, 120–121; and Coomára Swámy 1874, 11.

43. Gethin 1998, 95. For a summary of the "tendency in Western scholarship to ignore world-engaging aspects of Buddhism," see Scott 2009, 19–28 (quotation on p. 20).

44. Olivelle 1995a, 12–13.

45. On the differences between monastic law codes and *sūtra* literature, see pp. 10–11. For references to the restriction of *vinaya* texts to a monastic audience, see Clarke 2009a, 18 n. 55.

46. Ray 1994, vii. See also Gethin 1998, 99. On forest monks and the rela-

tionship to the Mahāyāna, see Boucher 2008. For modern examples of the importance of cults of forest monks, see Tambiah 1984; Tiyavanich 1997.

47. See, for instance, the numerous studies of monks and their property rights collected in Schopen 2004a. On wealth and prosperity in contemporary Thai Buddhism, see Scott 2009.

48. Tyagi 2007, 277, for instance, recognizes that monks "could continue with their kinship ties determined by birth." Liz Wilson 1996, 29: "Familial relationships need not be completely severed by the renouncer as long as such relationships are reconfigured to resemble the utopian family of the *sangha*."

49. Chakravarti 1987, 30.

50. Young 2004, 37, without reference to any *vinaya* passage.

51. Michaels 2006, 161–162. For a similar statement, see the early remark in Kellogg 1885, 316–317.

52. Wijayaratna 1990, 89.

53. Commenting on the content of the Buddha's *First Sermon,* Monier-Williams (1889, 44–45) noted that "... 'right resolve' means abandoning one's wife and family as the best method of extinguishing the fires of the passions." See also his pp. 125, 253, 561.

54. Lamotte [1958] 1988, 65: "... since he was devoted to a very pure ideal of renunciation, the Blessed One reserved his favours for those who gave up family life in order to embrace the condition of a religious mendicant...."

55. For another early example, see Hopkins 1918, 189: "to the Buddhist mendicant, love and even affection were as dangerous as passion. He must break all home ties; must not be fettered by a love of family any more than by a love of woman. Buddha himself set the example of abandoning those who loved him."

56. See, for instance, n. 90 below.

57. In his review of Wijayaratna's study "of how Buddhist monks and nuns were supposed to live," Gombrich writes: "Oddly enough, no such account has been published before. Most authors who have written on the Sangha have concerned themselves with the Buddha's doctrine and monastic spirituality, giving pride of place to the inner life... rather than focusing on what it was like to be an early Buddhist monk or nun" (1986, 387–388).

58. Liz Wilson 1996, 19, cites the *Rhinoceros Horn Sutta* as a "poem in praise of the celibate life that warns of the filial and social obligations that entrap the householder." She then notes (19–20) that "from the perspective of these mendicants who renounce their land, property, and familial life, the wealthy householder with many sons to carry on the family lineage is caught in a web of social obligations." It is nowhere established, however, that "these mendicants" in fact are Buddhist mendicants; see p. 7 on the Rhinoceros Horn as an ideal not of mainstream monks but of *pratyekabuddhas*.

59. Liz Wilson 1996, 20.

60. Hume ([1924] 1942, 69) cites *Therīgāthā* 301: "Forsake [their] children, wealth and kin." Spiro ([1984] 1986, 49) cites the *Vessantara Jātaka* as the *locus*

classicus for the view that Buddhists give up their wives and children. Gombrich (Cone and Gombrich 1977, xv) notes that "the selfless generosity of Vessantara, who gave away everything, even his children and wife, is the most famous story in the Buddhist world.... even the biography of the Buddha is not better known." Further on, he states (xxv) that "a serious Buddhist was—and is—supposed to become a monk or nun, renouncing material possessions and family ties—almost like Vessantara." Moreover, (xxii) "Parents in Buddhist countries do not lose their children by death alone. Many of them go so far as to give away their sons, not indeed to slavery, but to a monastery.... Parents lose their emotional relationship with them, and in many cases physical proximity as well." As far as I can see, the story of Vessantara is not about renunciation or giving up one's children. It is, as Gombrich himself notes (xvii), "an example of the perfection of giving." Moreover, as also noted by Gombrich (xv), Vessantara gets—actually buys (see p. 160)—not only his wife back, but also his children: "the family is reunited, Vessantara becomes king, and all live happily ever after" (xvi). The whole story in many ways mirrors the life story of the Buddha, and in fact is a previous-life story of the Bodhisattva, as Gombrich also notes (xviii).

61. Examples include Edkins 1881, 72: "Thus to become a monk and abandon family life is the first step." Lingat 1937, 415: "Le premier acte du bouddhiste qui désire entrer dans les ordres est le 'départ de la maison,' c'est-à-dire l'abandon de son foyer et de ses biens. Cet abandon constitue une rupture unilatérale des liens sociaux." Singh 1954, 151: "Any system that aims at the disolution [*sic*] of the family life, and renunciation of the world...." Lancaster [1984] 1986, 139: "No institution of Buddhism had more far reaching effect than the monastery with its inhabitants who took a vow of celibacy and separated themselves from their families." See also p. 145: "Buddhism in East Asia achieved a working relationship with the family system... the monks and nuns were weaned away from filial responsibilities of the sort commonly practiced by the laity and these ordained members transferred loyalty to the Buddhist community in which no kinship ties existed." Frances Wilson 1985, 82: "Society forced women to sever their family ties before joining the order." See also p. 79: "A man was ultimately to renounce the family for religion. Family and religion are mutually exclusive for a man." Paul 1985, 6: "The male novitiate left his wife and family for the order." See also p. 10: "The pragmatic concerns of the monastic order to preserve and stabilize their organization demanded the exclusion of familial responsibilities, particularly to the wife." Gombrich and Obeyesekere 1988, 233: "The vast majority of Protestant Buddhists do not go the whole way and renounce family life." Wickremeratne 2006, 181: "The life style of a monk is different from that of a layperson.... Once a monk enters the order to become a *bhikkhu*, he distances himself from society, from family ties and lay life." Ohnuma 2012, 192: "Those who became pregnant *after* ordination were guilty of committing a *pārājika* offense and liable to immediate expulsion from the Saṃgha" (emphasis in original).

62. On this last question, see Clarke 1999, 2000, 2009a, and 2009b.

63. A number of interesting projects have been under way and are reaching completion. See Sasson 2013 on children and childhood in Buddhism, and Liz Wilson 2013 (unseen) on family in Buddhism.

64. This quest for "original Buddhism" has been abandoned more or less, particularly in North American scholarly circles, where, as Ray (1994, 9) tells us, "it has come to be widely agreed that nothing definitive can be known about the Buddha himself or the Buddhism he founded." But this is not universally agreed. See, for instance, Gombrich 2009.

65. Schopen (2000a) 2004a, 2, states that "we need no longer be implicitly or explicitly concerned primarily with the question of what Buddhist monasticisms originally were. We might be equally—and probably more fruitfully—concerned with what at given places at given points in time they had become."

66. See, for instance, Mills 2003, 69: "So, if Tibetan Buddhist monks appear not to fulfil the classic South Asian definition of the Buddhist renouncer—the *anagarika* or 'homeless one'—then how *are* we to understand their social and religious role?" (emphasis in original).

67. On schools that reject the *abhidharma,* the third "basket" of the *tripiṭaka* or Buddhist canon, see Lamotte [1958] 1988, 181.

68. See n. 45 above.

69. At least as they have come down to us, monastic law codes have little, if anything, to do with Buddhist ethics or morality, as is often erroneously asserted. This has been correctly noted by Skilton [1994] 1997, 78, and Prebish 2003, 58, among others.

70. Schopen (1996b) 2004a, 329; Schmithausen 2003, 43.

71. Schopen (1995a) 2004a, 96.

72. For an example of criticism from modest monks, see: *Pārivāsikavastu,* GMs iii 3:96.12–.15; for criticism of monks by nuns, see *Kṣudrakavastu,* sTog, *'Dul ba,* THA 261a6, in which the criticism falls like a thunderbolt (see n. 75 below); for *tīrthikas*, see *Bhaiṣajyavastu,* GMs iii 1:236.9–.13; for a king, see *Kṣudrakavastu,* sTog, *'Dul ba,* THA 51a7–b1; for brahmins and householders, see *Bhaiṣajyavastu,* GMs iii 1:44.10–.17.

73. Schopen 2004c, 167.

74. *Pravrajyāvastu,* Eimer 1983, 2:201.24–202.1; 2:205.15–.18; *Vinayavibhaṅga,* T. 1442 (xxiii) 691a14 (*juan* 12). For a sample of parallels in other *vinaya*s, see: *Mahāsāṅghika-vinaya,* T. 1425 (xxii) 308a5–6 (*juan* 9); *Mahīśāsaka-vinaya,* T. 1421 (xxii) 5c23–24 (*juan* 1); Pāli Vinaya, Vin 3:44.22–.25; *BD* 1:70; *Sarvāstivāda-vinaya,* T. 1435 (xxiii) 109a15–16 (*juan* 15).

75. See, for instance, *Kṣudrakavastu,* sTog, *'Dul ba,* TA 339a1; 339a4–5; 341a3–4; 344b5–6; THA 54b1–2.

76. On the ten benefits, see Hirakawa 1993–1995, 1:148–154.

77. T. 1428 (xxii) 640a14–641a10 (*juan* 11).

78. T. 1428 (xxii) 640a14–27 (*juan* 11).

79. T. 1428 (xxii) 640b7–8 (*juan* 11).

80. T. 1428 (xxii) 640b8–11 (*juan* 11).

81. T. 1428 (xxii) 640b18–19 (*juan* 11).

82. For one early and quite colorful call to read the literature of Tibet, including the *Mūlasarvāstivāda-vinaya,* see Anonymous [1890] 1957, reprinted and attributed to A. Braustein in Nagendra Singh 1999, 2206–2225. Note also the preface by C. A. F. Rhys Davids to Ralston's English translation of von Schiefner's *Tibetan Tales.* In claiming that half of the tales translated from Tibetan had no known Indian origin, Rhys Davids suggested that they "may have been rejected by the Buddhist canonical editors as too un- or im-moral" (von Schiefner 1882, ii). It now turns out that most, if not all, of them are canonical and Indian; they are from the *Mūlasarvāstivāda-vinaya.*

83. For the story, see Chap. 2, Sec. 7.

84. T. 1428 (xxii) 982b13–15 (*juan* 56).

85. I discuss this passage in detail in Chap. 3, Sec. 4.

86. T. 1421 (xxii) 94c14–15 (*juan* 14).

87. See the comment by Dayal to the effect that advanced bodhisattvas must be married, quoted in Chap. 3, n. 271.

88. I deal with this narrative in Chap. 4, Sec. 4.

89. *Kṣudrakavastu,* sTog, *'Dul ba,* THA 215a1–4; T. 1451 (xxiv) 360c3–7 (*juan* 31).

90. There are Pāli parallels to all three passages presented above. For the Pāli parallel to the story about a father who leaves home with his son, see *BD* 1:138–139; on the nun-wife's fanning her monk-husband, see *BD* 3:252–253; for the story about a nun who has given birth to a baby boy requesting authorization to sleep in the same room as her son, see *BD* 5:385–386.

91. See pp. 3–5 and n. 60 above.

92. Nattier 2003, 66. In her discussion of the *Ugraparipṛcchā,* Nattier notes that "when the author of the *Ugra* tells us, in the course of a discussion of how the bodhisattva should use his worldly belongings, that the bodhisattva should bestow wealth upon his male and female ṣlaves (*dāsa* and *dāsī*), he is not making an argument for or against the institution of slavery, but is merely revealing that it exists. He is also letting us know, again inadvertently, that the category of 'bodhisattva' included at least some individuals of considerable wealth" (ibid., 66–67).

93. Schopen 2004a.

94. Schopen 2004b, 26. On the degree to which the authors/redactors of the *vinaya* texts seem to be uninterested in meditation, which has often been taken as one of the mainstays of Buddhism, see ibid. See also Bronkhorst 2006.

95. See, for instance, the comment in Young 2004, 37, cited in n. 50 above, that "the *vinayas*... required [monastics] to abandon all family life."

96. That there is a difference is not often noted. Oldenberg ([1879–1883] 1969–1982, 1:xiii) states: "The difference between the Dhamma and Vinaya cannot be very clearly defined, and it would be difficult to lay down any very broad

line of distinction between the two. Many sections of the Vinaya are met with again in the Dhamma, and not unfrequently are repeated word for word."

97. See Gombrich's comments to this effect in his review of Wijayaratna's (1983) *Le moine bouddhiste selon les textes du Theravāda* (1986, 387–388). Gombrich's observations are further discussed in the introduction to the English translation of Wijayaratna 1983 by Collins (1990). This focus is also noted in Reynolds' review of the state of the field in the United States between 1972 and 1997 (2000, 120).

98. See, for instance, Holt [1981] 1995; Wijayaratna 1983 and 1990. On nuns, see Horner [1930] 1999; Wijayaratna 1991 and 2001; Hüsken 1997.

99. See Lamotte [1958] 1988, 517–548; on the formation of *nikāya*s, see Bechert 1973 and 1993. See also Nalinaksha Dutt 1978. *Nikāya*s are sometimes referred to as "schools" or "sects." Throughout I generally use the Indic term.

100. Epigraphically we can locate far more *nikāya*s than those few for which we have textual materials. See Lamotte [1958] 1988, 523–529, 529–548. See also Bareau 1955. Both surveys need to be updated; for one list of recent references, see von Hinüber 2008b, 34–35.

101. Although a number of important Mahāsāṅghika-Lokottaravādin texts have survived in Sanskrit (e.g., Roth 1970), we do not possess a complete version of their *vinaya*.

102. Norman, for instance, states that "it is known that the Pāli canon is a translation from some earlier tradition, and cannot be regarded as a primary source" (1984, 37). On Pāli as an "artificial language," see von Hinüber 1982. The utility of the Pāli Vinaya for the study of Indian Buddhism has been called into question on a number of occasions. Most recently, see Clarke 2009a, 31–35 (note also the references in n. 6 to the work of Schopen and rejoinders from Pāli scholars). Referring to it as "a work belonging to the Sinhalese Theravādins," Lamotte tells us that it "circulated on the island of Ceylon but never seems to have been used on the mainland" ([1958] 1988, 167–168). On quotations from a South Indian commentary (*Andhaka-aṭṭhakathā*) in the *Samantapāsādikā*, see Kieffer-Pülz 1993 and 2010a for the commentaries.

103. Oldenberg's edition of the Pāli text appeared between 1879 and 1883; three volumes of the Pāli Vinaya were translated into English in the *Sacred Books of the East* series (Rhys Davids and Oldenberg [1882–1885] 1996), but a full translation did not appear until Horner ([1938–1966] 1996–1997; see Kieffer-Pülz 2001 on Horner's untranslated passages). A Japanese translation of the Pāli Vinaya appeared from 1936 to 1940 (Takakusu [1936–1940] 1970).

104. For a detailed bibliographic survey of *vinaya* texts, including editions and translations, see Yuyama 1979, supplemented by Yamagiwa 2007b. Prebish 1994 is of limited utility. On the limits of the *prātimokṣa*s for the study of Indian Buddhist monasticisms, see the discussion on pp. 32–34 and Chap. 4, Sec. 5.

105. See now the collected works of Schopen (1997 and 2004a) dealing with the *Mūlasarvāstivāda-vinaya*.

106. In describing the state of the field from 1972 to 1997, Gombrich (2000, 179–180) notes that in the "anthropological (and, to a lesser extent, sociological) study of Buddhist communities and traditions...it is undoubtedly Theravâda Buddhist studies that have led the field, both in Britain and worldwide." In terms of textual studies, Gombrich (ibid., 183) notes that "British scholars have published little research about Srâvakayâna traditions other than the Theravâda."

107. See Boucher 2008, 201 n. 59.

108. On the split, see Lamotte [1958] 1988, 286–292, 517–518, and the references cited therein. Note that the Sthaviras are not to be confused with the Theravāda; on the confusion, see Skilton [1994] 1997, 66–67.

109. For a critique of the principle of higher criticism, see Schopen 1985. See also Clarke 2009a, 25–26.

110. I leave aside discussion of the important but very fragmentary Sanskrit *vinaya* manuscripts belonging to the *Sarvāstivāda-vinaya*. For a useful survey, see, with caution as to identification of Chinese parallels, Chung 2002.

111. Lamotte [1958] 1988, 167–171; Wang 1994, 168–170.

112. Wang 1994, 182. Note, however, that one text, the *Vinayakārikā* (T. 1459), was translated by Yijing somewhat earlier, while he was still in Nālandā; see the colophon at T. 1459 (xxiv) 657b20–22 (*juan* c).

113. For the dates of a number of *vinaya* texts preserved in Chinese from Dunhuang, see Giles 1957, 118–121. For dated colophons, see Ikeda 1990 and Giles 1935 for fifth- to sixth-century manuscripts in the Stein Collection.

114. A good sense of the coverage of *vinaya* materials in the Shōgozō 聖語藏 manuscripts, an incomplete Japanese collection kept by the Imperial Household, can be gleaned from Kokusai bukkyōgaku daigakuin daigaku gakujutsu furontia jikkō iinkai 2006, 223–243.

115. For recent discussions of Chinese canons and printed editions, see Zacchetti 2005, 74–142; Deleanu 2006, 1:110–132, and 2007. For a useful chronological list of editions of the Buddhist canon in Chinese, see Deleanu 2006, 1:113–115.

116. The Nanatsudera collection is still largely inaccessible, although slowly it is being digitized. On this collection, see Makita and Ochiai 1994–2001; Ochiai 1991. On texts copied and known in Nara-period Japan, see Ishida [1930] 1966. Note, however, the recent work of Ochiai 2004 on the Kongōji 金剛寺 collection of mid-Heian (901–1085) to late-Kamakura (1222–1287) manuscripts. For an overview of the Japanese manuscript traditions, see the Eight Canon Catalogue edited by the Kokusai bukkyōgaku daigakuin daigaku gakujutsu furontia jikkō iinkai (2006). See Ochiai 2007, vol. 2, for a catalogue of the Kongōji material.

117. Daizōkai 1964, 36–39. See also Buswell 2004. On the source of the so-called "second carving," see Ochiai 2012, 39 n. 2.

118. There seems to be some disagreement as to the exact dates of compilation for the Taishō canon: Demiéville (1978, 1), Vita (2003, 235), and Zacchetti

(2005, 74) give 1924–1932; Deleanu (2006, 1:114) gives 1922–1933; and Sueki (2008, 212) gives 1924–1934.

119. For the calculation of one-quarter, see Clarke 2010b, 1–2 n. 2.

120. Sander 1968, 159–161. Most recently, see Sander 2007, 131, on the script used in the manuscript of the *Mūlasarvāstivāda-vinaya* (known variously as Gilgit/Bāmiyān, Type II; Proto-Śāradā; and Siddhamātṛkā—see ibid., 129). Sander notes the use of two different scripts at Gilgit; the calligraphic ornate Gilgit/Bāmiyān, Type I, used primarily in Mahāyāna *sūtra*s and the Siddhamātṛkā used mainly in Mūlasarvāstivāda literature (ibid., 130 n. 62). Why the scripts should be so used is yet to be explained. More fragments of the *Mūlasarvāstivāda-vinaya* have come to light in recent years. Wille, for instance, notes the existence of three manuscripts of the *Vinayavastu* in Gilgit/Bamiyan Type II; for an overview of these recent manuscript finds, see Hartmann and Wille, forthcoming.

121. Hirakawa [1960] 1999–2000, 1:77. For a list of Tibetan *vinaya* texts reported in the early ninth-century *lHan (lDan) kar ma* translation catalogue, see Herrmann-Pfandt 2008, 277–292 [entries 483–513]; for the contemporaneous *'Phang thang ma* catalogue, see Kawagoe 2005, 23–24 [452–470] and 33–34 [687–691]. On the completeness of the Tibetan translation, see Clarke 2002a. I leave aside questions of Mongolian or Xixia editions since these are secondary translations, generally translated from Tibetan and Chinese, respectively.

122. Steinkellner 1994, 117, says it was "presumably written between the 11th and 17th–18th centuries"; Scherrer-Schaub 2000, 116, says "presumably dating from the Xth to the XVI–XVIIth c."

123. For Tibetan *vinaya* texts from Dunhuang, see La Vallée Poussin 1962, 1–21 (nos. 1–47), and Yamaguchi et al. 1977, 1–51, on the Stein Collection, and Lalou 1939–1961 on the Pelliot Collection. For an overview, see Okimoto 1985. A systematic survey of the Tibetan *vinaya* material at Dunhuang and Tabo is an urgent desideratum.

124. On the Yongle Kanjur, see Silk 1996. Silk reproduces (p. 181) the comparative tables of Sakai Shinten (Shirō), in which thirteen *vinaya* volumes are reported.

125. The Lithang Kanjur, for instance, is dated to 1608–1621; see, for convenience, Harrison 1992, 80, and references therein. The Phug brag manuscript Kanjur is dated to 1696–1706; see Samten 1992, iv.

126. von Hinüber 1978, 49.

127. von Hinüber 1991.

128. von Hinüber 1996, 4. On the re-importation of *vinaya* texts from Siam in the 18th century, see the references cited in Clarke 2009a, 24 n. 75.

129. Evidence from the colophon gives a fifth century date (429/430 C.E.), although it might also correspond to a date in the fourth century (369/370 C.E.); see von Hinüber 1996, 104. The text is attributed to Buddhaghosa, but both the attribution and his dates are contested; see von Hinüber 1996, 103–109, esp. 109. See, most recently, von Hinüber 2006, 19, on "the unknown author(s) of

the *Samantapāsādikā*." On Buddhaghosa, see Pind 1992. It should be noted that the *Samantapāsādikā* contains quotations from earlier commentaries; see von Hinüber 1996, 104–105, and Kieffer-Pülz 1993.

130. Schopen (1999) 2005a, 76, quoting Lamotte 1966 to give a revised view of Lamotte's earlier date. Note also the discussions in Schopen 2004a (see his index entry [p. 420] under *Mūlasarvāstivāda-vinaya:* date and place of origin), and the references cited there. Note also Schopen 2004b, 20. See also Schopen 2010b, 885 n. 9, where he refines this date to "the 2nd century C.E." on the basis of Falk's dating of Kaniṣka.

131. Schopen (1994a) 2004a, 74; (2000a) 2004a, 1–2.

132. Schopen (1994a) 2004a, 74.

133. Ibid.; Schopen (2000a) 2004a, 1–2.

134. Schopen (1985) 1997, 26–27.

135. This study does not attempt to date the composition of the *vinaya*s with any precision. Although an important concern, it cannot be undertaken here.

136. For the story of Nanda's renunciation and the embedded *Garbhāvakrānti-sūtra* (on which see de Jong 1977 and Kritzer 2012), see *Kṣudrakavastu,* T. 1451 (xxiv) 251a15–262a19 (*juan*s 11–12); sTog, *'Dul ba,* TA 181a4–240a4. For Nanda's doodling, see *Kṣudrakavastu,* T. 1451 (xxiv) 252a15–22; sTog, *'Dul ba,* TA 185b1–7. The best-known version of this story is undoubtedly Aśvaghoṣa's tale; for an English translation, see Johnston 1932 and Covill 2007; for a Japanese translation and study, see Matsunami 1981. For a bibliography of important early studies on this text, see Shastri 1939, 11–13. See also the additional references in Panglung 1981, 175–176. The version preserved in the *Mūlasarvāstivāda-vinaya* deserves a separate study; see Formigatti 2009.

137. For convenience, see Rockhill [1884a] 2007, 54, 57–58. Unfortunately, given the dearth of English translations from the *Mūlasarvāstivāda-vinaya,* we still must rely on the remarkable, albeit dated, translation by Rockhill.

138. For the story of a woman who was the Buddha's mother in a previous life, see Durt 2005 and Muldoon-Hules 2009.

139. Rockhill [1884a] 2007, 14; Durt 2002, 2003, and 2004.

140. Rockhill [1884a] 2007, 58–62.

141. Ibid., 40–41.

142. Ibid., 53. For detailed studies on Śuddhodana, see Minori Nishimura 2003a, 2003b, and 2004.

143. Rockhill [1884a] 2007, 55–56.

144. Ibid., 51.

145. Ibid., 52.

146. Ibid., 56–57.

147. Ibid., 56; Strong 1997.

148. The emphasis on the Buddha's own family was recognized early on by Henry S. Olcott in his *Buddhist Catechism;* see Olcott [1881] 1982, 22–24.

149. Young 2004, 86.

150. Ohnuma 2012, 182.

151. No source is cited, but note Horner's comment on p. 25.

152. Ohnuma 2012, 182; emphasis in original.

153. See Liz Wilson 1994, 9, and similar comments about leaving "grieving loved ones in their wake" on p. 11; 1996, 22 and 24. See also Bond 1980, which discusses ascetic practices required for Buddhist novices during "initiation rituals," all of which "symbolize death, the candidate's death to the world" (pp. 250, 252).

154. The same deep-rooted assumptions about Buddhist monasticisms can be seen in Chen 2002. Although aware of the problematic assumption that "many scholars seem to assume...that a Buddhist monk or nun automatically and permanently severed ties with his or her family" (p. 51), Chen's focus on family background seems to result in his support for this tenuous generalization.

155. Spiro [1984] 1986, 49.

156. Ibid., 50; emphasis in original. Whether families shared cells within communities is not known. See, however, Chap. 4 on nuns' giving birth and authorizations to dwell together with their newborn sons.

157. Ohnuma 2012, 182; emphasis in original.

158. See also the passage by Ohnuma cited on p. 6.

159. Cole 2004, 280. Cole 2006 is an expansion of this essay, but his basic premise remains the same: "Family life is something that needs to be overcome and left behind" (p. 304); "becoming a Buddhist cleric formally required the breaking of familial bonds" (p. 307).

160. As we will see in Chap. 2, the Sanskrit term *pravrajyā* does not mean "leaving the family." Moreover, *pravrajyā* is not "the technical term for becoming a monk or nun." One who has "gone forth" is neither monk nor nun; that requires ordination (*upasaṃpadā*). *Pravrajyā* refers to going forth, usually from the home, but neither "home" nor "family" is conveyed by the term itself; these have to be supplied, as they are, for instance, in the stock phrase found throughout the Pāli canon: *agārasmā anagāriyaṃ pabbajati* "he goes forth *from home to homelessness.*" For a discussion of this phrase, see Chap. 2, Sec. 2. Cole is presumably influenced by non-*vinaya* understandings of Chinese *chujia* 出家. See also Cole 2005, 25, where he asserts that "Buddhism was constructed around the act of 'leaving the family.'"

161. Cole 2004, 280.

162. Ibid.

163. Cole 2006, 313–316.

164. See, for instance, p. 81.

165. *BD* 4:56.

166. Bailey and Mabbett 2003, 165 n. 14.

167. In her study of *Monastic Life in Medieval Daoism,* Kohn, for instance, states that "monastics of all traditions describe their leader as father; monks and nuns become brothers and sisters" (2003, 59). The same has also been said

of Egyptian monasticism: Krawiec, for instance, notes Shenoute's use of "family imagery" and "fictive kinship" in his construction of a monastic family, one in which "not only did husbands and wives address each other as 'brother' and 'sister,' but so too 'father,' 'mother,' 'son,' and 'daughter' could be used for more distant kin" (2002, 146). See also her discussion of "family language" on p. 136. Krawiec notes the presence of biological kin in the White Monastery.

168. Why this should be so has not been explained adequately. That it should be so, however, does make a certain amount of sense if we accept the presence of actual biological kin within the conventual confines. See also n. 12 above. On the Buddha as a (metaphorical) mother, see Liz Wilson 1996, 29–32, and n. 48 above.

169. *BD* 1:xlii. Note, however, that this does not mean that monks, for instance, are not to view and treat their preceptors as they would their own biological fathers; clearly they were—see *BD* 4:58–59: "The preceptor, monks, should arouse in the one who shares his cell the attitude of a son; the one who shares his cell should arouse in the preceptor the attitude of a father." An indication of how uncommon such statements are, however, can be gauged from the *Index to the Vinaya-piṭaka* (Ousaka et al. 1996) in which we see only two entries under *pitucittaṃ*, Horner's "the attitude of a father." See also VSS_{MsB} *sūtra* no. 64 (VSPVSG 2005, 60–61).

170. *BD* 1:xliii. See also pp. xl–l and l–lv on "monk" for Pāli *bhikkhu*. On the existence of the term *dharmabhrāt*ṛ in the *Mūlasarvāstivāda-vinaya*, see Schopen (2001) 2004a, 165 n. 41. See Schopen 2008b on *dharmabhaginī*.

171. *BD* 1:xliii.

172. Note, however, Crosby 2005, 164.

173. Bareau 1976.

174. Schopen 1995b.

175. Schopen 2007a. See also Wayman [1966–1968] 1997 for a brief study of parents of Buddhist monks.

176. Schopen 1984.

177. Strong 1997. Note also Namikawa 1997; Tatelman 1998. On Yaśodharā, see Devee 1989; Tatelman 1999; and Ranjini Obeyesekere 2009.

178. Yamagiwa 2004.

179. Yamagiwa 2007a.

180. Sasaki 1999, 156–158.

181. "こうした親族の情愛を仏教は否定しない" (ibid., 156); "もとの親戚との絶縁が奨励されることは決してなかった" (ibid.).

182. On differences between Theravādin and Mūlasarvāstivādin monasticisms, see, for instance, Schopen 1989 and 1992. On legal and financial aspects of Indian Buddhist monasticism, see the articles collected in Schopen 1997 and 2004a. For an important new study on "Theravāda Buddhisms," note Skilling et al. 2012.

183. Cf. n. 65 above.

184. Young, for instance, asserts that "Buddhist texts are perfectly silent about the lives of such deserted women, except for those instances when they mustered the courage to approach their monk-husbands" (2004, 87). Accordingly, she suggests that the lives of Buddhist monks' wives "be imagined...from what we do know about the lives of non-Buddhist Indian widows." This is premised on the problematic acceptance of primarily prescriptive law codes such as *Dharmaśāstra*—codes that lack the narrative description of Buddhist *vinaya*s—as somehow reflecting historical reality.

185. Boswell 1988, 4–5.

186. Other important sources include accounts of early Chinese pilgrims, archaeology, iconography, and inscriptions; see Wang 2005.

187. The structure of the *Mahāsāṅghika-vinaya* differs from that of the Sthavira *vinaya*s. On the structure of the *vinaya*s, see Frauwallner 1956. For a critique of Frauwallner's handling of the *Mahāsāṅghika-vinaya*—not, *pace* Sasaki 2006, his entire thesis—see Clarke 2004a and Clarke 2009b, 123 n. 26. On the structure of the Pāli Vinaya, see von Hinüber 1995, 20.

188. The *vinaya*s all differ in the exact number of rules given for monks and nuns. For convenience, see Pachow [1955] 2000 on monks' rules and Kabilsingh 1998 on nuns' rules.

189. Lévi [1923] 1992, 167.

190. Pāli *ādikammika;* Skt. *ādikarmika;* Chi. *chuzuo* 初作; Tib. *las dang po pa.* The *Mahāsāṅghika-vinaya* does not seem to recognize "first offenders," at least not explicitly.

191. For a full discussion, see Chap. 2, Sec. 3, and n. 103 for references.

192. On the dating of the *prātimokṣa*s, see p. 76.

193. I do not deny the general scholarly value of the *prātimokṣa*s.

194. Faure 1998, 79; Clasquin 2001; and Siegel 1987, 4–5. See also Schopen 2007b and Clarke 2009c.

195. See p. 123.

196. Ibid.

Chapter 2: Family Matters

1. For a sampling of references, see n. 23 below.

2. Schopen utilized this same corpus of epigraphical material to show, for instance, that Indian Buddhist monks and nuns actively participated in religious giving and that there is nothing typically Chinese about filial piety among Chinese Buddhists: Indian Buddhist monks were just as concerned with the welfare of their parents as were their Chinese brethren. Schopen 1984 and 1985.

3. For dates and stratification of the inscriptional evidence at Sāñcī, see Dani 1963, 64–65; Dehejia 1972, 35–38.

4. The translations of inscriptional material presented below are not new translations. I have generally accepted, and slightly reworked, the earlier transla-

tions of specialists. No attempt has been made to Sanskritize proper nouns. Some technical terms such as *bhichu* (Skt. *bhikṣu*), however, have been Sanskritized. For references to Majumdar, see Marshall and Foucher 1940, vol. 1.

5. The same inscription was engraved three times: see Tsukamoto (Sāñcī) §§134–135.

6. See also Bühler 1894, 371 (§137).

7. It is perhaps worth further investigating teacher/disciple relationships as found in both epigraphical and textual sources. In this inscription, a male monk seems to have had a female nun disciple (*antevāsin*). This could turn out to be interesting, especially if one accepts the etymological definition of *antevāsika* given by Upasak 1975, 18, s.v., *antevāsika:* "one who resides with the Ācariya." Note also Law 1939–1940, 32.

8. See also VSS$_{\text{MsB}}$ *sūtra* nos. 78–79 (VSPVSG 2007, 39–40).

9. Note Horner's comments on the use of *bhaginī* on p. 26; see also the references to Schopen's work in Chap. 1, n. 170.

10. The exact sense of *caityavandaka* or *caitya* worshipper is not agreed upon; see Schopen (1996a) 2004a, 250 n. 31.

11. It is often impossible to distinguish between joint gifts and those in which the donor associates others with the gift and thus the resultant merit; both interpretations seem possible. See Schopen (1984) 1997, 69–70 n. 35 on the *sahā* formula.

12. "Superintendent of construction" is not a particularly good translation for *navakarmaka/navakarmika,* but the fact remains that we do not fully understand this term. For recent investigations thereof, see Silk 2008, 75–99; Kieffer-Pülz 2010b, 77–78. See also Schopen 2006, 231–236.

13. For a sample, see Tsukamoto [Amarāvatī] §§29, 49.4, 51 (here Tsukamoto omits the term *bhikṣuṇī* in his translation), 56, 63, 148 (there are many more).

14. Sankalia 1942, 351, suggests that "the suffix *rakhita* seems to be . . . the special contribution of Buddhism. For it is after the advent of Buddhism and all through its subsequent history that names with this suffix are met with."

15. Whether Buddhist monks and nuns in India took on new names when they were ordained is not entirely clear. See, however, T. 1443 (xxiii) 1005b11–19 and 1008b1–6 (*juan* 18) for at least two pieces of evidence for ordination names in the *Mūlasarvāstivāda-vinaya*. For an important passage in the *Kriyāsaṃgraha,* see Tanemura 1993, 41, and 1994. See Peters 1997, 283 (and Frankfurter 1883, 149–150) for a Burmese Pāli ecclesiastical formula for bestowing monastic names (*nāmasammuti*). On the usage of temporary names (Nāga and Tissa) in ordination ceremonies, see Kieffer-Pülz 1997.

16. Dehejia 1997, 170.

17. Basham 1981, 33.

18. See, however, Sankalia 1942, Shobana Gokhale 1957, Mulay 1972, and Shah 2001.

19. On the Pāli phrase *agārasmā anagāriyaṃ pabbajati,* Trenckner's *A Critical Pāli Dictionary* (1924–2011) gives "a house, household life" for *agāra* (q.v.) and "houseless" for *anagāra* (q.v.). See also Childers [1875] 1979; Rhys Davids and Stede [1921–1925] 1997, s.v., *agāra;* and Cone 2001, s.v., *agāra: anagāra.* Whereas Trenckner gives only "houseless," Rhys Davids and Stede favor "homeless" over the wooden term "houseless." So too Cone 2001. Our modern lexicographers are careful, however, not to suggest that one leaves one's "family"; see Childers [1875] 1979; Rhys Davids and Stede [1921–1925] 1997, s.vv., *pabbajati, pabbajjā.* In rendering this and similar phrases, I have generally used "home" and "homelessness" but I do not take these terms to encompass any notion of family.

20. Collins 1982, 171.

21. Ibid.; see also Collins 1988, 105.

22. Hamilton 2000, 102–103, notes a metaphorical usage of the phrase, but takes it to imply that one who is "homeless" is "free from the home in which one is tied to and by one's desires."

23. For a small sampling of works in which the phrase seems to be accepted at face value, see the following: Fausböll 1881, xv; Thomas [1933] 2002, 44–45; Dissanayake 1977, 33; Misra 1979, 4; Olivelle 1981, 268, and 1984, 131 n. 87; Bronkhorst [1993] 1998, 81; Findly 2003, 297; Mills 2003, 57, cf. 69; Gutschow 2004, 175.

24. Spiro [1984] 1986, 50; see also his p. 48.

25. Masson 1976, 620. Note, however, the balanced observations of Sukumar Dutt [1962] 1988, 45: "World-forsaking does not mean for the world-forsaker a stepping out into solitude or lapse into a social vacuum.... 'Homelessness' does not necessarily mean a state of aloofness or companionlessness: such a condition for the world-forsaker is optional."

26. Nyanatiloka [1952] 1956, s.v., *pabbajjā:* "'The Going Forth from Home to the Homeless Life' of a monk... consists in severing all family and social ties to live the pure life of a monk." On "the going into homelessness (pabbajjā)," Grimm 1958, 305, states: "The Buddha demands of him who wants to go the highest way, to give up wife and child, house and home, money and fortune." Yu 1997, 122, observes: "To take... 'holy orders' from the Buddhist sangha... represents... Buddhism's most severe conflict with the social and ethical ideals of Chinese culture. To be committed to the life of *pravarājya* [*sic*] (*chujia,* literally, leaving one's family), is to renounce those ties to the family that the Chinese... most deeply cherish."

27. Kohn 2003, 57.

28. Olivelle 1975, 75.

29. On Sudinna, see Freiberger 2005, 243–245.

30. For select, partial translations, see Anālayo 2012. For a partial translation of the Tibetan version, see Martini 2012.

31. sTog, *'Dul ba,* CA 32a4–40b4; T. 1442 (xxiii) 628a14–629c1 (*juan* 1).

See Hiraoka 2002, 157 (3.A.a) for the full form of this stock phrase. See also Demoto 1998, 37 (7.1).

32. sTog, *'Dul ba,* CA 32b2; T. 1442 (xxiii) 628a20–21 (*juan* 1). The *Samantapāsādikā* (Sp 1:203.25–.29) contains a gloss on our phrase "to leave home for 'homelessness,'" one that is also found in various other commentarial texts. It is conveniently translated by Masefield (2008–2009, 2:586) in the commentary to the *Itivuttaka* (Bose [1934–1936] 1977, 2:73.10–.13), for instance, as follows: "And, in this connection, since that which is to the well-being of the home, such as activities involving ploughing and trade and so on, is spoken of as 'home[li]ness', and [since] going forth has none of this, therefore going forth is to be known as 'homelessness'" (square brackets in original). Masefield (1994–1995, 2:778) also translates the gloss in the commentary to the *Udāna* (Woodward [1926] 1977, 309.6–.8). For the corresponding passage in what has been taken to be the Chinese version of the *Samantapāsādikā,* see Bapat and Hirakawa 1970, 150. At least for the authors of the commentarial tradition, then, the homeless state has, by definition, nothing to do with leaving one's family.

33. The similarities were noticed already in Horner [1957] 1970, 2:251 n. 2; see also von Hinüber [1976] 1994, 71–72, and 1996, 13. On Raṭṭhapāla as one of the foremost disciples, see *Aṅguttara-nikāya* (Morris [1885] 1961, 24.16–.18). For an English translation, see Woodward [1932] 1960, 18.

34. Sudinna's ordination seems not to be mentioned in either the Chinese or the Tibetan text. It is mentioned in other *vinayas*: *Mahīśāsaka-vinaya,* T. 1421 (xxii) 2c28–29 (*juan* 1); Pāli Vinaya, Vin 3:15.1–.2; *BD* 1:26; *Sarvāstivāda-vinaya,* T. 1435 (xxiii) 1a11–12 (*juan* 1).

35. sTog, *'Dul ba,* CA 32b3; T. 1442 (xxiii) 628a21–22 (*juan* 1). Anālayo 2012, 408 n. 23, "doubts the present instance depicts a monk who actually lives at home." Note, however, his translation (408): "[Despite] having gone forth, he dwelled in close association with his kinsfolk" (square brackets in original). Martini 2012, 442, seems less uncertain: "In this way he went forth, but he continued to mix and *stay* with his relations as he had when he was [still] a householder" (my emphasis; square brackets in original).

36. On ordination by messenger and Dharmadinnā, see Hirakawa [1960] 1999–2000, 2:164–165; Finnegan 2009, 156–163 and 201–209 (Dharmadattā); Yao 2011; and Anālayo 2011. The importance of this story was noted already by Nishimoto (1933–1938, 26:405–406).

A number of different types of ordination are recognized in various texts; see Hirakawa [1960] 1999–2000, 2:160–178; Hakamaya 2011. In the lists of ten types of ordination in the *Abhidharmakośabhāṣya,* a text known as the *Sapoduobu pini modeleqie* 薩婆多部毘尼摩得勒伽 (T. 1441), and the *Mātṛkā* of the *Uttaragrantha* of the *Mūlasarvāstivāda-vinaya,* Dharmadinnā is cited as the example of ordination by messenger. For convenience, see Pruden 1988–1990, 2:592; a little less convenient: T. 1441 (xxiii) 594a18–b9 (*juan* 5); sTog, *'Dul ba,* NA 340a6–341a6, esp. the discussion of three types of ordination for nuns

(NA 341a1–6). On the *Sapoduobu pini modeleqie* and its close affinity to parts of the *vinaya* of the Mūlasarvāstivādins, specifically various sections of the *Uttaragrantha,* see Clarke 2004a, 84–86; 2004b, 339; 2006a, 11–12; Kishino 2008; and Clarke 2010b.

37. For the tale of Ardhakāśī, see *Mahīśāsaka-vinaya,* T. 1421 (xxii) 189a26–b15 (*juan* 29); *Sarvāstivāda-vinaya,* T. 1435 (xxiii) 295b13–296a22 (*juan* 41); Pāli Vinaya, Vin 2:277.3–278.12; *BD* 5:383–384 (Aḍḍhakāsī). In the Mahāsāṅghika traditions, the nun is said to be a disciple of Dharmadinnā: T. 1425 (xxii) 474a3–c2 (*juan* 30), translated in Hirakawa 1982, 76–81; Roth 1970, §§70–82, translated in Nolot 1991, 37–42. For the *Dharmaguptaka-vinaya,* see T. 1428 (xxii) 926b7–c14 (*juan* 48).

38. T. 1451 (xxiv) 366b14–c8 (*juan* 32); sTog, *'Dul ba,* THA 239b6–241b2.

39. T. 1451 (xxiv) 366b24–28 (*juan* 32); sTog, *'Dul ba,* THA 240b5–241a1.

40. T. 1451 (xxiv) 366c14–17 (*juan* 32); sTog, *'Dul ba,* THA 241b7–242a2. For another story of a woman who chooses the life of a nun over marriage, see Muldoon-Hules, forthcoming (a).

41. T. 1451 (xxiv) 366c17–20 (*juan* 32); sTog, *'Dul ba,* THA 242a2–4.

42. T. 1451 (xxiv) 366c20–367a8 (*juan* 32); sTog, *'Dul ba,* THA 242a4–243a2.

43. T. 1451 (xxiv) 367a8–14 (*juan* 32); sTog, *'Dul ba,* THA 243a2–6. She is told to wait in the Chinese only.

44. T. 1451 (xxiv) 367a14–18 (*juan* 32); sTog, *'Dul ba,* THA 243a6–b1. Tonsure seems to be mentioned only in the Chinese.

45. T. 1451 (xxiv) 367a18–23 (*juan* 32); sTog, *'Dul ba,* THA 243b1–4.

46. T. 1451 (xxiv) 367a23–26 (*juan* 32); sTog, *'Dul ba,* THA 243b4–6.

47. T. 1451 (xxiv) 367a26–b3 (*juan* 32); sTog, *'Dul ba,* THA 243b6–244a4.

48. T. 1451 (xxiv) 367b3–23 (*juan* 32); sTog, *'Dul ba,* THA 244a4–245a5.

49. T. 1451 (xxiv) 368b2–11 (*juan* 32); sTog, *'Dul ba,* THA 248b1–7. On the *brahmacaryopasthāna-saṃvṛti,* see Kishino 2011.

50. T. 1451 (xxiv) 368b11–13 (*juan* 32); sTog, *'Dul ba,* THA 248b7–249a2.

51. T. 1451 (xxiv) 368b13–14 (*juan* 32); sTog, *'Dul ba,* THA 249a2–3.

52. T. 1451 (xxiv) 368b15–20 (*juan* 32); sTog, *'Dul ba,* THA 249a3–b1.

53. T. 1451 (xxiv) 368b20–28 (*juan* 32); sTog, *'Dul ba,* THA 249b1–5.

54. T. 1451 (xxiv) 368b29–c2 (*juan* 32); sTog, *'Dul ba,* THA 249b6–7.

55. T. 1451 (xxiv) 368c2–6 (*juan* 32); sTog, *'Dul ba,* THA 250a1–4.

56. T. 1451 (xxiv) 368c14–16 (*juan* 32); sTog, *'Dul ba,* THA 250b3–5.

57. T. 1451 (xxiv) 368c16–22 (*juan* 32); sTog, *'Dul ba,* THA 250b5–251a4.

58. T. 1451 (xxiv) 368c22–25 (*juan* 32); sTog, *'Dul ba,* THA 251a4–6.

59. T. 1451 (xxiv) 368c25–369a5 (*juan* 32); sTog, *'Dul ba,* THA 251b2–6.

60. T. 1451 (xxiv) 369a6–7 (*juan* 32); sTog, *'Dul ba,* THA 252a1–2.

61. T. 1451 (xxiv) 369a7–b16 (*juan* 32); sTog, *'Dul ba,* THA 252a2–254a3.

62. There are a number of minor differences between the Chinese and Tibetan here.

63. T. 1442 (xxiii) 628a22–25 (*juan* 1); sTog, *'Dul ba,* CA 32b3–5.

64. sTog, *'Dul ba,* CA 32b5–6; T. 1442 (xxiii) 628a25–26 (*juan* 1).

65. It is often incorrectly assumed that Sudinna was expelled; for examples, see Liz Wilson 1994, 11–12; Faure 1998, 76; Powers 2009, 71 and n. 14. Gyatso 2005, 282, correctly notes that Sudinna was not expelled. Malalasekera [1937] 1960, s.v., Sudinna Kalandakaputta, notes that Sudinna became guilty of the first *pārājika,* but then adds in a footnote a reference to the *ādikammika* rule in the *Samantapāsādikā* whereby the "first offender" is not guilty.

66. See Olivelle's comment that sex as a duty does not necessarily constitute a breach of celibacy, quoted in Chap. 5, n. 8.

67. Kings in India were inclined to confiscate the estates of those who died sonless. See Schopen (2000a) 2004a, 5.

68. When Sudinna returns home, he addresses his mother in Tibetan with the honorific form *yum,* "Mother." Likewise, Sudinna's mother refers to him as "Son, Sudinna" (*bu bzang byin*); sTog, *'Dul ba,* CA 34a2, 34a7.

69. Parental consent is a generally accepted monastic requirement found throughout the *vinayas.*

70. T. 1421 (xxii) 2c8–9 (*juan* 1).

71. T. 1421 (xxii) 2c15–16 (*juan* 1).

72. T. 1421 (xxii) 2c19–20 (*juan* 1). For the Pāli version of the Sudinna story, see *BD* 1:25, where Sudinna's friends assure his parents that "after he has gone forth [they] may see him again."

73. T. 1421 (xxii) 2c24 (*juan* 1). The Pāli version of the Sudinna story does not seem to contain the promise, but the refrain is found twice in the *Raṭṭhapāla-sutta* (Chalmers [1898] 1960, 60.11–.12 and .21–.22; Horner [1957] 1970, 2:254–255; Ñāṇamoli and Bodhi [1995] 2001, 680).

74. See Chap. 3, Sec. 1, for a similar agreement made between husband and wife.

75. Waldschmidt tells us that in the *Rāṣṭrapāla-sūtra,* Rāṣṭrapāla is granted permission to join the monastic order only on the "condition that he would visit his parents some day after his ordination" (1980, 361).

76. For the *sutta,* see Chalmers [1898] 1960, 62.27–.28; Horner [1957] 1970, 2:257; Ñāṇamoli and Bodhi [1995] 2001, 682.

77. For the Pāli Vinaya, see Vin 3:16.6–.7; *BD* 1:28. For the *sutta,* see references in n. 76 above.

78. Steinthal [1885] 1948, 5–6. For a full translation of the story, see Masefield 1994, 6–7. For an English translation of the story of Saṅgāmaji as preserved in the (Shorter) Chinese *Saṃyukta-āgama,* see Bingenheimer 2006, 39–40. See also Bailey and Mabbett 2003, 164. Note also the comments by Axel Michaels in Luz and Michaels 2006, 162.

79. On this term, see pp. 81–82.

80. Masefield 1994, 6.

81. The silence here is probably best understood not as a sign of assent,

as is common in *vinaya* texts, but as one of disapproval or dissent. See Schopen (1995b) 2004a, 180, for silence as a sign of "consternation."

82. Masefield 1994, 7.

83. See Woodward [1926] 1977, 70–74, for the Pāli text. For a translation, see Masefield 1994–1995, 1:108–113.

84. He had gone forth while his wife was pregnant; see Masefield 1994–1995, 1:110.

85. Ibid., 1:109.

86. Ibid.

87. Ibid., 1:110.

88. Ibid.

89. Ibid., 1:111.

90. Masefield 1994, 7.

91. Ibid.

92. Masefield 1994–1995, 1:112.

93. Ibid., 1:233 n. 1117.

94. Ibid., 1:110.

95. Ibid., 1:108.

96. Ibid., 1:233 n. 1117.

97. Ibid.

98. Materials for Raṭṭhapāla's or Saṅgāmaji's families are much more sparse. Note, however, that Saṅgāmaji's brother was also a monk (Posiya Thera, who also had a wife and son); see Malalasekera [1937] 1960, s.vv., Saṅgāmaji Thera; Posiya Thera.

99. The *Dharmaguptaka-*, *Mahīśāsaka-*, *Mūlasarvāstivāda-*, and *Sarvāstivāda-vinayas* mention only the son: T. 1428 (xxii) 570a24–27 (*juan* 1); T. 1421 (xxii) 3a28–29 (*juan* 1); sTog, *'Dul ba,* CA 37b5–6; T. 1442 (xxiii) 629a10–13 (*juan* 1); T. 1435 (xxiii) 1b14–15 (*juan* 1). We do not know where Sudinna's renunciant family lived, and whether or not they lived together. Sudinna's wife presumably lived in a nunnery; Sudinna and son may have dwelt in the same monastery.

100. The Pāli mentions both mother and son; Vin 3:19.11–.12; Sp 1:215.24–.26; *BD* 1:34.

101. *Dharmaguptaka-vinaya,* T. 1428 (xxii) 570a27–29 (*juan* 1); *Mahīśāsaka-vinaya,* T. 1421 (xxii) 3a28–29 (*juan* 1); *Mūlasarvāstivāda-vinaya,* sTog, *'Dul ba,* CA 37b6–38a6; T. 1442 (xxiii) 629a13–22 (*juan* 1); *Sarvāstivāda-vinaya,* T. 1435 (xxiii) 1b15–16 (*juan* 1).

102. Vin 3:19.7–.12; *BD* 1:33–34; Malalasekera [1937] 1960, s.v., Bījaka.

103. This stock phrase appears throughout the *Mūlasarvāstivāda-vinaya* with some variation. The monk (or nun) is generally asked if he (or she) is visiting the house of a relative or of his/her donor or family. In addition to the two narratives dealing with barbers (references in next note), see the narratives cited in n. 105 below on leather work and bowl mending. Note that the full text of

the stock phrase is often abbreviated, as is the case in the Sanskrit and Chinese versions of the leather-work narrative.

104. *Kṣudrakavastu,* sTog, *'Dul ba,* TA 300a5–301a3; T. 1451 (xxiv) 275a3–19 (*juan* 15). For a parallel story for nuns, see sTog, *'Dul ba,* TA 306a6–307a5; T. 1451 (xxiv) 276a23–26 (*juan* 16). For a narratively sparser version of the allowance of barbering tools to monks, see the *Sarvāstivāda-vinaya,* T. 1435 (xxiii) 280b2–5 (*juan* 39); for nuns, see T. 1435 (xxiii) 280c17–20 (*juan* 39).

105. The *Mūlasarvāstivāda-vinaya* allows monks who are skilled in secular crafts to continue to practice their crafts subsequent to ordination provided they do so *pratigupte:* in private/hidden/secluded—the meaning is not entirely clear. For a sample of such stories, see the following: on leather work (*Carmavastu,* GMs iii 4:210.6–.14; sTog, *'Dul ba,* KA 395b6–396a7; T. 1447 [xxiii] 1057b11–18 [*juan* b]); mending bowls (*Kṣudrakavastu,* sTog, *'Dul ba,* TA 45a6–46a1; T. 1451 [xxiv] 217b23–c12 [*juan* 3]); barbering (*Kṣudrakavastu,* sTog, *'Dul ba,* TA 300a5–301a3; T. 1451 [xxiv] 275a3–19 [*juan* 15]—this is to be done in a secluded place, according to Yijing's Chinese translation, lest the laity give rise to contempt [勿使俗流致生譏笑]); and dressing wounds (*Kṣudrakavastu,* sTog, *'Dul ba,* THA 51b2–52a7; T. 1451 [xxiv] 327c8–19 [*juan* 25]—here too the Chinese is particularly clear: one must not let the laity see this [勿令俗見]). This list is not intended to be comprehensive. On nuns with barbering skills, see *Kṣudrakavastu,* sTog, *'Dul ba,* TA 306a6–307a5; T. 1451 (xxiv) 276a23–26 (*juan* 16). A full study of these practices, all polluting in brahmanical India, is a desideratum. For another example, see the story of father and son barbers on pp. 69–70.

106. On monks and their relations with craftsmen, see Schopen (2001) 2004a, 130–131.

107. See also the story in Chap. 3, Sec. 1, on monks visiting their wives. For an example of a father visiting his son, now a monk, in the monastery, see *Kṣudrakavastu,* sTog, *'Dul ba,* TA 275a7–276a5; T. 1451 (xxiv) 269c26–270a10 (*juan* 14).

108. T. 1421 (xxii) 169b9–11 (*juan* 26).

109. T. 1421 (xxii) 169b7–9 (*juan* 26).

110. The Indic term given here as *pācattika* appears in various forms, each *nikāya* using a slight variant. For convenience, I have here used the Mahāsāṅghika-Lokottaravādin term. The Mahīśāsaka form remains, as far as I know, unknown; a Sanskrit text has yet to surface. See also Chap. 4, n. 47.

111. T. 1421 (xxii) 55b20–23 (*juan* 8). Note also the rule in this *vinaya* that makes it a *pācattika* offense for monks who are not sick to eat more than one meal at a luncheon invitation (T. 1421 [xxii] 51b8–9 [*juan* 7]). The *vibhaṅga,* however, stipulates that "if it is the house of a relative, exceeding one meal is an offense of wrongdoing" (T. 1421 [xxii] 51b15 [*juan* 7]). See n. 123 below on offenses of wrongdoing.

112. Note, however, a passage in the *Mūlasarvāstivāda-vinaya* which indicates an awareness that some monks in fact did enter the religious life for the

food; see GMs iii 4:52.1–.7; Eimer 1983, 2:307.1–.11; T. 1444 (xxiii) 1038b27–c5 (*juan* 4). A detailed study of diet in Buddhist monasteries is a desideratum.

113. The same was said long ago about medieval English monasticism; see Jessopp 1889, 155–156.

114. *Mūlasarvāstivāda-vinaya Nidāna,* T. 1452 (xxiv) 432c14–21 (*juan* 5); sTog, *'Dul ba,* NA 188b5–189a5.

115. It is unclear whether this is the father's or daughter's line.

116. *Mūlasarvāstivāda-vinaya Nidāna,* T. 1452 (xxiv) 432c21–28 (*juan* 5); sTog, *'Dul ba,* NA 189a5–b2.

117. *Mūlasarvāstivāda-vinaya Nidāna,* T. 1452 (xxiv) 433a1–4 (*juan* 5); sTog, *'Dul ba,* NA 189b3–5. I am tempted to ignore the *zhuzhi* 住止 translated here as "stay"; it is not found in the Tibetan translation where we simply find *gnyen dang lhan cig 'dre bar nye spyod kyi sdom pa* "permission to partake [of food, etc.] in union with relatives," nor in the collection of formal ecclesiastical acts preserved in the *Mūlasarvāstivāda-vinaya Ekaśatakakarman,* T. 1453 (xxiv) 486a22–b19 (*juan* 7). There is a parallel text preserved in Tibetan (Tōhoku 4118, *Las brgya rtsa gcig pa*), but the Chinese and Tibetan do not correspond very well; see Chap. 4, n. 138, on the existence of at least two Mūlasarvāstivādin *vinaya* traditions, of which this discrepancy may provide further evidence. I do not understand this passage to allow nuns to live at home, although other passages clearly do allow such.

118. *Mūlasarvāstivāda-vinaya Nidāna,* T. 1452 (xxiv) 433a8–10 (*juan* 5); sTog, *'Dul ba,* NA 190a7–b2. This is a very minor class of offense, one not recognized in the *prātimokṣa*s.

119. See also the passage in the *Mahīśāsaka-vinaya* about nuns who run to the safety of their relatives' homes when they become frightened in the midst of their travels (T. 1421 [xxii] 80a26–28 [*juan* 11]).

120. See the comment by Olivelle on renouncers who return home for meals on p. 156.

121. See n. 117 above.

122. An ellipsis in the Chinese text, and possibly in the underlying Indic.

123. This type of offense, translated here as "wrongdoing" (Sanskrit *duṣkṛta*), is only to be confessed, and even then not necessarily to another monk, but to oneself. A monk is to think to himself, "I should not do that." See Hirakawa [1964] 2000, 1:309–315.

124. T. 1421 (xxii) 96b13–19 (*juan* 14).

125. The same rule is also found in the Pāli Vinaya, but there is no mention of houses of relatives (*BD* 3:275–276).

126. T. 1428 (xxii) 928a17–21 (*juan* 49).

127. See, however, the story of Dharmadinnā on pp. 48–49. See also n. 117 above. It may be useful here to consider the practice of "home asceticism" in late antiquity. Elizabeth Clark (1999, 34) tells us that "simply adopting an ascetic lifestyle while residing at home was another popular option, especially for female

ascetics, some of whom stayed in their parental households, or, as widows, in their own homes."

128. T. 1435 (xxiii) 151b4–22 (*juan* 21).

129. T. 1435 (xxiii) 151b6–7 (*juan* 21).

130. See the comments of Kohn (2003, 57) on p. 46.

131. Monier-Williams [1899] 2000, s.v., *pra√vraj*. See n. 19 above for the Pāli equivalent.

132. T. 1435 (xxiii) 151b8–9 (*juan* 21).

133. T. 1435 (xxiii) 151b14–15 (*juan* 21). For a discussion of nuns who become pregnant, see Chap. 4, Sec. 4; for monks who have sex, see Clarke 2009a.

134. T. 1435 (xxiii) 151b21–22 (*juan* 21).

135. Clearly, part of the problem is the public nature of the declaration, and not the fact that the monk and novice continue to refer to each other with biological kinship terms; see also the story (p. 71) in which rather than enacting a general rule against pushing people, the Buddha is made to admonish one for pushing his father.

136. T. 1428 (xxii) 810c16–23 (*juan* 34).

137. This might simply refer to an elderly monk, although the term is often used to indicate monastic seniority.

138. Eimer 1983, 2:193.7–195.7; T. 1444 (xxiii) 1032c7–29 (*juan* 3).

139. Yijing translates this criticism as "How is it that *bhikṣus* initiate their own flesh and blood?" (何故苾芻度此血團). This, however, does not fit the context since in Yijing's translation neither are the onlookers informed that this novice is the son of the monk nor does the novice refer to his father as such. I have followed the Tibetan.

140. T. 1421 (xxii) 115c22–116a3 (*juan* 17).

141. For a parallel, see the story about the newly delivered mother who carries her baby in one arm and her bowl in another as she goes for alms; *Mahīśāsaka-vinaya,* T. 1421 (xxii) 92b7–12 (*juan* 13). For further details, see p. 130.

142. It makes little sense to suggest that the infant or baby—a child who was, or perhaps had to be, carried around—was considered to be a novice, although that is what would be required if we accept the text as it stands. There are no reported textual variants, but Nishimoto (1932–1935, 14:52) long ago suggested that we understand the object of the verb as "one holding a small child." In other words, one should not initiate a man carrying a small child. I remain unconvinced.

143. Vin 1:78.33–79.6; *BD* 4:98–99.

144. Vin 1:79.5–.6; cf. *BD* 4:99.

145. For the *Mahīśāsaka-vinaya,* see T. 1421 (xxii) 117a16–28 (*juan* 17). For the *Dharmaguptaka-vinaya,* see T. 1428 (xxii) 810c24–811a3 (*juan* 34); no lower age limit is specified, but the child must be able to chase away crows. For a detailed discussion of the initiation of novices, see Hirakawa [1964] 2000, 2:162–168, esp. 165–167. For the *Mūlasarvāstivāda-vinaya,* see Eimer 1983,

2:219.3–221.20; see also *Mūlasarvāstivāda-vinaya Nidāna,* T. 1452 (xxiv) 415b21–25 (*juan* 1); sTog, *'Dul ba,* NA 102a7–b3. See also VSS$_{MsB}$ *sūtra* no. 111 (VSPVSG 2009, 96). The *Mahāsāṅghika-vinaya* lists three categories of novices at T. 1425 (xxii) 461b9–12 (*juan* 29): ages 7–13, 14–19, and 20–70.

146. *BD* 4:99 n. 3.

147. T. 1435 (xxiii) 151b23–c1 (*juan* 21).

148. This rule is also found in the Pāli Vinaya, although there is no suggestion that the children are in any way related to Ānanda. See *BD* 4:99.

149. Note also the story in the *Mūlasarvāstivāda-vinaya* about a woman who leaves home for the religious life with her son and four daughters. The son makes a robe, which he wishes to give to his mother. His sisters, however, covet the robe, and this brings about the establishment of a rule concerning the exchange of robes. T. 1443 (xxiii) 1011a25–b11 (*juan* 19). This rule seems not to have a parallel in the Tibetan *Bhikṣuṇī-vibhaṅga.* See, however, the *Ārya-sarvāstivādi-mūla-bhikṣuṇī-prātimokṣa-sūtra-vṛtti,* which is similar to the Chinese but not identical: Peking, bstan 'gyur, *'Dul ba'i 'grel pa,* (vol. 122) DZU [DSU] 150b7–151a5.

150. See Chap. 1, n. 187.

151. See n. 145 above.

152. For a parallel in the *Dharmaguptaka-vinaya,* see T. 1428 (xxii) 874a13–25 (*juan* 42). There both father and son are clearly identified as monks, unlike the *Mahāsāṅghika-vinaya* in which the son might be a novice. In the former, the monks make money by barbering, and then use the money to make an offering to the Buddha. Also see the Mūlasarvāstivāda version at GMs iii 1:280.8–281.18; sTog, *'Dul ba,* GA 50b1–51a7.

153. T. 1425 (xxii) 463a17–b1 (*juan* 29).

154. This father and son barbering team causes other problems in the *Mahāsāṅghika-vinaya.* They are ordained with their tools of trade, and this gives rise to criticism. They are told to throw away their tools but then are allowed to use borrowed tools. This provision also applies to a number of other craftsmen: blacksmiths, carpenters, gold and silver smiths, leather workers, and weavers. T. 1425 (xxii) 489b28–c8 (*juan* 32). For another brief reference to this father and son, see T. 1425 (xxii) 477a17–20 (*juan* 31).

155. T. 1428 (xxii) 982b9–13 (*juan* 56).

156. T. 1428 (xxii) 982b13–20 (*juan* 56). For three separate, and characteristically elliptical, versions of this story in the Pāli Vinaya, see, for convenience, *BD* 1:138–139.

157. See p. 13.

158. T. 1425 (xxii) 523c3–4 (*juan* 37); for an English translation, see Hirakawa 1982, 183. Cf. the Lokottaravādin parallel in Roth 1970, §172; for a French translation, see Nolot 1991, 153.

159. T. 1425 (xxii) 523c4–5 (*juan* 37). With regard to the Lokottaravādin parallel, Roth (1970, §172 n. 1) notes that the mother "asks her daughter to

come over to see her, and the daughter replies that she cannot come like that." The *Mahāsāṅghika-vinaya* (Chinese) is much clearer.

160. On family-friendly Jainism, see Granoff 2006, and the discussion in Chap. 5, Sec. 3.

161. T. 1425 (xxii) 528a13–14 (*juan* 38); for an English translation, see Hirakawa 1982, 249. For a regulation concerning family members on different paths, see the *Mahāsāṅghika-vinaya:* T. 1425 (xxii) 373c28–374a1 (*juan* 18). Cf. Roth 1970, §185; for a French translation, see Nolot 1991, 211.

162. T. 1425 (xxii) 528a14–b4 (*juan* 38). It seems permissible, however, if a factotum (*kalpikārika;* 淨人—on this term, see the references cited in Clarke 2009a, 27 n. 86) makes the donation. For another story of family members following separate religious paths, see Chap. 3, n. 112. For a husband and wife on separate paths, see p. 112.

163. Madan 1987, 17.

164. Olivelle 1995b, 188.

165. Dumont 1960, 38.

166. Ibid., 44.

167. Olivelle 1995b, 188.

168. See, for instance, Schopen 2004d, 236–237.

169. T. 1428 (xxii) 759c7–760a7 (*juan* 28); for an English translation, see Heirman 2002, 2:821–823.

170. Schopen 1985.

171. von Hinüber 1978, 49.

172. Rhys Davids and Oldenberg [1882–1885] 1996, 1:ix. For a detailed analysis of the Theravāda *pātimokkha,* see von Hinüber 1999.

173. Pruitt and Norman 2001, 31; square brackets in original. There are also similar rules for nuns; see nuns' *nissaggiya-pācittiya*s 16–19, 28; Pruitt and Norman 2001, 151, 153, 161.

174. *BD* 2:49.

175. See also *nissaggiya-pācittiya*s 7, 8, 9, 27; Pruitt and Norman 2001, 31, 33, 43; *BD* 2:52, 57, 60–61, 150.

176. Pruitt and Norman 2001, 29–31; square brackets in original. On these rules, see most recently Yamagiwa 2004. See also *nissaggiya-pācittiya* 17, *pācittiya*s 25–26, *pāṭidesanīya* 1; Pruitt and Norman 2001, 39, 53–55, 85. On the rule about having an unrelated nun do one's laundry, see Chap. 3, Sec. 5.

177. *BD* 2:31, and see Horner's n. 6 for further references. See also Chap. 3, n. 143.

Chapter 3: Former Wives from Former Lives

1. Jenner 1993, 1:449. Cf. Waley [1943] 1980, 157.

2. On loss of communion and not expulsion as the punishment for *pārājika* offenses, see Clarke 2009b.

3. *Kṣudrakavastu,* sTog, *'Dul ba,* TA 151a4–154b3; T. 1451 (xxiv) 244a25–245a12 (*juan* 9).

4. For a sampling, see *Vinaya-vibhaṅga,* T. 1442 (xxiii) 805a6–10 (*juan* 32); sTog, *'Dul ba,* CHA 414b3–6 (here the wife also decides to leave home); *Vinaya-vibhaṅga,* T. 1442 (xxiii) 822c11–15 (*juan* 36); sTog, *'Dul ba,* CHA 492b5–493a1; *Pravrajyāvastu,* T. 1444 (xxiii) 1032c7–12 (*juan* 3); Eimer 1983, 2:193.7–.21 (here the householder's son decides to join the order together with his father); *Kṣudrakavastu,* T. 1451 (xxiv) 249b20–23 (*juan* 10); sTog, *'Dul ba,* TA 174a6–b3; *Kṣudrakavastu,* T. 1451 (xxiv) 358c13–17 (*juan* 31); sTog, *'Dul ba,* THA 206a5–b2 (here too the wife leaves home with her husband); *Bhikṣuṇī-vibhaṅga,* T. 1443 (xxiii) 998b22–26 (*juan* 17) (here too the wife also decides to join the order); sTog, *'Dul ba,* NYA 358a5–6 (the Tibetan says that the householder left home together with his wife, and the text is somewhat abbreviated in comparison to the Chinese [the stock phrase is not found in the Tibetan]: *khyim bdag cig chung ma dang lhan cig khyim nas khyim med par rab tu byung nas*). Parallels in the *Bhikṣuṇī-vibhaṅga* in Tibetan are quite often shorter or more abridged than their Chinese counterparts; on the *Bhikṣuṇī-vibhaṅga* and the problems associated with it, see Chap. 4, n. 138, and references therein.

5. Here, in both the recollection and recounting of his promise, the monk refers to his wife as his "former" wife, and this is clearly marked in the Tibetan by the term *sngon* "former, previous" (*sngon gyi chung ma* and *sngon gyi mchis brang*). Tibetan *sngon gyi chung ma* is listed in the *Mahāvyutpatti* (no. 9262) as a standard translation for Sanskrit *purāṇa-dvitīyā* (Ishihama and Fukuda 1989, no. 9197). This term is listed in Monier-Williams' *Sanskrit-English Dictionary* ([1899] 2000, q.v.) as meaning "former wife," but the authority given is the lexicographers. Unfortunately, this term is rarely defined, and even when it is, the definitions seem to say little about the formal marriage tie; see, for instance, Sp 1:211.29–.31. There is evidence to suggest that as a masculine noun this term refers to a "former" husband.

6. The preceptor's use of the term "son" seems to be an example of the use of familial language; see pp. 25–26.

7. The Chinese version of this passage differs slightly.

8. *Kṣudrakavastu,* T. 1451 (xxiv) 244b27–29 (*juan* 9).

9. See, for example, *Kṣudrakavastu,* T. 1451 (xxiv) 251c27 (*juan* 11); sTog, *'Dul ba,* TA 184b1. See also *Kṣudrakavastu,* T. 1451 (xxiv) 357a14–17 (*juan* 30); sTog, *'Dul ba,* THA 200a1–5.

10. The Chinese states that "when he was touched, his mind was thereupon roiled and gave rise to evil thoughts. Thereupon, they had intercourse."

11. The Chinese reads: "I wish to return to the monastery."

12. That this is how laymen usually address their wives—and, according to our texts, they sometimes had multiple wives—is not in doubt, and examples are available in abundance; see, for convenience, Hiraoka 2002, 164 (M). Note, however, that where the Tibetan is precise with its use of a feminine suffix (*bzang*

mo), the Chinese term (*xianshou* 賢首) is not: more often than not it simply means "sir."

13. In discussing Sanskrit drama, Lévi [1890] 1978, 1:109, notes that "the wife always calls her husband '*āryaputra*.' "

14. Oldenberg [1882] 1998, 355.

15. Oldenberg continues: "It is in no way inconsistent with this, if the family of a monk, which desires his return to a worldly status, looks upon his marriage and his rights of property as continuing. . . ." (ibid. n. 2).

16. Schopen (1995b) 2004a, 172.

17. This was made even more explicit by Lingat: "il n'y a rien de changé, légalement, dans les rapports entre les deux époux" (1937, 415).

18. On *kārṣāpaṇa*s, see Thakur 1973, 269–270, and Jain 1995 (see index). See also n. 71 below.

19. *Kṣudrakavastu,* T. 1451 (xxiv) 244c15 (*juan* 9).

20. This rule has been interpreted variously as one against touching/handling/receiving gold/silver/money. See Schopen (2000a) 2004a, 11–15.

21. Although we should probably not make too much of this one passage, note that this woman, "deserted" by her husband, was clearly not left destitute. The woman, in fact, was able to offer her husband some cash for the road.

22. A book-length study of the Group-of-Six is a desideratum. Oldenberg noted long ago that "the longest catalogue of crimes attaches to the Chabbaggiyas, six monks associated together in all mischievous artifices. . . . The Chabbaggiyas figure everywhere as the archcriminals, whose new discoveries in all regions of mischief the spiritual legislation enacted by Buddha follows step by step" ([1882] 1998, 335–336). On Udāyin, a key member of the Group-of-Six, see also nn. 118–119 below. On the Group-of-Six monks, see Schopen 2004c, 176–178; on their humor, see Schopen 2007b and Clarke 2009c. For further references, see Clarke 2009c, 315 n. 19.

23. Monier-Williams ([1899] 2000) gives Agati Grandiflora for *bakapuṣpa* (q.v.), and notes that *baka* is a heron or crane. For *bakapuṣpam*, see *Mahāvyutpatti,* no. 6213 (Ishihama and Fukuda 1989, no. 6191). Note also Bloomfield on the heron "as the typical sham ascetic" (1924, 211–212).

24. See VSSMsB *sūtra* no. 35 (VSPVSG 2004, 65).

25. Skt. *mahallaka*. For a study, see Durt 1980. Note also von Hinüber 1997 and Schopen 2010a.

26. *Kṣudrakavastu,* T. 1451 (xxiv) 245a9–10 (*juan* 9).

27. The Chinese suggests that the four *pārājika*s are to be taught as soon as one is ordained (i.e., as a monk), whereas the Tibetan suggests that this is done upon initiation (i.e., as a novice). At least for adult males, according to some textual traditions, both the initiation and ordination seem to have been performed at the same time. See, for convenience, Bapat and Gokhale 1982, xxv–xxvi.

28. See VSSMsB *sūtra* no. 61 (VSPVSG 2005, 60).

29. *Kṣudrakavastu,* T. 1451 (xxiv) 245a10–12 (*juan* 9).

30. sTog, *'Dul ba,* TA 154b2–3.

31. The sDe dge edition adds no such emendation (sDe dge, *'Dul ba,* THA 102a5).

32. This ruling is not unique to the *Mūlasarvāstivāda-vinaya;* it is also found, for instance, in the monastic codes of the Dharmaguptakas and the Theravādins: T. 1428 (xxii) 815b6–22 (*juan* 35); *BD* 4:124.

33. Liz Wilson 1994, 9.

34. Ohnuma 2000, 51; repeated with minor modification at Ohnuma 2007, 116.

35. The Chinese here reads *wuxiang* 無相, which might also be translated as "undistinguished" or "without characteristics." Tentatively, I have taken this as a translation of Sanskrit *alakṣaṇa,* for which Monier-Williams ([1899] 2000, q.v.) lists, *inter alia,* "inauspicious."

36. Lit., not mutually know (不相知).

37. T. 1425 (xxii) 275b18–c6 (*juan* 6). On this passage, see Durt 1980, 96–97.

38. On this class of offenses, see Chap. 2, n. 118.

39. *Saṅghāvaśeṣa* offenses constitute the second most serious category of ecclesiastical transgressions. See Upasak 1975, s.v., *saṅghādisesa;* Thanissaro 1994, 90, on the category, and 117–119, on this rule; and Prebish 2003, 50.

40. For further examples from the *Mūlasarvāstivāda-vinaya,* see the following stories in which Udāyin visits the house of Guptā, his "former" wife, on or after his alms round: *Vinaya-vibhaṅga,* T. 1442 (xxiii) 710a28–b29 (*juan* 16); sTog, *'Dul ba,* CA 456a3–4 (note that the Tibetan, unlike the Chinese, here and below gives Guptā as the householder's wife [*khyim bdag gi chung ma sbed ma*]; on the complexities surrounding the exact nature of their relationship, see n. 124 below; note also that this is exactly what Udāyin himself calls her [see pp. 100–101]); *Vinaya-vibhaṅga,* T. 1442 (xxiii) 807b25–c27 (*juan* 33); sTog, *'Dul ba,* CHA 430a2–3; *Vinaya-vibhaṅga,* T. 1442 (xxiii) 720c7–9 (*juan* 18); sTog, *'Dul ba,* CHA 1b2–2a3 (summarized on pp. 99–104), and a version in the *Bhikṣuṇī-vibhaṅga,* T. 1443 (xxiii) 952a15–17 (*juan* 9); cf. sDe dge, *'Dul ba,* TA 231a4–5: note here, however, that at least according to the sDe dge edition, Udāyin visits *sbed ma'i khyim* (Guptā's house); note also that the sTog Palace edition does not seem to include this story (sTog, *'Dul ba,* NYA 311a7ff.). For more examples, see n. 164 below.

41. This term usually refers to attempted offenses (i.e., attempted murder vs. murder). In this case, a *sthūlātyaya* would refer to an attempted *saṅghāvaśeṣa.* See Upasak 1975, s.v., *thullaccaya.* Note also Rhys Davids and Oldenberg [1882–1885] 1996, 1:xxv.

42. T. 1425 (xxii) 275c6–13 (*juan* 6).

43. T. 1421 (xxii) 12a16–13a11 (*juan* 2); T. 1428 (xxii) 582c15–584a15 (*juan* 3); T. 1435 (xxiii) 18a11–20b6 (*juan* 3); T. 1442 (xxiii) 685c24–688a17 (*juan* 12); sTog, *'Dul ba,* CA 327a6–344a4; *BD* 1:229–245. For the rules con-

cerning nuns: T. 1421 (xxii) 79a12–17 (*juan* 11); T. 1425 (xxii) 517c1–3 (*juan* 36); T. 1428 (xxii) 718b2–8 (*juan* 22); T. 1443 (xxiii) 931c13–933c13 (*juan* 5); sTog, *'Dul ba,* NYA 117a4–130a6. Note, however, that some traditions do not list this rule separately for nuns in their *vibhaṅgas* since it is already explained in the monks' text; see Hirakawa 1982, 135–137 nn. 1 and 3.

44. For the definition of illicit relationships, see *Vinayasaṃgraha,* T. 1458 (xxiv) 542c27–28 (*juan* 3).

45. T. 1443 (xxiii) 931c13–26 (*juan* 5); sTog, *'Dul ba,* NYA 118b3–119a1. Note that directly before this (sTog, *'Dul ba,* NYA 117a4–118b3), the Tibetan but not the Chinese text includes the story about Kāla Mṛgāraputra (*ri dags 'dzin gyi bu nag po;* 黑鹿子), found also in the *Vinaya-vibhaṅga* (T. 1442 [xxiii] 685c24–686a25 [*juan* 12]; sTog, *'Dul ba,* CA 327a6–331a1). At the end of both *bhikṣu* and Tibetan *bhikṣuṇī* versions, it is specifically stated that the Buddha did *not* establish a rule in this regard (*de ni re zhig byung ba yin gyi / sangs rgyas bcom ldan 'das kyis re zhig 'dul ba la nyan thos rnams kyi bslab pa'i gzhi bca' ba ni ma mdzad do //;* 然世尊尙未爲諸聲聞弟子於毘奈耶制其學處; quote from *bhikṣu* version). Viśeṣamitra, on the other hand, mentions the frame-story of Kāla Mṛgāraputra and not the one connected with the Group-of-Six (*Vinayasaṃgraha,* T. 1458 [xxiv] 542c8–13 [*juan* 3]; Peking, bstan 'gyur, *'Dul ba'i 'grel pa,* [vol. 120] PHU 166b7–8). These discrepancies may be further evidence of multiple Mūlasarvāstivādin traditions; see Chap. 4, n. 138. Note that in the *Sarvāstivāda-vinaya,* the rule about matchmaking is delivered on account of the story of the monk Kāla Mṛgāraputra (T. 1435 [xxiii] 18a11–c2 [*juan* 3]). The statement that the Buddha did *not* establish a rule with regard to specific incidents is found throughout the *Mūlasarvāstivāda-vinaya* in numerous places.

46. Bloomfield 1924, 238.

47. Warder 1972–2011, 4:273; Kher 1979; and Chapekar 2003.

48. Baldissera 2005, 77–78.

49. See, for convenience, Ryder 1927, 89 and 178ff. Dharmarakṣitā is apparently called a *śākyabhikṣukī* (Bloomfield 1924, 239).

50. See Kāle 1967, 15ff., for a summary of the plot. Also noticed in Kher 1979, 212.

51. Bloomfield 1924, 238.

52. See, for instance, Doniger and Kakar 2002, 119 (5.4.43); and Kangle 1965–1972, 3:154 and 206 on nuns as spies.

53. Sarma 1931. Cf. Kane 1941, 620: "The position of the writers on dharmaśāstra is that marriage is a saṁskāra. . . ." See also Sharma 1993. The same seems to hold for modern Hindu law; see Menski 2001, 12.

54. Kapadia 1958, 168–169. See also Virdi 1972, 1–2 and 19–20.

55. Kane 1941, 620, and Virdi 1972, 26. Virdi adds that "both in abandonment and supersession the wife retained her status of a wife and had to be maintained" (p. 31); see the useful section on "The Distinction Between Abandonment and Supersession" (pp. 27–32). In a discussion of alternatives to divorce,

Lariviere 1991, 38, cites a passage in the *Nāradasmṛti* that requires women to supersede their husbands in the event of "five catastrophes," one of which is the husband's world renunciation.

56. Kane 1941, 620.

57. Ibid. Sarma 1931 uses the term "divorce" uncritically. See also Sharma 1993, 36–40.

58. Virdi 1972, 25. See also Banerjee 1879, 182.

59. Commenting on an early passage in the *Arthaśāstra* that seems to allow divorce (see n. 74 below), Basham suggests that "these provisions . . . do not appear in later lawbooks, and were probably forgotten by Gupta times" ([1954] 1959, 173).

60. In the following, I neither distinguish between, nor employ in a technical sense, the terms "divorce," "(marital) dissolution," or "annulment." Scholars of brahmanical law seem not to agree on usage here, either. Note Banerjee, for instance, who states—and here we introduce another term, "separation"—that "though the Hindu law does not allow divorce, it is not so unreasonable as to compel married parties to live together as man and wife under all possible circumstances. . . . Separation, called in Hindu law desertion (*tyag*), differs from divorce . . . it can never have the effect of dissolving the marriage tie completely" (1879, 186).

61. Sharma 1993, 40, states that "we do not find any specific reference to divorce in Buddhist text. Instances of remarriage are there but their number is small." Note, however, the previous statement that "in the Baudhdha [*sic*] literature, there are instances of divorce" (p. 38).

62. T. 1425 (xxii) 273b7 (*juan* 6). Tai 1978, 77, lists *fang* 放 "to send away" and *li* 離 "to part" (see n. 100 below) as traditional expressions "meaning to divorce and terminate all relations with the wife."

63. The earliest occurrence of the term *lihun* 離婚 may well be in this *vinaya* (translated 416–418 C.E.). In non-Buddhist Chinese texts this term is found at least as early as the fifth-century *Shishuo xinyu* 世說新語; see Morohashi [1955–1960] 1986, 11.42140.70. Tai 1978, 77, states that "the term now employed, *li-hun,* was not used, although it was in existence as early as the Nan-Pei dynasty (A.D. 420–477)." Tai further cites Chen Guyuan (Ch'en Ku-yüan) 陳顧遠 in noting a passage in the *Jinshu* 晉書 (*Annals of the Jin;* compiled 644, covering the period 265–419; see Wilkinson 2000, 503) in which we find the phrase *zhao ting lihun* 詔聽離婚 "The Emperor permits divorce" (p. 77 n. 13; Tai's translation). Tai tells us that in China, unlike in India, "since ancient times, divorce has been the means for effective dissolution of a valid marriage. The marital relationship of a husband and wife is terminated from the time of the divorce onward" (p. 75). On divorce in premodern China, see also Dull 1978, 52–64. We must be careful not to assume that modern notions or concepts of divorce can be directly mapped on to *lihun* 離婚 in our texts.

64. T. 1425 (xxii) 273b7–8 (*juan* 6).

65. Jamison 1996, 253.

66. Virdi 1972, 19 and 29. Doniger and Smith 1991, 202, citing Manu ix 46, translate: "A wife is not freed from her husband by sale or rejection." See also Olivelle 2005, 192. This passage is widely cited as the justification for the claim that divorce (or marital dissolution) is not recognized in brahmanical law (see, for instance, Banerjee 1879, 182 and 184).

67. Lingat [1973] 1993, 177.

68. Ibid., 195. See also Virdi 1972, 32: "How then [i.e., if *Dharmaśāstra* does not permit divorce] is it possible to claim that Hindus in India are familiar with divorce? The answer lies in the field of custom."

69. The dating is that offered by Lariviere 1989, 2:xxii (see also xix). Lariviere suggests that "there was no single 'author'" of the *Nāradasmṛti* (xxiii).

70. Ibid., 2:11 (*Nārada* 1.34).

71. It seems that there are nineteen coins (*qian* 錢) to a *kārṣāpaṇa*. See T. 1425 (xxii) 242c22 (*juan* 3).

72. On this form of cotton, see Ayyar and Aithal 1964.

73. T. 1425 (xxii) 273b8–10 (*juan* 6).

74. Kangle 1965–1972, 2:203 (3.3.16). Traditional brahmanical society recognized various types of "approved" marriages, but "if the marriage is in an unapproved form," Virdi notes, "then it can be dissolved by mutual consent, if both [parties] have come to hate each other" (1972, 14, citing *Arthaśāstra* 3.3.16). See also Altekar 1962, 84–85.

75. For the *Mūlasarvāstivāda-vinaya,* see *Vinaya-vibhaṅga,* T. 1442 (xxiii) 686b14–c5 (*juan* 12); sTog, *'Dul ba,* CA 332a5–333b7. Also see the *Bhikṣuṇī-vibhaṅga,* T. 1443 (xxiii) 932a1–22 (*juan* 5); sTog, *'Dul ba,* NYA 119a2–120b4. See also Viśeṣamitra's commentary: *Vinayasaṃgraha,* T. 1458 (xxiv) 542c17–27 (*juan* 3); Peking, bstan 'gyur, *'Dul ba'i 'grel pa,* (vol. 120) PHU 167a2–5. For the *Sarvāstivāda-vinaya,* see T. 1435 (xxiii) 18c14–25 (*juan* 3). Some monastic codes mention ten forms of matrimony. *BD* 1:237 gives ten types. Ten types of women are given in the *Mahīśāsaka-vinaya* (T. 1421 [xxii] 12c9–16 [*juan* 2]), and twenty in the *Dharmaguptaka-vinaya* (T. 1428 [xxii] 583a19–b4 [*juan* 3]). See also *Mahāsāṅghika-vinaya,* T. 1425 (xxii) 272c28–273a24 (*juan* 6).

76. For the brahmanical forms of marriage, see Sternbach 1965 and Jamison 1996, 210–218. Note also Muldoon-Hules, forthcoming (b).

77. The Sanskrit terms are supplied from the *Mahāvyutpatti,* nos. 9448–9454, with corrections from Ishihama and Fukuda 1989, nos. 9380–9385 and 9395, and confirmed by a Sanskrit parallel in the *Dharmaskandha* edited from the Gilgit manuscripts in Matsuda 1986, 14–15.

78. There are minor differences between the definitions found in Tibetan and Chinese. sTog, *'Dul ba,* CA 332a6–b1; T. 1442 (xxiii) 686b19–21 (*juan* 12). The Chinese text adds *fu* 婦 "wife" to all of these terms; the Tibetan adds *chung ma*. See also Matsuda 1986, folio 21r11.

79. sTog, *'Dul ba,* CA 332b1–3; T. 1442 (xxiii) 686b22–23 (*juan* 12). See also Matsuda 1986, folio 21r11–12.

80. sTog, *'Dul ba,* CA 332b3–333a2; T. 1442 (xxiii) 686b23–27 (*juan* 12). See also Matsuda 1986, folio 21r12–13.

81. sTog, *'Dul ba,* CA 333a2–5; T. 1442 (xxiii) 686b27–29 (*juan* 12). See also Matsuda 1986, folio 21v1.

82. sTog, *'Dul ba,* CA 333a5–b1; T. 1442 (xxiii) 686b29–c2 (*juan* 12). See also Matsuda 1986, folio 21v1–2.

83. sTog, *'Dul ba,* CA 333b1–5; T. 1442 (xxiii) 686c2–4 (*juan* 12). See also Matsuda 1986, folio 21v2–3. Cf. *BHSD,* s.v., *samajīvikā.*

84. sTog, *'Dul ba,* CA 333b5–7; T. 1442 (xxiii) 686c4–5 (*juan* 12). See also Matsuda 1986, folio 21v4, although there are only a few *akṣaras* here.

85. The Chinese text is briefly discussed in Hirakawa 1993–1995, 1:428. There seems to be a partial overlap between this list and the types of slaves studied in Schopen 2010c.

86. The Tibetan suggests that these are stages. The text runs through the list some eight times, with a successive step being completed each time. The Chinese is more explicit about the fact that we are dealing with marital annulment.

87. The Mūlasarvāstivādin *Vinayasaṃgraha* attributed to Viśeṣamitra analyzes each rule in the *Vinaya-vibhaṅga* into some twenty-one categories, one of which is the *kleśa* or *upakleśa* associated with each offense; T. 1458 (xxiv) 530c21–531c2 (*juan* 2); Peking, bstan 'gyur, *'Dul ba'i 'grel pa,* (vol. 120) PHU 133b7–136a3. For a similar classification for nuns' rules, again into twenty-one categories, see *Ārya-sarvāstivādi-mūla-bhikṣuṇī-prātimokṣa-sūtra-vṛtti* (Peking, bstan 'gyur, *'Dul ba'i 'grel pa,* [vol. 122] DZU [DSU] 34b1–36a1); on this text, see Chap. 4, n. 138.

The author of the *Vinayasaṃgraha* uses a system of twenty-seven *kleśa*s (煩惱) in the Chinese translation (T. 1458 [xxiv] 531a21–b1 [*juan* 2]) and twenty-five specified in Tibetan (*nyon mongs pa ni…nyi shu rtsa lnga'o*), although I count twenty-six (Peking, bstan 'gyur, *'Dul ba'i 'grel pa,* [vol. 120] PHU 134b7–135a5). I have not been able to identify the source of this *kleśa/upakleśa* list. With regard to the offense of matchmaking, the mental affliction or *kleśa* involved in this offense is related to conflict (*rtsod pa byung ba'i nyon mongs pa;* 諍恨) (*Vinayasaṃgraha,* Peking, bstan 'gyur, *'Dul ba'i 'grel pa,* [vol. 120] PHU 166b7–8; T. 1458 [xxiv] 542c10 [*juan* 3]).

As noted in Clarke 2009c, 322 n. 34, this type of *kleśa* analysis is also found in the Mūlasarvāstivādin *Prātimokṣa-sūtra-paddhati,* but, interestingly, this text does not always agree with the *Vinayasaṃgraha* in terms of the *kleśa*s associated with specific rules. With regard to this rule, the fifth *saṅghāvaśeṣa,* for instance, the *kleśa* is said to be that of lust (Peking, bstan 'gyur, *'Dul ba'i 'grel pa,* [vol. 120] PU 63a2: *nyon mongs pa ni 'dod chags*). Note also that the *Prātimokṣa-sūtra-paddhati* attributes this rule to the actions of the Group-of-Six (*gang zag ni drug sde*), whereas, as mentioned in n. 45 above, the *Vinayasaṃgraha* mentions only the narrative of Kāla Mṛgāraputra. The *Prātimokṣa-sūtra-ṭīkā-vinaya-samuccaya* by Vimalamitra takes a middle position, giving the protagonist as Kāla Mṛgāraputra but the *kleśa* as lust: *gang zag ni ri dags 'dzin gyi bu nag po / nyon mongs pa ni 'dod chags /* (Peking, bstan 'gyur, *'Dul ba'i 'grel pa,* [vol. 120] BU 96a7).

88. The wife here is restricted to one of the first three types given above.

89. The Chinese text is somewhat abridged, giving us little more than an enumeration of the seven. Consequently, unlike the Tibetan (and Sanskrit—see n. 91 below), the Chinese terms are not given in the negative: *'thabs pa nyid kyi mod yin la;* 正鬪即離. The English glosses are tentative, and await further study. Here again there is some variation between the Tibetan and Chinese (and Sanskrit).

90. *'thabs pa'i 'og ma yin pa;* 鬪後方離.

91. *tilintilikācchinnatva; dum pa ma bcad pa;* 折草三段離. Sanskrit equivalents given here and below are from Guṇaprabha's *Vinayasūtra* (Sankrityayana 1981, 24.27–.29, with corrections based on *sūtra* 2.498 of the text input by Yonezawa Yoshiyasu et al. available at http://gretil.sub.uni-goettingen.de/gretil/1_sanskr/4_rellit/buddh/vinsutru.htm; Peking, bstan 'gyur, *'Dul ba'i 'grel pa,* [vol. 123] ZU 24b1–2), and not the *Mūlasarvāstivāda-vinaya* itself. For Guṇaprabha's *Autocommentary,* see Peking, bstan 'gyur, *'Dul ba'i 'grel pa,* (vol. 124) 'U [ḤU] 142b2ff. For a short definition of these seven, see *Prātimokṣa-sūtra-ṭīkā-vinaya-samuccaya,* Peking, bstan 'gyur, *'Dul ba'i 'grel pa,* (vol. 120) BU 101a2–b2. See also *Vinayasaṃgraha,* T. 1458 (xxiv) 543a21–27 (*juan* 3); Peking, bstan 'gyur, *'Dul ba'i 'grel pa,* (vol. 120) PHU 168a2–3.

92. *trisaṅkarāparitatva; rde'u gsum ma gtor ba;* 三方擲瓦離.

93. *ācārapratiniḥsṛṣṭatva; cho ga ma btang ba;* 依法對親離. The *Prātimokṣa-sūtra-ṭīkā-vinaya-samuccaya* (Peking, bstan 'gyur, *'Dul ba'i 'grel pa,* [vol. 120] BU 101b1) gives *cho ga btang ba zhes bya ba ni khyim so 'am khyim thab kyi rkang pa bkru ba la sogs pa phral gyi bya ba ni cho ga ste / de btang ba'o //.*

94. *abhāryānuśrāvitatva; chung ma ma yin par ma bsgrags pa;* 言非我婦離.

95. *ghaṇṭā ca ghuṣṭatva; dril ma bsgrags pa;* 普告衆人離.

96. sTog, *'Dul ba,* CA 342b4–343b7; T. 1442 (xxiii) 687a4–13 (*juan* 12).

97. Or just the husband? This remains unclear.

98. A *sthūlātyaya* is more serious than an offense of wrongdoing, but still less serious than a *saṅghāvaśeṣa* offense, which incurs a probation of six days and nights.

99. The Tibetan and Sanskrit suggest "sounded by a bell." Vinītadeva's *Vinaya-vibhaṅga-pada-vyākhyāna* adds that this is performed at a "temple and so forth" (**devakula, lha'i gnas*) (Peking, bstan 'gyur, *'Dul ba'i 'grel pa,* [vol. 122] WU 107b6).

100. See n. 62 above. *Li* 離 is one of the terms used in traditional Chinese law as "what may be considered equivalent to the term 'divorce' within the meaning of the present law" (Tai 1978, 77).

101. At stage six, a monk incurs three offenses of wrongdoing, two *sthūlātyaya* offenses, and a *saṅghāvaśeṣa;* at stage seven, three, four, and two offenses, respectively. A *saṅghāvaśeṣa* offense is deemed to have taken place at

stages six or seven, but this is only the case for any of the first three classes of wife. For the other four classes of wife—and this seems to suggest their inferiority—a monk incurs a *saṅghāvaśeṣa* offense for reconciling a couple at any of the seven stages.

102. Hirakawa 1993–1995, 1:433–434, refers to this rule with the Japanese term *rikon* 離婚 "divorce." Hirakawa suggests that "divorce" is only recognized at the seventh stage for any of the first three types of wives, and Yijing's Chinese text seems to support this view. The Tibetan, however, suggests that this is equally valid for the sixth stage as well. At least this follows if one accepts that "divorce" is established at the stage at which a monk incurs a *saṅghāvaśeṣa* offense. Horner also mentions divorce (*BD* 1:244 n. 2).

103. See, for convenience, Hirakawa 1982, 60. On parental permission, see Crosby 2005. Note also the case of Dharmadinnā (Chap. 2, Sec. 2), who is ordained by messenger against her parents' wishes.

104. See n. 1 above.

105. Liz Wilson 1994, 8.

106. Cf. *BD* 3:252–253. For a further sample of passages dealing with men and women leaving home for the religious life together, see *Dharmaguptaka-vinaya,* T. 1428 (xxii) 738c20–739a20 (*juan* 25); and *Mahāsāṅghika-vinaya,* T. 1425 (xxii) 532c26–533a8 (*juan* 38). For the *Mūlasarvāstivāda-vinaya,* see—again as a sample—references in n. 4 above. See also n. 115 below.

107. Or perhaps "diffidently" (輒).

108. T. 1421 (xxii) 94c14–26 (*juan* 14).

109. T. 1421 (xxii) 94c23–25 (*juan* 14).

110. Basing her comments on the Pāli version of this story, Horner (*BD* 3:252 n. 2) suggests that "nuns had access to the monks' quarters." I can see nothing in her text, however, to suggest this, and the Chinese parallel in fact suggests quite the opposite. Note also the *Mūlasarvāstivāda-vinaya* passage translated in part in Schopen (1996b) 2004a, 342, in which the Buddha is made to require nuns to seek permission to enter monasteries, and to submit to body searches for concealed weapons.

111. The Pāli parallel (Vin 4:263–264) clearly refers to the wife as a "former wife": *purāṇa-dutiyikā*. See n. 5 above on the Sanskrit equivalent for this term.

112. T. 1425 (xxii) 530a22–b13 (*juan* 38). The Lokottaravādin parallel to this states that their son also left home for the religious life, albeit not among the Śākyas (Roth 1970, §193). For a French translation, see Nolot 1991, 230–231. For an English translation of the Chinese, see Hirakawa 1982, 265–266. See also T. 1463 (xxiv) 827c18–25 (*juan* 5).

113. T. 1425 (xxii) 530b12 (*juan* 38).

114. T. 1425 (xxii) 530b12–13 (*juan* 38).

115. Note also the rule in this monastic code in which it is made an offense for a nun to censure a monk directly to his face. The exceptions state that if the nun has a brother or [male] relative who has gone forth into the religious life,

and even if that person does not uphold the practice of the precepts, a nun is not to rebuke him; she should remonstrate with soft words (T. 1425 [xxii] 532c26–533a19 [*juan* 38]). This rule is also introduced with a narrative in which a husband and wife have left home for the religious life together (有夫婦出家). For a translation, see Hirakawa 1982, 284–286.

116. See nn. 4, 106, and 115 above for further references.

117. *Kṣudrakavastu,* T. 1451 (xxiv) 358c20–21 (*juan* 31): 夫妻能發此勝妙心。俱共出家斯爲好事; sTog, *'Dul ba,* THA 206b3–4: *bu khyod chung ma dang bcas te sems bskyed pa ni legs te /.*

118. On Udāyin, "le moine dissolu," see Feer 1883, 34. It is a shame that Feer's project never came to fruition: "Je m'étais proposé de recueillir tous les textes où se trouve le nom de Char-ka [= Udāyin], pour en faire une sorte de monographie; j'en ai été détourné par d'autres préoccupations" (ibid.).

119. A novel by the little-known Japanese author Adachi Kin'ichi 足立欽一 (1893–1953) was based on the life story of the monk Udāyin. Entitled *Gedō zanmai* 外道三昧 (*Heretics' Samādhi,* with the double meaning *Heretics Galore*), this 1923 novel was banned ten days after publication. It was republished under the title *Karudai* (i.e., Kālodāyin) 迦留陀夷 in 1924. For a brief account of his experience with the censors, see the afterword in Adachi 1924 (内検の濟んだ日に). The 1923 version preserves the subsequently censored passages, easily enabling the student of Japanese literature to compare the pre- and post-censorship books. See, *inter alia,* the account on the front page of the *Yomiuri* newspaper (Nov. 1, 1924, morning edition).

120. Below I give snippets from the story in the hope of conveying the flavor of the original.

121. *Vinaya-vibhaṅga,* T. 1442 (xxiii) 716a23–722a24 (*juans* 17–18); sTog, *'Dul ba,* CA 495b4–CHA 8b4.

122. Nishimoto 1933–1938, 20:14 gives Gopana for Tibetan *sbed pa.* Cf. Feer 1883, 38, where he has taken the name as Guptika. A Sanskrit fragment (Private Collection Virginia, F2.2) of this story has recently come to light, dispelling any uncertainty regarding the form of the names of Guptā and her husband. I wish to thank Jens-Uwe Hartmann and Kazunobu Matsuda for providing me with a photo of this fragment and a transliterated text made by Klaus Wille.

123. The Chinese suggests Udāyin was himself a minister. The Tibetan seems to have only Gupta as a minister of the state.

124. The Tibetan term *kha dum pa* is not entirely straightforward. When Feer translated part of this story 130 years ago, he seems to have understood the Tibetan term to mean that "il arriva que Udâyî et Guptikâ approchèrent leurs bouches l'une de l'autre" (1883, 38). Yijing's Chinese translation of this passage gives *gongxing feifa* 共行非法, which suggests something along the lines of "[they] together performed unrighteous [acts]"; in other words, Yijing suggests that they had sex. Given that later on in the same story Guptā is referred to as Udāyin's "former" wife (*'char kha'i sngon gyi chung ma*), it seems to make sense

that we understand the Tibetan *kha dum pa* in its attested technical sense as the sixth of the seven types of wives recognized by the authors/redactors of this monastic code: *samajīvikā* (*kha dum pa;* 共活): "(a wife) in a partnership [wherein both parties combine their property]." See n. 83 above.

125. The Chinese says that he thought of killing them both.

126. Gupta realized he could not kill a brahmin "for the sake of a woman's body" (sTog, *'Dul ba,* CA 499a4–5; T. 1442 [xxiii] 716b27 [*juan* 17]).

127. See Chap. 2, n. 67.

128. See n. 25 above.

129. sTog, *'Dul ba,* CHA 4a5–b2; T. 1442 (xxiii) 721a14–24 (*juan* 18).

130. sTog, *'Dul ba,* CHA 5a6; T. 1442 (xxiii) 721b5–6 (*juan* 18).

131. sTog, *'Dul ba,* CHA 5a6–b1; T. 1442 (xxiii) 721b6–9 (*juan* 18).

132. sTog, *'Dul ba,* CHA 5b1–4. The Chinese just has him state that he does not wish to stay: T. 1442 (xxiii) 721b10–13 (*juan* 18). On *caitya* pilgrims, see Chap. 2, n. 10.

133. sTog, *'Dul ba,* CHA 5b4–5; T. 1442 (xxiii) 721b13–15 (*juan* 18).

134. sTog, *'Dul ba,* CHA 6a4–6; T. 1442 (xxiii) 721b27–c3 (*juan* 18).

135. sTog, *'Dul ba,* CHA 6a6–b3; T. 1442 (xxiii) 721c3–9 (*juan* 18).

136. sTog, *'Dul ba,* CHA 6b3–4; T. 1442 (xxiii) 721c9–11 (*juan* 18).

137. On temples, especially empty ones, as "the resort or home of the socially broken," see Schopen 2010b (quotation from p. 886).

138. sTog, *'Dul ba,* CHA 6b4–6; T. 1442 (xxiii) 721c11–12 (*juan* 18).

139. sTog, *'Dul ba,* CHA 6b6–7a3; T. 1442 (xxiii) 721c12–17 (*juan* 18).

140. sTog, *'Dul ba,* CHA 7a3–4; T. 1442 (xxiii) 721c17–19 (*juan* 18).

141. sTog, *'Dul ba,* CHA 7a4–5; T. 1442 (xxiii) 721c19–20 (*juan* 18).

142. sTog, *'Dul ba,* CHA 7a5–b4; T. 1442 (xxiii) 721c20–28 (*juan* 18).

143. A wife is not considered a relative in this literature. Relatives are defined as blood-relations up to seven generations; see the *vibhaṅga* definition of a relative: sTog, *'Dul ba,* CHA 8b5–6; T. 1442 (xxiii) 722a26–27 (*juan* 18). So too in brahmanical literature; see Manu v 60, and s.v. "relative" in the index to Doniger and Smith 1991. See also p. 104.

144. In some other versions the semen was orally ingested, but our text clearly states that it was placed into her vagina as well (the Chinese gives both accounts). In a version of Guptā's not-so-immaculate conception preserved in the *Sarvāstivāda-vinaya,* Guptā orally ingests one-half of the semen. This led the Buddha to make a rule that a nun commits a *pāyattika* offense in drinking semen (若比丘尼飲精、波夜提) (T. 1435 [xxiii] 344b29–c23 [*juan* 47]). This must have produced a few giggles when recited by nuns every fortnight. Another version preserved in this monastic code states that she became pregnant through inserting the semen into her vagina: T. 1435 (xxiii) 43a26–b27 (*juan* 6). In the *Mahīśāsaka-vinaya,* we find a rule making it an offense for a nun to inseminate herself: T. 1421 (xxii) 98b19–28 (*juan* 14). In this *vinaya,* the nun is Sthūlanandā and the monk Upananda (see n. 162 below).

145. sTog, *'Dul ba,* CHA 8a2–3; T. 1442 (xxiii) 722a11–12 (*juan* 18).

146. sTog, *'Dul ba,* CHA 8a3–4; T. 1442 (xxiii) 722a12–13 (*juan* 18).

147. sTog, *'Dul ba,* CHA 7b7; T. 1442 (xxiii) 722a7–8 (*juan* 18).

148. Clarke 2009b.

149. Clarke 2009a.

150. On the female penitent, see Clarke 2000. The applicability of this penitential status to nuns is explicitly mentioned in the Dharmaguptaka, Mahāsāṅghika, Sarvāstivāda, and Mūlasarvāstivāda *vinaya*s. In the case of the *Mahīśāsaka-vinaya,* the applicability to *bhikṣuṇī*s can be assumed. For a comparative chart of the details of this penance, see Clarke 1999, 212–215. The details of the nun's penance differ between traditions, as does the name for this status; some call her a *śikṣādattā-śrāmaṇerī* and others simply a *śikṣādattā*. On the status of the *pārājika* penitent in general, see Clarke 2009a.

151. Clarke 1999 and 2009a. On Nandika in medieval China, see Greene 2012, chap. 5.

152. In fact, in most versions, Nandika seems to have sex with a dead royal horse into which the goddess had disappeared; see Clarke 2009a.

153. Such conceptions are common in Indian literature; see Masson 1976.

154. This story is well known in Buddhist monastic law codes. Its popularity may well have prevented it from being discarded or reworked to avoid the somewhat unconvincing—apparently even to the authors/redactors themselves—fact that this nun became pregnant without having sex. The story of Udāyin (or Kālodāyin, "Udāyin the Black") and Guptā, for instance, was clearly very important to a number of Buddhists. Lamotte tells us that the Kāśyapīya or Suvarṣaka *nikāya* traces its roots back to "Suvarṣa, the son of Kāḷodāyi and the nun Guptā" ([1958] 1988, 576).

155. See n. 143 above.

156. On incest in India, see Silk 2009.

157. sTog, *'Dul ba,* CHA 8a5; T. 1442 (xxiii) 722a14–15 (*juan* 18).

158. See Chap. 4, Sec. 4, for further details on the birth.

159. sTog, *'Dul ba,* CHA 8a6–b1; T. 1442 (xxiii) 722a16–18 (*juan* 18). For the attainment of arhatship by Udāyin, see T. 1442 (xxiii) 860a18–c4 (*juan* 42); sTog, *'Dul ba,* JA 206b4–217a5. The Chinese text is abbreviated considerably; the Tibetan includes a version of Udāyin's tour of the Jetavana, on which see Sec. 6 below.

160. This is one of the longest narratives in the *Mūlasarvāstivāda-vinaya,* or in any other Buddhist monastic law code for that matter. I have been able to summarize it only very briefly.

161. sTog, *'Dul ba,* CHA 8b3–4; T. 1442 (xxiii) 722a23–24 (*juan* 18).

162. T. 1421 (xxii) 26c14–27a1 (*juan* 4). The Mahīśāsaka frame-story is based on an episode involving the monk Upananda and the nun Sthūlanandā. A rule is established that makes it an offense for any nun to wash, dye, or beat a monk's robes. The phenomenon of old, sick monks who could not do their own

laundry then caused this to be amended to allow related nuns to wash monks' robes (27a1–8). In the Mahāsāṅghika version, Udāyin has Mahāprajāpatī Gautamī dye his robe, but she then ends up with dye all over her hands. Udāyin is criticized for having a nun who was practicing religious exertion dye his robes (T. 1425 [xxii] 300b22–c2 [*juan* 9]). The rule is established in reference to a story with Ānanda and his "former" wife Sthūlanandā (!) (T. 1425 [xxii] 300c2–25 [*juan* 9]). For the *Dharmaguptaka-vinaya,* see T. 1428 (xxii) 607a26–b25 (*juan* 6); *Sarvāstivāda-vinaya,* see T. 1435 (xxiii) 43a26–b27 (*juan* 6). For the story in the Pāli Vinaya, see *BD* 2:30–32. On this rule, see Hirakawa 1993–1995, 2:118–130, and, most recently, Yamagiwa 2004.

163. On the "domestication" of nuns by monks and the contemporary situation of Tibetan Buddhism in Zangskar, see Gutschow 2001, 49; for a modification of her earlier view, see Gutschow 2004, 160.

164. See also the following stories from the *Mūlasarvāstivāda-vinaya:* the nun Guptā, whose robes are in tatters, visits Udāyin, who embroiders an image of himself and Guptā embracing each other on her robe, much to her embarrassment (*Vinaya-vibhaṅga,* T. 1442 [xxiii] 805b28–806a14 [*juan* 33]; sTog, *'Dul ba,* CHA 418a4–420a6); Udāyin visits Guptā in the nunnery (*Vinaya-vibhaṅga,* T. 1442 [xxiii] 808a8–29 [*juan* 33]; sTog, *'Dul ba,* CHA 432b4–434a6; note here Guptā is described as an **upadhivārikā* [*dge skos* 授事], a form of monastic office—on monastic offices, see Silk 2008); Guptā gets into trouble for being alone with Udāyin in both secluded and open areas (*Bhikṣuṇī-vibhaṅga,* T. 1443 [xxiii] 999b23–c1 [*juan* 17]; sTog, *'Dul ba,* NYA 360b5–7 [the Tibetan adds that Udāyin visits the nuns' convent (*dge slong ma'i dbyar khang*)]; T. 1443 [xxiii] 999c17–21 [*juan* 17]; sTog, *'Dul ba,* NYA 361b1–2, respectively).

165. Oldenberg [1882] 1998, 380–381.

166. Hirakawa [1990] 1998, 64–65.

167. Horner [1930] 1999, 59.

168. Workman [1913] 1962, 141.

169. von Schiefner 1882, 186–205.

170. This story has been discussed in terms of its doctrinal jokes in Schopen 2007b, 211–214.

171. *Vinaya-vibhaṅga,* T. 1442 (xxiii) 681c19–26 (*juan* 11); sTog, *'Dul ba,* CA 294b7–295a3.

172. T. 1442 (xxiii) 681c29–682a2 (*juan* 11); sTog, *'Dul ba,* CA 295a7–b2.

173. T. 1442 (xxiii) 682a2–11 (*juan* 11); sTog, *'Dul ba,* CA 295b2–7.

174. T. 1442 (xxiii) 682a11–19 (*juan* 11); sTog, *'Dul ba,* CA 295b7–296b1.

175. The *Catalogue of Buddhist Teachings [compiled in the] Kaiyuan Period* (*Kaiyuan shijiao lü* 開元釋教録; 730 C.E.) contains two separate lists of *sūtra*s which seem to have circulated independently before they were removed from the Chinese canon on account of the cataloguer's stated wish to avoid duplication. The first list contains nine *sūtra*s from the *Vinaya-vibhaṅga* of the *Mūlasarvāstivāda-vinaya* (T. 2154 [lv] 699a4–13 [*juan* 20]); the second, some

thirty-two *sūtras* from the *Kṣudrakavastu* (T. 2154 [lv] 699a14–b20 [*juan* 20]). Although only one of these *sūtras* has survived (Ochiai 1994, 448), what is undoubtedly our story about Udāyin the tour guide is reported in a one-fascicle (*juan* 卷) length work entitled *The Sūtra on Venerable Udāyin Guiding People to Pay Homage to the Buddha and Saṅgha* (尊者鄔陀夷引導諸人禮佛僧經) (T. 2154 [lv] 699a5 [*juan* 20]).

176. T. 1442 (xxiii) 682a23–24 (*juan* 11); sTog, *'Dul ba,* CA 296b2–3.

177. T. 1442 (xxiii) 682b9–12 (*juan* 11); sTog, *'Dul ba,* CA 297a4–6.

178. T. 1442 (xxiii) 682b15–20 (*juan* 11); sTog, *'Dul ba,* CA 297b3–5. Only the Chinese refers to her as a wife (妻).

179. Cf. Yijing's travel record: T. 2125 (liv) 228b4 (*juan* 4); Takakusu 1896, 167.

180. T. 1442 (xxiii) 682b25–27 (*juan* 11); sTog, *'Dul ba,* CA 298a2–3.

181. T. 1442 (xxiii) 682c6–7 (*juan* 11); sTog, *'Dul ba,* CA 298a7; "crownless reign" (*cod pan med pa'i rgyal srid*) is not found in the Chinese.

182. T. 1442 (xxiii) 682c11–12 (*juan* 11); sTog, *'Dul ba,* CA 298b3.

183. T. 1442 (xxiii) 682c16–17 (*juan* 11); sTog, *'Dul ba,* CA 298b5–7.

184. T. 1442 (xxiii) 682c22–23 (*juan* 11); sTog, *'Dul ba,* CA 299a1–2; the Tibetan reads *gcung po sru'i sras.*

185. T. 1442 (xxiii) 682c26–27 (*juan* 11); sTog, *'Dul ba,* CA 299a3–4.

186. T. 1442 (xxiii) 683a1–2 (*juan* 11); sTog, *'Dul ba,* CA 299a6–7. The Tibetan lists Chanda before Aśvaka and Punarvasuka.

187. T. 1442 (xxiii) 683a2 (*juan* 11); sTog, *'Dul ba,* CA 299a7.

188. See Schopen 2007b, 212.

189. T. 1442 (xxiii) 683a2–b26 (*juan* 11); sTog, *'Dul ba,* CA 299b1–301b3.

190. T. 1442 (xxiii) 683b29–c2 (*juan* 11); sTog, *'Dul ba,* CA 301b5–7.

191. T. 1442 (xxiii) 682b22–24 (*juan* 11); sTog, *'Dul ba,* CA 297b7–298a1.

192. Ray 1994, 105.

193. von Schiefner 1882, 186–205. The German edition, although now reprinted, remains relatively unknown (Silk 2010, 65, paraphrasing the new editors).

194. In Clarke 2011a, 2011b, and 2012a, I have argued that there exist at least two separate Mūlasarvāstivādin traditions of rules for nuns. Hence, we must begin to talk not about the singular *vinaya* of the Mūlasarvāstivādins, but rather about their *vinayas* in the plural. See also Chap. 4, n. 138.

195. Hirakawa 1998, 96.

196. *Mahīśāsaka-vinaya,* T. 1421 (xxii) 77b28–78a3 (*juan* 11); *Mahāsāṅghika-vinaya,* T. 1425 (xxii) 514a26–517b28 (*juan* 36); *Dharmaguptaka-vinaya,* T. 1428 (xxii) 714a7–715a5 (*juan* 22); *Sarvāstivāda-vinaya,* T. 1435 (xxiii) 302c15 (*juan* 42); the Pāli Vinaya omits this rule since it is shared with monks (see Pruitt and Norman 2001, 117, for the *pātimokkha* rule).

197. *Bhikṣuṇī-vibhaṅga,* T. 1443 (xxiii) 908b10–20 (*juan* 1); sTog, *'Dul ba,* NYA 35b2–5. The Tibetan version is generally fuller than the Chinese. The sum-

mary below follows von Schiefner 1882, 186–205; sometimes I summarize the Tibetan, sometimes the Chinese.

198. T. 1443 (xxiii) 908b20–909a14 (*juan* 1); sTog, *'Dul ba,* NYA 35b5–41b3.

199. T. 1443 (xxiii) 909a14–b6 (*juan* 1); sTog, *'Dul ba,* NYA 41b3–42b2.

200. T. 1443 (xxiii) 909b10–26 (*juan* 1); sTog, *'Dul ba,* NYA 42b2–43b5.

201. T. 1443 (xxiii) 909b26–c2 (*juan* 1); sTog, *'Dul ba,* NYA 43b7–44a6.

202. T. 1443 (xxiii) 909c3–17 (*juan* 1); sTog, *'Dul ba,* NYA 44a6–45a3.

203. T. 1443 (xxiii) 909c17–18 (*juan* 1); sTog, *'Dul ba,* NYA 45a3–4.

204. T. 1443 (xxiii) 909c18–910a15 (*juan* 1); sTog, *'Dul ba,* NYA 45a4–47b6.

205. T. 1443 (xxiii) 910a18–20 (*juan* 1); sTog, *'Dul ba,* NYA 47b6–48a2.

206. sTog, *'Dul ba,* NYA 48a2–4; T. 1443 (xxiii) 910a20–22 (*juan* 1). This conversation is found only in the Tibetan.

207. T. 1443 (xxiii) 910a22–27 (*juan* 1); sTog, *'Dul ba,* NYA 48a4–b2.

208. T. 1443 (xxiii) 910a27–28 (*juan* 1); sTog, *'Dul ba,* NYA 48b2–3.

209. T. 1443 (xxiii) 910a28–b1 (*juan* 1); sTog, *'Dul ba,* NYA 48b3–4.

210. T. 1443 (xxiii) 910b1–2 (*juan* 1); sTog, *'Dul ba,* NYA 48b4–6.

211. sTog, *'Dul ba,* NYA 48b6–49a2.

212. sTog, *'Dul ba,* NYA 49a2–4.

213. T. 1443 (xxiii) 910b2–9 (*juan* 1); sTog, *'Dul ba,* NYA 49a4–b1.

214. sTog, *'Dul ba,* NYA 49b1–3.

215. sTog, *'Dul ba,* NYA 49b3–4. Cf. T. 1443 (xxiii) 910b26–28 (*juan* 1).

216. T. 1443 (xxiii) 910b9–26 (*juan* 1); sTog, *'Dul ba,* NYA 49b5–50a5.

217. See von Schiefner 1882, 253–256; for the *Mahābhārata* story, see van Buitenen 1975, 431–441. See also p. 83 on women as poison to the touch.

218. sTog, *'Dul ba,* NYA 50a5–7.

219. T. 1443 (xxiii) 910c2–911a1 (*juan* 1); sTog, *'Dul ba,* NYA 50a7–52a2.

220. sTog, *'Dul ba,* NYA 52a2–6.

221. T. 1443 (xxiii) 912a3–5 (*juan* 2); sTog, *'Dul ba,* NYA 52a6–b3.

222. T. 1443 (xxiii) 912a5–7 (*juan* 2); sTog, *'Dul ba,* NYA 52b3–7. von Schiefner 1882, 202.

223. T. 1443 (xxiii) 911a2–912a3 (*juan*s 1–2); sTog, *'Dul ba,* NYA 52b7–56a3.

224. T. 1443 (xxiii) 912a17–20 (*juan* 2); sTog, *'Dul ba,* NYA 56a3–b1.

225. T. 1443 (xxiii) 912a20–b7 (*juan* 2); sTog, *'Dul ba,* NYA 56b1–6.

226. T. 1443 (xxiii) 912b7–14 (*juan* 2); sTog, *'Dul ba,* NYA 56b6–57a3.

227. T. 1443 (xxiii) 912b14–17 (*juan* 2); sTog, *'Dul ba,* NYA 57a3–4. The authorization is found only in the Chinese. In the Tibetan, Mahākāśyapa acts on his own authority.

228. T. 1443 (xxiii) 912b17–20 (*juan* 2); sTog, *'Dul ba,* NYA 57a4–6.

229. *Kṣudrakavastu,* T. 1451 (xxiv) 359a3–5 (*juan* 31); sTog, *'Dul ba,* THA 207a4–6.

230. *Bhikṣuṇī-vibhaṅga,* T. 1443 (xxiii) 912b20–24 (*juan* 2); sTog, *'Dul ba,* NYA 57a6–7.

231. This is a stock phrase in the *Mūlasarvāstivāda-vinaya.*

232. *Bhikṣuṇī-vibhaṅga,* T. 1443 (xxiii) 912b25–26 (*juan* 2); sTog, *'Dul ba,* NYA 57a7–b2.

233. T. 1443 (xxiii) 912b27–c7 (*juan* 2); sTog, *'Dul ba,* NYA 57b3–58a7.

234. T. 1443 (xxiii) 912c16–18 (*juan* 2); sTog, *'Dul ba,* NYA 58b6–7.

235. T. 1443 (xxiii) 913a9–14 (*juan* 2); sTog, *'Dul ba,* NYA 60b2–61a1. Tibetan: *khyod kyis bdag gir ma byas sam,* and Chinese: 汝受樂不. The divergence here may be attributable to different interpretations of Sanskrit *svī√kṛ;* cf. Chandra Vidyabhusana's translation of this verb from the Tibetan *Bhikṣu-prātimokṣa* ([1915] 2000, 53.15: *nyug pa bdag gir byed na*) as "touches...for enjoyment" (ibid., 13 [*saṅghāvaśeṣa* 2]).

236. T. 1443 (xxiii) 913a14–15 (*juan* 2). Expressed only in the Chinese.

237. T. 1443 (xxiii) 913a19–21 (*juan* 2); sTog, *'Dul ba,* NYA 61b1–3.

238. T. 1443 (xxiii) 914b15–16 (*juan* 2). These previous-life stories are found in the Tibetan *'Dul ba* between *pārājika* rules four and five (sTog, *'Dul ba,* NYA 81b3–98a3), as opposed to the Chinese, where they are appended to the first *pārājika.* The Tibetan and Chinese texts do not match exactly. For a summary of the stories in Tibetan, see Panglung 1981, 163–166.

239. T. 1443 (xxiii) 914b16–915c7 (*juan* 2).

240. T. 1443 (xxiii) 914c11–12 (*juan* 2).

241. T. 1443 (xxiii) 914c6–22 (*juan* 2). References to the "solitary rhinoceros" in *vinaya* literature are relatively rare. This previous-life story seems not to be included in the series of *avadāna*s in the Tibetan *'Dul ba* appearing between *pārājika*s four and five. In the Chinese, it appears as the second *avadāna* discussing how Mahākāśyapa and Bhadrā came to extinguish their desires. It is located before the *avadāna* of Mahākāśyapa and Bhadrā as farmer and farmer's wife, and directly after the story about the potter and wife who encounter four *pratyekabuddha*s.

242. On the dating of these documents, see Brough 1965, 602–605.

243. We find *viharavala* (*vihārapāla*) in document no. 489 (for translations, see Burrow 1940; for the texts, see Boyer et al. 1920–1929). See also *vihāra* in document no. 511. On this document and parallels to the *Avadānaśataka,* see Hasuike 1996; on document no. 510, see Hasuike 1997. See also Ichikawa 1999. Note also Atwood 1991, esp. 173–175.

244. Hoernle 1916; Inokuchi 1995, 329–351; and Bongard-Levin 1975–1976.

245. *Śramaṇa*s are not necessarily ordained monks, and they may have had good reason to remain as novices. This requires further research.

246. Document no. 418. I have adopted the romanization of Atwood (1991, 174) over that of Burrow.

247. Document no. 474. Atwood 1991, 171–172, notes that his wife bore him two sons: Dharmapri and Sumudata; see document no. 481.

248. Document nos. 418–419. Atwood 1991, 174.

249. Document no. 621.

250. Document no. 655.

251. For a recent discussion, see Hansen 2004. Note also Insler 1998 and von Hinüber 2006, 25–26. Atwood 1991, 174, draws an unfortunate distinction between "ordinary Buddhist practice" and monks who marry and have children.

252. Agrawala 1954, 174 (I have romanized the Devanāgarī). Note also Hao 1998, in which he makes the case that monks in Dunhuang from the late Tang to early Song periods often lived at home with their families; see, for convenience, the review by Kieschnick (2000) and Hao 2010.

253. On Japanese clerical marriage, see Jaffe 2001. Married "monks" living at home, usually in family temples, with their wives and children are certainly not to be found in the monasticisms envisioned and sanctioned by our Indian monastic codes. Although clerical marriage in Japan can be traced back to a specific set of unique (or at least uniquely documented) historical circumstances, a comparative study of married monks in Newar Buddhism and Japanese "monasticisms" may prove interesting.

254. Sagaster 2007, 426, states: "It goes without saying that married monks cannot leave their families behind. Because of this, Mongolian Buddhism is reproached by the Tibetans as no longer 'pure.'"

255. Gellner 1992, 58.

256. Ibid., 165.

257. Allen 1973, 6. Allen states that *saṅgha* is "a Sanskrit word which means 'celibate monastic order.'" *Saṅgha,* in fact, is not originally a monastic/religious term, but one for commercial guilds. Nalinaksha Dutt [1941] 1981, 73, for instance, states that "the term *Saṅgha* or *Gaṇa* literally means a multitude.... It was applied generally to a political, professional or commercial body." In political usage, it is, according to Kangle, "best rendered by 'oligarchy'" (1965–1972, 2:454). For a good overview of the pre-Buddhistic uses of the term *saṅgha,* see Hirakawa [1964] 2000, 1:3–12 and the sources cited. Hirakawa [1990] 1998, 62, notes that "during the time of the Buddha, political groups and trade guilds were called *saṅgha.*" The term *saṅgha* carries with it no inherent, implicit, or any other sense of "celibacy."

258. Samuel 1993, 286–289; see also pp. 274–278.

259. Aziz 1978, 53; cf. pp. 77ff. on the *ser-ky'im gön-pa* of D'ing-ri. See also Yotsuya 2004 and the comments in Ray 1994, 446.

260. Stein [1900] 1961, 1:73–74. For an alternative interpretation of this passage, see Kieffer-Pülz 2000, 307; note, however, von Hinüber 2002, 82. See also Xuanzang's (602–664 C.E.) observations concerning Sind(hu): "All the people, whether male or female, and regardless of nobility or lowliness, shave off their hair and beards and dress in religious robes, thus giving the appearance of being *bhikṣus* (and *bhikṣunīs* [*sic*]), yet engaging in secular affairs." Li 1996, 346, translating T. 2087 (li) 937b10–11 (*juan* 11).

261. Gombrich 1988, 167, citing *Mahāvaṃsa* lxxviii, 3–4. See Rickmer's

note of caution on the interpretation of this passage (Geiger [1929] 1998, 2:101–102). Note Leider 2006 on Burmese *gāmavāsī* monks.

262. For textual evidence suggesting that not all monastics had left home physically, see Chap. 2, Sec. 2, esp. the stories of Sudinna and Dharmadinnā.

263. Banerji-Sastri 1940, 250 (§84). Tsukamoto 1996–2003, 1:191 (Kurkihar §72).

264. Tsukamoto 1996–2003, 1:188–189 (Kurkihar §§58–59). Banerji-Sastri 1940, 250 (§§58–59).

265. A full study of the various inhabitants of monasteries, including, but not limited to, *ārāmika*s, *paścācchramaṇa*s, and *upasthāyaka*s, is a desideratum. For a start, on *ārāmika*s in particular, see Schopen 1994b and Yamagiwa 2002 (and the references in his n. 1). On *paścācchramaṇa*s "attending menials," see Schopen 2013. Note also Yamagiwa 2009. On the "landlord ascetic" (*samaṇa-kuṭimbika*), see von Hinüber 1997, 74; 2002, 82; 2004, 311–314; and 2006, 24–25.

266. Boucher 2008, 138 (square brackets in original); cf. Ensink 1952, 29.

267. Vaidya 1961, 307.19–.21; paraphrased in Studholme 2002, 153.

268. Note Studholme 2002, 81, on the Dharma preacher or *dharmabhāṇaka* in the *Kāraṇḍavyūha-sūtra*. Studholme states that "this type of reviled married practitioner also happens to be one of the most highly revered personages in the whole work."

269. Boucher 2008, 139.

270. von Rospatt suggests that we understand Newar Buddhism "as an alternative model of Buddhist monasticism, rather than as a mere 'aberration from true monkhood'" (2005, 209 n. 34).

271. For further references in Mahāyāna literature to acerbic attacks on monks for having families, see Schopen (2000b) 2005a, 15, and the references cited. For references to married bodhisattvas in a positive light, see Dayal [1932] 1978, 174–175, 178, 201, and 222–224. According to Dayal, "it is indeed necessary for an advanced *bodhisattva* to be married in order that he may be able to exhibit this virtue [i.e., giving away his wife and children] in its perfection!" ([1932] 1978, 175). For further references to married monks and the need for a systematic study of this issue, see also von Hinüber 2002, 82–83. Note also Tāranātha's reference to married monks in India cited in Ray 1994, 445.

272. Leclercq 1979, 14.

Chapter 4: Nuns Who Become Pregnant

1. John Wilson [1936] 1961, 62.

2. On the structure of the Pāli *Suttavibhaṅga*, see von Hinüber 1996, 13, and Kieffer-Pülz 2012.

3. See, however, Wang 1994, 183–186; note also Bianchi 2001 and Clarke 2006a.

4. For other translations, see Kabilsingh 1998, 194; Tsomo 1996, 54; Wu 2001, 99–100; and Heirman 2002, 2:763. For the view that pregnant women and nursing mothers cannot be ordained, see, *inter alia,* Wu 2001, 99–100.

5. See Chap. 2, n. 110.

6. Rather than "give the full precepts," I translate Chinese *yu shoujuzu jie* 與受具足戒 as "ordain."

7. T. 1431 (xxii) 1037b20–23.

8. For the Mahīśāsaka and Mūlasarvāstivāda schools, see their respective nuns' *prātimokṣas*: T. 1423 (xxii) 211b9–10 and T. 1455 (xxiv) 514c12. The Mūlasarvāstivāda *Bhikṣuṇī-prātimokṣa* contains the rule pertaining to the ordination of pregnant women, but not that of nursing mothers. For the Theravāda tradition, see Pruitt and Norman 2001, 183; see also the rules embedded in the nuns' *vibhaṅga:* Vin 4:317–318 (*BD* 3:361–363). See also n. 63 below.

9. See pp. 32–34.

10. Hart [1961] 1988, 27.

11. Ibid., 35.

12. For evidence of an awareness of this distinction from within the commentarial tradition, see VSSMsB *sūtra* no. 95 (VSPVSG 2007, 43), esp. with reference to *prajñapti* connected to rules-of-training and *pratikṣepa.*

13. These rules vary from *vinaya* to *vinaya*. The *Sarvāstivāda-vinaya,* for instance, in the rule which was brought about by the admission of those who were ugly (see n. 16 below), states that such people should not be initiated. At the same time, it also makes it an offense of wrongdoing if one in fact does initiate an ugly person.

14. As with most Buddhist monastic legislation, rules are given first and foremost in reference to monks. Some categories, such as castrates, obviously will not apply to nuns, but those that could are undoubtedly applicable.

15. The diseases listed in the *Dharmaguptaka-vinaya* are not all easily identifiable, as is often the case with Indian terms preserved only in Chinese. The Pāli Vinaya lists boils, consumption, eczema, epilepsy, and leprosy as "stumbling-blocks" to ordination (*BD* 4:120). For a Mūlasarvāstivādin list, see Schopen 2004d, 237, in which we find, *inter alia,* asthma, cough, fatigue, goiter, hemorrhoids, jaundice, liver disease, rheumatism, and wheezing.

16. See, for instance, T. 1435 (xxiii) 155a3–29 (*juan* 21), where the Group-of-Six gets into trouble for initiating the ugly (醜陋).

17. T. 1428 (xxii) 814a18–b20 (*juan* 35). See, *inter alia,* Sasaki 1999, 79–104, and Sasaki 1996 for the Theravādin tradition; also Irisawa 1989. For the *Mūlasarvāstivāda-vinaya,* see Schopen 2004d. See also Vogel and Wille 2002, 59–64. Similar lists are found throughout *vinaya* literature.

18. T. 1428 (xxii) 814b19–20 (*juan* 35).

19. There are exceptions. See, for instance, the questions by Upāli on ordination in the *Mūlasarvāstivāda-vinaya* (*Nidāna, Muktaka,* and *Upālipariprcchā*) discussed in Clarke 2010a.

20. A clause in the rule in the Pāli Vinaya making it an offense to ordain someone under twenty years of age deserves our attention. Horner's translation reads (*BD* 3:12): "Whatever monk should knowingly confer the *upasampadā* ordination on an individual under twenty years of age, both that individual is not ordained and these monks are blameworthy...." This last clause invalidates the ordination, but no such clause is found in the rules concerning the ordination of pregnant or nursing women.

21. T. 1431 (xxii) 1036b23.

22. T. 1431 (xxii) 1036b27. For a comparative study of humor in a *vinaya* story about nuns and dildos, see Clarke 2009c, 323–327.

23. T. 1431 (xxii) 1036c6.

24. These rules seem to refer specifically to "ordination" and not "initiation." If they referred to the latter, then, presumably, there would be no problem: the pregnancy would be detected during the nun's normal two-year probationary period. The textual traditions are not uniform (all but the *Mūlasarvāstivāda-vinaya* suggest "ordination"): Pāli (Vin 4:317.21–.25; *BD* 3:361.18–.25): *yā pana bhikkhunī gabbhiniṃ vuṭṭhāpeyya, pācittiyan ti*... (and the word commentary) *vuṭṭhāpeyyā 'ti upasampādeyya*. On the Pāli verb *vuṭṭhāpeti*, see *BD* 3:xlvff. and Norman 2001. Norman translates this as to "sponsor (for ordination)" (2001, 131). The *Dharmaguptaka-vinaya* gives "initiate and confer ordination" (T. 1428 [xxii] 754c2–3 [*juan* 27]); the *Mahīśāsaka-vinaya* gives "confer ordination" (T. 1421 [xxii] 92b3–4 [*juan* 13]); Yijing's translation of the Mūlasarvāstivāda *Bhikṣuṇī-vibhaṅga* gives "initiation," and the word commentary states that this means the rules-of-training for novices (T. 1443 [xxiii] 1006a2–4 [*juan* 18]); the Tibetan Mūlasarvāstivāda *Bhikṣuṇī-vibhaṅga* gives *pra√vraj* and not *upasaṃ√pad* (initiate, not ordain) (sTog, *'Dul ba*, NYA 381b5–7). Note, however, that the frame-story makes it clear that the pregnant woman was already showing, i.e., this is not a case of a woman who only later found out that she was pregnant. As Horner translates, she was already "heavy with child" (*BD* 3:361).

25. T. 1428 (xxii) 754c16–755a3 (*juan* 27). This passage makes it clear that we cannot always take *du* 度 as "initiate" as opposed to "ordain." A couple of lines down this woman is referred to as a nun. The Chinese adds *tuo* 他 "another" here and below. If the intended sense is that she was breast-feeding another's child, then the syntax seems to be wrong. This is probably best understood in the sense of "a certain" (cf. *BHSD*, s.v., *anyatara*).

26. T. 1428 (xxii) 754c17–18 (*juan* 27).

27. T. 1428 (xxii) 754c18–21 (*juan* 27).

28. T. 1428 (xxii) 755a2–3 (*juan* 27).

29. T. 1428 (xxii) 755a4–5 (*juan* 27).

30. T. 1428 (xxii) 755a5–6 (*juan* 27).

31. T. 1428 (xxii) 755a7–12 (*juan* 27).

32. T. 1428 (xxii) 755a13–15 (*juan* 27).

33. On the unquestioned validity of "faulty" ordinations, see Clarke 2010a.

34. I take the opening referent, "that mother" (其母), to refer to the newly ordained nursing mother whose ordination sparked the establishment of the rule concerning the ordination of a breast-feeding woman.

35. Heirman (2002, 2:766) translates "nurses and raises" and this seems to capture the sense well. The binomial compound *ruyang* 乳養 seems to be a contraction of *rubu zhangyang* 乳哺長養 found in the rule directly preceding this, and discussed on p. 127. On breast-feeding in premodern traditions, see Stuart-Macadam 1995, 75.

36. T. 1428 (xxii) 755a15–16 (*juan* 27). For another translation, see Heirman 2002, 2:766.

37. See Monier-Williams [1899] 2000, q.v.; Bechert 1968; cf. Schopen (1998) 2004a, 282–283 n. 56; and Schopen (1996a) 2004a, 235. The same argument has been made by Schopen (2007a) with reference to monks' obligations to look after their parents; Schopen's paper provides the model for the present line of argumentation. See Chung and Wille 1997, 73 (8r4–5), for an attested correspondence between Sanskrit *anu√jñā* and Chinese *ting* 聽 in a *Dharmaguptaka-vinaya* fragment (T. 1428 [xxii] 584a16–18 [*juan* 3]). See also Hirakawa's *Buddhist Chinese-Sanskrit Dictionary,* although no authorities are cited (Hirakawa 1997, s.v., 2981). Here I have translated Chinese *ting* 聽 in the sense of *anu√jñā,* usually with "authorize."

38. T. 1428 (xxii) 755a16–18 (*juan* 27).

39. See the rule in the Dharmaguptaka *Bhikṣuṇī-vibhaṅga* addressing this at T. 1428 (xxii) 734c14 (*juan* 24) and in the nuns' *prātimokṣa* at T. 1431 (xxii) 1034c15. The other possibility, although much less probable, is that this was written with the rule making it an offense to share sleeping quarters with an unordained female in mind. **Pācattika* no. 5 for nuns in the *Dharmaguptaka-vinaya* reads: "Whatever nun spends the night in the same room together with an unordained woman, if she spends more than three nights incurs a **pācattika*" (T. 1428 [xxii] 734c15–16 [*juan* 24]). That the issue here is the gender of the child is clear from parallels in this and other *vinayas*; see, for instance, the story delivered in connection with the rule directly preceding this one, discussed on pp. 128–129.

40. T. 1428 (xxii) 754b12–14 (*juan* 27).

41. T. 1428 (xxii) 754b14–15 (*juan* 27). There is no plural marker, and a translation along the lines of "This nun" may be more justified. This stock phrase, however, often seems to be more general than specific.

42. T. 1428 (xxii) 754b15–17 (*juan* 27).

43. T. 1428 (xxii) 754b26–27 (*juan* 27).

44. T. 1428 (xxii) 754b27–c3 (*juan* 27). The *vibhaṅga* commentary here too provides for a gradation of offenses (T. 1428 [xxii] 754c3–9 [*juan* 27]).

45. T. 1428 (xxii) 754c11–12 (*juan* 27).

46. T. 1428 (xxii) 754c12–14 (*juan* 27).

47. As far as I know, the exact terminology for the Dharmaguptaka tradition is still unknown. Here and above I have followed Hirakawa (1993–1995,

2:49) in using the Mahāsāṅghika-Lokottaravādin form of the word; see Chap. 2, n. 110. T. 1428 (xxii) 734c14 (*juan* 27). See rule 4 in Tsomo 1996, 42, and Kabilsingh 1998, 181; also Heirman 2002, 2:530.

48. On monastic celibacy, see Clarke 2009a and 2009b.

49. T. 1421 (xxii) 92a24–28 (*juan* 13).

50. T. 1421 (xxii) 92b7–12 (*juan* 13).

51. T. 1421 (xxii) 92b4–6 (*juan* 13). In the *Mahīśāsaka-vinaya,* the ruling has not been amended to incorporate this provision. Other traditions have incorporated these provisions into their versions of the rule, thus making it an offense to ordain a pregnant woman intentionally. In this case, the Mahīśāsaka rule appears to preserve an older stratum of legislation.

52. T. 1423 (xxii) 211b9–10.

53. See pp. 32–34.

54. See Chap. 2, n. 81, on meanings of silence.

55. T. 1421 (xxii) 189c19–26 (*juan* 29).

56. T. 1421 (xxii) 189c26–28 (*juan* 29).

57. In translating these passages I have supplied the definite article, as this seems to be the desired sense. Context suggests that these two nuns are the mother and her helper.

58. The wording here is unclear. There are no variants listed in the Taishō, and *ming* 鳴 usually means "to cry" (e.g., a bird or animal) or "to sound" (e.g., a drum). Possibly, we should understand *ming* 鳴 for the graphically similar *wu* 嗚, which Mathews' *Chinese English Dictionary* gives as "an exclamation of regret" (1943, s.v., *wu* [no. 7167]). The authoritative Morohashi gives the same ([1955–1960] 1986, 2.4084.A1: 歎息の聲; 嗚呼、歎辭). Not only does grief or regret not work here, but one would expect a verb. Using the bird imagery in both characters ([mouth + bird] and [mouth + crow]), one might translate it as "to coo." Clearly, the nuns dressed the child up and made a fuss.

59. T. 1421 (xxii) 189c28–190a1 (*juan* 29).

60. On ages at weaning among humans (as opposed to primates), see Dettwyler 1995, 45 and 66.

61. T. 1421 (xxii) 117a16–28 (*juan* 17).

62. On the age of majority, see Fezas 2001.

63. Nishimoto 1928, comparative table 4.2 (比丘尼波逸提法其二). Hirakawa 1998, 552. Waldschmidt [1926] 1979, 135, gives (Pā 61 = Dha 119 = Mī 116 = Mū 111 = T 87). See table 2 (*bikuni kaihon* 比丘尼戒本) in *Nanden daizōkyō,* which for nuns only compares the Pāli, Dharmaguptaka, and Mahīśāsaka *prātimokṣa*s (Takakusu [1936–1940] 1970, 5:21, last numbered section from front—there are at least three pages numbered "21" in this volume).

64. T. 1435 (xxiii) 326b5–14 (*juan* 45).

65. Much work remains to be done on the *śikṣamāṇā* (and *gurudharma*s), particularly the origins of this status and how it was understood and implemented in various schools. For a good start, see Naoko Nishimura 1999. There are

parallels if not direct borrowings between the *śikṣamāṇā* and the *śikṣādattaka* (on which see Clarke 2009a) in the Mahāsāṅghika tradition—see Clarke 1999, 118ff. As noted by, *inter alia,* Naoko Nishimura 1999, 110, the *śikṣamāṇā* status is supposedly imposed on all women regardless of age and seems not to be, as some have suggested, a training period only for young girls (*pace* Lamotte [1958] 1988, 57). The Sarvāstivāda (rule no. 1) and Mūlasarvāstivāda *vinaya*s (rule no. 2) do not seem to mention this two-year period in their list of *gurudharma*s; see T. 1435 (xxiii) 345c8–18 (*juan* 47); *Kṣudrakavastu,* T. 1451 (xxiv) 351a1–25 (*juan* 29). There seems to be a major difference between the Sarvāstivāda and Mūlasarvāstivāda *vinaya*s on the one hand and the remaining *vinaya*s on the other with regard to the formation of the rule requiring a two-year training period.

66. T. 1435 (xxiii) 326b16–18 (*juan* 45). Apparently it is only the *Sarvāstivāda-vinaya* that explicitly mentions this as the reason for introducing the rules for a *śikṣamāṇā* (Hirakawa [1964] 2000, 2:242–243; Sasaki 1999, 285 n. 11; Naoko Nishimura 1999, 114).

67. The other possibility is that the canonical authors/redactors overlooked this apparent incongruence.

68. The frame-story for the Sarvāstivādin *śikṣamāṇā* rules suggests that her co-religionists did not take kindly to what they perceived to be a breach of celibacy; those nuns, we are told, threw the pregnant nun out of her cell.

69. T. 1435 (xxiii) 28b9–c3 (*juan* 4).

70. T. 1435 (xxiii) 43a26–b25 (*juan* 6); T. 1435 (xxiii) 84b22–c13 (*juan* 12); T. 1435 (xxiii) 344b29–c23 (*juan* 47).

71. T. 1435 (xxiii) 43a26–b25 (*juan* 6); T. 1435 (xxiii) 344b29–c23 (*juan* 47). See Chap. 3, n. 144.

72. T. 1435 (xxiii) 293a4–5 (*juan* 40).

73. T. 1435 (xxiii) 293a4–8 (*juan* 40).

74. T. 1435 (xxiii) 293a9–13 (*juan* 40).

75. T. 1435 (xxiii) 293a7 (*juan* 40).

76. T. 1435 (xxiii) 293a7–8 (*juan* 40). On offenses of wrongdoing, see Chap. 2, n. 123.

77. T. 1435 (xxiii) 293a12–13 (*juan* 40). On this type of offense, see Chap. 2, n. 110.

78. That Guptā was a nun is beyond any doubt, and is confirmed later in the text. As it stands, this passage presupposes a familiarity with this nun on the part of the monastic audience or readership.

79. The wording here is interesting, and I have so far not been able to trace it exactly (especially the addition that a nun should share the cell). The closest in this *vinaya* seems to be the rule that came about after a nun by the name of *Bhadrā, a daughter of a Kapila brahmin, returned to her elder sister's husband's house, seemingly upon hearing of the news of her sister's death. After expounding the Dharma until dusk, she decided that it might be too dangerous to return

to the convent and spent the night there. The widower, however, misunderstood her intentions: "That this nun does not leave is certainly because she wishes to break her rules-of-training; I ought to seek her in place of her elder sister." The husband propositions the nun, asking her to become his wife and stepmother to his child. Too afraid to say anything, she sits there all night and is again propositioned in the middle and last watches of the night, until she finally escapes at daybreak. T. 1435 (xxiii) 307c15–308a8 (*juan* 42).

80. T. 1435 (xxiii) 293a14–19 (*juan* 40).

81. An ecclesiastical act consisting of a motion and the passing of a resolution as the second part.

82. T. 1435 (xxiii) 293a23–27 (*juan* 40).

83. I do not mean to suggest that the circumstances of Guptā's conception were not somewhat problematic. Other versions of this story supply slightly different details, but in all it seems that the baby boy grew up to be the very successful monk Kumāra-Kāśyapa. The story seems to have made its way even into *Abhidharma* discussions; see La Vallée Poussin's footnote ([1923–1971] 1971, 3:213 n. 5; and Pruden 1988–1990, 2:751 n. 467). T. 1562 (xxix) 588c10ff. For further details on this monastic family, and the life of Kumāra-Kāśyapa, see Chap. 3, Sec. 5.

84. Enomoto 1998 and 2000. See Yao 2007 on the shortcomings of Enomoto's thesis. Note also the early discussion in Tokuoka 1960, in his review of Frauwallner 1956. Wynne 2008 adds little.

85. It now appears that there may have been at least two *Mūlasarvāstivāda-vinayas*. See Clarke 2011a, 2011b, 2012a, and n. 138 below.

86. See Clarke 2010b.

87. On the dating of this text, see p. 20.

88. See next note for the *vibhaṅga* reference.

89. *Kṣudrakavastu*, sTog, *'Dul ba*, THA 213b3–4; T. 1451 (xxiv) 360b4–6 (*juan* 31). The term for "semen" here is *bujing* 不淨 (lit. "impure"), which is often found in *vinaya* texts in this sense. The Tibetan has *gcin* ("urine"). In the full version in the *vibhaṅga*, to which this passage appears to be alluding, the Tibetan (at least in the sTog) gives *khu ba* and the Chinese *jing* 精, both of which mean "semen." For the *vibhaṅga*, see sTog, *'Dul ba*, CHA 7b6–7; T. 1442 (xxiii) 722a6–7 (*juan* 18).

90. See p. 102.

91. *Kṣudrakavastu*, sTog, *'Dul ba*, THA 213b4–7; T. 1451 (xxiv) 360b6–10 (*juan* 31).

92. sTog, *'Dul ba*, THA 213b7; T. 1451 (xxiv) 360b10 (*juan* 31).

93. T. 1451 (xxiv) 360b11–12 (*juan* 31).

94. sTog, *'Dul ba*, THA 214a1–2.

95. In the story to which our *Kṣudrakavastu* passage seems to be alluding, the following is put into the mouth of the Buddha: "Monks, since that nun did not commit a *pārājika*, in this manner she is to be placed in a concealed place (the

Chinese gives "screened room" 屏室), and you must not let her be without alms, and having given birth to a child named Kumāra-Kāśyapa, he, having gone forth in my Teaching, through the removal of all impurities will directly attain arhatship, and in this manner, that monk, Kumāra-Kāśyapa, will become the foremost among. . . ." sTog, *'Dul ba,* CHA 8a5–b1; T. 1442 (xxiii) 722a15–18 (*juan* 18). Giving birth is one of many things that monastics may do as long as it is done in a concealed place (*pratigupte pradeśe*); see Chap. 2, n. 105.

96. *Kṣudrakavastu,* sTog, *'Dul ba,* THA 214a2–6; T. 1451 (xxiv) 360b13–17 (*juan* 31).

97. See n. 100 below.

98. sTog, *'Dul ba,* THA 214b2–216a5; T. 1451 (xxiv) 360b25–c28 (*juan* 31). For Guṇaprabha's discussion of this in his *Autocommentary,* see, for convenience, Jyväsjärvi 2011, 563. For a tale about incest resulting from a nun's spending the rainy season with her son, see *Aṅguttara-nikāya* (Hare [1934] 1961, 55–57).

99. The Chinese clearly mentions that it was night.

100. According to the Chinese translation, Guptā requests a "*karman* [to allow her] to spend the night together in the same room with [her] child" (與子同室宿羯磨). The Tibetan gives, to cite the shorter form, *bu dang lhan cig khang pa gcig tu nyal ba'i sdom pa.* Tibetan *sdom pa* is from the verb "to bind" and seems to mean "resolution" or "permission" (see Kieffer-Pülz 1992, 369, for *sdom pa* as a translation of Sanskrit *saṃvṛti;* also Kishino 2011). Note the Tibetan gives *khang pa* "house"; I have translated with the Chinese *shi* 室 "room." In both the Tibetan and the Chinese the ruling here seems to be picking up on, and thus dependent on, the terminology of the original rule: a nun must not sleep together in the same house/room with a man. This phrase might be best translated as "under one roof."

101. On the urban location of nunneries, see Schopen 2008a, 2008b, and 2009.

102. See pp. 18–19. For references to reservations expressed concerning the principle of higher criticism, see Chap. 1, n. 109.

103. T. 1425 (xxii) 380a24–28 (*juan* 19). The rule that this narrative goes on to introduce has nothing to do with the ordination of pregnant women. It is a rule about playing in water.

104. T. 1425 (xxii) 536a15–28 (*juan* 39); Roth 1970, 247 (§216). For an English translation of the Chinese text, see Hirakawa 1982, 311–312. For a French translation of Roth's text, see Nolot 1991, 267–268.

105. On various problems surrounding the enigmatic expulsion of a pregnant nun, see Clarke 2008.

106. Roth 1970, 247 (§216); T. 1425 (xxii) 536a17–20 (*juan* 39).

107. The Indic text uses the verb *upa√sthā,* which Nolot translates as "prendre en charge." The Chinese, however, consistently has *yu shoujuzu* 與受具足, and this undoubtedly translates a form of *upa-saṃ√pad.* Nolot 1991, 393–395,

notes that these two verbs seem to be used interchangeably. The same pattern is also seen in Pāli; see n. 24 above.

108. Lit. "yet" (未).

109. Lit. "grass-mattress." The term *ru* 蓐 of *caoru* 草蓐 is clearly connected with maternity. See Morohashi [1955–1960] 1986, 9.31660.5: 産室 "birthing chamber, delivery room."

110. T. 1425 (xxii) 536a20–24 (*juan* 39).

111. See n. 63 above.

112. According to the Chinese text, when she leaves the maternity mattress. The Prakrit text gives, to use Nolot's translation (1991, 268), "la chambre."

113. See Nattier and Prebish 1977.

114. I have yet to come across Mahāsāṅghika parallels to the rules in other traditions dealing with the provision of childcare assistance, separate living quarters, and special permission to share sleeping quarters with one's son.

115. *BD* 3:361–363; *pācittiya*s lxi–lxii.

116. T. 1428 (xxii) 754c2–3 (*juan* 27); T. 1428 (xxii) 755a5–6 (*juan* 27). The *Dharmaguptaka-vinaya* contains rules concerning the ordination of both nursing and pregnant women. For references to these rules in the extant *vinaya*s, see Hirakawa 1998, 551–553. The situation for the *Mūlasarvāstivāda-vinaya* is complicated. The *Mūlasarvāstivāda-vinaya* seems to contain only the rule concerning the initiation (not ordination) of pregnant women, not one about nursing mothers. Note, however, that the initial (and sole) formulation of the rule in the Tibetan *Bhikṣuṇī-vibhaṅga* already includes the term "knowingly" (*shes bzhin du*); sTog, *'Dul ba,* NYA 381b5–6. The *Ārya-sarvāstivādi-mūla-bhikṣuṇī-prātimokṣa-sūtra-vṛtti* makes it an offense if the initiation is carried out knowingly and not an offense if performed unknowingly; Peking, bstan 'gyur, *'Dul ba'i 'grel pa,* (vol. 122) DZU [DSU] 143b3–4. In the Chinese, there is no mention of initiating one "knowingly"; T. 1443 (xxiii) 1006a2 (*juan* 18).

117. On the relative date of the *anāpatti* formulas as "younger," see von Hinüber 1996, 14.

118. A comparative study of the various strata of rulings across the extant *vinaya*s is a desideratum.

119. *BD* 5:385; Vin 2:278–279.

120. See pp. 133–134.

121. *BD* 5:354 n. 2.

122. This has been noted by Hüsken 1997, 258, in reference to the Pāli Vinaya. On the foundation of the order of nuns, see von Hinüber 2008a and Anālayo 2008. On the establishment of the *bhikṣuṇī saṅgha* and the Buddha's debt to his mother, see Ohnuma 2006.

123. See p. 126 on the translation of *anu√jñā*.

124. For the nun's statement, see *BD* 5:385; Vin 2:278.31–.33. For the Buddha's authorization, see Vin 2:278.35–279.1. Horner translates: "I allow them, monks, having agreed upon one nun, to give her to that nun as a companion."

Again, here "allow" probably should be emended to "authorize" or something to that effect. The Pāli text then goes on to give the ecclesiastical act in detail. For an earlier translation of these three passages, see Rhys Davids and Oldenberg [1882–1885] 1996, 3:364–365; note, however, Rhys Davids and Oldenberg translate *gabbho vuṭṭhāsi* (Horner's "she was delivered of a child") as "her womb moved within her."

125. *BD* 5:386; Vin 2:279.15–.17.

126. As Horner notes in her translation (*BD* 5:386 n. 1), the fifth-century (?) commentary to the Pāli Vinaya, the *Samantapāsādikā,* adds that the mother—that is, the nun-mother—may, for example, bathe, feed, and dress him (Sp 6:1295.23–.24).

127. While there may have been other positions, the dearth of sources does not allow us to make statements about monastic traditions such as the Haimavatas, Vātsīputrīyas, Kāśyapīyas, and Bahuśrutīyas.

128. Nishimoto 1928, comparative table 4.3 (比丘尼波逸提法其三).

129. Rockhill 1884c, 182 (rule no. 109). Perhaps not able to believe that this was a rule about nuns selling (*vendre*) infants, Rockhill appears to have doubted the reading *bu hts'ong* (*'tshong*) *na,* which could be translated, as he remarks in a footnote, only as "si elle vend un enfant." The reading *'tshong* may be nothing more than a scribal error for *'tsho* "to nourish, rear, bring up." Rockhill notes the *vibhaṅga* reading *bu len na,* which is glossed with *rtse na* (si elle amuse). We have, then, two divergent translations of this rule. Rockhill suggests that it is a rule about nuns looking after (*soigner*) small infants, while Tsomo finds that it refers to nuns "raising" children. On the selling of children, see p. 160.

130. Tsomo 1996, 112 (rule no. 109).

131. It is not clear to me which edition Tsomo 1996 translates.

132. Kawaguchi manuscript, *'Dul ba,* CA 25a5; sNar thang, *'Dul ba,* TA 28b5 (reading unclear); sTog, *'Dul ba,* NYA 27a3.

133. sDe dge, *'Dul ba,* TA 20a1; Urga, *'Dul ba,* TA 20a1; lHa sa, *'Dul ba,* TA 27b1.

134. Co ne, *'Dul ba,* TA 21a2. See Jäschke [1881] 1958, q.vv. for the definitions.

135. T. 1455 (xxiv) 515a24–25.

136. Waldschmidt [1926] 1979, 167, translates the Chinese *jiyang* 給養 with the German verb *pflegen,* and this seems to be very close to Rockhill's *soigner.* Waldschmidt (ibid.) translates the Tibetan *'tsho* with German *nähren:* "W. f. e. N. ein Kind nährt. . . ." sDe dge, *'Dul ba,* TA 20a1.

137. Waldschmidt (ibid.) translates "ein fremdes Kind." That there is no offense in touching one's own child is made explicit in the commentarial tradition preserved in Tibetan. Guṇaprabha's *Autocommentary* reads (Peking, bstan 'gyur, *'Dul ba'i 'grel pa,* [vol. 124] YU 40b4–5): *gang gi bu la reg pa rjes su gnang ba'i phyir rang gi bu 'tsho ba la ni nyes pa med do //.*

138. sTog, *'Dul ba,* NYA 398a3–399a7; sDe dge, *'Dul ba,* TA 297b1–

298a7. T. 1443 (xxiii) 1010c11–1011a1 (*juan* 19). There are some interesting yet irreconcilable differences between the Tibetan and Chinese texts here. The rule is also found, again in quite some detail, in the little-studied *Ārya-sarvāstivādi-mūla-bhikṣuṇī-prātimokṣa-sūtra-vṛtti* (Peking, bstan 'gyur, *'Dul ba'i 'grel pa,* [vol. 122] DZU [DSU] 149b2–150a5). On problems associated with this text, see the appendix in Schopen 2004c. It now appears that we have two Mūlasarvāstivāda *vinaya* traditions preserved in the corpus of rules for nuns. In the fourteenth century, the great Tibetan polymath Bu sTon noted that the *Bhikṣuṇī-vibhaṅga* and the *Bhikṣuṇī-prātimokṣa* preserved in Tibetan do not match (Claus Vogel 1985). He drew what must have seemed the only possible conclusion: that one of the texts belongs to another school. Bu sTon concluded that what we now know as the Mūlasarvāstivādin *Bhikṣuṇī-vibhaṅga* is in fact not Mūlasarvāstivādin at all. But Bu sTon did not have access to perhaps the most credible eyewitness to the Mūlasarvāstivādin tradition(s) in India: Yijing. The Chinese translation of the Mūlasarvāstivādin *Bhikṣuṇī-vibhaṅga* generally matches the Tibetan *Bhikṣuṇī-vibhaṅga* against the Tibetan *Bhikṣuṇī-prātimokṣa.* In speaking of the "tangled ball of issues associated with Mūlasarvāstivādin rules for nuns," Schopen 2004c, 181, posited that "the agreement between the Tibetan *Vibhaṅga* and the Chinese *Prātimokṣa*... may suggest that it might not be the Tibetan *Vibhaṅga* that was derived from a non-Mūlasarvāstivādin source, but rather the Tibetan *Bhikṣuṇī-prātimokṣa* and that the problem lies with it." I rashly concurred (2006b, 319 n. 124). It now turns out that Guṇaprabha, the foremost exegete of the *Mūlasarvāstivāda-vinaya,* confirms the authenticity of the Tibetan *Bhikṣuṇī-prātimokṣa* insofar as his order of presentation of the *prātimokṣa* rules for nuns almost perfectly matches the extant Tibetan *Bhikṣuṇī-prātimokṣa.* We have, then, two competing traditions, both of which seem to be Mūlasarvāstivādin. On the basis of this evidence, I have suggested that we can no longer talk about the *Mūlasarvāstivāda-vinaya* in the singular; we have not one, but at least two Mūlasarvāstivādin *vinaya* traditions (Clarke 2011a and 2011b). This is particularly clear in the case of the Mūlasarvāstivādin nuns' corpus. Although somewhat less conclusive, there is mounting evidence to suggest that this situation also holds for the monks' texts (Clarke 2012a; and now Emms 2012).

139. T. 1443 (xxiii) 1010c12–13 (*juan* 19); sTog, *'Dul ba,* NYA 398a3–4.

140. sTog, *'Dul ba,* NYA 398a4–b1; cf. T. 1443 (xxiii) 1010c13–16 (*juan* 19).

141. sTog, *'Dul ba,* NYA 398b1–2; cf. T. 1443 (xxiii) 1010c16–19 (*juan* 19); Peking, bstan 'gyur, *'Dul ba'i 'grel pa,* (vol. 122) DZU [DSU] 149b4–5.

142. sTog, *'Dul ba,* NYA 398b2–5; T. 1443 (xxiii) 1010c19–21 (*juan* 19).

143. sTog, *'Dul ba,* NYA 398b6–399a1; cf. T. 1443 (xxiii) 1010c22–23 (*juan* 19); Peking, bstan 'gyur, *'Dul ba'i 'grel pa,* (vol. 122) DZU [DSU] 148b8–150a1.

144. sTog, *'Dul ba,* NYA 399a1–3; T. 1443 (xxiii) 1010c23–25 (*juan* 19); Peking, bstan 'gyur, *'Dul ba'i 'grel pa,* (vol. 122) DZU [DSU] 150a1–3.

145. Havnevik 1989, 90. The children are described as orphans or "put in the nunnery by their parents so they could be fed."

146. Peking, bstan 'gyur, *'Dul ba'i 'grel pa,* (vol. 122) DZU [DSU] 150a4–5.

147. Note, for instance, the Mūlasarvāstivādin (n. 95 above) stance which requires the mother's removal to a concealed place.

148. Pachow [1955] 2000; Prebish [1975] 1996; Tsomo 1996; and Kabilsingh 1998. On the relationship between the *prātimokṣas* and the *vibhaṅgas*, see Schlingloff 1964. See also Schopen (2000a) 2004a, 12–13.

149. Tsomo 1996, x.

150. Clarke 2008, 115.

151. Clarke 2008.

152. Ohnuma 2012, 191–192; emphasis in original. Ohnuma's evidence for this claim is problematic; she cites my own study of the nun Mettiyā, discussed above. The case of Mettiyā, albeit admittedly one of a pregnant nun who was expelled, is not evidence for a legal stance on monastic motherhood at all.

153. Reis 1983.

Chapter 5: Reconsidering Renunciation

1. See Chap. 3, n. 154.

2. See Chap. 1, Secs. 1 and 2.

3. Workman [1913] 1962, 125. Elizabeth Clark 1999, 33, tells us that scholars "question the degree to which anchoritic monasticism was truly solitary."

4. Workman [1913] 1962, 124.

5. Ibid., 125. Workman's work should be read in light of the foreword to the 1962 edition by David Knowles.

6. See p. 117 and Chap. 3, n. 271.

7. See Schopen 2005b.

8. Olivelle 1993, 167, notes that the Prājāpatya student is regarded as celibate despite the fact that he maintains sexual relations with his wife: "The assumption here is that he does so not for pleasure but for duty, and thus can be recognized as a celibate, an assumption common in later literature."

9. See Schopen 2004a.

10. On the "gift" in Indian Buddhism, see Ohnuma 2005.

11. Olivelle 2008a, 78. See also Olivelle 1993, 165–170.

12. Olivelle 1993, 113.

13. Olivelle 2005, 148, translating Manu vi 3; my emphasis.

14. Deo 1956, 466.

15. Ibid., 465.

16. Ibid., 490.

17. Ibid., 506.

18. Dayal [1932] 1978, 132. Dayal goes on to say that the Buddhists "had approved of the new mode of life, which was adopted by the unmarried *muni,* the lonely hermit and thinker."

19. Olivelle 2008b, xxx. Compare the prediction in the *Mūlasarvāstivāda-vinaya,* mentioned on p. 99.

20. See Clarke 2009b.

21. As evinced by the numerous rules in extant Buddhist monastic law codes expressly addressing the safety of nuns. For a discussion of this issue, see Jyväsjärvi 2011, esp. chap. 3.

22. Deo 1956, 466.

23. Ibid., 467.

24. Ibid., 490.

25. Ibid.

26. Ibid.; see also 494.

27. Ibid., 490–491.

28. Jyväsjärvi 2011, 456 (v. 4141); square brackets in original.

29. Bapat 1979, 48–49. For unmarried women, the minimum ages for initiation and ordination were eighteen and twenty, respectively. Altekar 1962, 55–56, notes that "soon after 100 A.D. . . . society definitely decided in favour of pre-puberty marriages." See also Kapadia 1958, 138–140.

30. See Chap. 3, n. 265.

31. Granoff 2006, 624; see also Deo 1956, 471. Note also Balbir 2001.

32. Granoff 2006, 624.

33. Ibid.

34. Schopen 2013, 21.

35. Ibid., 21–24.

36. Ibid., 21 n. 11.

37. The *Vessantara Jātaka* is mentioned in this context also by Granoff 2006, 618 n. 33. See also Chap. 1, n. 60.

38. Schopen 2013, 25–41.

39. Granoff 2006, 628.

40. See Boucher 2008, esp. chap. 4.

41. Ñāṇamoli and Bodhi [1995] 2001, 1104.

42. Ibid., 1105.

43. Boucher 2008, 233 n. 234.

44. See now Ohnuma 2012 on motherhood imagery in Indian Buddhist texts.

45. Almond 1988, 37.

46. Very conservatively, I estimate that we are probably at least half a century away from being able to read all canonical *vinaya* literature in English, to say nothing of the voluminous commentarial tradition preserved in Pāli, Sanskrit, Chinese, and Tibetan.

47. Krawiec 2002, 162.

48. Ibid., 10–11.

49. Ibid., 169: "Monks were to be separated from their kin so that their old family order did not affect their new monastic rank."

50. Constable 1978, 206–207.

51. Ibid., 207.

52. Boswell 1988, 456.

53. Constable 1978, 214, states that Aelred does not tell us what happened to the baby.

54. Boswell 1988, 371–372.

55. Constable 1978, 214; also quoted in Boswell 1988, 372.

56. Abbott [1999] 2001, 177.

57. For two recent examples, see Gyatso 2005 and Powers 2009.

58. T. 1441 (xxiii) 584a6–14 (*juan* 3); sTog, *'Dul ba,* DA 405a2–7. For a Sanskrit fragment, see SHT (V) 1063 (Sander and Waldschmidt 1985), discussed in detail in Clarke 2012b. Chung (2002, 93) identifies the Sanskrit fragment with T. 1441, which he takes as belonging to the *Sarvāstivāda-vinaya.* On problems associated with Chung's identifications, see Clarke 2010b.

59. *Kṣudrakavastu,* sTog, *'Dul ba,* THA 212a7–213b2; T. 1451 (xxiv) 360a9–b3 (*juan* 31).

60. T. 1428 (xxii) 930a9–15 (*juan* 49).

61. *Vinaya-vibhaṅga,* T. 1442 (xxiii) 662b12–15 (*juan* 7); sTog, *'Dul ba,* CA 206b2–5. Here I read with the Tibetan; the Chinese suggests that the monk or nun "tramples her belly" (蹂蹋其腹). *Bhikṣuṇī-vibhaṅga,* T. 1443 (xxiii) 925c19–22 (*juan* 4). The Tibetan translation of the *Bhikṣuṇī-vibhaṅga* differs markedly from the Chinese; see Chap. 4, n. 138, for further references.

62. On the possible applicability of *pārājika* penance to all *pārājika* offenses, see Clarke 2000, 154–157.

63. See Schopen 2007c. Textual evidence for such enterprising nuns is not limited to the *Mūlasarvāstivāda-vinaya.* The *Mahīśāsaka-vinaya,* for instance, mentions nuns who were criticized for operating taverns (作酒沽) (T. 1421 [xxii] 190a19–20 [*juan* 29]), lending money on interest (出息) (T. 1421 [xxii] 190a23–25 [*juan* 29]), running brothels (畜婬女坐肆賃之) (T. 1421 [xxii] 190a25–26 [*juan* 29]), pressing and selling oil (壓油賣) (T. 1421 [xxii] 190a26–27 [*juan* 29]), keeping fields, draught cattle, slaves, and supervising the ploughing and sowing of fields (畜田犁牛奴自看耕種) (T. 1421 [xxii] 190a20–23 [*juan* 29]). These references have been discussed briefly in Clarke 2002b. The *Dharmaguptaka-vinaya* contains a short episode about nuns' dealing in alcohol (酤酒) (T. 1428 [xxii] 928a23–24 [*juan* 49]) and what seems to be the establishment of a brothel (安婬女在住處) (T. 1428 [xxii] 928a24–25 [*juan* 49]). The *Sarvāstivāda-vinaya* contains a story about a nun who set up a tavern (立沽酒店) (T. 1435 [xxiii] 294c25–29 [*juan* 40]), one who made alcohol (作酒) (T. 1435 [xxiii] 297c18–22 [*juan* 41]), and one who rented out stores (賃舍) (T. 1435 [xxiii] 297c23–28 [*juan* 41]). The *Mahāsāṅghika-vinaya* mentions nuns of noble backgrounds who made their livelihood from putting their servants to work as prostitutes (貴人女將使人出家。使人端正。令與外人交通以自活命) (T. 1425 [xxii] 545b3–9 [*juan* 40]). Undoubtedly, there are many more such references, all of which deserve a separate treatment.

Works Consulted

Abbott, Elizabeth. [1999] 2001. *A History of Celibacy.* New York: Da Capo Press.

Adachi Kin'ichi 足立欽一. 1923. *Gedō zanmai* 外道三昧. Tokyo: Seichōsha 青潮社.

———. 1924. *Karudai* 迦留陀夷. Tokyo: Shūhōkaku 聚芳閣.

Agrawala, Ratna Chandra. 1954. "Life of Buddhist Monks in Chinese Turkestan." In *Sarūpa-bhāratī; or, The Homage of Indology: Being the Dr. Lakshman Sarup Memorial Volume,* ed. Nath Agrawal Jagan and Dev Shastri Bhim, 173–181. Hoshiarpur: Vishveshvaranand Institute Publications.

Allen, Michael. 1973. "Buddhism without Monks: The Vajrayana Religion of the Newars of Kathmandu Valley." *South Asia: Journal of South Asian Studies* 3:1–14.

Almond, Philip C. 1988. *The British Discovery of Buddhism.* Cambridge: Cambridge University Press.

Altekar, A. S. 1962. *The Position of Women in Hindu Civilization from Prehistoric Times to the Present Day.* 3rd ed. Delhi: Motilal Banarsidass.

Anālayo. 2008. "Theories on the Foundation of the Nuns' Order—A Critical Evaluation." *Journal of the Centre for Buddhist Studies, Sri Lanka* 6:105–142.

———. 2011. "*Chos sbyin gyi mdo*—Bhikṣuṇī Dharmadinnā Proves Her Wisdom." *Chung-Hwa Buddhist Journal* 24:3–33.

———. 2012. "The Case of Sudinna: On the Function of *Vinaya* Narrative, Based on a Comparative Study of the Background Narration to the First *Pārājika* Rule." *Journal of Buddhist Ethics* 19:396–438.

Anonymous. [1890] 1957. "The Literature of Tibet." In *The Life and Teachings of Buddha,* by Alexander Csoma Korosi, 104–137. Calcutta: Susil Gupta (India) Private Limited.

Atwood, Christopher. 1991. "Life in Third-fourth Century Cadh'ota: A Survey of Information Gathered from the Prakrit Documents Found North of Minfeng (Niyä)." *Central Asiatic Journal* 35, nos. 3/4:161–199.

Ayyar, V. Ramanatha, and K. Parameswara Aithal. 1964. "Kārpāsa Cotton: Its Origin and Spread in Ancient India." *Adyar Library Bulletin* 28, nos. 1/2:1–40.

Aziz, Barbara Nimri. 1978. *Tibetan Frontier Families: Reflections of Three Generations from D'ing-ri*. New Delhi: Vikas Publishing House.

Bailey, Greg, and Ian Mabbett. 2003. *The Sociology of Early Buddhism*. Cambridge: Cambridge University Press.

Balbir, Nalini. 2001. "La question de l'ordination des enfants en milieu jaina." In *Les âges de la vie dans le monde indien*, ed. Christine Chojnacki, 153–183. Paris: Distributed by De Boccard.

Baldissera, Fabrizia. 2005. *The Narmamālā of Kṣemendra: Critical Edition, Study, and Translation*. Beiträge zur Südasienforschung 197. Würzburg: Ergon Verlag.

Banerjee, Gooroodass. 1879. *The Hindu Law of Marriage and Stridhan*. Calcutta: Thacker, Spink, and Co.

Banerji-Sastri, A. 1940. "Ninety-three Inscriptions on the Kurkihar Bronzes." *Journal of the Bihar and Orissa Research Society* 26, no. 3:236–251.

Bapat, P. V. 1979. "Guṇaprabha's *Vinaya-sūtra* and His Own Commentary on the Same." *Journal of the International Association of Buddhist Studies* 1, no. 2:47–51.

Bapat, P. V., and V. V. Gokhale. 1982. *Vinaya-sūtra and Auto-Commentary on the Same by Guṇaprabha*. Tibetan Sanskrit Works Series 22. Patna: K. P. Jayaswal Research Institute.

Bapat, P. V., and Akira Hirakawa. 1970. *Shan-Chien-P'i-P'o-Sha: A Chinese Version by Saṅghabhadra of Samantapāsādikā*. Bhandarkar Oriental Series 10. Poona: Bhandarkar Oriental Research Institute.

Bareau, André. 1955. *Les sectes bouddhiques du petit véhicule*. Paris: Publications de l'École française d'Extrême-Orient.

———. 1976. "Les reactions des familles dont un membre devient moine selon le canon bouddhique pali." In *Malalasekera Commemoration Volume*, ed. O. H. de A. Wijesekera, 15–22. Colombo: Malalasekera Commemoration Volume Editorial Committee.

Barnett, L. D. 1924. "Some Notes on the Matta-Vilasa." *Bulletin of the School of Oriental Studies, University of London* 3, no. 2:281–285.

———. 1930. "Matta-Vilasa: A Farce." *Bulletin of the School of Oriental Studies, University of London* 5, no. 4:697–717.

Basham, A. L. [1954] 1959. *The Wonder That was India: A Survey of the History and Culture of the Indian Sub-Continent before the Coming of the Muslims*. New York: Grove Press.

———. 1966. *Aspects of Ancient Indian Culture*. Bombay: Asia Publishing House.

———. 1981. "The Evolution of the Concept of the Bodhisattva." In *The Bodhisattva Doctrine in Buddhism*, ed. Leslie S. Kawamura, 19–59. Waterloo: Wilfrid Laurier University Press.

Bechert, Heinz. 1968. "Some Remarks on the Kaṭhina Rite." *Journal of the Bihar Research Society* 54, nos. 1/4:319–329.

———. 1973. "Notes on the Formation of Buddhist Sects and the Origins of

Mahāyāna." In *German Scholars on India: Contributions to Indian Studies*, ed. Cultural Department of the Embassy of the Federal Republic of Germany, New Delhi, 1:6–18. Varanasi: Chowkhamba Sanskrit Series Office.

———. 1993. "On the Origination and Characteristics of Buddhist Nikāyas, or Schools." In *Premier Colloque Étienne Lamotte (Bruxelles et Liège 24–27 Septembre 1989)*, 51–56. Publications de l'Institut Orientaliste de Louvain. Louvain-la-Neuve: Institut Orientaliste.

Bianchi, Ester. 2001. *The Iron Statue Monastery: "Tiexiangsi," a Buddhist Nunnery of Tibetan Tradition in Contemporary China*. Firenze: L. S. Olschki.

Bigandet, P. [1879] 1979. *The Life or Legend of Gaudama, the Buddha of the Burmese*. 3rd ed. 2 vols. Varanasi: Bharatiya Publishing House.

Bingenheimer, Marcus. 2006. "The Shorter Chinese *Saṃyukta Āgama:* Preliminary Findings and Translation of Fascicle 1 of the *Bieyi za ahan jing* 別譯雜阿含經 (T.100)." *Buddhist Studies Review* 23, no. 1:21–60.

Bloch, T. 1905–1906. "Two Inscriptions on Buddhist Images." *Epigraphia Indica* 8:179–182.

Bloomfield, Maurice. 1924. "On False Ascetics and Nuns in Hindu Fiction." *Journal of the American Oriental Society* 44, no. 3:202–242.

Bond, George D. 1980. "Theravada Buddhism's Meditations on Death and the Symbolism of Initiatory Death." *History of Religions* 19, no. 3:237–258.

Bongard-Levin, G. M. 1975–1976. "New Sanskrit and Prakrit Texts from Central Asia." *Indologica Taurinensia* 3–4:73–80.

Bose, M. M., ed. [1934–1936] 1977. *Paramattha-Dīpanī Iti-Vuttakaṭṭhakathā (Iti-Vuttaka Commentary) of Dhammapālâcariya*. 2 vols. bound as one. London: Pali Text Society.

Boswell, John. 1988. *The Kindness of Strangers: The Abandonment of Children in Western Europe from Late Antiquity to the Renaissance*. New York: Pantheon Books.

Boucher, Daniel. 2008. *Bodhisattvas of the Forest and the Formation of the Mahāyāna: A Study and Translation of the Rāṣṭrapālaparipṛcchā-sūtra*. Honolulu: University of Hawai'i Press.

Boyer, A. M., E. J. Rapson, and E. Senart, eds. 1920–1929. *Kharoṣṭhī Inscriptions Discovered by Sir Aurel Stein in Chinese Turkestan*. 3 vols. Oxford: Clarendon Press.

Brobjer, Thomas H. 2004. "Nietzsche's Reading About Eastern Philosophy." *Journal of Nietzsche Studies* 28:3–35.

Bronkhorst, Johannes. 1986. *The Two Traditions of Meditation in Ancient India*. Alt- und neu-indische Studien 28. Stuttgart: Steiner Verlag.

———. [1993] 1998. *The Two Sources of Indian Asceticism*. Delhi: Motilal Banarsidass.

———. 2006. "The Context of Indian Philosophy." In *Conflict between Tradition and Creativity in Indian Philosophy: Text and Context*, ed. Toshihiro Wada, 9–22. Nagoya: Graduate School of Letters, Nagoya University.

Brough, John. 1965. "Comments on Third-Century Shan-Shan and the History of Buddhism." *Bulletin of the School of Oriental and African Studies, University of London* 28, no. 3:582–612.

Buchanan, Francis. 1799. "*On the* Religion *and* Literature *of the* Burmas." *Asiatick Researches; or, Transactions of the Society Instituted in Bengal, for Inquiring into the History and Antiquities, the Arts, Sciences, and Literature, of Asia* 6:163–308.

Bühler, G. 1894. "Further Inscriptions from Sânchi." *Epigraphia Indica* 2:366–408.

Buitenen, J. A. B. van. 1975. *The Mahābhārata*. Vol. 2. Chicago: University of Chicago Press.

Burnouf, Eugène. [1844] 1876. *Introduction à l'histoire du buddhisme indien*. 2nd ed. Paris: Maisonneuve et Cie, Libraires-Éditeurs.

———. 2010. *Introduction to the History of Indian Buddhism*. Translated by Katia Buffetrille and Donald S. Lopez Jr. Chicago: University of Chicago Press.

Burrow, T. 1940. *A Translation of the Kharoṣṭhi Documents from Chinese Turkestan*. London: Royal Asiatic Society.

Buswell, Robert E., Jr. 2004. "Sugi's *Collation Notes* to the Koryŏ Buddhist Canon and Their Significance for Buddhist Textual Criticism." *Journal of Korean Studies* 9, no. 1:129–184.

Caner, Daniel. 2002. *Wandering, Begging Monks: Spiritual Authority and the Promotion of Monasticism in Late Antiquity*. Berkeley: University of California Press.

Chakravarti, Uma. 1987. *The Social Dimensions of Early Buddhism*. Delhi: Oxford University Press.

Chalmers, Robert. [1898] 1960. *The Majjhima-nikāya*. Vol. 2. London: Published for the Pali Text Society by Messrs. Luzac & Co.

———. 1932. *Buddha's Teachings, Being the Sutta-Nipāta or Discourse-Collection*. Harvard Oriental Series 37. Cambridge, MA: Harvard University Press.

Chandra Vidyabhusana, Satis, ed. and trans. 2000. *So-sor thar pa (Khrims): Vol. 5 of the Dulwa Portion of the Kangyur (Leaves 1–29 and Top Line of Leaf 30)*. Calcutta: R. N. Bhattacharya. Previously published as "So-sor-thar-pa; or, a Code of Buddhist Monastic Laws: Being the Tibetan version of Prātimokṣa of the Mūla-sarvāstivāda School." *Journal of the Asiatic Society of Bengal* 11 (1915): 29–139.

Chapekar, Nalinee. 2003. "Buddhists [*sic*] Characters in Sanskrit Literature." In *Buddhism in Global Perspective,* ed. Kalpakam Sankarnarayan, Ichijo Ogawa, and Ravindra Panth, 2:431–450. Mumbai: Somaiya Publications.

Chen, Jinhua. 2002. "Family Ties and Buddhist Nuns in Tang China: Two Studies." *Asia Major,* 3rd ser., 15, no. 2:51–85.

Ch'en, Kenneth K. S. 1968. *Buddhism: The Light of Asia*. Woodbury, NY: Barron's Educational Series.

Childers, Robert Cæsar. [1875] 1979. *A Dictionary of the Pali Language*. New Delhi: Cosmo Publications.

Chung, Jin-il. 2002. "Sanskrit-Fragmente des sogenannten Daśādhyāya-vinaya aus Zentralasien: eine vorläufige Auflistung." In *Sanskrit-Texte aus dem buddhistischen Kanon: Neuentdeckungen und Neueditionen IV*, ed. Jin-il Chung, Claus Vogel, and Klaus Wille, 77–104. Sanskrit-Wörterbuch der buddhistischen Texte aus den Turfan-Funden 9. Göttingen: Vandenhoeck & Ruprecht.

Chung, Jin-il, and Klaus Wille. 1997. "Einige Bhikṣuvinayavibhaṅga-Fragmente der Dharmaguptakas in der Sammlung Pelliot." In *Untersuchungen zur buddhistischen Literatur: Zweite Folge*, ed. Heinz Bechert, Sven Bretfeld, and Petra Kieffer-Pülz, 47–94. Sanskrit-Wörterbuch der buddhistischen Texte aus den Turfan-Funden 8. Göttingen: Vandenhoeck & Ruprecht.

Clark, Elizabeth A. 1999. *Reading Renunciation: Asceticism and Scripture in Early Christianity*. Princeton, NJ: Princeton University Press.

Clark, Gillian, trans. 2000. *Porphyry: On Abstinence from Killing Animals*. Ithaca, NY: Cornell University Press.

Clarke, Shayne. 1999. "Pārājika: the Myth of Permanent and Irrevocable Expulsion from the Buddhist Order: A Survey of the Śikṣādattaka in Early Monastic Buddhism." MA thesis, University of Canterbury.

———. 2000. "The Existence of the Supposedly Non-existent *Śikṣādattā-śrāmaṇerī*: A New Perspective on *Pārājika* Penance." *Bukkyō kenkyū* 仏教研究 29:149–176.

———. 2002a. "The *Mūlasarvāstivādin Vinaya*: A Brief Reconnaissance Report." In *Sakurabe Hajime hakushi kiju kinen ronshū: Shoki bukkyō kara abidaruma e* 櫻部建博士喜寿記念論集·初期仏教からアビダルマへ, ed. Sakurabe Hajime hakushi kiju kinen ronshū kankōkai 櫻部建博士喜寿記念論集刊行会, 45–63. Kyoto: Heirakuji shoten 平樂寺書店.

———. 2002b. "Hallowed Harrowing and Fields of Merit: Share-cropping Monks in Buddhist India." Paper presented at the 13th Congress of the International Association of Buddhist Studies, Bangkok, December 8–13, 2002.

———. 2004a. "*Vinaya Mātṛkā*—Mother of the Monastic Codes, or Just Another Set of Lists? A Response to Frauwallner's Handling of the Mahāsāṃghika *Vinaya*." *Indo-Iranian Journal* 47, no. 2:77–120.

———. 2004b. "Right Section, Wrong Collection: An Identification of a Canonical Vinaya Text in the Tibetan *bsTan 'gyur—Bya ba'i phung po zhes bya ba (Kriyāskandha-nāma)*." *Journal of the American Oriental Society* 124, no. 2:335–340.

———. 2006a. "Miscellaneous Musings on Mūlasarvāstivāda Monks: The *Mūlasarvāstivāda Vinaya* Revival in Tokugawa Japan." *Japanese Journal of Religious Studies* 33, no. 1:1–49.

———. 2006b. "Family Matters in Indian Monastic Buddhism." PhD diss., University of California, Los Angeles.

———. 2008. "The Case of the Nun Mettiyā Reexamined: On the Expulsion of a Pregnant *Bhikṣuṇī* in the *Vinaya* of the Mahāsāṅghikas and Other Indian Buddhist Monastic Law Codes." *Indo-Iranian Journal* 51, no. 2:115–135.

———. 2009a. "Monks Who Have Sex: *Pārājika* Penance in Indian Buddhist Monasticisms." *Journal of Indian Philosophy* 37, no. 1:1–43.

———. 2009b. "When and Where Is a Monk No Longer a Monk? On Communion and Communities in Indian Buddhist Monastic Law Codes." *Indo-Iranian Journal* 52, nos. 2/3:115–141.

———. 2009c. "Locating Humour in Indian Buddhist Monastic Law Codes: A Comparative Approach." *Journal of Indian Philosophy* 37, no. 4:311–330.

———. 2010a. "Creating Nuns Out of Thin Air: Problems and Possible Solutions Concerning the Ordination of Nuns according to the Tibetan Monastic Code." In *Dignity and Discipline: Reviving Full Ordination for Buddhist Nuns,* ed. Thea Mohr and Jampa Tsedroen, 227–238. Boston: Wisdom Publications.

———. 2010b. "Towards a Comparative Study of the *Sarvāstivāda-* and *Mūlasarvāstivāda-vinaya*s: Studies in the Structure of the *Uttaragrantha* (1): *Kathāvastu*—A Preliminary Survey." Unpublished manuscript.

———. 2011a. "Guṇaprabha, Yijing, Bu sTon and the Lack of a Coherent System of Rules for Nuns in the Tibetan Tradition of the *Mūlasarvāstivāda-vinaya.*" Paper presented at Buddhist Nuns in India, University of Toronto, April 15–17, 2011.

———. 2011b. "On the Mūlasarvāstivādin Affiliations of the *Bhikṣuṇī Vibhaṅga* and *Bhikṣuṇī Prātimokṣa* Preserved in Tibetan." Paper presented at the 16th Congress of the International Association of Buddhist Studies, Jinshan, Taiwan, June 20–25, 2011.

———. 2012a. "Multiple Mūlasarvāstivādin Monasticisms: On the Affiliation of the Tibetan Nuns' Lineages and Beyond." Paper presented at the Oslo Buddhist Studies Forum, University of Oslo, June 12, 2012.

———. 2012b. "An Unnoticed Collection of Indian Buddhist Case Law: The *'Dul bar byed pa* of the Mūlasarvāstivādin *Uttaragrantha.*" Paper presented at the International Institute for Buddhist Studies, Tokyo, November 30, 2012.

Clasquin, Michel. 2001. "Real Buddhas Don't Laugh: Attitudes towards Humour and Laughter in Ancient India and China." *Social Identities* 7, no. 1:97–116.

Cole, Alan. 2004. "Family, Buddhism and the." In *Encyclopedia of Buddhism,* ed. Robert E. Buswell Jr., 1:280–281. New York: Macmillan Reference USA.

———. 2005. *Text as Father: Paternal Seductions in Early Mahāyāna Buddhist Literature*. Berkeley: University of California Press.

———. 2006. "Buddhism." In *Sex, Marriage, and Family in World Religions,* ed. Don S. Browning, M. Christian Green, and John Witte Jr., 299–366. New York: Columbia University Press.

Collins, Steven. 1982. *Selfless Persons: Imagery and Thought in Theravāda Buddhism.* Cambridge: Cambridge University Press.

———. 1988. "Monasticism, Utopias and Comparative Social Theory." *Religion* 18:101–135.

———. 1990. Introd. to *Buddhist Monastic Life: According to the Texts of the Theravāda Tradition,* by Môhan Wijayaratna, ix–xxiv. Cambridge: Cambridge University Press.

———. 1992. "Problems with Pacceka-buddhas." Review of *Ascetic Figures before and in Early Buddhism: The Emergence of Gautama as the Buddha,* by Martin G. Wiltshire. *Religion* 22:271–278.

Cone, Margaret. 2001. *A Dictionary of Pāli. Part 1. a—kh.* Oxford: Pali Text Society.

Cone, Margaret, and Richard F. Gombrich. 1977. *The Perfect Generosity of Prince Vessantara: A Buddhist Epic; Translated from the Pali and Illustrated by Unpublished Paintings from Sinhalese Temples.* Oxford: Clarendon Press.

Constable, Giles. 1978. "Aelred of Rievaulx and the Nun of Watton: An Episode in the Early History of the Gilbertine Order." In *Medieval Women,* ed. Derek Baker, 205–226. Oxford: Basil Blackwell.

Coomaraswamy, Ananda. [1916] 1956. *Buddha and the Gospel of Buddhism.* Bombay: Asia Publishing House.

Coomára Swámy, M. 1874. *Sutta Nipáta; or, Dialogues and Discourses of Gotama Buddha; Translated from the Páli, with Introduction and Notes.* London: Trübner & Co.

Costelloe, M. Joseph. 1992. *The Letters and Instructions of Francis Xavier.* St. Louis, MO: Institute of Jesuit Sources.

Cousins, L. S. 1985. Review of *The Group of Discourses (Sutta-nipāta),* vol. 1, by K. R. Norman. *Journal of the Royal Asiatic Society of Great Britain and Ireland* 2:219–220.

Covill, Linda. 2007. *Handsome Nanda.* New York: JJC Foundation; New York University Press.

Crosby, Kate. 2005. "'Only If You Let Go of That Tree': Ordination without Parental Consent in Theravāda Vinaya." *Buddhist Studies Review* 22, no. 2:155–173.

Daizōkai 大蔵会, ed. 1964. *Daizōkyō: Seiritsu to hensen* 大蔵経・成立と変遷. Kyoto: Hyakka-en 百華苑.

Dani, Ahmad Hasan. 1963. *Indian Palaeography.* Oxford: Clarendon Press.

Das Gupta, C. C. 1949–1950. "Shelarwadi Cave Inscription." *Epigraphia Indica* 28:76–77.

Dayal, Har. [1932] 1978. *The Bodhisattva Doctrine in Buddhist Sanskrit Literature.* Delhi: Motilal Banarsidass.

Dehejia, Vidya. 1972. *Early Buddhist Rock Temples: A Chronology.* Ithaca, NY: Cornell University Press.

———. 1997. *Discourse in Early Buddhist Art: Visual Narratives of India*. New Delhi: Munshiram Manoharlal Publishers Pvt.

Deleanu, Florin. 2006. *The Chapter on the Mundane Path (Laukikamārga) in the Śrāvakabhūmi: A Trilingual Edition (Sanskrit, Tibetan, Chinese), Annotated Translation, and Introductory Study*. Studia Philologica Buddhica. Monograph Series 20. 2 vols. Tokyo: International Institute for Buddhist Studies of the International College for Postgraduate Buddhist Studies.

———. 2007. "The Transmission of Xuanzang's Translation of the Yogācārabhūmi in East Asia: With a Philological Analysis of Scroll XXXIII." In *Kongōji issaikyō no sōgōteki kenkyū to Kongōji shōgyō no kisoteki kenkyū* 金剛寺一切経の総合的研究と金剛寺聖教の基礎的研究, ed. Ochiai Toshinori 落合俊典 et al., 1:1–44. Tokyo: Kokusai bukkyōgaku daigakuin daigaku 国際仏教学大学院大学.

Demiéville, Paul, Hubert Durt, and Anna Seidel, comps. 1978. *Répertoire du canon bouddhique Sino-Japonais: Édition de Taishō (Taishō Shinshū Daizōkyō)*. Paris/Tokyo: Librairie d'Amérique et d'Orient Adrien-Maisonneuve.

Demoto Mitsuyo 出本充代. 1998. "*Avadānaśataka* no bon-kan hikaku kenkyū *Avadānaśataka*の梵漢比較研究." PhD diss., Kyoto University.

Deo, Shantaram Bhalchandra. 1956. *History of Jaina Monachism: From Inscriptions and Literature*. Deccan College Dissertation Series 17. Poona: Deccan College Postgraduate and Research Institute.

Dettwyler, Katherine A. 1995. "A Time to Wean: The Hominid Blueprint for the Natural Age of Weaning in Modern Human Populations." In *Breastfeeding: Biocultural Perspectives*, ed. Patricia Stuart-Macadam and Katherine A. Dettwyler, 39–74. New York: Aldine De Gruyter.

Devee, Sunity. 1989. *The Life of Princess Yashōdara: Wife and Disciple of the Lord Buddha*. Jammu Tawi: Jay Kay Book House.

Dietz, Maribel. 2005. *Wandering Monks, Virgins, and Pilgrims: Ascetic Travel in the Mediterranean World, A.D. 300–800*. University Park: Pennsylvania State University Press.

Dissanayake, Piyasena. 1977. *Political Thoughts of the Buddha*. Colombo: Department of Cultural Affairs.

Doniger, Wendy, and Sudhir Kakar, trans. 2002. *Kamasutra: A New, Complete English Translation of the Sanskrit Text with Excerpts from the Sanskrit Jayamangala Commentary of Yashodhara Indrapada, the Hindi Jaya Commentary of Devadatta Shastri, and Explanatory Notes by the Translators*. Oxford: Oxford University Press.

Doniger, Wendy, and Brian K. Smith, trans. 1991. *The Laws of Manu: With an Introduction and Notes*. London: Penguin Books.

Don Peter, W. L. A. 1990. *Buddhist and Benedictine Monastic Education: A Comparative Study of the Educational Implications of the Vinaya and the Rule of St. Benedict*. Colombo: Evangel Press.

Dull, Jack L. 1978. "Marriage and Divorce in Han China: A Glimpse at 'Pre-Confucian' Society." In *Chinese Family Law and Social Change: In Histori-*

cal and Comparative Perspective, ed. David C. Buxbaum, Asian Law Series 3:23–74. Seattle: University of Washington Press.

Dumont, Louis. 1960. "World Renunciation in Indian Religions." In *Contributions to Indian Sociology,* ed. Louis Dumont and D. Pocock, 4:33–62. Paris: Mouton & Co.

Durt, Hubert. 1980. "Mahalla/Mahallaka et la crise de la communauté après le Parinirvāṇa du Buddha." In *Indianisme et bouddhisme: Mélanges offerts à Mgr Étienne Lamotte,* Publications de l'Institut Orientaliste de Louvain, 23:79–99. Louvain-la-Neuve: Université catholique de Louvain, Institut Orientaliste.

———. 2002. "The Pregnancy of Māyā: I. The Five Uncontrollable Longings (*dohada*)." *Journal of the International College for Advanced Buddhist Studies* 5:43–66.

———. 2003. "The Pregnancy of Māyā: II. Māyā as Healer." *Journal of the International College for Advanced Buddhist Studies* 6:43–62.

———. 2004. "On the Pregnancy of Māyā III: Late Episodes." *Journal of the International College for Advanced Buddhist Studies* 7:55–72.

———. 2005. "Kajaṅgalā, Who Could Have Been the Last Mother of the Buddha." *Journal of the International College for Postgraduate Buddhist Studies* 9:65–90.

Dutt, Nalinaksha. [1941] 1981. *Early Monastic Buddhism.* 2nd ed. Calcutta: Firma K. L. Mukhopadhyay.

———, ed. [1942–1950] 1984. *Gilgit Manuscripts.* Vol. 3 in 4 parts. Bibliotheca Indo-Buddhica 16–19. 2nd ed. Delhi: Sri Satguru.

———. 1978. *Buddhist Sects in India.* 2nd ed. Delhi: Motilal Banarasidass Publishers.

Dutt, Sukumar. [1924] 1996. *Early Buddhist Monachism.* New Delhi: Munshiram Manoharlal Publishers.

———. 1957. *The Buddha and Five After-Centuries.* London: Luzac & Company Limited.

———. [1962] 1988. *Buddhist Monks and Monasteries of India: Their History and Their Contribution to Indian Culture.* Delhi: Motilal Banarsidass.

Edgerton, Franklin. [1953] 1998. *Buddhist Hybrid Sanskrit Dictionary.* Delhi: Motilal Banarsidass.

Edkins, J. 1881. "The Nirvana of the Northern Buddhists." *Journal of the Royal Asiatic Society of Great Britain and Ireland,* n.s., 13:59–79.

Eimer, Helmut. 1983. *Rab tu ʾbyuṅ ba'i gži. Die tibetische Übersetzung des Pravrajyāvastu im Vinaya der Mūlasarvāstivādins.* Asiatische Forschungen 82. 2 vols. Wiesbaden: Otto Harrassowitz.

Elm, Susanna. 1994. *"Virgins of God": The Making of Asceticism in Late Antiquity.* Oxford: Clarendon Press.

Emms, Christopher. 2012. "Evidence for Two Mūlasarvāstivādin *Vinaya* Traditions in the Gilgit *Prātimokṣa-sūtras.*" MA thesis, McMaster University.

Enomoto Fumio 榎本文雄. 1998. "'Konponsetsuissaiubu' to 'Setsuissaiubu' 「根

本説一切有部」と「説一切有部」." *Indogaku bukkyōgaku kenkyū* 印度學佛教學研究 47, no. 1:111–119.

———. 2000. "'Mūlasarvāstivādin' and 'Sarvāstivādin.'" In *Vividharatnakaraṇḍaka: Festgabe für Adelheid Mette,* ed. Christine Chojnacki, Jens-Uwe Hartmann, and Volker M. Tschannerl, Indica et Tibetica 37:239–250. Swisttal-Odendorf: Indica et Tibetica.

Ensink, Jacob. 1952. *The Question of Rāṣṭrapāla.* Zwolle: J. J. Tijl.

Faure, Bernard. 1998. *The Red Thread: Buddhist Approaches to Sexuality.* Princeton, NJ: Princeton University Press.

———. 2003. *The Power of Denial: Buddhism, Purity, and Gender.* Princeton, NJ: Princeton University Press.

Fausböll, V., trans. 1881. *The Sutta-nipâta: A Collection of Discourses; Being One of the Canonical Books of the Buddhists.* Sacred Books of the East 10, pt. 2. Oxford: Clarendon Press.

Feer, Léon. 1883. *Fragments extraits du Kandjour.* Annales du Musée Guimet 5. Paris: Ernest Leroux.

Fezas, Jean. 2001. "Responsabilité, âge de raison et indépendance dans la tradition juridique hindoue." In *Les âges de la vie dans le monde indien,* ed. Christine Chojnacki, 51–64. Paris: Distributed by De Boccard.

Findly, Ellison Banks. 2003. *Dāna: Giving and Getting in Pali Buddhism.* Buddhist Tradition Series 52. Delhi: Motilal Banarsidass.

Finnegan, Damchö Diana. 2009. "'For the Sake of Women, Too': Ethics and Gender in the Narratives of the *Mūlasarvāstivāda Vinaya.*" PhD diss., University of Wisconsin-Madison.

Flood, Gavin. 2004. *The Ascetic Self: Subjectivity, Memory, and Tradition.* Cambridge: Cambridge University Press.

Formigatti, Camillo Alessio. 2009. "The Story of Sundarī and Nanda in the *Mūlasarvāstivādavinaya.*" In *Pāsādikadānaṁ: Festschrift für Bhikkhu Pāsādika,* ed. Martin Straube, Roland Steiner, Jayandra Soni, Michael Hahn, and Mitsuyo Demoto, Indica et Tibetica 52:129–155. Marburg: Indica et Tibetica.

Frankfurter, O. 1883. *Handbook of Pāli: Being an Elementary Grammar, a Chrestomathy, and a Glossary.* London: Williams and Norgate.

Frauwallner, Erich. 1956. *The Earliest Vinaya and the Beginnings of Buddhist Literature.* Serie Orientale Roma 8. Rome: Istituto Italiano per il Medio ed Estremo Oriente.

Freiberger, Oliver. 2005. "Resurrection from the Dead? The Brāhmaṇical Rite of Renunciation and Its Irreversibility." In *Words and Deeds: Hindu and Buddhist Rituals in South Asia,* ed. Jörg Gengnagel, Ute Hüsken, and Srilata Raman, 235–256. Wiesbaden: Harrassowitz Verlag.

Fry, Timothy, ed. 1981. *RB 1980: The Rule of St. Benedict in Latin and English with Notes.* Collegeville, MN: Liturgical Press.

Geiger, Wilhelm. [1929] 1998. *Cūḷavaṃsa: Being the More Recent Part of the*

Mahāvaṃsa. Edited by C. Mabel Rickmers. 2 vols. New Delhi: Asian Educational Services.

Gellner, David N. 1992. *Monk, Householder, and Tantric Priest: Newar Buddhism and Its Hierarchy of Ritual*. Cambridge: Cambridge University Press.

Gethin, Rupert. 1998. *The Foundations of Buddhism*. Oxford: Oxford University Press.

Giles, Lionel. 1935. "Dated Chinese Manuscripts in the Stein Collection." *Bulletin of the School of Oriental Studies* 7:810–836.

———. 1957. *Descriptive Catalogue of the Chinese Manuscripts from Tunhuang in the British Museum*. London: Trustees of the British Museum.

Gokhale, B. G. 1965. "The Theravāda-Buddhist View of History." *Journal of the American Oriental Society* 85, no. 3:354–360.

Gokhale, Shobhana. 1957. "Cultural Significance of the Personal and Place Names from Vākāṭaka Inscriptions." *Bulletin of the Deccan College Research Institute* 18:173–185.

Gombrich, Richard. 1975. "Buddhist Karma and Social Control." *Comparative Studies in Society and History* 17, no. 2:212–220.

———. 1986. Review of *Le moine bouddhiste selon les textes du Theravāda,* by Môhan Wijayaratna. *Religion* 16:387–389.

———. 1988. *Theravāda Buddhism: A Social History from Ancient Benares to Modern Colombo*. London: Routledge & Kegan Paul.

———. 2000. "Buddhist Studies in Britain." In *The State of Buddhist Studies in the World, 1972–1997,* ed. Donald K. Swearer and Somparn Promta, 171–189. Bangkok: Center for Buddhist Studies, Chulalongkorn University.

———. 2009. *What the Buddha Thought*. London: Equinox Pub.

Gombrich, Richard, and Gananath Obeyesekere. 1988. *Buddhism Transformed: Religious Change in Sri Lanka*. Princeton, NJ: Princeton University Press.

Granoff, Phyllis. 2006. "Fathers and Sons: Some Remarks on the Ordination of Children in the Medieval Śvetāmbara Monastic Community." *Asiatische Studien/Études Asiatiques* 60:607–633.

Greene, Eric. 2012. "Meditation, Repentance, and Visionary Experience in Early Medieval Chinese Buddhism." PhD diss., University of California, Berkeley.

Grimm, George. 1958. *The Doctrine of the Buddha: The Religion of Reason and Meditation*. Translated from the German by Bhikkhu Sīlācāra. 2nd rev. ed. Berlin: Akademie-Verlag.

Gutschow, Kim. 2001. "The Women Who Refuse to Be Exchanged: Nuns in Zangskar, Northwest India." In *Celibacy, Culture, and Society: The Anthropology of Sexual Abstinence,* ed. Elisa J. Sobo and Sandra Bell, 47–64. Madison: University of Wisconsin Press.

———. 2004. *Being a Buddhist Nun: The Struggle for Enlightenment in the Himalayas*. Cambridge, MA: Harvard University Press.

Gyatso, Janet. 2005. "Sex." In *Critical Terms for the Study of Buddhism,* ed. Donald S. Lopez Jr., 271–290. Chicago: University of Chicago Press.

Hakamaya Noriaki 袴谷憲昭. 2011. "10 shu upasaṃpad(ā) to kaitai no mondai 10種upasaṃpad(ā)と戒体の問題." *Komazawa daigaku bukkyōgakubu kenkyū kiyō* 駒澤大學佛教學部研究紀要 69:1–45.

Hamilton, Sue. 2000. *Early Buddhism: A New Approach; The I of the Beholder.* Curzon Critical Studies in Buddhism. Richmond: Curzon.

Hansen, Valerie. 2004. "Religious Life in a Silk Road Community: Niya during the Third and Fourth Centuries." In *Religion and Chinese Society,* ed. John Lagerwey, 1:279–315. Hong Kong: Chinese University Press; Paris: École française d'Extrême-Orient.

Hao Chunwen 郝春文. 1998. *Tang houqi wudai songchu Dunhuang sengni de shehui shenghuo* 唐后期五代宋初敦煌僧尼的社会生活. Beijing: Zhongguo shehui kexue chubanshe 中国社会科学出版社.

———. 2010. "The Social Life of Buddhist Monks and Nuns in Dunhuang during the Late Tang, Five Dynasties, and Early Song." *Asia Major,* 3rd ser., 23, no. 2:77–95.

Hardy, R. Spence. [1850] 1989. *Eastern Monachism: An Account of the Origin, Laws, Discipline, Sacred Writings, Mysterious Rites, Religious Ceremonies, and Present Circumstances of the Order of Mendicants Founded by Gautama Buddha.* Bibliotheca Indo-Buddhica Series 49. Delhi: Sri Satguru.

Hare, Edward M., trans. [1934] 1961. *The Book of the Gradual Sayings (Anguttara-nikāya); or, More-Numbered Suttas.* Vol. 3. London: Published for the Pali Text Society by Luzac.

Harrison, Paul. 1992. "Meritorious Activity or Waste of Time? Some Remarks on the Editing of Texts in the Tibetan Kanjur." In *Tibetan Studies: Proceedings of the 5th Seminar of the International Association of Tibetan Studies, Narita 1989,* ed. Shōren Ihara and Zuihō Yamaguchi, 1:77–93. Narita: Naritasan Shinshoji.

Hart, H. L. A. [1961] 1988. *The Concept of Law.* Clarendon Law Series. Oxford: Clarendon Press.

Hartmann, Jens-Uwe, and Klaus Wille. Forthcoming. "The Manuscript of the *Dīrghāgama* and the Private Collection in Virginia." In *From Birch Bark to Digital Data: Recent Advances in Buddhist Manuscript Research,* ed. Paul Harrison and Jens-Uwe Hartmann.

Hasuike Toshitaka 蓮池利隆. 1996. "Shinkyō Niya iseki shutsudo no bukkyō bunken ni tsuite (1) 新疆ニヤ遺跡出土の仏教文献について(1)." *Indogaku bukkyōgaku kenkyū* 印度學佛教學研究 44, no. 2:164–166.

———. 1997. "Shinkyō Niya iseki shutsudo no bukkyō bunken ni tsuite (2) 新疆ニヤ遺跡出土の仏教文献について(2)." *Indogaku bukkyōgaku kenkyū* 印度學佛教學研究 45, no. 2:183–187.

Havnevik, Hanna. 1989. *Tibetan Buddhist Nuns: History, Cultural Norms and Social Reality.* Oslo: Institute for Comparative Research in Human Culture, Norwegian University Press.

Heesterman, J. C. 1985. *The Inner Conflict of Tradition: Essays in Indian Ritual, Kingship, and Society.* Chicago: University of Chicago Press.

Heirman, Ann. 2002. *Rules for Nuns according to the Dharmaguptakavinaya: The Discipline in Four Parts.* 3 vols. Delhi: Motilal Banarsidass.

Herrmann-Pfandt, Adelheid. 2008. *Die lHan kar ma: Ein früher Katalog der ins Tibetische übersetzten buddhistischen Texte.* Beiträge zur Kultur- und Geistesgeschichte Asiens 59. Vienna: Verlag der Österreichischen Akademie der Wissenschaften.

Hinüber, Oskar von. [1976] 1994. "Linguistic Observations on the Structure of the Pāli Canon." In *Selected Papers on Pāli Studies,* 62–75. Oxford: Pali Text Society.

———. 1978. "On the Tradition of Pāli Texts in India, Ceylon and Burma." In *Buddhism in Ceylon and Studies on Religious Syncretism in Buddhist Countries,* ed. Heinz Bechert, 48–57. Göttingen: Vandenhoeck & Ruprecht.

———. 1982. "Pāli as an Artificial Language." *Indologica Taurinensia* 10:133–140.

———. 1991. *The Oldest Pāli Manuscript: Four Folios of the Vinaya-Piṭaka from the National Archives, Kathmandu.* Abhandlungen der Geistes- und Sozialwissenschaftlichen Klasse; Jg. 1991, no. 6. Stuttgart: Franz Steiner Verlag.

———. 1995. "Buddhist Law according to the Theravāda-Vinaya: A Survey of Theory and Practice." *Journal of the International Association of Buddhist Studies* 18, no. 1:7–45.

———. 1996. *A Handbook of Pāli Literature.* Berlin: Walter de Gruyter.

———. 1997. "Old Age and Old Monks in Pāli Buddhism." In *Aging: Asian Concepts and Experiences, Past and Present,* ed. Susanne Formanek and Sepp Linhart, 65–78. Vienna: Österreichische Akademie der Wissenschaften.

———. 1999. *Das Pātimokkhasutta der Theravādin.* Studien zur Literatur des Theravāda-Buddhismus 2. Mainz: Akademie der Wissenschaften und der Literatur.

———. 2002. Review of *Der Buddhismus 1,* by H. Bechert. *Indo-Iranian Journal* 45, no. 1:77–86.

———. 2004. Review of *Bauern, Buddhisten und Brahmanen: Das frühe Mittelalter in Gujarat,* by Marlene Njammasch. *Indo-Iranian Journal* 47, nos. 3/4:308–320.

———. 2006. "Everyday Life in an Ancient Indian Buddhist Monastery." *Annual Report of the International Research Institute for Advanced Buddhology at Soka University for the Academic Year 2005* 9:3–31.

———. 2008a. "The Foundation of the Bhikkhunīsaṃgha: A Contribution to the Earliest History of Buddhism." *Annual Report of the International Research Institute for Advanced Buddhology at Soka University for the Academic Year 2007* 11:3–29.

———. 2008b. "The Pedestal Inscription of Śirika." *Annual Report of the International Research Institute for Advanced Buddhology at Soka University for the Academic Year 2007* 11:31–35.

Hirakawa Akira 平川彰. [1960] 1999–2000. *Ritsuzō no kenkyū* 律蔵の研究. Hirakawa Akira chosakushū 平川彰著作集, 9–10. 2 vols. Tokyo: Shunjūsha 春秋社.

———. [1964] 2000. *Genshi bukkyō no kyōdan soshiki* 原始仏教の教団組織. Hirakawa Akira chosakushū 平川彰著作集, 11–12. 2 vols. Tokyo: Shunjūsha 春秋社.

———. 1982. *Monastic Discipline for the Buddhist Nuns: An English Translation of the Chinese Text of the Mahāsāṃghika-Bhikṣuṇī-Vinaya*. Tibetan Sanskrit Works Series 21. Patna: Kashi Prasad Jayaswal Research Institute.

———. [1990] 1998. *A History of Indian Buddhism: From Śākyamuni to Early Mahāyāna*. Translated by Paul Groner. Delhi: Motilal Banarsidass.

———. 1993–1995. *Nihyaku gojikkai no kenkyū* 二百五十戒の研究. Hirakawa Akira chosakushū 平川彰著作集, 14–17. 4 vols. Tokyo: Shunjūsha 春秋社.

———. 1997. *A Buddhist Chinese-Sanskrit Dictionary: Bukkyō kan-bon daijiten* 佛教漢梵大辭典. Tokyo: Reiyukai.

———. 1998. *Bikuni ritsu no kenkyū* 比丘尼律の研究. Hirakawa Akira chosakushū 平川彰著作集, 13. Tokyo: Shunjūsha 春秋社.

Hiraoka Satoshi 平岡聡. 2002. *Setsuwa no kōkogaku: Indo bukkyō setsuwa ni himerareta shisō* 説話の考古学・インド仏教説話に秘められた思想. Tokyo: Daizō shuppan 大蔵出版.

Hodgson, Brian Houghton. [1828] 1972. *Essays on the Languages, Literature and Religion of Nepal and Tibet; Together with Further Papers on the Geography, Ethnology and Commerce of These Countries*. Corrected and augmented edition... with a supplement of additions and corrections from the author's copy, edited by Mahadeva Prasad Saha and with other additions, omitted in the former edition. Amsterdam: Philo Press.

Hoernle, A. F. R. 1916. *Manuscript Remains of Buddhist Literature Found in Eastern Turkestan*. Oxford: Oxford University Press.

Holt, John Clifford. [1981] 1995. *Discipline: The Canonical Buddhism of the Vinayapiṭaka*. 2nd ed. Delhi: Motilal Banarsidass.

Hopkins, E. Washburn. 1906. "The Buddhistic Rule against Eating Meat." *Journal of the American Oriental Society* 27:455–464.

———. 1918. *The History of Religions*. New York: MacMillan Company.

Horner, I. B. [1930] 1999. *Women under Primitive Buddhism: Laywomen and Almswomen*. Delhi: Motilal Banarsidass.

———, trans. [1938–1966] 1996–1997. *The Book of the Discipline*. Sacred Books of the Buddhists. 6 vols. London: Pali Text Society.

———, trans. [1957] 1970. *The Collection of the Middle Length Sayings (Majjhima-nikāya)*. 3 vols. London: Published for the Pali Text Society by Luzac.

Hume, Robert Ernest. [1924] 1942. *The World's Living Religions: With Special Reference to Their Sacred Scriptures and in Comparison with Christianity; An Historical Sketch*. Rev. ed. New York: Charles Scribner's Sons.

Hüsken, Ute. 1997. *Die Vorschriften für die buddhistische Nonnengemeinde im Vinaya-Piṭaka der Theravādin*. Monographien zur indischen Archäologie, Kunst und Philologie 11. Berlin: Dietrich Reimer.

Ichikawa Yoshifumi 市川良文. 1999. "Niya iseki o meguru shomondai: Toku ni Chadōta ni okeru bukkyōsō no jittai o chūshin to shite ニヤ遺跡をめぐる諸問題・特にチャドータにおける仏教僧の実態を中心として." *Bukkyō shigaku kenkyū* 佛教史學研究 42, no. 1:1–37.

Ikeda On 池田温. 1990. *Chūgoku kodai shahon shikigo shūroku* 中國古代寫本識語集録. Tokyo: Daizō shuppan 大蔵出版.

Inokuchi Taijun 井ノ口泰淳. 1995. *Chūō Ajia no gengo to bukkyō* 中央アジアの言語と仏教. Kyoto: Hōzōkan 法藏館.

Insler, Stanley. 1998. "Buddhism in the Niya Documents." Paper presented at the Silk Road Conference, Yale University, July 10–12, 1998.

Irisawa Takashi 入澤崇. 1989. "Gusokukai o sazuku bekarazaru nijūnin 具足戒を授くべからざる二十人." *Pārigaku bukkyō bunkagaku* パーリ学仏教文化学 2:105–117.

Ishida Mosaku 石田茂作. [1930] 1966. *Shakyō yori mitaru narachō bukkyō no kenkyū* 寫經より見たる奈良朝佛教の研究. Tokyo: Tōyō bunko 東洋文庫.

Ishihama Yumiko 石濱裕美子, and Fukuda Yōichi 福田洋一. 1989. *A New Critical Edition of the Mahāvyutpatti: Sanskrit-Tibetan-Mongolian Dictionary of Buddhist Terminology* 新訂翻訳名義大集. Studia Tibetica 16. Tokyo: Tōyō bunko 東洋文庫.

Jaffe, Richard M. 2001. *Neither Monk nor Layman: Clerical Marriage in Modern Japanese Buddhism*. Princeton, NJ: Princeton University Press.

Jain, Rekha. 1995. *Ancient Indian Coinage: A Systematic Study of Money Economy from Janapada Period to Early Medieval Period (600 BC to AD 1200)*. Reconstructing Indian History and Culture 8. New Delhi: D. K. Printworld.

Jamison, Stephanie W. 1996. *Sacrificed Wife/Sacrificer's Wife: Women, Ritual, and Hospitality in Ancient India*. New York: Oxford University Press.

Jäschke, H. A. [1881] 1958. *A Tibetan-English Dictionary*. London: Routledge & Kegan Paul.

Jenner, W. J. F. 1993. *Journey to the West*. 4 vols. Beijing: Foreign Languages Press.

Jessopp, Augustus. 1889. *The Coming of the Friars and Other Historical Essays*. New York: G. P. Putnam's Sons.

Johnston, E. H. 1932. *The Saundarananda; or, Nanda the Fair*. Panjab University Oriental Publications 14. London: Oxford University Press.

Jong, J. W. de. 1977. "The *Bodhisattvāvadānakalpalatā* and the *Ṣaḍdantāvadāna*." In *Buddhist Thought and Asian Civilization: Essays in Honor of Herbert V. Guenther on His Sixtieth Birthday*, ed. Leslie S. Kawamura and Keith Scott, 27–38. Emeryville, CA: Dharma Publishing.

———. 1997. *A Brief History of Buddhist Studies in Europe and America*. Tokyo: Kōsei Publishing.

Jyväsjärvi, Mari Johanna. 2011. "Fragile Virtue: Interpreting Women's Monastic Practice in Early Medieval India." PhD diss., Harvard University.

Kabilsingh, Chatsumarn. 1998. *The Bhikkhunī Pātimokkha of the Six Schools*. Delhi: Sri Satguru Publications.

Kaempfer, Engelbert. [1727] 1998. *A Description of the Kingdom of Siam, 1690.* Itineraria Asiatica, Thailand 4. Bangkok: Orchid Press.

Kāle, M. R. 1967. *Bhavabhūti's Mālatīmādhava: With the Commentary of Jagaddhara.* Delhi: Motilal Banarsidass.

Kane, Pandurang Vaman. 1941. *History of Dharmaśāstra: Ancient and Mediæval Religious and Civil Law.* Government Oriental Series, Class B, no. 6. Vol. 2, pt. 1. Poona: Bhandarkar Oriental Research Institute.

Kangle, R. P. 1965–1972. *The Kauṭilīya Arthaśāstra.* 3 vols. Delhi: Motilal Banarsidass.

Kapadia, K. M. 1958. *Marriage and Family in India.* 2nd ed. Bombay: Oxford University Press.

Kawagoe Eishin 川越英信. 2005. *dKar chag 'Phang thang ma.* Sendai: Tōhoku Indo-Chibetto kenkyūkai 東北インド・チベット研究会.

Kellogg, Samuel H. 1885. *The Light of Asia, and the Light of the World: A Comparison of the Legend, the Doctrine, and the Ethics of the Buddha with the Story, the Doctrine, and the Ethics of Christ.* London: Macmillan and Co.

Kher, C. V. 1979. "Buddhism and the Non-Philosophical Brahmanical Literature." In *Studies in Pali and Buddhism: A Memorial Volume in Honor of Bhikkhu Jagdish Kashyap,* ed. A. K. Narain, 207–216. Delhi: B. R. Publishing Corporation.

Kieffer-Pülz, Petra. 1992. *Die Sīmā: Vorschriften zur Regelung der buddhistischen Gemeindegrenze in älteren buddhistischen Texten.* Berlin: Dietrich Reimer.

———. 1993. "Zitate aus der Andhaka-Aṭṭhakathā in der Samantapāsādikā." In *Studien zur Indologie und Buddhismuskunde: Festgabe des Seminars für Indologie und Buddhismuskunde für Professor Dr. Heinz Bechert,* ed. Reinhold Grünendahl, Jens-Uwe Hartmann, and Petra Kieffer-Pülz, Indica et Tibetica 22:171–212. Bonn: Indica et Tibetica Verlag.

———. 1997. "Nāgas Ordained and Sīmās Connected: The Importance of the Vimativinodanīṭīkā for Vinaya Studies." In *Untersuchungen zur buddhistischen Literatur: Zweite Folge,* ed. Heinz Bechert, Sven Bretfeld, and Petra Kieffer-Pülz, Sanskrit-Wörterbuch der buddhistischen Texte aus den Turfan-Funden 8:239–253. Göttingen: Vandenhoeck & Ruprecht.

———. 2000. "Die buddhistische Gemeinde." In *Der Buddhismus 1: Der indische Buddhismus und seine Verzweigungen,* vol. 24 of *Religionen der Menschheit,* 1:281–402. Stuttgart: W. Kohlhammer.

———. 2001. "*Pārājika* 1 and *Saṅghādisesa* 1: Hitherto Untranslated Passages from the *Vinayapiṭaka* of the Theravādins." *Traditional South Asian Medicine* 6:62–84.

———. 2010a. "Zitate aus der Andhakaṭṭhakathā in den Subkommentaren." *Studien zur Indologie und Iranistik* 27:147–235.

———. 2010b. Review of *Managing Monks: Administrators and Administrative Roles in Indian Buddhist Monasticism,* by Jonathan Silk. *Indo-Iranian Journal* 53, no. 1:71–88.

———. 2012. "The Law of Theft: Regulations in the Theravāda Vinaya and the Law Commentaries." *Journal of the Pali Text Society* 31:1–56.

Kieschnick, John. 2000. Review of *Tang houqi wudai songchu Dunhuang sengni de shehui shenghuo* 唐后期五代宋初敦煌僧尼的社会生活, by Hao Chunwen 郝春文. *Journal of the American Oriental Society* 120, no. 3:477–478.

Kishino Ryōji 岸野亮示. 2008. "'Satsubatabu bini matoroka' wa 'Jūjuritsu' no chūshakusho ka? 『薩婆多部毘尼摩得勒伽』は『十誦律』の注釈書か?" *Indogaku bukkyōgaku kenkyū* 印度學佛教學研究 56, no. 2:183–186.

———. 2011. "On Possible Misunderstandings of the *Brahmacaryopasthānasaṃvṛti* Requirement for Female Ordination in the *Mūlasarvāstivāda-vinaya*." Paper presented at Buddhist Nuns in India, University of Toronto, April 15–17, 2011.

Kloppenborg, Ria. 1974. *The Paccekabuddha: A Buddhist Ascetic; A Study of the Concept of the Paccekabuddha in Pāli Canonical and Commentarial Literature*. Orientalia Rheno-Traiectina 20. Leiden: E. J. Brill.

Kohn, Livia. 2003. *Monastic Life in Medieval Daoism: A Cross-Cultural Perspective*. Honolulu: University of Hawai'i Press.

Kokusai bukkyōgaku daigakuin daigaku gakujutsu furontia jikkō iinkai 国際仏教学大学院大学学術フロンティア実行委員会, ed. 2006. *Nihon genzon hasshu issaikyō taishō mokuroku* 日本現存八種一切経対照目録. Tokyo: Kokusai bukkyōgaku daigakuin daigaku 国際仏教学大学院大学.

Krawiec, Rebecca. 2002. *Shenoute and the Women of the White Monastery: Egyptian Monasticism in Late Antiquity.* New York: Oxford University Press.

Kritzer, Robert. 2012. "Tibetan Texts of *Garbhāvakrāntisūtra:* Differences and Borrowings." *Annual Report of the International Institute for Advanced Buddhology at Soka University for the Academic Year 2011* 15:131–145.

Lalou, Marcelle. 1939–1961. *Inventaire des Manuscrits tibétains de Touenhouang conservés à la Bibliothèque Nationale (Fonds Pelliot tibétain)*. 3 vols. Paris: Librairie d'Amérique et d'Orient (vol. 1); Bibliothèque Nationale (vols. 2–3).

Lamotte, Étienne. [1958] 1988. *History of Indian Buddhism: From the Origins to the Śaka Era*. Translated by Sara Webb-Boin. Louvain-Paris: Peeters Press.

———. 1966. "Vajrapāṇi en Inde." In *Mélanges de Sinologie offerts à Monsieur Paul Demiéville,* 1:113–159. Paris: Presses universitaires de France.

Lancaster, Lewis R. [1984] 1986. "Buddhism and Family in East Asia." In *Religion and the Family in East Asia,* ed. George A. De Vos and Takao Sofue, 139–154. Berkeley: University of California Press.

Lariviere, Richard W. 1989. *The Nāradasmṛti*. University of Pennsylvania Studies on South Asia 4–5. 2 vols. Philadelphia: Department of South Asia Regional Studies, University of Pennsylvania.

———. 1991. "Matrimonial Remedies for Women in Classical Indian Law: Alternatives to Divorce." In *Rules and Remedies in Classical Indian Law,* ed.

Julie Leslie, Panels of the 7th World Sanskrit Conference 9:37–45. Leiden: E. J. Brill.

La Vallée Poussin, Louis de. [1923–1971] 1971. *L'Abhidharmakośa de Vasubandhu: Traduction et annotations*. Mélanges chinois et bouddhiques 16. 6 vols. Brussels: Institut Belge des Hautes Études Chinoises.

———. 1962. *Catalogue of the Tibetan Manuscripts from Tun-huang in the India Office Library: With an Appendix on the Chinese Manuscripts by Kazuo Enoki*. Oxford: Oxford University Press.

Law, Bimala Churn. 1939–1940. "Bhikshunis in Indian Inscriptions." *Epigraphia Indica* 25:31–34.

Leclercq, Jean. 1979. *Monks and Love in Twelfth-Century France: Psycho-Historical Essays*. Oxford: Oxford University Press.

Leider, Jacques P. 2006. "*Araññavāsī* and *Gāmavāsī* Monks: Towards Further Study of Variant Forms of Buddhist Monasticism in Myanmar." In *Buddhist Legacies in Mainland Southeast Asia*, ed. François Lagirarde and Paritta Chalermpow Koanantakool, 113–137. Paris: École française d'Extrême-Orient.

Lévi, Sylvain. [1890] 1978. *The Theatre of India*. Translated from the French by Narayan Mukherji. 2 vols. Calcutta: Writers Workshop.

———. [1923] 1992. "Constitution of the Buddhist Canon." In *Literary History of Sanskrit Buddhism*, translated by J. K. Nariman, 2nd ed., 162–176. Delhi: Motilal Banarsidass.

Li, Rongxi. 1996. *The Great Tang Dynasty Record of the Western Regions*. BDK English Tripiṭaka 79. Berkeley, CA: Numata Center for Buddhist Translation and Research.

Lingat, Robert. 1937. "Vinaya et droit laique." *Bulletin de l'école française d'extrême-orient* 37:415–477.

———. [1973] 1993. *The Classical Law of India*. Translated from the French with additions by J. Duncan M. Derrett. New Delhi: Munishiram Manoharlal.

Lopez, Donald S., Jr. 2004. "The Ambivalent Exegete: Hodgson's Contributions to the Study of Buddhism." In *The Origins of Himalayan Studies: Brian Houghton Hodgson in Nepal and Darjeeling, 1820–1858*, ed. David M. Waterhouse, 49–76. London: RoutledgeCurzon.

Lüders, H. 1912. *A List of Brāhmī Inscriptions from the Earliest Times to about A.D. 400 with the Exception of those of Aśoka*. Appendix to Epigraphia Indica and Record of the Archaeological Survey of India 10. Calcutta: Superintendent Government Printing, India.

———. 1963. *Bhārhut Inscriptions*. Revised and supplemented by E. Waldschmidt and M. A. Mehendale. Corpus Inscriptionum Indicarum 2, pt. 2. Ootacamund: Government Epigraphist for India.

Luz, Ulrich, and Axel Michaels. 2006. *Encountering Jesus and Buddha: Their Lives and Teachings*. Translated by Linda M. Maloney. Minneapolis: Fortress Press.

Madan, T. N. 1987. *Non-Renunciation: Themes and Interpretations of Hindu Culture*. Delhi: Oxford University Press.

Makita Tairyō 牧田諦亮, and Ochiai Toshinori 落合俊典, eds. 1994–2001. *Nanatsudera koitsu kyōten kenkyū sōsho* 七寺古逸經典研究叢書. 6 vols. Tokyo: Daitō shuppansha 大東出版社.

Malalasekera, George Peiris. [1937] 1960. *Dictionary of Pāli Proper Names*. 2 vols. London: Published for the Pali Text Society by Luzac.

Marshall, John, and Alfred Foucher. 1940. *The Monuments of Sāñchī*. Inscriptions edited, translated, and annotated by N. G. Majumdar. 3 vols. London: Probsthain.

Martini, Giuliana. 2012. "The Story of Sudinna in the Tibetan Translation of the Mūlasarvāstivāda *Vinaya*." *Journal of Buddhist Ethics* 19:439–450.

Masefield, Peter. 1994. *The Udāna: Translated from the Pāli*. Sacred Books of the Buddhists 42. Oxford: Pali Text Society.

———. 1994–1995. *The Udāna Commentary (Paramatthadīpanī nāma Udānaṭṭhakathā) by Dhammapāla*. 2 vols. Oxford: Pali Text Society.

———. 2008–2009. *The Commentary on the Itivuttaka: The Itivuttaka-aṭṭhakathā (Paramatthadīpanī II) of Dhammapāla*. 2 vols. Oxford: Pali Text Society.

Masson, J. Moussaieff. 1976. "The Psychology of the Ascetic." *Journal of Asian Studies* 35, no. 4:611–625.

Masuzawa, Tomoko. 2005. *The Invention of World Religions; or, How European Universalism Was Preserved in the Language of Pluralism*. Chicago: University of Chicago Press.

Mathews, R. H. 1943. *Mathews' Chinese English Dictionary*. Rev. American ed. Cambridge, MA: Harvard University Press.

Matsuda, Kazunobu. 1986. *Newly Identified Sanskrit Fragments of the Dharmaskandha in the Gilgit Manuscripts: (1) Sanskrit Fragments Transliterated*. Kyoto: Bun'eido.

Matsunami Seiren 松涛誠廉. 1981. *Memyō tansei naru Nanda* 馬鳴端正なる難陀. Edited by Matsunami Seiren sensei ikōshū kankōkai 松涛誠廉先生遺稿集刊行会. Tokyo: Sankibō busshorin 山喜房仏書林.

Menski, Werner F. 2001. *Modern Indian Family Law*. Richmond: Curzon Press.

Michaels, Axel. 2006. "Monks and Laity in Early Buddhism." In *Encountering Jesus and Buddha: Their Lives and Teachings*, ed. Ulrich Luz and Axel Michaels, trans. Linda M. Maloney, 159–172. Minneapolis: Fortress Press.

Mills, Martin A. 2003. *Identity, Ritual and State in Tibetan Buddhism: The Foundations of Authority in Gelukpa Monasticism*. RoutledgeCurzon Studies in Tantric Traditions. Richmond: Curzon.

Misra, G. S. P. 1979. "Some Reflections on Early Jaina and Buddhist Monachism." In *Jain Thought and Culture*, ed. G. C. Pande, 4–15. Jaipur: Department of History and Indian Culture, University of Rajasthan.

Monier-Williams, Monier. 1889. *Buddhism: In Its Connexion with Brāhmanism and Hindūism, and in Its Contrast with Christianity*. 2nd ed. New York: Macmillan and Co.

———. [1899] 2000. *A Sanskrit-English Dictionary: Etymologically and Philologically Arranged with Special Reference to Cognate Indo-European Languages*. Oxford: Oxford University Press.

Morohashi Tetsuji 諸橋轍次, ed. [1955–1960] 1986. *Dai kan-wa jiten* 大漢和辭典. Rev. ed. 13 vols. Tokyo: Taishūkan shoten 大修館書店.

Morris, Richard, ed. [1885] 1961. *The Aṅguttara-nikâya*. Vol. 1. 2nd ed. Revised by A. K. Warder. London: Published for the Pali Text Society by H. Luzac.

Mulay, Sumati. 1972. *Studies in the Historical and Cultural Geography and Ethnography of the Deccan: Based Entirely on the Inscriptions of the Deccan from the 1st–13th Century A.D.* Deccan College Dissertation Series, D. 68. Poona: Deccan College, Postgraduate and Research Institute.

Muldoon-Hules, Karen. 2009. "Of Milk and Motherhood: The Kacaṅgalā *Avadāna* Read in a Brahmanical Light." *Religions of South Asia* 3, no. 1:111–124.

———. Forthcoming (a). "Brides of the Buddha: How Brahmanical Marital Motifs Served Buddhist Ends." In *Conference Proceedings of the 4th International Sanskrit Workshop*.

———. Forthcoming (b). "The Role of Brahmanical Marriage in a Buddhist Text." In *Women in Early Indian Buddhism: Comparative Textual Studies*, ed. Alice Collett. Oxford: Oxford University Press.

Murakami Shinkan 村上真完, and Oikawa Shinsuke 及川真介. 1985. *Hotoke no kotoba chū: Paramatta-jōtikā* 仏のことば註・パラマッタ・ジョーティカー. Vol. 1. Tokyo: Shunjūsha 春秋社.

Namikawa Takayoshi 並川孝義. 1997. "Rāfura (Ragora) no meimei to shakuson no shukke ラーフラ (羅睺羅) の命名と釈尊の出家." *Bukkyō daigaku sōgō kenkyūsho kiyō* 佛教大学総合研究所紀要 4:17–34.

Ñāṇamoli, Bhikkhu, and Bhikkhu Bodhi. [1995] 2001. *The Middle Length Discourses of the Buddha: A Translation of the Majjhima Nikāya*. 2nd ed. Boston: Wisdom Publications.

Nattier, Jan. 2003. *A Few Good Men: The Bodhisattva Path according to the Inquiry of Ugra (Ugraparipṛcchā)*. Honolulu: University of Hawai'i Press.

Nattier, Janice J., and Charles S. Prebish. 1977. "Mahāsāṃghika Origins: The Beginnings of Buddhist Sectarianism." *History of Religions* 16, no. 3:237–272.

Nishimoto Ryūzan 西本龍山. 1928. "Rajū-yaku Jūju bikuni haradaimokusha kaihon no shutsugen narabi ni shobu sōni kaihon no taishō kenkyū 羅什譯十誦比丘尼波羅提木叉戒本の出現並諸部僧尼戒本の對照研究." *Ōtani gakuhō* 大谷學報 9, no. 2:27–60.

———, trans. 1932–1935. Ritsubu 律部. Vols. 13–14 of *Kokuyaku issaikyō* 國譯一切經. Tokyo: Daitō shuppansha 大東出版社.

———, trans. 1933–1938. Ritsubu 律部. Vols. 19–26 of *Kokuyaku issaikyō* 國譯一切經. Tokyo: Daitō shuppansha 大東出版社.

Nishimura Minori 西村実則. 2003a. "Jōbon-ō no bannen (jō) 浄飯王の晩年 (上)." *Sankō bunka kenkyūsho nenpō* 三康文化研究所年報 34:87–143.

———. 2003b. "Jōbon-ō no bannen (ge) 浄飯王の晩年 (下)." In *Satō Ryōjun kyōju koki kinen ronbunshū: Indo bunka to bukkyō shisō no kichō to tenkai* 佐藤良純教授古稀記念論文集・インド文化と仏教思想の基調と展開, ed. Satō Ryōjun kyōju koki kinen ronbunshū kankōkai 佐藤良純教授古稀記念論文集刊行会, 1:87–128. Tokyo: Sankibō busshorin 山喜房佛書林.

———. 2004. "Jōbon-ō no sōgi: 'Jōbon-ō hatsu nehan gyō' kara 'Konjaku monogatari' e 浄飯王の葬儀・『浄飯王般涅槃経』から『今昔物語』へ." In *Miyabayashi Akihiko kyōju koki kinen ronbunshū: Bukkyō shisō no juyō to tenkai* 宮林昭彦教授古稀記念論文集・仏教思想の受容と展開, ed. Miyabayashi Akihiko kyōju koki kinen ronbunshū kankōkai 宮林昭彦教授古稀記念論文集刊行会, 1:99–134. Tokyo: Sankibō busshorin 山喜房佛書林.

Nishimura Naoko 西村直子. 1999. "Ritsuzō ni mirareru josei shukkesha no seikatsu: Shikishamana o chūshin to shite 律蔵に見られる女性出家者の生活・式叉摩那を中心として." *Bukkyōgaku* 佛教學 40:109–131.

Nolot, Édith. 1991. *Règles de discipline des nonnes bouddhistes: Le Bhikṣuṇīvinaya de l'école Mahāsāṃghika-Lokottaravādin.* Publications de l'Institut de Civilisation Indienne 60. Paris: Collège de France. Distributed by De Boccard.

Norman, K. R. 1983a. "The Pratyeka-Buddha in Buddhism and Jainism." In *Buddhist Studies: Ancient and Modern,* ed. Philip Denwood and Alexander Piatigorsky, Collected Papers on South Asia 4:92–106. London: Curzon Press and Barnes & Noble.

———. 1983b. *Pāli Literature: Including the Canonical Literature in Prakrit and Sanskrit of All the Hīnayāna Schools of Buddhism.* Wiesbaden: Otto Harrassowitz.

———. 1984. "The Value of the Pāli Tradition." In *Collected Papers,* 3:33–44. Oxford: Pali Text Society.

———. [1984] 1996. *The Rhinoceros Horn and Other Early Buddhist Poems: The Group of Discourses (Sutta-Nipāta); With Alternative Translations by I. B. Horner and Walpola Rahula.* Pali Text Society Translation Series 44. Oxford: Pali Text Society.

———. [1992] 2001. *The Group of Discourses (Sutta-nipāta).* 2nd ed. Oxford: Pali Text Society.

———. 2001. "Vuṭṭhāpeti, Vuṭṭhāna, and Related Matters." *Indologica Taurinensia* 27:121–137.

Nyanatiloka. [1952] 1956. *Buddhist Dictionary: Manual of Buddhist Terms and Doctrines.* 2nd rev. ed. Colombo: Frewin & Co.

Obeyesekere, Gananath. 2002. *Imagining Karma: Ethical Transformation in Amerindian, Buddhist, and Greek Rebirth.* Berkeley: University of California Press.

Obeyesekere, Ranjini. 2009. *Yasodharā, the Wife of the Bōdhisattva: The Sinhala Yasodharāvata (The Story of Yasodharā) and the Sinhala Yasodharāpadānaya (The Sacred Biography of Yasodharā).* Albany: State University of New York Press.

Ochiai Toshinori 落合俊典. 1991. *Manuscripts of Nanatsu-dera: A Recently Discovered Treasure-House in Downtown Nagoya.* Translated and edited by Silvio Vita. Italian School of East Asian Studies. Occasional Papers 3. Kyoto: Istituto Italiano di Cultura, Scuola di studi sull'Asia Orientale.

———. 1994. "Nanatsudera issaikyō to koitsu kyōten 七寺一切經と古逸經典." In *Chūgoku senjutsu kyōten (sono ichi)* 中國撰述經典 (其之一), ed. Makita Tairyō 牧田諦亮 and Ochiai Toshinori, Nanatsudera koitsu kyōten kenkyū sōsho 七寺古逸經典研究叢書 1:433–477. Tokyo: Daitō shuppansha 大東出版社.

———, ed. 2004. *Kongōji issaikyō no kisoteki kenkyū to shinshutsu butten no kenkyū* 金剛寺一切経の基礎的研究と新出仏典の研究. Tokyo: Kokusai bukkyōgaku daigakuin daigaku 国際仏教学大学院大学.

———. 2012. "On Ancient Japanese Manuscript Copies of the *Dīrghanakha-paripṛcchā sūtra* 長爪梵志請問經." *Journal of the International College for Postgraduate Buddhist Studies* 16:39–47.

Ochiai Toshinori et al., eds. 2007. *Kongōji issaikyō no sōgōteki kenkyū to Kongōji shōgyō no kisoteki kenkyū* 金剛寺一切経の総合的研究と金剛寺聖教の基礎的研究. 2 vols. Tokyo: Kokusai bukkyōgaku daigakuin daigaku 国際仏教学大学院大学.

Ohnuma, Reiko. 2000. "Internal and External Opposition to the Bodhisattva's Gift of His Body." *Journal of Indian Philosophy* 28, no. 1:43–75.

———. 2005. "Gift." In *Critical Terms for the Study of Buddhism,* ed. Donald S. Lopez Jr., 103–123. Chicago: University of Chicago Press.

———. 2006. "Debt to the Mother: A Neglected Aspect of the Founding of the Buddhist Nuns' Order." *Journal of the American Academy of Religion* 74, no. 4:861–901.

———. 2007. *Head, Eyes, Flesh, and Blood: Giving Away the Body in Indian Buddhist Literature.* New York: Columbia University Press.

———. 2012. *Ties That Bind: Maternal Imagery and Discourse in Indian Buddhism.* New York: Oxford University Press.

Okimoto Katsumi 沖本克己. 1985. "Ritsu bunken 律文献." In *Tonkō kogo bunken* 敦煌胡語文献, ed. Yamaguchi Zuihō 山口瑞鳳, Kōza Tonkō 講座敦煌 6:395–418. Tokyo: Daitō shuppansha 大東出版社.

Olcott, Henry Steel. [1881] 1982. *The Buddhist Catechism.* 2nd Quest ed. Wheaton, Ill.: Theosophical Publishing House.

Oldenberg, Hermann, ed. [1879–1883] 1969–1982. *The Vinaya Piṭakaṃ: One of the Principal Buddhist Holy Scriptures in the Pāli Language.* 5 vols. London: Pali Text Society.

———. [1882] 1998. *Buddha: His Life, His Doctrine, His Order.* Translated by William Hoey. Delhi: Pilgrims Books Pvt.

———. 1896. *Ancient India: Its Languages and Religions.* Chicago: Open Court Publishing Company.

Olivelle, Patrick. 1975. "A Definition of World Renunciation." *Wiener Zeitschrift für die Kunde Südasiens* 19:75–83.

———. 1981. "Contributions to the Semantic History of Saṃnyāsa." *Journal of the American Oriental Society* 101, no. 3:265–274.

———. 1984. "Renouncer and Renunciation in the *Dharmaśāstras*." In *Studies in Dharmaśāstra,* ed. Richard W. Lariviere, 81–152. Calcutta: Firma KLM Private Limited.

———. 1993. *The Āśrama System: The History and Hermeneutics of a Religious Institution*. New York: Oxford University Press.

———. 1995a. *Rules and Regulations of Brahmanical Asceticism: Yatidharma-samuccaya of Yādava Prakāśa*. New York: State University of New York Press.

———. 1995b. "Deconstruction of the Body in Indian Asceticism." In *Asceticism,* ed. Vincent L. Wimbush and Richard Valantasis, 188–210. New York: Oxford University Press.

———. 2005. *Manu's Code of Law: A Critical Edition and Translation of the Mānava-Dharmaśāstra*. South Asia Research. Oxford: Oxford University Press.

———. 2008a. *Ascetics and Brahmins: Studies in Ideologies and Institutions*. Collected Essays 2. Firenze: Firenze University Press.

———. 2008b. *Life of the Buddha by Ashva-ghosha*. Clay Sanskrit Library. New York: NYU Press.

Ousaka, Y., M. Yamazaki, and K. R. Norman, comps. 1996. *Index to the Vinaya-piṭaka*. Oxford: Pali Text Society.

Pachow, W. [1955] 2000. *A Comparative Study of the Prātimokṣa: On the Basis of its Chinese, Tibetan, Sanskrit and Pali Versions*. Buddhist Tradition Series 31. Delhi: Motilal Banarsidass.

Panglung, Jampa Losang. 1981. *Die Erzählstoffe des Mūlasarvāstivāda-Vinaya: Analysiert auf Grund der tibetischen Übersetzung*. Studia Philologica Buddhica. Monograph Series 3. Tokyo: Reiyukai Library.

Paul, Diana Y. 1985. *Women in Buddhism: Images of the Feminine in Mahāyāna Tradition*. 2nd ed. Berkeley, CA: Asian Humanities Press.

Peters, Anne. 1997. "Die birmanischen Kammavācā-Sammlungen mit neun Abschnitten." In *Untersuchungen zur buddhistischen Literatur: Zweite Folge,* ed. Heinz Bechert, Sven Bretfeld, and Petra Kieffer-Pülz, Sanskrit-Wörterbuch der buddhistischen Texte aus den Turfan-Funden 8:273–284. Göttingen: Vandenhoeck & Ruprecht.

Pind, Ole Holten. 1992. "Buddhaghosa—His Works and Scholarly Background." *Bukkyō kenkyū* 佛教研究 21:135–156.

Powers, John. 2009. *A Bull of a Man: Images of Masculinity, Sex, and the Body in Indian Buddhism*. Cambridge, MA: Harvard University Press.

Prebish, Charles S. [1975] 1996. *Buddhist Monastic Discipline: The Sanskrit*

Prātimokṣa Sūtras of the Mahāsāṃghikas and Mūlasarvāstivādins. Delhi: Motilal Banarsidass.
———. 1994. *A Survey of Vinaya Literature*. The Dharma Lamp Series 1. Taipei: Jin Luen Publishing House.
———. 2003. "Varying the Vinaya: Creative Responses to Modernity." In *Buddhism in the Modern World: Adaptations of an Ancient Tradition,* ed. Steven Heine and Charles S. Prebish, 45–73. Oxford: Oxford University Press.
Pruden, Leo M. 1988–1990. Abhidharmakośabhāṣyam: *Being a translation of Louis de La Vallée Poussin's* L'Abhidharmakośa de Vasubandhu. 4 vols. Berkeley, CA: Asian Humanities Press.
Pruitt, William, ed., and K. R. Norman, trans. 2001. *The Pātimokkha*. Sacred Books of the Buddhists 39. Oxford: Pali Text Society.
Radhakrishnan, [S]. [1929] 1971. *Indian Philosophy*. 2 vols. 2nd ed. London: George Allen & Unwin.
Ray, Reginald A. 1994. *Buddhist Saints in India. A Study in Buddhist Values and Orientations*. Oxford: Oxford University Press.
Reed, Annette Yoshiko. 2009. "Beyond the Land of Nod: Syriac Images of Asia and the Historiography of 'The West.'" *History of Religions* 49, no. 1:48–87.
Reis, Ria. 1983. "Reproduction or Retreat: The Position of Buddhist Women in Ladakh." In *Recent Research on Ladakh: History, Culture, Sociology, Ecology; Proceedings of a Conference Held at the Universität Konstanz, 23–26 November 1981*, 217–229. München: Weltforum Verlag.
Reynolds, Frank E. 2000. "Buddhist Studies in the United States." In *The State of Buddhist Studies in the World, 1972–1997,* ed. Donald K. Swearer and Somparn Promta, 110–143. Bangkok: Center for Buddhist Studies, Chulalongkorn University.
Rhys Davids, T. W., and Hermann Oldenberg. [1882–1885] 1996. *Vinaya Texts*. 3 vols. Delhi: Motilal Banarsidass.
Rhys Davids, Thomas William, and William Stede. [1921–1925] 1997. *Pali-English Dictionary*. Delhi: Motilal Banarsidass.
Rockhill, William Woodville. [1884a] 2007. *The Life of the Buddha: Derived from Tibetan Works in the Bkah-Hgyur and Bstan-Hgyur*. London: Kegan Paul.
———. 1884b. "Le Traité d'émancipation ou Pratimoksha sutra." *Revue de l'Histoire des Religions* 9, no. 1:3–26.
———. 1884c. "Le Traité d'émancipation ou Pratimoksha sutra." *Revue de l'Histoire des Religions* 9, no. 2:167–201.
Rospatt, Alexander von. 2005. "The Transformation of the Monastic Ordination (*pravrajyā*) into a Rite of Passage in Newar Buddhism." In *Words and Deeds: Hindu and Buddhist Rituals in South Asia,* ed. Jörg Gengnagel, Ute Hüsken, and Srilata Raman, 199–234. Wiesbaden: Harrassowitz Verlag.
Roth, Gustav, ed. 1970. *Bhikṣuṇī-Vinaya: Including Bhikṣuṇī-Prakīrṇaka and a*

Summary of the Bhikṣu-Prakīrṇaka of the Ārya-Mahāsāṃghika-Lokottaravādin. Tibetan Sanskrit Works Series 12. Patna: Kashi Prasad Jayaswal Research Institute.

Rousseau, Philip. [1985] 1999. *Pachomius: The Making of a Community in Fourth-Century Egypt*. Berkeley: University of California Press.

Ryder, Arthur W. 1927. *Dandin's Dasha-kumara-charita: The Ten Princes*. Chicago: University of Chicago Press.

Sagaster, Klaus. 2007. "The History of Buddhism among the Mongols." In *The Spread of Buddhism*, ed. Ann Heirman and Stephan Peter Bumbacher, 379–432. Leiden: Brill.

Sakaki Ryōzaburō 榊亮三郎. [1916] 1998. *Bon-zō-kan-wa shiyaku taikō hon'yaku myōgi taishū* 梵藏漢和四譯對校飜譯名義大集. 2 vols. Kyoto: Rinsen shoten 臨川書店.

Salomon, Richard. 2000. *A Gāndhārī Version of the Rhinoceros Sūtra*. Seattle: University of Washington Press.

Samten, Jampa. 1992. *A Catalogue of the Phug-Brag Manuscript Kanjur*. Dharamsala: Library of Tibetan Works and Archives.

Samuel, Geoffrey. 1993. *Civilized Shamans: Buddhism in Tibetan Societies*. Washington, DC: Smithsonian Institution Press.

Sander, Lore. 1968. *Paläographisches zu den Sanskrithandschriften der Berliner Turfansammlung*. Verzeichnis der orientalischen Handschriften in Deutschland. Supplementband 8. Wiesbaden: Franz Steiner Verlag.

———. 2007. "Confusion of Terms and Terms of Confusion in Indian Palaeography." In *Expanding and Merging Horizons: Contributions to South Asian and Cross-Cultural Studies in Commemoration of Wilhelm Halbfass*, ed. Karin Preisendaz, Beiträge zur Kultur- und Geistesgeschichte Asiens 53:121–139. Vienna: Österreichische Akademie der Wissenschaften.

Sander, Lore, and Ernst Waldschmidt, eds. 1985. *Sanskrithandschriften aus den Turfanfunden*. Verzeichnis der orientalischen Handschriften in Deutschland 10, bk. 5. Stuttgart: Franz Steiner Verlag.

Sankalia, H. D. 1942. "Cultural Significance of the Personal Names in the Early Inscriptions of the Deccan." *Bulletin of the Deccan College Research Institute* 3, no. 3:349–391.

Sankrityayana, Rahul. 1981. *Vinayasūtra of Bhadanta Gunaprabha*. Singhi Jain Śāstra Śiksāpītha Singhi Jain Series 74. Bombay: Bharatiya Vidya Bhavan.

Sarma, R. Naga Raja. 1931. "Ethics of Divorce in Ancient India." *International Journal of Ethics* 41, no. 3:329–342.

Sasaki Shizuka 佐々木閑. 1996. "Biku ni narenai hitobito 比丘になれない人々." *Hanazono daigaku bungakubu kenkyū kiyō* 花園大学文学部研究紀要 28:111–148.

———. 1999. *Shukke to wa nani ka* 出家とはなにか. Tokyo: Daizō shuppan 大蔵出版.

———. 2006. "Ritsuzō no seiritsu mondai ni kansuru genzai no jōkyō 律蔵の成

立問題に関する現在の状況." *Indogaku bukkyōgaku kenkyū* 印度學佛教學研究 54, no. 2:175–182.

Sasson, Vanessa R., ed. 2013. *Little Buddhas: Children and Childhoods in Buddhist Texts and Traditions*. New York: Oxford University Press.

Scherrer-Schaub, Cristina. 2000. "Tibetan Manuscripts around the First Millenium: A New Chapter in the Buddhist Text Transmission." *Journal of the International College for Advanced Buddhist Studies* 3:109–132.

Schiefner, F. Anton von. 1882. *Tibetan Tales: Derived from Indian Sources*. Translated from the German by W. R. S. Ralston. London: George Routledge & Sons.

Schlingloff, Dieter. 1964. "Zur Interpretation des Prātimokṣasūtra." *Zeitschrift der Deutschen Morgenländischen Gesellschaft* 113:536–551.

Schmithausen, Lambert. 2003. *Buddhism and Nature*. Studia Philologica Buddhica. Occasional Papers Series 7. Tokyo: International Institute for Buddhist Studies.

Schopen, Gregory. 1984. "Filial Piety and the Monk in the Practice of Indian Buddhism: A Question of 'Sinicization' Viewed from the Other Side." *T'oung Pao, Revue internationale de sinologie* 70:110–126. In Schopen 1997, 56–71.

———. 1985. "Two Problems in the History of Indian Buddhism: The Layman/Monk Distinction and the Doctrines of the Transference of Merit." *Studien zur Indologie und Iranistik* 10:9–47. In Schopen 1997, 23–55.

———. 1989. "The *Stūpa* Cult and the Extant Pāli *Vinaya*." *Journal of the Pali Text Society* 13:83–100. In Schopen 1997, 86–98.

———. 1992. "The Ritual Obligations and Donor Roles of Monks in the Pāli *Vinaya*." *Journal of the Pali Text Society* 16:87–107. In Schopen 1997, 72–85.

———. 1994a. "Doing Business for the Lord: Lending on Interest and Written Loan Contracts in the *Mūlasarvāstivāda-vinaya*." *Journal of the American Oriental Society* 114, no. 4:527–554. In Schopen 2004a, 45–90.

———. 1994b. "The Monastic Ownership of Servants or Slaves: Local and Legal Factors in the Redactional History of Two *Vinayas*." *Journal of the International Association of Buddhist Studies* 17, no. 2:145–173. In Schopen 2004a, 193–218.

———. 1995a. "Deaths, Funerals, and the Division of Property in a Monastic Code." In *Buddhism in Practice*, ed. D. S. Lopez Jr., 473–502. Princeton, NJ: Princeton University Press. In Schopen 2004a, 91–121.

———. 1995b. "Monastic Law Meets the Real World: A Monk's Continuing Right to Inherit Family Property in Classical India." *History of Religions* 35, no. 2:101–123. In Schopen 2004a, 170–192.

———. 1996a. "The Lay Ownership of Monasteries and the Role of the Monk in Mūlasarvāstivādin Monasticism." *Journal of the International Association of Buddhist Studies* 19, no. 1:81–126. In Schopen 2004a, 219–259.

———. 1996b. "The Suppression of Nuns and the Ritual Murder of Their Special Dead in Two Buddhist Monastic Codes." *Journal of Indian Philosophy* 24:563–592. In Schopen 2004a, 329–359.

———. 1997. *Bones, Stones, and Buddhist Monks. Collected Papers on the Archaeology, Epigraphy, and Texts of Monastic Buddhism in India*. Honolulu: University of Hawai'i Press.

———. 1998. "Marking Time in Buddhist Monasteries: On Calendars, Clocks, and Some Liturgical Practices." In *Sūryacandrāya: Essays in Honour of Akira Yuyama on the Occasion of His 65th Birthday,* ed. P. Harrison and G. Schopen, Indica et Tibetica 35:157–179. Swisttal-Odendorf: Indica et Tibetica Verlag. In Schopen 2004a, 260–284.

———. 1999. "The Bones of a Buddha and the Business of a Monk: Conservative Monastic Values in an Early Mahāyāna Polemical Tract." *Journal of Indian Philosophy* 27:279–324. In Schopen 2005a, 63–107.

———. 2000a. "The Good Monk and His Money in a Buddhist Monasticism of 'the Mahāyāna Period'." *The Eastern Buddhist,* n.s., 32, no. 1:85–105. In Schopen 2004a, 1–18.

———. 2000b. "The Mahāyāna and the Middle Period in Indian Buddhism: Through a Chinese Looking-glass." *The Eastern Buddhist,* n.s., 32, no. 2:1–25. In Schopen 2005a, 3–24.

———. 2001. "Dead Monks and Bad Debts: Some Provisions of a Buddhist Monastic Inheritance Law." *Indo-Iranian Journal* 44, no. 2:99–148. In Schopen 2004a, 122–169.

———. 2004a. *Buddhist Monks and Business Matters: Still More Papers on Monastic Buddhism in India.* Honolulu: University of Hawai'i Press.

———. 2004b. "Art, Beauty, and the Business of Running a Buddhist Monastery in Early Northwest India." In Schopen 2004a, 19–44.

———. 2004c. "On Buddhist Monks and Dreadful Deities: Some Monastic Devices for Updating the Dharma." In *Gedenkschrift J. W. de Jong,* ed. H. W. Bodewitz and Minoru Hara, 161–184. Tokyo: International Institute for Buddhist Studies.

———. 2004d. "Making Men into Monks." In *Buddhist Scriptures,* ed. D. S. Lopez Jr., 230–251. London: Penguin.

———. 2005a. *Figments and Fragments of Mahāyāna Buddhism in India: More Collected Papers.* Honolulu: University of Hawai'i Press.

———. 2005b. "On Sending the Monks Back to Their Books: Cult and Conservatism in Early Mahāyāna Buddhism." In Schopen 2005a, 108–153.

———. 2006. "On Monks and Menial Laborers: Some Monastic Accounts of Building Buddhist Monasteries." In *Architetti, capomastri, artigiani: L'organizzazione dei cantieri e della produzione artistica nell'Asia ellenistica. Studi offerti a Domenico Faccenna nel suo ottantesimo compleanno,* ed. P. Callieri, Serie Orientale Roma 100:225–245. Rome: Istituto Italiano per L'Africa e L'Oriente.

———. 2007a. "The Buddhist *Bhikṣu*'s Obligation to Support His Parents in Two Vinaya Traditions." *Journal of the Pali Text Society* 29:107–136.

———. 2007b. "The Learned Monk as a Comic Figure: On Reading a Buddhist Vinaya as Indian Literature." *Journal of Indian Philosophy* 35, no. 3:201–226.

———. 2007c. "The Life and Times of Buddhist Nuns in Early North India." Paper presented at McMaster University, October 17, 2007.

———. 2008a. "On Emptying Chamber Pots without Looking and the Urban Location of Buddhist Nunneries in Early India Again." *Journal Asiatique* 296, no. 2:229–256.

———. 2008b. "Separate but Equal: Property Rights and the Legal Independence of Buddhist Nuns and Monks in Early North India." *Journal of the American Oriental Society* 128, no. 4:625–640.

———. 2009. "The Urban Buddhist Nun and a Protective Rite for Children in Early North India." In *Pāsādikadānaṁ: Festschrift für Bhikkhu Pāsādika*, ed. Martin Straube, Roland Steiner, Jayandra Soni, Michael Hahn, and Mitsuyo Demoto, Indica et Tibetica 52:359–380. Marburg: Indica et Tibetica.

———. 2010a. "On Incompetent Monks and Able Urbane Nuns in a Buddhist Monastic Code." *Journal of Indian Philosophy* 38, no. 2:107–131.

———. 2010b. "On the Underside of a Sacred Space: Some Less Appreciated Functions of the Temple in Classical India." In *From Turfan to Ajanta: Festschrift for Dieter Schlingloff on the Occasion of his Eightieth Birthday,* ed. Eli Franco and Monika Zin, 2:883–895. Rupandehi: Lumbini International Research Institute.

———. 2010c. "On Some Who Are Not Allowed to Become Buddhist Monks or Nuns: An Old List of Types of Slaves or Unfree Laborers." *Journal of the American Oriental Society* 130, no. 2:225–234.

———. 2010d. "Trois morceaux en forme de poire: Réflexions sur la possibilité d'un monachisme comparatif." *Religions et Histoire,* Hors-série no. 3:14–21.

———. 2013. "A New Hat for Hārītī: On 'Giving' Children for Their Protection to Buddhist Monks and Nuns in Early India." In Sasson 2013, 17–42.

Scott, Rachelle M. 2009. *Nirvana for Sale? Buddhism, Wealth, and the Dhammakāya Temple in Contemporary Thailand.* Albany: State University of New York Press.

Senart, E. 1902–1903. "The Inscriptions in the Caves at Karle." *Epigraphia Indica* 7:47–74.

Shah, Kirit K. 2001. *The Problem of Identity: Women in Early Indian Inscriptions.* New Delhi: Oxford University Press.

Sharma, Mani Ram. 1993. *Marriage in Ancient India.* Delhi: Agam Kala Prakashan.

Shastri, Haraprasad. 1939. *Saundarananda Kāvya of Ārya Bhadanta Aśvaghoṣa.* Re-issued with additions by Chintaharan Chakravarti. Calcutta: Royal Asiatic Society of Bengal.

Shizutani Masao 静谷正雄. 1979. *Indo bukkyō himei mokuroku* インド仏教碑銘目録. Kyoto: Heirakuji shoten 平楽寺書店.

Siegel, Lee. 1987. *Laughing Matters: Comic Tradition in India.* Chicago: University of Chicago Press.

Silber, Ilana Friedrich. 1981. "Dissent through Holiness: The Case of the Radical Renouncer in Theravada Buddhist Countries." *Numen* 28, no. 2:164–193.

———. 1995. *Virtuosity, Charisma, and Social Order: A Comparative Sociological Study of Monasticism in Theravada Buddhism and Medieval Catholicism.* Cambridge: Cambridge University Press.

Silk, Jonathan A. 1996. "Notes on the History of the Yongle Kanjur." In *Suhṛllekhāḥ: Festgabe für Helmut Eimer,* ed. Michael Hahn, Jens-Uwe Hartmann, and Roland Steiner, Indica et Tibetica 28:153–200. Swisttal-Odendorf: Indica et Tibetica.

———. 2008. *Managing Monks: Administrators and Administrative Roles in Indian Buddhist Monasticism.* Oxford: Oxford University Press.

———. 2009. *Riven by Lust: Incest and Schism in Indian Buddhist Legend and Historiography.* Honolulu: University of Hawai'i Press.

———. 2010. Review of *Übersetzungen aus dem tibetischen Kanjur: Beiträge zur Buddhismuskunde und zur zentralasiatischen Märchenforschung,* ed. Hartmut Walravens. *Indo-Iranian Journal* 53:65–70.

Singh, Madan Mohan. 1954. "Life in the Buddhist Monastery during the 6th Century B.C." *Journal of the Bihar Research Society* 40, no. 2:131–154.

Singh, Nagendra Kr., ed. 1999. *International Encyclopaedia of Buddhism,* vol. 71 (Tibet). New Delhi: Anmol Publications Pvt.

Sivaramamurti, C. [1942] 1998. *Amaravati Sculptures in the Chennai Government Museum.* Chennai: Thiru S. Rangamani.

Skilling, Peter, Jason A. Carbine, Claudio Cicuzza, and Santi Pakdeekham, eds. 2012. *How Theravāda Is Theravāda? Exploring Buddhist Identities.* Chiang Mai: Silkworm Books.

Skilton, Andrew. [1994] 1997. *A Concise History of Buddhism.* 2nd ed. Birmingham: Windhorse.

Spiro, Melford E. 1969. "Religious Symbolism and Social Behavior." *Proceedings of the American Philosophical Society* 113, no. 5:341–349.

———. [1970] 1982. *Buddhism and Society: A Great Tradition and Its Burmese Vicissitudes.* 2nd expanded ed. Berkeley: University of California Press.

———. [1984] 1986. "Some Reflections on Family and Religion in East Asia." In *Religion and the Family in East Asia,* ed. George A. De Vos and Takao Sofue, 35–54. Berkeley: University of California Press.

Stein, M. A. [1900] 1961. *Kalhaṇa's Rājataraṅgiṇī: A Chronicle of the Kings of Kaśmīr.* 2 vols. Delhi: Motilal Banarsidass.

Steinkellner, E. 1994. "A Report on the 'Kanjur' of Ta pho." *East and West* 44, no. 1:115–136.

Steinthal, Paul, ed. [1885] 1948. *Udāna.* London: Oxford University Press.

Sternbach, Ludwik. 1965. "Forms of Marriage in Ancient India and Their Development." In *Juridical Studies in Ancient Indian Law,* ed. Ludwik Sternbach, 1:347–438. Delhi: Motilal Banarasidass.

Stoneman, Richard. 1995. "Naked Philosophers: The Brahmans in the Alexander Historians and the Alexander Romance." *Journal of Hellenic Studies* 115:99–114.

Strong, John. 1997. "A Family Quest: The Buddha, Yaśodharā, and Rāhula in the *Mūlasarvāstivāda Vinaya.*" In *Sacred Biography in the Buddhist Traditions of South and Southeast Asia,* ed. Juliane Schober, 113–128. Honolulu: University of Hawai'i Press.

Stuart-Macadam, Patricia. 1995. "Breastfeeding in Prehistory." In *Breastfeeding: Biocultural Perspectives,* ed. Patricia Stuart-Macadam and Katherine A. Dettwyler, 75–100. New York: Aldine De Gruyter.

Studholme, Alexander. 2002. *The Origins of Oṃ Maṇipadme Hūṃ: A Study of the Kāraṇḍavyūha Sūtra.* Albany: State University of New York Press.

Sueki, Yasuhiro. 2008. *Bibliographical Sources for Buddhist Studies from the Viewpoint of Buddhist Philology.* 2nd rev. and enlarged ed. Tokyo: International Institute for Buddhist Studies.

Tai, Yen-hui. 1978. "Divorce in Traditional Chinese Law." In *Chinese Family Law and Social Change: In Historical and Comparative Perspective,* ed. David C. Buxbaum, Asian Law Series 3:75–106. Seattle: University of Washington Press.

Takakusu Junjirō 高楠順次郎. 1896. *A Record of the Buddhist Religion as Practised in India and the Malay Archipelago (A.D. 671–695) by I-Tsing.* Oxford: Clarendon Press.

———, ed. [1936–1940] 1970. *Nanden daizōkyō* 南傳大藏經. Ritsuzō 律藏. 5 vols. Tokyo: Taishō shinshū daizōkyō kankōkai 大正新脩大藏經刊行會.

Takakusu, Junjirō, and Makoto Nagai, eds. [1924] 1975–1976. *Samantapāsādikā: Buddhaghosa's Commentary on the Vinaya Piṭaka.* 8 vols. London: Pali Text Society.

Takakusu Junjirō 高楠順次郎 and Watanabe Kaikyoku 渡邊海旭, eds. 1924–1935. *Taishō shinshū daizōkyō* 大正新脩大藏經. 100 vols. Tokyo: Taishō issaikyō kankōkai 大正一切經刊行會.

Talbot, Alice-Mary. 1990. "The Byzantine Family and the Monastery." *Dumbarton Oaks Papers* 44:119–129.

Tambiah, Stanley Jeyaraja. 1984. *The Buddhist Saints of the Forest and the Cult of Amulets: A Study in Charisma, Hagiography, Sectarianism, and Millennial Buddhism.* Cambridge: Cambridge University Press.

Tanemura Ryūgen 種村隆元. 1993. "The Four *Nikāyas* Mentioned in the *Gaṇḍīlakṣaṇa* Chapter of the *Kriyāsaṃgraha.*" *Indogaku bukkyōgaku kenkyū* 印度學佛教學研究 41, no. 2:40–42.

———. 1994. "Kriyāsaṃgraha no shukke sahō Kriyāsaṃgrahaの出家作法." *Indo tetsugaku bukkyōgaku kenkyū* インド哲学仏教学研究 2:53–66.

Tatelman, Joel. 1998. "The Trials of Yaśodharā and the Birth of Rāhula: A Synopsis of Bhadrakalpāvadāna II–IX." *Buddhist Studies Review* 15, no. 1:3–42.

———. 1999. "'The Trials of Yaśodharā': The Legend of the Buddha's Wife in the *Bhadrakalpāvadāna*." *Buddhist Literature* 1:176–261.

Thakur, Upendra. 1973. "Early Indian Mints." *Journal of the Economic and Social History of the Orient* 16, nos. 2/3:265–297.

Thanissaro Bhikkhu (Geoffrey DeGraff). 1994. *The Buddhist Monastic Code: The Patimokkha Training Rules*. Valley Center, CA: Metta Forest Monastery.

Thomas, Edward J. [1933] 2002. *The History of Buddhist Thought*. 2nd ed. Mineola, NY: Dover Publications.

Tiyavanich, Kamala. 1997. *Forest Recollections: Wandering Monks in Twentieth-Century Thailand*. Honolulu: University of Hawai'i Press.

Tokuoka Ryōei 徳岡亮英. 1960. "Indo bukkyō ni okeru buha no seiritsu ni tsuite: Furauwarunā no kincho o yonde 印度仏教における部派の成立について・フラウワルナーの近著を読んで." *Ōtani gakuhō* 大谷學報 40, no. 3:43–69.

Trenckner, V., ed. 1924–2011. *A Critical Pāli Dictionary*. Revised, continued, and edited by Dines Andersen, Helmer Smith, Ludwig Alsdorf, Kenneth Roy Norman, Oskar von Hinüber, and Ole Holten Pind. Copenhagen: Royal Danish Academy.

Tsomo, Karma Lekshe. 1996. *Sisters in Solitude: Two Traditions of Buddhist Monastic Ethics for Women; A Comparative Analysis of the Chinese Dharmagupta and the Tibetan Mūlasarvāstivāda Bhikṣuṇī Prātimokṣa Sūtras*. Albany: State University of New York Press.

Tsukamoto Keishō 塚本啓祥. 1996–2003. *Indo bukkyō himei no kenkyū* インド仏教碑銘の研究. 3 vols. Kyoto: Heirakuji shoten 平樂寺書店.

Tyagi, Jaya. 2007. "Organized Household Production and the Emergence of the *Sangha*." *Studies in History* 23:271–287.

Upasak, C. S. 1975. *Dictionary of Early Buddhist Monastic Terms: Based on Pali Literature*. Varanasi: Bharati Prakashan.

Vaidya, P. L. 1961. *Mahāyāna-sūtra-saṁgraha, Part 1*. Darbhanga: Mithila Institute of Post-Graduate Studies and Research in Sanskrit Learning.

Vinayasūtra's Pravrajyāvastu Study Group. 2003–2011. "The *Pravrajyāvastu* of the *Vinayasūtra* and its *Vṛtti:* Sanskrit Text and Japanese Translation (1–7)." *Annual of the Institute for Comprehensive Studies of Buddhism Taisho University* 25 (2003): 44–93; 26 (2004): 54–73; 27 (2005): 50–76; 29 (2007): 26–65; 31 (2009): 83–125; 32 (2010): 48–84; 33 (2011): 65–104.

Virdi, P. K. 1972. *The Grounds for Divorce in Hindu and English Law: A Study in Comparative Law*. Delhi: Motilal Banarsidass.

Vita, Silvio. 2003. "Printings of the Buddhist 'Canon' in Modern Japan." In *Buddhist Asia 1: Papers from the First Conference of Buddhist Studies Held in Naples in May 2001*, ed. Giovanni Verardi and Silvio Vita, 217–245. Kyoto: Italian School of East Asian Studies.

Vogel, Claus. 1985. "Bu-ston on the Schism of the Buddhist Church and on the

Doctrinal Tendencies of Buddhist Scriptures." In *Zur Schulzugehörigkeit von Werken der Hīnayāna-Literatur,* ed. Heinz Bechert, 1:104–110. Göttingen: Vandenhoeck & Ruprecht.

Vogel, Claus, and Klaus Wille. 2002. "The Final Leaves of the Pravrajyāvastu Portion of the Vinayavastu Manuscript Found Near Gilgit, Part 2: Nāgakumārāvadāna and Lévi Text, with Two Appendices Containing a Turfan Fragment of the Nāgakumārāvadāna and a Kučā Fragment of the Upasaṃpadā Section of the Sarvāstivādins." In *Sanskrit-Texte aus dem buddhistischen Kanon: Neuentdeckungen und Neueditionen 4,* ed. Jin-il Chung, Claus Vogel, and Klaus Wille, Sanskrit-Wörterbuch der buddhistischen Texte aus den Turfan-Funden 9:11–76. Göttingen: Vandenhoeck & Ruprecht.

Vogel, J. Ph. 1905–1906. "Epigraphical Discoveries at Sarnath." *Epigraphia Indica* 8:166–179.

Waldschmidt, Ernst. [1926] 1979. *Bruchstücke des Bhikṣuṇī-Prātimokṣa der Sarvāstivādins.* Kleinere Sanskrit-Texte Heft 3. Wiesbaden: Franz Steiner Verlag.

———. 1980. "The Rāṣṭrapālasūtra in Sanskrit Remnants from Central Asia." In *Indianisme et bouddhisme: Mélanges offerts à Mgr Étienne Lamotte,* 359–374. Louvain-la-neuve: Université catholique de Louvain, Institut orientaliste.

Waley, Arthur, trans. [1943] 1980. *Monkey.* New York: Grove Press.

Wang, Bangwei. 1994. "Buddhist Nikāyas through Ancient Chinese Eyes." In *Untersuchungen zur buddhistischen Literatur,* ed. Frank Bandurski et al., Sanskrit-Wörterbuch der buddhistischen Texte aus den Turfan-Funden 5:165–203. Göttingen: Vandenhoeck & Ruprecht.

———. 2005. "Rules and Practice in Buddhist Monastic Life in 7th Century India: A Textual Analysis of Yijing's Accounts." In *Im Dickicht der Gebote: Studien zur Dialektik von Norm und Praxis in der Buddhismusgeschichte Asiens,* ed. Peter Schalk, Max Deeg, Oliver Freiberger, Christoph Kleine, and Astrid van Nahl, 85–97. Stockholm: Uppsala Universitet.

Warder, A. K. 1972–2011. *Indian Kāvya Literature.* 8 vols. Delhi: Motilal Banarsidass.

Wayman, Alex. [1966–1968] 1997. "Parents of the Buddhist Monks." In *Untying the Knots in Buddhism: Selected Essays,* ed. Alex Wayman, 149–162. Delhi: Motilal Banarsidass.

Wickremeratne, Swarna. 2006. *Buddha in Sri Lanka: Remembered Yesterdays.* Albany: State University of New York Press.

Wijayaratna, Môhan. 1983. *Le moine bouddhiste selon les textes du Theravāda.* Paris: Éditions du Cerf.

———. 1990. *Buddhist Monastic Life: According to the Texts of the Theravāda Tradition.* Translated by Claude Grangier and Steven Collins. Cambridge: Cambridge University Press.

———. 1991. *Le moniales bouddhistes: Naissance et développement du monachisme féminin.* Paris: Éditions du Cerf.

———. 2001. *Buddhist Nuns: The Birth and Development of a Women's Monastic Order.* Colombo: Wisdom.

Wilkinson, Endymion. 2000. *Chinese History: A Manual, Revised and Enlarged.* Cambridge, MA: Harvard University Press.

Wilson, Elizabeth [Liz]. 1994. "Henpecked Husbands and Renouncers Home on the Range: Celibacy As Social Disengagement in South Asian Buddhism." *Union Seminary Quarterly Review* 48, nos. 3/4:7–28.

———. 1996. *Charming Cadavers: Horrific Figurations of the Feminine in Indian Buddhist Hagiographic Literature.* Chicago: University of Chicago Press.

———. 2013. *Family in Buddhism.* Albany: State University of New York Press.

Wilson, Frances. 1985. "The Nun." In *Women in Buddhism: Images of the Feminine in the Mahāyāna Tradition,* ed. Diana Y. Paul, 77–105. 2nd ed. Berkeley, CA: Asian Humanities Press.

Wilson, John Dover, ed. [1936] 1961. *The Tragedy of Hamlet, Prince of Denmark.* The Works of Shakespeare. 2nd ed. Cambridge: Cambridge University Press.

Wiltshire, Martin Gerald. 1990. *Ascetic Figures before and in Early Buddhism: The Emergence of Gautama as the Buddha.* Berlin: Mouton de Gruyter.

Woodward, F. L., ed. [1926] 1977. *Paramattha-Dīpanī Udānaṭṭhakathā (Udāna Commentary) of Dhammapālâcariya.* London: Pali Text Society.

———, trans. [1932] 1960. *The Book of the Gradual Sayings (Anguttara-nikāya); or, More-Numbered Suttas: With an Introduction by Mrs. Rhys Davids.* Vol. 1. London: Published for the Pali Text Society by Luzac & Co.

Workman, Herbert B. [1913] 1962. *The Evolution of the Monastic Ideal from the Earliest Times Down to the Coming of the Friars.* Boston: Beacon Press.

Wu Yin. 2001. *Choosing Simplicity: A Commentary on the Bhikshuni Pratimoksha.* Translated by Jendy Shih. Edited by Thubten Chodron. Ithaca: Snow Lion Publications.

Wynne, Alexander. 2008. "On the Sarvāstivādins and Mūlasarvāstivādins." *The Indian International Journal of Buddhist Studies* 9:243–266.

Yamagiwa Nobuyuki 山極伸之. 2002. "*Ārāmika*—Gardener or Park Keeper? One of the Marginals around the Buddhist *Saṃgha.*" In *Buddhist and Indian Studies in Honour of Professor Sodo Mori,* 363–385. Hamamatsu: Kokusai Bukkyoto Kyokai.

———. 2004. "Ritsuzō ga shimesu biku to kazoku no kankei 律蔵が示す比丘と家族の関係." In *Kazoku no arikata to bukkyō* 家族のあり方と仏教, ed. Nihon bukkyō gakkai 日本仏教学会, 49–64. Kyoto: Heirakuji shoten 平楽寺書店.

———. 2007a. "Samantapāsādikā ga shimesu biku to shinzoku no kankei サマンタ・パーサーディカーが示す比丘と親族の関係." *Indogaku bukkyōgaku kenkyū* 印度學佛教學研究 55, no. 1:136–142.

———. 2007b. "Vinaya Manuscripts: State of the Field." In *Indica et Tibetica: Festschrift für Michael Hahn Zum 65. Geburtstag von Freunden und Schülern überreicht,* ed. Konrad Klaus and Jens-Uwe Hartmann, Wiener Studien zur Tibetologie und Buddhismuskunde 66:607–616. Vienna: Arbeitskreis für Tibetische und Buddhistische Studien Universität Wien.

———. 2009. "Indo buha bukkyō kyōdanron to ritsuzō no rekishi インド部派仏教教団論と律蔵の歴史." DLitt diss., Bukkyo University.

Yamaguchi Zuihō 山口瑞鳳 et al., eds. 1977. Sutain shūshū chibettogo bunken kaidai mokuroku スタイン蒐集チベット語文献解題目録. Vol. 1. Tokyo: Tōyō bunko 東洋文庫.

Yao Fumi 八尾史. 2007. "'Konponsetsuissaiubu' to iu meishō ni tsuite「根本説一切有部」という名称について." *Indogaku bukkyōgaku kenkyū* 印度學佛教學研究 55, no. 2:132–135.

———. 2011. "The Story of Dharmadinnā: Ordination by Messenger in the *Mūlasarvāstivāda-vinaya*." Paper presented at Buddhist Nuns in India, University of Toronto, April 15–17, 2011.

Yotsuya Kōdō 四津谷孝道. 2004. "Chibetto bukkyō ni okeru keishō, sōzoku チベット仏教における継承・相続." In *Kazoku no arikata to bukkyō* 家族のあり方と仏教, ed. Nihon bukkyō gakkai 日本仏教学会, 95–103. Kyoto: Heirakuji shoten 平楽寺書店.

Young, Serinity. 2004. *Courtesans and Tantric Consorts: Sexualities in Buddhist Narrative, Iconography, and Ritual*. New York: Routledge.

Yu, Anthony C. 1997. *Rereading the Stone: Desire and the Making of Fiction in* Dream of the Red Chamber. Princeton, NJ: Princeton University Press.

Yuyama, Akira. 1979. *Vinaya-Texte*. Systematische Übersicht über die buddhistische Sanskrit-Literatur 1. Wiesbaden: Franz Steiner Verlag.

Zacchetti, Stefano. 2005. *In Praise of the Light: A Critical Synoptic Edition with an Annotated Translation of Chapters 1–3 of Dharmarakṣa's Guang zan jing* 光讚經, *Being the Earliest Chinese Translation of the Larger Prajñāpāramitā*. Bibliotheca Philologica et Philosophica Buddhica 8. Tokyo: International Research Institute for Advanced Buddhology, Soka University.

Index of Texts

Abhidharmakośabhāṣya, 189n36
Andhaka-aṭṭhakathā, 180n102
Aṅguttara-nikāya, 189n33, 222n98
Arthaśāstra, 91, 94, 201n52, 202n59, 203n74
Ārya-sarvāstivādi-mūla-bhikṣuṇī-prātimokṣa-sūtra-vṛtti, 145–146, 196n149, 204n87, 223n116, 224n138, 225n141, 225nn143–144, 226n146
Avadānaśataka, 213n243

Bṛhat-kalpa-bhāṣya (of Saṅghadāsa), 159
Buddhacarita "Life of the Buddha" (of Aśvaghoṣa), 157

Cullaniddesa, 175n42

Dakkhiṇāvibhaṅga-sutta, 161
Daśakumāracarita "The Ten Princes" (of Daṇḍin), 91
Dhammapada, 173n28
Dharmaguptaka-vinaya (T. 1428), 12, 13, 55, 63, 66, 67, 70–72, 75, 123, 124–129, 131, 132, 133, 135, 142, 168, 178nn77–79, 179nn80–81, 179n84, 190n37, 192n99, 192n101, 194n126, 195n136, 195n145, 196n152, 196nn155–156, 197n169, 200n32, 200n43, 203n75, 206n106, 209n150, 209n162, 211n196, 216n15, 216nn17–18, 217nn24–32, 218nn34–47, 223n116, 228n60, 228n63
  Bhikṣuṇī-prātimokṣa (T. 1431), 121, 134, 142, 216n7, 217nn21–23, 218n39, 219n63
Dharmaskandha, 203nn77–79, 204nn80–84
Divyāvadāna, 31

Ekaśatakakarman (T. 1453), 194n117

Garbhāvakrānti-sūtra, 183n136
Gedō zanmai, 207n119

Itivuttaka commentary, 189n32

Kaiyuan shijiao lü catalogue (T. 2154), 210n175
Kāmasūtra, 91, 201n52
Kāraṇḍavyūha-sūtra, 117, 215nn267–268
Karudai, 207n119
Kriyāsaṃgraha, 187n15

lHan (lDan) kar ma catalogue, 182n121

Mahāsāṅghika-Lokottaravāda Bhikṣuṇī-vinaya, 141, 180n101, 190n37, 193n110, 196nn158–159, 197n161, 206n112, 222n104, 222n106–107, 223n112
Mahāsāṅghika-vinaya (T. 1425), 69–70, 72–73, 87–90, 93–94, 96, 98, 104–105, 140–141, 178n74, 186n190, 190n37, 195n145, 196nn152–154, 196nn158–159, 197nn161–162, 200nn35–37, 200nn42–43, 202n62, 202n64, 203n71, 203n73, 203n75, 206n106, 206nn112–115, 209n150, 209n162, 211n196, 219n65, 222nn103–104, 222nn106–107, 223nn108–110, 223n112, 223n114, 228n63
Mahāvaṃsa, 214n261
Mahāvyutpatti, 198n5, 199n23, 203n77
Mahīśāsaka-vinaya (T. 1421), 1, 14, 52, 55, 58–59, 62–63, 66–67, 96–97, 104–105, 129–133, 135, 142, 171n1, 178n74, 179n86, 189n34, 190n37, 191nn70–73, 192n99, 192n101,

193nn108–111, 194n119, 194n124, 195nn140–142, 195n145, 200n43, 203n75, 206nn108–109, 208n144, 209n150, 209n162, 211n196, 217n24, 219nn49–51, 219nn55–59, 219n61, 228n63
Bhikṣuṇī-prātimokṣa (T. 1423), 122, 124, 131, 142, 216n8, 219n52, 219n63
Majjhima-nikāya, 47, 161
Mālatīmādhava (of Bhavabhūti), 91
Manusmṛti, 93, 156, 203n66, 208n143, 226n13
Mūlasarvāstivāda-vinaya, 185n170, 206n110, 209n150, 209n160, 216n15, 216n17, 219n65
Bhaiṣajyavastu (T. 1448, and Skt., and Tib.), 178n72, 196n152
Bhikṣuṇī-prātimokṣa (T. 1455 and Tib.), 122, 124, 144, 216n8, 224nn132–137, 224n138
Bhikṣuṇī-vibhaṅga (T. 1443 and Tib.), 90–91, 110–114, 144–145, 187n15, 196n149, 198n4, 200n40, 200n43, 201n45, 203n75, 210n164, 211n197, 212nn198–216, 212nn218–228, 213n230, 213nn232–241, 217n24, 223n116, 224n129, 224n138, 225nn139–144, 228n61
Bhikṣu-prātimokṣa (T. 1454, and Skt., and Tib.), 213n235
Carmavastu (T. 1447, and Skt., and Tib.), 193n105
Kṣudrakavastu (T. 1451 and Tib.), 15, 48–49, 56–57, 80–86, 98–99, 137–139, 168, 178n72, 178n75, 179n89, 183n136, 190nn38–61, 193nn104–105, 193n107, 198nn3–4, 198nn7–11, 199n19, 199nn26–27, 199n29, 200nn30–31, 207n117, 210n175, 212n229, 219n65, 221n89, 221nn91–95, 222n96, 222n98, 228n59
Mātṛkā (*ma lta bu;* in *Uttaragrantha*; Tib. and T. 1441), 189n36
Muktaka (*rkyang pa;* in *Uttaragrantha*; T. 1452, *juans* 6–10, and Tib.), 216n19
Nidāna (*gleng gzhi;* in *Uttaragrantha*; T. 1452, *juans* 1–5, and Tib.), 60–61, 194n114, 194nn116–118, 195n145, 216n19
Pārivāsikavastu, 178n72
Pravrajyāvastu (T. 1444, and Skt., and Tib.), 66, 67, 178n74, 193n112, 195nn138–139, 195n145, 198n4
Upālipariprcchā (*upalis zhus pa;* in *Uttaragrantha*; Tib. and T. 1441), 216n19
Vinaya-vibhaṅga (T. 1442 and Tib.), 47, 50–51, 55, 94–95, 99–102, 104, 107–109, 168, 178n74, 188n31, 189n32, 189n35, 191nn63–64, 191n68, 192n99, 192n101, 198n4, 200n40, 200n43, 201n45, 203n75, 203nn78–79, 204nn80–84, 204n87, 205n96, 207n121, 208n126, 208nn129–136, 208nn138–143, 209nn145–147, 209n157, 209nn159–161, 210n164, 210nn171–175, 211nn176–178, 211nn180–187, 211nn189–191, 221n89, 221n95, 228n61
Vinītaka (*'dul bar byed pa;* in *Uttaragrantha*; Tib. and T. 1441), 228n58

Nanhai jigui neifazhuan (T. 2125), 211n179
Nāradasmṛti, 93, 201n55, 203nn69–70
Narmamālā "Garland of Satires" (of Kṣemendra), 91
Nyāyānusāra (of Saṅghabhadra; T. 1562), 221n83

Pāli (Theravāda) Vinaya, 25, 52, 55, 67, 76, 103, 142–143, 148, 178n74, 179n90, 184n165, 185n169, 189n34, 190n37, 191nn72–73, 191n77, 192n100, 192n102, 194n125, 195nn143–144, 196n148, 196n156, 197nn174–175, 197n177, 200n32, 200n43, 203n75, 206n102, 206n106, 206nn110–111, 209n162, 211n196, 216n8, 216n15, 216n17, 217n20, 217n24, 222n107, 223n115, 223n119, 223n124, 224n125
Bhikkhunī-pātimokkha, 122, 124, 142, 197n173, 211n196, 216n8, 219n63
Bhikkhu-pātimokkha, 76–77, 197nn172–173, 197nn175–176
Paramatthajotikā, 7, 175n42
'Phang thang ma catalogue, 182n121
Pinimu-jing (T. 1463), 206n112
Prātimokṣa-sūtra-paddhati (Tib.), 204n87
Prātimokṣa-sūtra-ṭīkā-vinaya-samuccaya (of Vimalamitra; Tib.), 204n87, 205n91, 205n93

Rājataraṅgiṇī, 116, 214n260
Rāṣṭrapālaparipṛcchā-sūtra, 117, 161, 215n266, 215n269
Rāṣṭrapāla-sūtra, 191n75
Raṭṭhapāla-sutta, 47, 52, 53, 191n73, 191n76
Rhinoceros Horn Sūtra/Sutta, 4–7, 10, 13, 16, 17, 25, 153, 172n14, 172n16, 173n26, 173n28, 174nn39–40, 175n41, 176n58

Sacred Books of the East, 175n41, 180n103
Samantapāsādikā, 20, 180n102, 182n129, 189n32, 191n65, 192n100, 198n5, 224n126
Samantapāsādikā (Chinese version, T. 1462), 189n32
Saṃyukta-āgama (T. 100), 191n78
Sapoduobu pini modeleqie (T. 1441; early trans. of *Uttaragrantha*), 189n36, 228n58
Sarvāstivāda-vinaya (T. 1435), 55, 64–66, 67–68, 94, 133, 134–137, 178n74, 189n34, 190n37, 192n99, 192n101, 193n104, 195nn128–129, 195nn132–134, 196n147, 200n43, 201n45, 203n75, 208n144, 209n150, 209n162, 211n196, 216n13, 216n16, 219nn64–65, 220n66, 220nn68–79, 221n80, 221n82, 228n63
  Bhikṣuṇī-prātimokṣa (T. 1437), 133
Saundarananda (of Aśvaghoṣa), 183n136
Sūtra on Venerable Udāyin Guiding People to Pay Homage to the Buddha and Saṅgha, 210n175
Sutta-nipāta, 4, 6, 172n14, 172n16, 173n28, 174n40, 175nn41–42

Therīgāthā, 176n60
Tibetan Tales, 179n82

Udāna, 53
Udāna commentary, 53–54, 189n32, 192n83
Ugraparipṛcchā, 179n92

Vessantara Jātaka, 160, 176n60, 227n37
Vinayakārikā (of Viśākhadeva; T. 1459, and Tib., and Skt.), 181n112
Vinayasaṃgraha (of Viśeṣamitra; T. 1458 and Tib.), 201nn44–45, 203n75, 204n87, 205n91
Vinayasūtra (of Guṇaprabha; Skt. and Tib.), 95, 199n27, 205n91
Vinayasūtravṛttyabhidhānasva-vyākhyāna (of Guṇaprabha; Skt. and Tib.), 185n169, 187n8, 195n145, 199n24, 199n28, 205n91, 216n12, 222n98, 224n137
Vinaya-vibhaṅga-pada-vyākhyāna (of Vinītadeva; Tib.), 205n99

Index of Authors/Subjects

Abbott, Elizabeth, 165
abortion, 168, 169
Adachi, Kin'ichi, 207n119
Aelred of Rievaulx, 164, 228n53
age: at initiation/ordination, 64–68, 132–133, 140, 141, 142, 159, 160, 195n145, 199n27, 217n20, 227n29 (*see also* "scarecrow" provision for novices); of majority, 133, 219n62; at weaning, 132, 133, 135, 141, 142, 159, 219n60
Agrawala, Ratna Chandra, 115–116
Allen, Michael, 116, 214n257
Almond, Philip, 162–163
antifamilial/antisocial/asocial: Buddhism as, 5, 9, 152–153, 173n28, 174n29, 174n38; Indian renunciation as, 5, 7; *pratyekabuddha* as, 114
anu√jñā (to authorize/command/order), 126, 143, 218n37, 223n124
asceticism, 17, 153–155, 158, 173n21, 174n40; conflation with monastic traditions, 7, 174n40; *dhūtaguṇa*s, 109; domestication of, 7; home asceticism in late antiquity, 194n127; of Mahākāśyapa, foremost Buddhist ascetic, 24, 80, 107–110, 112, 114, 152; monastic ambivalence toward, 17, 113, 161; rhetoric of, 7; sham ascetics, 199n23
Aśvaghoṣa, 157, 183n136
*avadāna*s (previous-life stories), 31, 49, 114, 213n238, 213n241

Bailey, Greg, 6, 25, 173n28
Bala, *bhikṣu*, 43–45
Bardesanes, 173n21
Bareau, André, 26
Basham, A. L., 44–45, 174n31, 202n59
Bechert, Heinz, 126
Benedict of Nursia, 3, 106–107, 172n11
bhikṣu/bhikṣuṇī: "monk"/"nun" and other terms for, 1, 2–3, 25–26, 163–164, 171n2, 171n6, 185n170
biological kin, presence of in monasteries, 9, 23–24, 54, 55–56, 74–75, 109, 161, 185n168; in Egyptian monasticism, 164, 184n167; in Jainism, 157; presupposed in *prātimokṣa*s, 28, 33, 39, 76–77
biological kinship terms, 24, 25–26, 184n167, 185n168, 195n135
Bloomfield, Maurice, 91
Boswell, John, 29, 164
Boucher, Daniel, 161
brahmanical treatises, 35–36, 91, 108, 151. See also *Arthaśāstra* and *Kāmasūtra* in Index of Texts
brothels, 168–169, 228n63
Buddhaghosa, 7, 175n42, 182n129
Buddhamitrā, *bhikṣuṇī,* 44–45
Buddha's family, 9, 21–23, 26, 109, 153, 156; Amṛtodana (uncle), 22; Ānanda (cousin; husband of Sthūlanandā), 21–22, 48, 49, 67–68, 108, 109, 196n148, 209n162; Aniruddha (cousin), 21–22, 108, 109; Bhadrika (cousin), 21–22; Devadatta (cousin), 21–22; Droṇodana (uncle), 22; Gopikā (wife), 22; Kacaṅgalā (mother in a previous life), 183n138; Mahāmāyā (mother), 22; Mahāprajāpatī Gautamī (aunt and stepmother), 22, 73, 98–99, 100–101, 112–113, 143, 145, 209n162; Mṛgajā (wife), 22; Nanda (half-brother; aka Sundarananda), 21, 108, 109, 183n136; Rāhula (son), 22, 23, 26, 108, 109; Śuddhodana (father),

22, 99, 183n142; Yaśodharā (wife), 22, 26, 185n177
Buddhism outside India, 10, 118, 154, 167; Central Asian, 10, 80, 115–116, 117–118, 154, 163; Chinese, 10, 25, 116; Dunhuang, 214n252; Japanese, 10, 25, 116, 214n253; Kaśmīri, 80, 117–118; Ladakhi, 148–149; Mongolian, 10, 116, 154, 163, 214n254; Newar, 10, 80, 116, 117–118, 154, 155, 163, 214n253, 215n270; Sind(hu), 214n260; Sri Lankan, 10, 80; Tibetan, 10, 25, 80, 116, 117–118, 154, 178n66, 210n163
Buddhist studies, 3, 10, 13, 17, 18, 24, 27, 162–163, 173n24, 181n106
business matters, monastic involvement in, 7, 16, 27, 155, 166, 167, 168–169, 185n182, 228n63
Bu sTon, 224n138

celibacy, 2, 9, 116, 134, 147, 171n2, 214n257, 219n48; *brahmacarya,* 52, 72, 130, 133; breaches of (*abrahmacarya*), 2, 9, 10, 30, 55, 83, 85–86, 103–104, 112, 114, 147–148, 155, 157–158, 162, 164–165, 166–167, 177n62, 195n133; definitions of, 155, 226n8; need to educate monks about, 79, 80, 86, 156, 199n27; for nuns, 110, 112, 114, 128, 129, 130, 133–134, 147–148; pact, 111; struggle with, 106–107; unfounded accusations concerning, 65, 66, 67, 104, 128, 130, 133, 148, 220n68; "vows" of, 2, 177n61
Chakravarti, Uma, 7–8
characters in Buddhist literature: Ajātaśatru (King), 114; Ājñātakauṇḍinya, 100, 108; Ardhakāśī, 48, 190n37; Aśvaka (Group-of-Six), 108; Bījaka (son of Sudinna), 55, 192n99; Bījakamātā (wife of Sudinna; mother of Bījaka), 55, 192n99; Chanda (Group-of-Six), 108; Dharmadinnā, 37, 48–49, 151, 189n36, 190n37; Gartodara, 73; Group-of-Six monks (*ṣaḍvargika; chabbaggiya*), 84, 90–91, 99, 108, 113, 199n22, 201n45, 204n87, 216n16; Group-of-Twelve nuns, 90–91; Gupta (Prasenajit's prime minister), 99, 100, 207nn122–123, 208n126; Guptā (wife of Udāyin; mother of Kumāra-Kāśyapa), 15, 80, 99–103, 104, 105, 113, 118, 134–139, 148, 152, 167, 200n40, 207n122, 207n124, 208n144, 209n154, 210n164, 220n78, 221n83, 222n100; Kāla Mṛgāraputra, 201n45, 204n87; Kālī (nun), 141; Kapila (father of Kapilabhadrā), 110–111; Kapilabhadrā (aka Bhadrā; wife of Mahākāśyapa), 80, 108, 109, 110–114, 118, 152, 213n241, 220n79; Kāśyapa brothers, 22; Kāśyapa Buddha, 49; Kumāra-Kāśyapa, 80, 104, 118, 134, 138–140, 152, 209n154, 221n83, 221n95; Mahākāśyapa (aka Kāśyapa; husband of Kapilabhadrā), 24, 80, 100, 107, 108, 109–114, 118, 152, 212n227, 213n241; Mahāmaudgalyāyana, 100, 108; Māra, daughters of, 103–104; Mettiyā (expelled nun), 148, 222n105, 226n152; Nanda (Group-of-Six), 108; Nandika (penitent monk), 103–104, 209nn151–152; Nirgrantha Pūraṇa, 112; Nyagrodha (father of Mahākāśyapa), 110, 111; Posiya (brother of Saṅgāmaji), 192n98; Prasenajit (King), 99, 100; Punarvasuka (Group-of-Six), 108; Rāṣṭrapāla/Raṭṭhapāla, 47, 52, 53, 189n33, 191n75, 192n98; Ṛṣyaśṛṅga, 112; Śakra (lord of gods), 112; Saṅgāmaji, 37–38, 53–54, 191n78, 192n98; Śāriputra, 100, 108; Siddhārtha Gautama, 21–22, 26, 99, 109, 145, 157; Sthūlanandā, 113, 145, 168, 208n144, 209n162; Sudinna (father of Bījaka), 37, 47, 50–52, 53, 54–56, 151, 188n29, 189nn34–35, 191n65, 191n68, 191nn72–73, 192n99; Sudinnā (pregnant nun), 141; Udāyin (aka Kālodāyin; husband of Guptā; Group-of-Six), 12, 22, 80, 99–102, 103, 105, 106, 107–109, 113, 114, 118, 134–135, 152, 163, 199n22, 200n40, 207nn118–119, 207nn123–124, 209n154, 209n159, 209n162, 210n164, 210n175; Upāli, 22; Upananda (Group-of-Six), 84–85, 108, 208n144, 209n162; Utpalavarṇā, 48, 49; Viḍūḍabha, 68; Viśākha (betrothed to Dharmadinnā), 48, 49. *See also* Buddha's family
childhood: in Buddhism, 178n63; definitions of, 132, 159

children: abuse of, 66; on alms rounds with parents, 64–67 (*see also* nursing nuns: on alms rounds; pregnant nuns: on alms rounds); in Buddhism, 178n63; oblates, 160; presence of in monasteries, 159–161; protective measures for, 160; sale of, 160, 176n60, 224n129. *See also* co-renunciation: with children
Chinese canon, 19, 181nn113–118, 210n175
chujia, 46, 64, 184n160, 188n26. See also going-forth into homelessness; *pra√vraj*
Clark, Elizabeth, 194n127, 226n3
Cole, Alan, 24–26, 184nn159–160
Collins, Steven, 46, 174n40
conception/impregnation/insemination: Guptā's immaculate conception, 102–103, 104, 134–135, 137–138, 148, 167, 208n144, 209n154; in Jainism, 158; of nuns by monks, 102–103
Constable, Giles, 164–165
co-renunciation, 56, 155, 157; brahmanical, 156; with children, 2, 9, 16, 28, 46, 64–66, 67, 68, 69, 74, 151; father and son, 13–14, 38, 67, 69–70, 71, 179n90, 196n152, 196n154, 198n4; husband and wife, 2, 9, 14, 16, 28–29, 46, 79–80, 96–99, 113, 114, 115, 117, 152, 156, 157, 179n90, 198n4, 206n106, 206n115; in Jainism, 156–157; mother with son and four daughters, 196n149. *See also* renunciation
"corrupt"/"degenerate" religious practices, 80, 115–118, 154, 162–163, 167
courtship and dating, 101
crafts, monastic practice of, 57, 193nn104–105, 196n154
craftsmen, monastic interaction with, 32, 56–57, 192n103, 193nn104–106
criminal law (modern), 122–123, 127

Dayal, Har, 157, 215n271, 226n18
decline, narratives of, 117–118, 162–163
Dehejia, Vidya, 43
Deo, S. B., 156–157, 158–159
devakula (temples), 101, 205n99, 208n137
Dharmaguptaka-vinaya (general), 120; *Bhikṣuṇī-prātimokṣa,* 121, 123, 134, 146–147; dating of, 19, 20, 21, 75, 134; as part of extant *vinaya* corpus, 18, 75, 143–144; as Sthavira *vinaya,* 68
Dharmaśāstra (brahmanical law), 92, 93, 100, 186n184, 201n53, 202nn59–60, 203n68
diet, 59, 193n112, 194n113
direct order/commands, 34, 123, 126, 143
divorce, 2, 28, 79, 82, 84, 92–96, 105, 202n61, 206n102; alternatives to, 201n55; in brahmanical law, 79, 92, 202n57, 202nn59–60, 203n66, 203n68, 203n74; declaration of, 95–96; as prerequisite for ordination, 28, 78, 79, 92, 96, 118, 151; by sale of wife, 93; taxes/fees, 93–94; terminology for, 93, 95, 202nn62–63, 205n100; two forms of, 93
doctrine, 17, 161–162
Dumont, Louis, 73–74, 173n28
Dutt, Sukumar, 172n11, 173n28, 174nn29–30, 188n25

ecclesiastical acts (*karman*), 61–62, 136–137, 194n117, 222n100, 223n124; twofold (*jñapti-dvitīya karman*), 1, 131, 137, 221n81
Elm, Susanna, 3
ethics, 11, 17, 173n28, 178n69, 188n26
expulsion, 2, 9, 55, 103–104, 146, 148, 157–159, 161, 162, 165, 177n61, 191n65, 197n2, 222n105, 226n152; definitions of, 158, 227n20

Faure, Bernard, 6
Fausböll, V., 4–5, 8, 9
filial piety, 26, 186n2
Flood, Gavin, 6
food, 58, 59; pollution and purity of, 58–59; scarcity of, 51, 59–61; storage/preparation of, 69–70
"former" wives (*purāṇa-dvitīyā/purāṇa-dutiyikā*): as "abandoned," 28, 87, 119, 186n184, 199n21; demands by for support from monks, 37–38, 53–54; monks' interaction with, 78–79, 82–83, 85, 86–87, 87–90, 92, 106, 115, 118, 151, 156, 161; monks' interaction with ordained, "former" lay wives, 14, 78–79, 96–98, 99, 100–102, 105–106, 107, 109, 112–114, 117, 118–119, 152; terminology for, 9, 28, 81–82, 84, 151, 198n5, 206n111
frame-stories, 31, 32, 33, 73, 86, 103, 110

Gellner, David N., 116
Gethin, Rupert, 7

go-betweens. *See* matchmaking
going-forth into homelessness: and abandonment of family, 8, 37, 46, 52, 55, 64, 68, 71, 74, 78, 150–151, 188n26; interpretations of phrase, 28, 37–38, 45–49, 64, 150–151, 184n160, 188n19, 188nn22–23, 189n32; and physical separation from kin, 37, 52, 74, 151. See also *chujia; pra√vraj*
Gokhale, B. G., 5, 174n38
Gombrich, Richard, 5, 116, 173n28, 174n38, 176n57, 176n60, 177n61, 181n106
Granoff, Phyllis, 160
Guṇaprabha, 95, 224n138

Hart, H. L. A., 122–123, 127
Hinüber, Oskar von, 20, 182n129
Hirakawa, Akira, 105, 110, 141, 206n102, 214n257
Hodgson, Brian Houghton, 3, 13, 171n7
Horner, I. B., 25–26, 67, 105–106, 142–143, 180n103, 206n110, 217n20, 217n24, 223n124, 224n126
humor in law codes, 97, 106, 145, 199n22, 210n170, 217n22

illicit relationships, 14, 91, 97, 201n44
incest, 104, 209n156, 222n98
inscriptions, 27–28, 29, 35, 74, 150, 151, 152, 153; from Amarāvatī, 41–43; from Bhārhut, 41; corpus of, 37, 39, 186n2; from Kārli, 41; from Kurkihar, 117; from Mathurā, 44; *nikāya*s in, 180n100; *sahā* formula in, 187n11 (*see also* merit: share of in donative inscriptions); from Śailārwāḍi, 41; from Sāñcī, 39–41; from Sārnāth, 44

Jyväsjärvi, Mari, 159

Kane, P. V., 92, 201n53
Kaniṣka, 44, 183n130
karma, mysterious workings of, 102, 104, 138
*kārṣāpaṇa*s (cash), 84, 85, 199n18, 199n21, 203n71
Kāśyapīyas, 152, 209n154, 224n127
Kharoṣṭhī documents, 115, 213nn242–243
Kohn, Livia, 46, 184n167
Krawiec, Rebecca, 184n167, 227n49

Lamotte, Étienne, 8, 152, 176n54, 180n102, 209n154, 219n65
law (monastic), types of: for individual monastics, 30, 32–34, 35, 131 (see also *prātimokṣa*s); institutional, 30, 32, 33–34, 35, 123, 131
Leclercq, Jean, 119
legal theory, 31, 120, 122–123
Lévi, Sylvain, 31, 199n13
Lingat, Robert, 93, 177n61, 199n17

Mabbett, Ian, 6, 25, 173n28
Mahāsāṅghika-Lokottaravāda-vinaya (general), 180n101
Mahāsāṅghika tradition(s), 19, 141–142
Mahāsāṅghika-vinaya: dating of, 19, 20, 21, 75, 202n63; as non-Sthavira *vinaya,* 68–69; as part of extant *vinaya* corpus, 18, 75, 143–144; structure of, 68–69, 186n187
Mahāyāna and *sūtra*s of, 117, 118, 154–155, 175n46, 182n120, 215n271
Mahīśāsaka-vinaya (general), 129; dating of, 1, 19, 20, 21, 75, 142, 219n51; as part of extant *vinaya* corpus, 18, 75, 143–144; as Sthavira *vinaya,* 68
marital dissolution. *See* divorce
marital ties: continuation of, 79, 87, 118; *ipso facto* cancellation of, 84; of monastics, 2, 28, 80, 84, 151–152, 155–156, 157, 167; between monastics and lay spouses, 78–79, 87; between monks and nuns, 2, 28–29, 78–79
marriage: brahmanical, eight forms of, 94, 203n74, 203n76; clerical (Japanese), 214n253; counseling, 95; as a sacrament, 92, 201n53; seven steps to annulment of, 95; types of, 94–95, 203n75
married bodhisattvas, 215n268, 215n271
married monastic couples, 2, 14, 78–80, 97–99, 104, 152. *See also* co-renunciation; “former” wives: monks’ interaction with ordained, “former” lay wives
married monks, 79–80, 115–117, 154, 214n251, 214nn253–254, 215n271
Masefield, Peter, 53–54, 189n32
Masson, J. Moussaieff, 46
matchmaking, 28, 35–36, 79, 88–92, 95, 151, 201n45, 204n87; in brahmanical texts, 35–36, 91
maternity chamber, 141, 223n109, 223n112

meditation, 17, 21, 104–105, 114, 179n94
merit, 85, 151, 161–162; as currency, 57; fields of, 155, 161; share of in donative inscriptions, 44–45, 151, 187n11
Michaels, Axel, 8
monastic designations: *ācārya*s (teachers), 85, 100, 187n7; *ādikarmika* (first offenders), 31, 86, 186n190, 191n65; *antevāsin*, 187n7; *ārāmika*s (monastic attendants), 215n265; *bare bhikṣu* (Newar), 116; *bhaginī* (sister), 26, 84; *bhātar* (brother), 25–26; *Brahmacarya Bhikṣu* (Newar), 116; *caitya* pilgrim/worshipper, 42, 101, 187n10; *dharmabhaginī* (sister in the Dharma), 185n170; *dharmabhāṇaka*, 215n268; *dharmabhrātṛ* (brother in the Dharma), 185n170; *dutiyikā bhikkhunī* (companion nuns), 143, 223n124; forest-renunciants, 7, 51, 174n40, 175n46; *gāmavāsī* monks (Burmese), 214n261; *gaṇinnānsē* (Sri Lankan), 116; guards, 20, 145; *kalpikārika* (factotum), 197n162; *mahallaka* (old uncle), 85, 100, 199n25; *navakarmaka*, 187n12; *ngag-pa* priests (Tibetan), 116; *paścācchramaṇa*s (attending menials), 145, 160, 215n265; *pratyekabuddhas/paccekabuddha*s (solitary buddhas), 7, 114, 175n42, 213n241; preceptress, 145; Śākyas (Newar), 116; *samaṇa-kuṭimbika* (landlord ascetic), 215n265; serfs, 20; *śikṣādattā/śikṣādattā-śrāmaṇerī* (penitent nun), 103, 157–158, 209n150; *śikṣādattaka* (penitent monk), 103, 157–158, 219n65; *śikṣamāṇā* (probationary nun), 48, 49, 62–63, 133–134, 141, 143, 171n2, 217n24, 219n65, 220n66, 220n68; slaves, 20, 115, 179n92, 204n85, 228n63; *śramaṇa*s (mendicants), 115, 171n2, 171n5, 173n21, 213n245; *śrāmaṇera*s (novices), 64–68, 115, 159, 171n2, 184n153, 195n145, 199n27, 213n245; *śrāmaṇerī*s (novice nuns), 48, 62–63, 133, 134, 159, 171n2; *upadhivārikā*, 210n164; *upādhyāya* (preceptor), 41–42, 82, 83, 85–86, 87, 100, 185n169, 198n6; *upāsaka* (devoted layman), 100; *upāsikā* (devoted laywoman), 48, 100; *upasthāyaka*s, 215n265; Vajrācāryas (Newar), 116, 171n7
monastic families, 26, 30, 54–55, 78, 80, 99, 152, 221n83
monastic ideals, 7, 74, 80, 117–118, 153, 154, 162–163; Benedictine influence on, 3
monasticisms: Benedictine, 3, 164, 172n11; Byzantine, 3; Christian, 2, 3, 119, 153–154, 163–165, 172n11, 194n113, 194n127; Daoist, 46, 184n167; as a degenerate form of Buddhism, 5, 162–163; Egyptian, 3, 164, 184n167; family-friendly, 29, 73, 76, 99, 117, 157, 160–161, 164; fully developed, 20; Jain, 156–157, 158–159, 160; lateness of sources for, 20–21, 75–76, 174n30; settled/sedentary, 7, 161, 174n40; spouse-friendly, 157; utility of term, 147, 163–164, 171n2
monastic offenses/rules, types of: *anāpatti*s (nonoffenses), 74, 98, 142, 223n117; *āsamudācārika-dharma* (rules of customary behavior), 81; *brahmacaryopasthāna-saṃvṛti*, 49, 190n49; *duṣkṛta*s (wrongdoing), 63, 95, 135, 193n111, 194n123, 205n98, 205n101, 216n13; *gurudharma*s, 143, 219n65; *nissaggiya-pācittiya*s and related terms (confiscation), 76, 104, 197n173, 197nn175–176; *pācattika*, 59, 62, 129, 193nn110–111, 218n39; *pācittiya*s, 197n176, 223n115; *pārājika*s, 30, 80, 86–87, 103, 104, 110, 114, 166, 168, 177n61, 191n65, 197n2, 199n27, 209n150, 213n238, 213n241, 221n95, 228n62 (see also *pārājika* penance); *pāṭidesanīya*s, 197n176; *pāyantika*s, 121, 144; *pāyattika*s, 135, 208n144; *śaikṣā* rules, 30; *saṃvṛti* (*sdom pa*), 15, 139, 194n117, 222n100; *saṅghāvaśeṣa*s, 89, 90, 95, 109, 200n39, 200n41, 204n87, 205n98, 205n101, 206n102, 213n235; *sthūlātyaya*s, 90, 95, 200n41, 205n98, 205n101; transgression against the rule of law, 61, 62, 86, 88, 89, 139, 194n118
Monier-Williams, Monier, 5, 8, 9, 173n24, 176n53
monks: contact with families, 2, 3, 8, 9, 12, 16, 26–27, 32, 87–88, 89–90, 150–151, 155–156, 161, 162, 167; dining with their families, 38, 58–59,

156; living at home, 37, 47, 50, 151, 189n35; obligations to support parents, 26, 218n37; ownership of personal property, 84, 155, 176n47; parents of, 44–45, 185n175; right to inherit, 26; as unmarried/no longer married, 8, 9, 151; visiting wives, 28, 79, 81, 82–87, 88–89, 92, 106, 117, 118, 151, 156, 200n40
motherhood (monastic), 2, 29, 35, 99, 120–121, 129, 133, 137, 139, 140, 143–144, 146, 147, 148–149, 152, 162, 164–165, 226n152; appointment of companion nuns, 1–2, 131–132, 143, 152, 223n114, 223n124; assignment of solitary cells for mother-nuns, 136–137, 223n114; authorizations for companion nuns to share sleeping quarters with baby boys, 1, 132, 152; authorizations for mother-nuns to share sleeping quarters with their sons, 1, 15, 126–127, 128–129, 132, 135, 136, 139, 152, 179n90, 222n100, 223n114; breast-feeding/nursing, 1, 29, 125–126, 127, 128, 132–133, 138, 147, 152, 162; fawning upon a nun's baby, 1, 132, 219n58; imagery, 227n44; legal precedent for, 133, 137, 148; monastic attitude to, 129, 142, 143–144, 147, 162, 164–165, 226n152; raising children, 9–10, 29, 121, 125–126, 127, 128, 129, 132–133, 138, 142–143, 144, 147, 149, 162, 164, 166, 224n129
Mūlasarvāstivāda-vinaya (general), 24, 27, 31, 32, 107, 110, 137, 160, 163, 166, 228n63; *Bhikṣuṇī-prātimokṣa,* 146–147, 211n194, 224n138; *Bhikṣuṇī-vibhaṅga,* 110, 198n4, 211n194, 224n138; call to read, 179n82; dating and place of composition, 19–20, 21, 137, 183n130; multiplicity of, 194n117, 201n45, 211n194, 221n85, 224n138; as part of extant *vinaya* corpus, 18, 75, 143–144; Sanskrit manuscripts of, 19, 182n120, 207n122; as Sthavira *vinaya,* 68; structure of, 30; studies of, 180n105; *sūtra*s in, 31, 210n75; Tibetan translation of, 19–20, 75–76, 182nn121–124; translations of, 183n137
murder, 13, 30, 70–71, 100, 122, 168, 200n41
names: ordination, 187n15; *rakhita* suffix, 187n14
Nattier, Jan, 16, 179n92
New Testament studies, 16
*nikāya*s, 18, 143–144, 178n67, 180nn99–100, 193n110, 224n127
nunneries: urban location of, 139, 222n101
nun of Watton (Gilbertine), 164–165
nuns: birth of babies to, 1, 9, 15, 29, 120, 127–128, 129, 131, 133, 134, 135–139, 140–143, 146–147, 148, 149, 162, 165, 179n90; body searches for, 206n110; in brahmanical literature, 91; foundation of order of, 143, 223n122; impregnated by monks, 102–103; living at home, 48–50, 194n117; living/staying in lay houses, 38, 62–63; looking after lay children, 121, 144–146, 224n129; as maidservants, 145; returning home for meals, 38, 59–62; security concerns for, 30, 38, 60–62, 113, 194n119, 227n21; separate dwelling for, 63; as spies, 201n52; and their daughters, 128, 133, 135, 141; vocation chosen over marriage, 190n40; waiting on monks, 14, 97–98, 179n90
nursing nuns, 124–129, 130, 136, 144, 146, 155, 157; on alms rounds, 124, 127, 128, 130, 146, 158, 195n141; expulsion of, 146, 159

Obeyesekere, Gananath, 6, 174n38, 177n61
obligations to family, 22, 79, 87, 89, 90, 118, 151
Ohnuma, Reiko, 6, 22–23, 148, 177n61, 226n152
Oldenberg, Hermann, 76, 84, 105, 173n24, 179n96, 180n103, 199n15, 199n22, 223n124
Olivelle, Patrick, 7, 47, 74, 156, 157, 226n8
ordination/initiation: of biological kin, 74–75; effects on familial and matrimonial ties, 8–9, 25, 84, 118; by messenger in absentia, 37, 48–49, 189n36; of nursing mothers, 9, 120, 121–123, 124–125, 126–127, 129, 130–131, 141–142, 146, 147–148, 152, 158, 216n4, 216n8, 217n20,

218n34, 223n116; permission for, 52, 53, 96, 191n69, 206n103; persons ineligible for, 34, 75, 123–124, 158, 216nn13–17, 216n19; of pregnant women, 9, 29, 32–33, 34, 120, 121–123, 124, 127–128, 129–131, 133–134, 140–143, 146, 147–148, 152, 158, 216n4, 216n8, 217n20, 217n24, 219n51, 222n103, 223n116; promises to return home after, 52, 53, 81–82, 191nn72–73, 191n75, 198n5; of prostitutes, 75; reactions of families to, 25, 26, 52; ten types of, 189n36; three types of for nuns, 189n36; validity of, 34, 124, 125, 127, 130, 140, 142, 217n20, 217n33

Pāli (Theravāda) Vinaya (general), 8, 18, 27, 103, 116, 129, 148, 165–166; dating of, 19, 20, 76, 142, 223n122; manuscript tradition of, 20; as part of extant *vinaya* corpus, 18, 75, 143–144; *pātimokkha,* 197n172; privileging of, 18, 103, 165–166, 168; as Sthavira *vinaya,* 68; structure of, 30, 186n187, 215n2; as a translation, 18, 180n102; translations of, 18, 180n103; utility of, 165–166, 168, 180n102

Pāli sources, privileging of, 17, 153, 162, 166, 168, 173n24

Palmo, Karma Kechog, *bhikṣuṇī* (Mrs. Freda Bedi), 145

Palmo, Yeshe, 145

pārājika penance, 103–104, 157–158, 166, 168, 209n150, 228n62. *See also* monastic designations: *śikṣādattā/śikṣādattā-śrāmaṇerī*; monastic designations: *śikṣādattaka*

pollution and purity, brahmanical concern for, 57, 58, 70, 193n105

pratigupte, 57, 193n105, 221n95

*prātimokṣa*s, 30, 32–34, 120–124, 125, 130, 131, 134, 152, 186n193, 226n148; dating of, 33, 76; as a deterrent, 34, 122; legal effectiveness of, 32–34, 122–123, 144; utility of, 146–147

pra√vraj, 24, 37, 64, 184n160, 217nn24–25. See also *chujia;* going-forth into homelessness

pregnant nuns, 9, 12–13, 35, 102–103, 104, 105, 121, 129, 130, 134–135, 142, 146–149, 152, 155, 157–158, 161, 167, 217n24; accommodation of in monastic law, 1–2, 16, 29, 134, 146, 167; on alms rounds, 129–130, 146, 158; in Christianity, 164–165; expulsion/eviction of, 133, 140, 141, 146, 148, 157–159, 161, 220n68, 222n105, 226n152; in Jainism, 158–159; legal precedent for, 136, 137, 148; "rule-breaking," 168

principles: of higher criticism, 19, 181n109; of irrelevance, 16

prohibitions, 32, 33–34, 98, 120, 122–124, 142, 216n12

prostitution, 228n63

public/corporate image, monastic concern for in negotiating issues, 11–12, 31, 59, 153, 165; of celibacy, 12–13, 16, 118–119, 134, 155–156, 160, 161; of children on alms rounds, 65, 67, 195n135; of expulsion of pregnant nuns and misbehaving monks, 157–158, 159, 161; of "former" wives, 106, 109, 156; of health care and liabilities, 123–124; of married monastic couples, 105, 106, 118–119; of motherhood, 29, 128, 149; of practice of crafts, 57; of pregnant nuns, 13, 29, 130–131, 146

Ralston, W. R. S., 112

rape, 112, 114, 147–148, 158–159

Ray, Reginald, 109–110, 178n64

Reis, Ria, 148–149

relatives, *vibhaṅga* definition of, 76–77, 208n143

religiosity, struggle with, 106–107

religious studies, 17, 24, 27, 165

renouncers, types of: hermit, 156, 226n18; *kuṭīcaka,* 156; *ṛṣi,* 157; *saṃnyāsin,* 156

renunciant ideal, 16, 74, 117–118

renunciation: by Buddha's family, 9, 21–23, 26; as a family, 24, 38, 78 (*see also* co-renunciation); with family members, 12, 24, 70 (*see also* co-renunciation); of family members on different paths, 72–73, 112, 197n161, 206n112; five merits of, 48; language of, 25, 162; non-Buddhist, 72–74, 112, 156–157, 158–160; as a rejection of family, 6, 23, 24; as requiring physical separation, 46, 50–51, 151; retiring to the forest, 156; rhetoric of, 162; as social death,

23, 150, 184n153; utility of term, 163–164. *See also* ordination/initiation
Rhinoceros Horn ideal, 4–7, 9, 10, 16, 17, 153, 154, 162, 174nn30–31, 174nn38–40
Rhys Davids, Thomas William, 76, 173n24, 223n124
Rockhill, William Woodville, 144, 183n137, 224n129, 224n136
romanticization of Indian Buddhism, 3–4, 29, 107, 116, 154

Salomon, Richard, 4, 174n40
samajīvikā, 94, 207n124
saṅgha, meanings of term, 214n257
Sanskrit drama, 35, 79, 91, 151, 199n13
Sarvāstivāda-vinaya: dating of, 19, 20, 21, 75; as part of extant *vinaya* corpus, 18, 75, 143–144; Sanskrit fragments of, 181n110, 228n58; as Sthavira *vinaya,* 68
Sarvāstivādins and Mūlasarvāstivādins, relationship between, 137, 219n65, 221n84
Sasaki, Shizuka, 26–27, 185n181, 186n187
"scarecrow" provision for novices, 67–68, 69, 132–133, 195n145
Schopen, Gregory, 11, 16–17, 20–21, 26, 27, 84, 160, 165, 166, 167, 178n65, 183n130, 186n2, 218n37, 224n138
sectarianism, development of, 18–19
sex, definitions of, 166–167. *See also* celibacy: breaches of
sexual assault, 147–148. *See also* rape
sexual desire, five demerits of, 48
sexuality, struggle with, 106–107
sexual relations: as a duty, 51, 226n8; between monks and "former" wives, 80, 83, 85–87; between monks and nuns, 102–104
Shenoute, 164, 184n167
silence, 53, 131, 137, 138; meanings of, 191n81
sociohistorical realities, 29–30, 35, 79, 90, 166–167, 186n184
Spiro, Melford, 5, 23, 46, 176n60
Sthaviras: conflation with Theravāda, 181n108; Sthavira–Mahāsāṅghika split, 18–19, 139–140; *vinaya*s, 19, 68–69, 139–140, 186n187
stock phrases: for independence, 113–114; for lay criticism of the religious life, 11, 65, 66, 124, 127; for monks seen frequenting lay houses/craftsmen, 32, 38, 56–57, 192n103; for motives for entering the order, 25, 64, 81, 98; for old monks, 85, 100; for taking a wife, 47, 188n31
sTog Palace recensional history, 86, 200n40
Strong, John, 26
sūtras/*suttas*, 10, 16–17, 31, 52–53, 161, 163; accessibility to laity, 10, 161, 163; collections from the *Mūlasarvāstivāda-vinaya,* 210n175; privileging of, 17, 29, 75, 116, 153, 162
Suvarṣakas, 152, 209n154
svī√kṛ, 213n235

Tāranātha, 215n271
taverns, 73, 168–169, 228n63
teacher/disciple relationships, 187n7
terms of address: for husband, 83, 199n13; for mother and son, 191n68; for wife, 83, 198n12; for women (*see* monastic designations: *bhaginī*)
Tilokpur Nunnery, 145, 225n145
Tsomo, Karma Lekshe, 144, 146–147, 224n129, 224n131

upa-saṃ√pad (to ordain), 217nn24–25, 222n107
upa√sthā, 222n107

*vibhaṅga*s (general), 32, 33, 200n43, 226n148
vinaya rules (general): exceptions for family members, 7–8, 26, 33, 59, 63, 68, 74, 76, 98, 129, 135, 193n111, 206n115, 224n137; *kleśa/upakleśa* analysis of offenses, 204n87; non-applicability to laity, 83, 122; ten benefits in promulgation of, 11–12, 178n76. *See also* law (monastic), types of
vinaya rules (specific, concerning): censuring monks, 206n115; drinking semen, 208n144; eating, 58–59, 124, 193n111; giving up talk of abandoning religious life, 72; laundry done by unrelated nuns, 76, 102, 104–105, 209n162; looking after lay children, 121, 144–146, 224n129; making/using dildos, 124, 217n22; physical contact with opposite sex, 109, 135, 138;

playing in water, 222n103; practice of crafts, 57, 193n105, 196n154; robes, 33, 73, 76, 196n149; self-insemination, 208n144; sharing alms with wives, 24, 113; sharing sleeping quarters, 15, 126, 128–129, 135–136, 139, 143, 218n39, 222n100; solitary travel by nuns, 60–62; staying in a lay house without permission, 62–63; teaching Dharma to laywomen, 12; touching another nun's child, 139; touching money, 84, 85, 199n20; use of large alms bowls, 168; use of latrines, elevated or suspended, 168; waiting on monks, 14, 97–98; watching live entertainment, 124

*vinaya*s: authorship of, 171n3; currently used to govern communities of nuns, 120, 121, 146–147, 215n3; dating of, 18–21, 119, 183n135, 223n118; in East Asia, 121, 215n3; extant corpus, 18–20, 75, 143–144, 180n104, 182n121, 182n123; as "in-house" documents, 2, 7, 10–11, 13, 35, 107, 151, 161, 163, 175n45; probative value of, 30, 35, 79, 91; structure of, 30, 34, 186n187; translation of, 18, 168, 227n46; utility of, 10–11, 38–39, 72, 121, 146–147, 165–169

Virdi, P. K., 92, 201n55, 203n68, 203n74

visions of religious life: Pāli Vinaya and *Mūlasarvāstivāda-vinaya,* differences between, 27, 185n182; *sūtra* and *vinaya,* differences between, 7, 10–17, 52, 75, 116, 153, 179n96

wealth, seizure of by kings, 51, 53, 100, 191n67

widowers, 220n79

widows, 25, 40, 133, 148, 186n184, 194n127

wife: not a relative, 208n143; as property, 93; sale of, 93, 160; types of, 94–95, 203n75, 205n101, 207n124

Wijayaratna, Môhan, 8, 9, 176n57, 180n97

Wilson, Elizabeth [Liz], 8–9, 23, 96, 176n48, 176n58

women: touch of, 83, 112; vulnerability of, 158, 227n21

Workman, Herbert B., 153–154, 226n5

Yamagiwa, Nobuyuki, 26

Yijing (635–713 C.E.), 19, 75–76, 181n112, 224n138

Young, Serinity, 8, 22, 179n95, 186n184

About the Author

Shayne Clarke is an associate professor in the Department of Religious Studies at McMaster University. Before completing his PhD at the University of California, Los Angeles, in 2006, Clarke studied Asian languages, Buddhist studies, and religious studies in New Zealand and Japan. He has published widely on Indian Buddhist monastic law codes, on topics such as clerical celibacy, the role of humor, and the problems surrounding the establishment of nuns' ordination lineages in Tibetan Buddhism.

Production Notes for Clarke/*Family Matters in Indian Buddhist Monasticisms*
Jacket design by Julie Matsuo-Chun
Composition by Wanda China with display and text in Sabon
Printing and binding by Sheridan Books, Inc.
Printed on 60 lb. House White, 444 ppi.